Deceptions
and
Doublecross

How the NHL
Conquered Hockey

Deceptions
and
Doublecross

Morey Holzman and
Joseph Nieforth

THE DUNDURN GROUP
TORONTO · OXFORD

Copyright © Morey Holzman and Joseph Nieforth, 2002

Copy-Editor: Lloyd Davis
Design: Jennifer Scott
Printer: Transcontinental

National Library of Canada Cataloguing in Publication Data

Holzman, Morey
Deceptions and doublecross : how the NHL conquered hockey/Morey Holzman and Joseph Nieforth.

Includes bibliographical references and index.
ISBN 1-55002-413-2

1. National Hockey League — History. I. Nieforth, Joseph II. Title.

GV847.8.N3H64 2002   796.962'06'071   C2002-902292-4

1 2 3 4 5   06 05 04 03 02

THE CANADA COUNCIL | LE CONSEIL DES ARTS
FOR THE ARTS | DU CANADA
SINCE 1957 | DEPUIS 1957

Canada

ONTARIO ARTS COUNCIL
CONSEIL DES ARTS DE L'ONTARIO

We acknowledge the support of the **Canada Council for the Arts** and the **Ontario Arts Council** for our publishing program. We also acknowledge the financial support of the **Government of Canada** through the **Book Publishing Industry Development Program** and **The Association for the Export of Canadian Books**, and the **Government of Ontario** through the **Ontario Book Publishers Tax Credit** program.

Dundurn Press
8 Market Street
Suite 200
Toronto, Ontario, Canada
M5E 1M6

Dundurn Press
73 Lime Walk
Headington, Oxford,
England
OX3 7AD

Dundurn Press
2250 Military Road
Tonawanda NY
U.S.A. 14150

Deceptions
and
Doublecross

Contents

Introduction and
Acknowledgements

*F*rank Calder, the first president of the National Hockey League, once told his friend and protégé Elmer Ferguson, "Some day I'm going to write the real story of professional hockey, with all its colour, its incident. Some day, when I get time, I'd like to write that book."[1]

That is the goal we have set for ourselves in *Deceptions and Doublecross* — though it's a safe bet that Calder's version would have cast the principals in a much more flattering light than the account we are about to present.

This book is written for the hockey fan, no matter what part of the globe he or she lives on. We feel we must warn you that you will need to suspend any knowledge you may have acquired about the history of the sport in order to understand fully the thoughts and actions of the players, owners and, most importantly, the fans themselves.

It is the fans who passed the game on to their children, who in turn passed the game on to *their* children, whose children have perfected the game to the form you see in a National Hockey League arena today. There is no question that the lessons Bobby Hull learned have filtered down to his son Brett, which may also account for some of the younger Hull's outspokenness. The trailblazing efforts by Ted Lindsay to form a players' union in the 1950s are certainly influenced by the experience of Terrible Ted's father, Bert, who was one of the game's pioneering goalies.

But to appreciate where the Hulls, Lindsays and others get their contrary opinions, one must understand the information they read and the reality in which they lived.

Revisiting the world of hockey as it was more than eighty years ago is a daunting proposition. More than football, baseball or basketball, the game of hockey has seen drastic changes over the years. Today's player takes a shift of between thirty and forty-five seconds, spends the next minute or two on the bench catching his breath, then returns to the ice for another concentrated burst of activity.

Today's rosters have twenty men, and each team carries two or three spares, or "black aces," who are usually found watching the games from the press box. In the NHL of today, size matters: players who fail to meet the unofficial standard of six feet tall and 200 pounds rarely make the grade. Teams play five men to a side, plus a goalie. Thanks to a recent innovation, should a game be tied at the end of regulation time, each team drops to four skaters for the overtime period. In the sport's established hotbeds, enthusiastic crowds approaching 20,000 are kept pumped up — if not by the action, then by the rock music that blares from the loudspeakers during every stoppage in play. Beyond the friendly confines of the rink, thousands more fans tune in to each game on the radio or television; in fact, a single game may be watched by millions around the world. Satellite and cable television companies offer packages in which viewers can receive just about every National Hockey League game — even those thrilling matchups between Nashville and Minnesota or Columbus and Tampa Bay. Big money is at stake — for the players, for the owners, even for the broadcasters.

It wasn't always this way. Some eighty-five years ago, the Montreal Wanderers played their home opener before a crowd of seven hundred — and that was only after free admission was offered to disabled World War I veterans. Sam Lichtenhein, the Wanderers' owner, could not even have dreamed of the concept of tapping "revenue streams" by selling advertising space on the boards; in fact, the boards themselves had only been introduced a few years earlier. And painting sponsor logos on the ice? Lichtenhein considered himself lucky that there *was* ice, since the Westmount Arena in which his "Redbands" played had only installed equipment to make artificial ice in 1915.

The league the Wanderers played in, the National Hockey League, was an unknown quantity, having been founded only three weeks prior to the opening of the 1917–18 hockey season. Unless you were fortunate enough to be at the arena, you would have to settle for second- or third-hand accounts of the action. In those days before radio and television, there was no Foster Hewitt broadcasting from his gondola in Maple Leaf Gardens. The first hockey play-by-play commentary was provided by newspaper reporters relaying information to runners, who telegraphed the message back to the visiting team's locale. As the telegraph operator received the message at the other end of the line, he would relay its contents to the crowd that had gathered around the front of the telegraph office, which was usually found in a corner drugstore. A good example of this system —

which was reserved for major events such as Stanley Cup games — is portrayed in the baseball movie *Eight Men Out*.

Here's a description of play-by-play as it was handled in Canada's capital in 1910 (when the redoubtable Foster Hewitt would have been nine years old):

> The *Citizen* will bulletin at the Town Hall, Rockland, this evening a complete running story of the Rockland-Hawkesbury match at Hawkesbury, giving a full description of the play from start to finish. A staff reporter will go to Rockland to supply the material while another member of The *Citizen* staff will receive and announce the news at Rockland, hockey enthusiasts of the latter town being invited to come to Town Hall this evening and hear at The *Citizen's* expense, a splendid hot-off-the-wire story of the game at Hawkesbury.[2]

Thanks to expansion and a round of franchise shifts, the National Hockey League now plays in Sun Belt cities where you can attend a mid-January tilt wearing shorts and a T-shirt — or your favourite team's jersey. That's a far cry from one 1911 game in which Wanderers defenceman Fred Povey got frostbite — while he was playing! Frostbite was also a common affliction amongst fans back when the game was played outdoors on natural ice surfaces that had been frozen by the sub-zero temperatures. Some spectators brought heated bricks to the rink to keep their feet warm — not that that would have helped Povey. Of course, there were other ways of keeping warm, as the Ottawa *Journal* reported:

> Hockey fans who have been in the habit in the past of taking "something on the hip" to the Arena to keep out the cold while watching the games may be interested to know that the authorities intend to do a little investigating. Any person caught taking a throat oiler while in the Arena will be pinched.[3]

During a dull game in a modern, climate-controlled NHL arena, fans would be more likely to need a "throat oiler" to keep awake. Fortunately, beer flows freely at the concession stands.

The outdoor setting could help create a home-ice advantage: during a 1911 game in Quebec City, the Bulldogs supporters were so upset with Ottawa that they pelted the Senators players with snowballs! On the other side of the coin, the Montreal Canadiens had to relocate more than one playoff game during the 1920s because unseasonably warm weather left them without home ice.

At five foot eleven, Ernie Johnson was considered a "Moose." Fred "Cyclone" Taylor stood five foot eight and weighed 165 pounds. By 1910 he was well on his way to becoming one of hockey's all-time legends, but a player of Cyclone's stature would be hard-pressed to garner a second look from today's NHL scouts, who are looking for the next Zdeno Chara (six foot nine). With a bit of luck, he might land a chance to ply his trade for one of the dozens of minor-league clubs that now dot the continent.

Just as the players were considerably smaller in those days, so were the rosters. In 1917, each NHL team was made up of only eleven men — and Toronto was the lone club that would employ two goalkeepers over the course of the season. Players routinely spent the full sixty minutes on the ice, and at one time there was even a rule in the National Hockey Association — the NHL's predecessor — that substitutions could not be made after the second period! If a player was injured, the other team had to agree to remove a player.

Not surprisingly, hockey games were played at a much slower pace; in fact, the action could usually be followed simply by watching the puck carrier. There were no loudspeakers blaring out rock music, but occasionally the home teams did have bands that would perform during stoppages. And big money? Most of it stayed firmly in the hands of the arena operators, who as a general rule kept 60 percent of the gate receipts to cover so-called "incidental expenses." The two opponents would split the rest, or at least what remained after paying the players and footing the costs of travel — by train, of course.

Because fewer people were paying attention to pro hockey in those days before such innovations as all-sports talk radio stations and specialty cable TV channels, the business of the league's administrators was transacted in a near-vacuum. Ethics therefore took a back seat to expediency. Until the 1910s, teams were operated by a few local sportsmen, and would change hands every year or two. The rink owners, who did no more than provide the venues, were content to pocket the lion's share of the money generated by hockey; there was no incentive to take on the extra costs and headaches posed by the players.

Joe Patrick contributed to a revolution in the business side of the sport when he used part of the fortune he had amassed in the lumber industry to set up his two sons, Frank and Lester, with their own arenas and bankroll their brainchild, the Pacific Coast Hockey Association. With this new league the brothers would enjoy unprecedented control over all aspects of their teams' operations. They would decide who played and for how much, as well as where and when. In the process they changed forever the face of hockey. Unfortunately, all this happened in and around Vancouver and Victoria, British Columbia, and the Patricks' influence on the game would not be fully appreciated by the majority of hockey observers until decades later. Back east — birthplace of the players, the game itself, and perhaps most importantly the Stanley Cup — the hockey establishment used unscrupulous tactics, bordering on the illegal, to try and gain some sort of financial edge on the Patricks. The PCHA was often slandered by eastern arena and team operators as "syndicate hockey," as if the Patricks were some sort of mob racketeers.

No analysis of this period in hockey's history would be complete without some mention of the cozy relationship between the media and the custodians of the game. Journalists have traditionally occupied the bottom of the financial food chain, and in Canada in the early years of the twentieth century it seemed as if all the nation's sports editors were moonlighting. In the Toronto-Ottawa-Montreal triangle, these second jobs usually involved hockey.

In Montreal, Frank Calder was the sports editor of the *Herald and Daily Telegraph*. Before quitting to make hockey his full-time occupation, Calder recruited Elmer Ferguson, a reporter from Moncton, New Brunswick, to succeed him. By the time of the NHL's foundation in 1917, Calder held the dual role of league president and secretary, while Ferguson was put on the payroll as official statistician. It may be a coincidence, but Ferguson never once criticized a Calder decision — not even after Calder's death. Oh, if we could all be so perfect!

Tommy Gorman, the co-owner of the Ottawa Senators, was a reporter and then a sports editor for the Ottawa *Citizen*. Gorman is best known for coaching seven Stanley Cup winners, despite never having played an organized game in his life. The sports editor of the Ottawa *Journal* was Philip Ross, who was also one of the original Stanley Cup trustees and a former teammate of two of Lord Stanley's sons on the Rideau Rebels amateur hockey team. Ross purchased the *Journal* in 1898 and twenty-one years later would add the Ottawa *Free Press* to his growing media portfolio.

In Toronto, the media/sports compact was even tighter. The owner of the *Evening Telegram* was John Ross Robertson, who doubled as a member of Parliament when he wasn't serving as president of the Ontario Hockey Association. Foster Hewitt's dad, William, spent a career as sports editor of the Toronto *News* and later the *Daily Star*. At one time, Charlie Querrie, who would become manager of the Arena

Gardens and owner of the NHL's Toronto St. Pats, was one of his columnists. As Hewitt became secretary of the OHA — a league that depended upon amateurism for its owners to make money — his personal stand against professionalism frequently found its way into the *News*'s sports pages. Robertson and Hewitt went as far as to disparage the International Hockey League by insisting on referring to it as the "International (Professional) Hockey League" — a designation that has been propagated by many researchers who have been unaware of its origin or intent. The future Maple Leafs owner Conn Smythe also cut his teeth in the newspaper business, working for his father at the Toronto *World*. Even the *Star*'s famed sportswriter, Lou Marsh, earned a little side cash officiating NHL games. And Mike Rodden, the Hall of Fame referee who worked more than 1,100 NHL games, became the assistant sports editor at the Toronto *Globe* in 1918, after a stint as a sports editor in North Bay, Ontario. While in Toronto he found time to coach the Argonauts and other football teams, before leading the Hamilton Tigers to back-to-back Grey Cup championships in 1927 and '28. Rodden later became the respected sports editor of the Kingston *Whig-Standard* until 1959.

What is disturbing is that, not only were these "legendary" journalists moonlighting, they were double-dipping: on the one hand, the leagues paid them to officiate while their newspapers paid them to report the very same games. A 1921 bankruptcy case even proved that many journalists were paid by the teams just to show up and report on the games.

Foster Hewitt, through his *Hockey Night in Canada* broadcasts, became a national institution. Yet the beginnings of his career were not so auspicious. The Toronto *Daily Star* had made a foray into the new medium of radio, and Foster's dad needed someone to go down to the arena on Mutual Street and announce the game. As it turned out, Foster liked the gig, and the elder Hewitt was able to keep his son out of his hair at the *Star*'s newsroom.

There should never be a question that these members of the media were biased and were certainly not about to let the truth interfere with their take on the facts. And if a rival newspaper in their town happened to disagree, it was less out of a need to set the record straight than the desire to embarrass a rival. This is doubly true where Ferguson and Gorman are concerned, as both of them held important positions in hockey.

As a result, a newspaper's hockey "reporter" tended to be more akin to a cheerleader. And the press could indulge in as much trash talk as could be heard on the ice. One example came prior to a February 1911 game at Quebec, when the Ottawa Senators talked of refusing to travel to face the Bulldogs. This is how Tommy Gorman reported the incident in the Ottawa *Citizen*:

> The new champions will not go to Quebec to fill their engagement unless the Ancient Capital club guaranteed them absolute protection from the hoodlums who, on the occasion of their appearance at the Rock City two weeks ago, pelted the red and white and black players with snow and ice…
>
> Yesterday, the Ottawas followed up their first protest with a request that the National association order the Quebec club to improve its lightning facilities. They say the rink at the Ancient Capital is about as dark as the Lovers' Walk around Parliament Hill and that each of the Ottawa players wanted to go out on to the ice surface armed with a searchlight for the purpose of discovering the puck and distinguishing his opponents.[4]

In the aftermath of the cancellation of the 1905 Stanley Cup series between the Ottawa Silver Seven and the Montreal Wanderers, the *Citizen* presented this assessment of the media's roles in the two towns:

> As usual, the Montreal papers, the *Herald* and the *Star* at least, all saw the Ottawa dirty work and are now hurling all sorts of anathemas at the Ottawa press for sticking up for its own. Of course Ottawa has a bad name — among the outsiders — and any dog in that predicament has no friends anyway.[5]

Even Lord Stanley understood the power of the press when he donated fifty dollars to purchase the silver bowl that future generations would spend tens of millions to capture for just one year. He appointed two men to act as the trophy's caretakers: one was the sheriff of Ottawa, while the other was a part-time defenceman — and full-time sports editor.

No effort in the field of hockey research should go without an acknowledgement of the pioneering efforts of Charles L. Coleman. In 1964, Coleman finished Volume One of *Trail of the Stanley Cup*, which covers the years 1891 through 1926. NHL president Clarence Campbell was so impressed that he commissioned Coleman to write two more volumes, spanning the years through 1967. Most of the legends and lore that have since been published under the "hockey history" rubric come straight out of these three books.

Trail is a good place to start any research of hockey's early years, but it doesn't tell the complete story. Coleman relied heavily upon newspaper accounts for the first volume, while for the latter two books he also had access to league files. His account is straightforward, as Coleman preferred to leave it to others to interpret and form opinions about his findings. His first major flaw was his failure to recognize the conflicts of interest, noted above, in which the men involved in writing the newspaper reports were involved. His second major mistake was that he researched only those Canadian newspapers he could obtain at the Montreal and Toronto public libraries.[6]

In his defence, the former mayor of North Hatley, Quebec, wrote the series for the love of the sport rather than the money. Coleman was rewarded, however, with a spot on the Hall's selection committee. We acknowledge Coleman for his efforts, and hope that, as he looks down upon us, he realizes we are attempting to build upon his legacy — even if we had the audacity to add the goings-on in the United States to the Canadian material he wrote about.

Coleman's work was the culmination of a lifelong dream. He claimed to have watched his first game in 1911, and was still attending matches when he completed the third and final volume of *Trail* in 1976. The Montreal native and McGill University graduate — class of 1927 — had spent a lifetime around his favourite sport, and in that regard, Coleman was typical of Canadian boys during those years. When the Hall of Fame goaltender Harry "Hap" Holmes was winding down his playing career with the Detroit Cougars of the NHL, he once tried to explain to the Detroit newspapers what hockey meant to children in Canada. "In Canada," said Holmes, "many babies grasp a hockey stick before they are able to walk, and they begin to skate soon after they learn to walk. For them, the game is less difficult; it is simple for none."[7]

The fans were clearly hooked.

And the promoters were taking advantage.

Elmer Ferguson once wrote, "Today's hockey promoter has become a little loose with the truth."[8]

Indeed. And Gordie Howe played a game or two in the NHL.

To put a book such as this one together requires the efforts of many people around the globe and thousands of hours of research at all hours of the day. This project could not even have been conceived ten years ago: only by tapping the power of the Internet were we able to elicit contributions from all over the world — from the remote village of Haileybury, Ontario, to cosmopolitan Stockholm, Sweden, and many places in between.

Lest the public be deceived into thinking we completed this project unaided, the authors would like to thank those who worked like tireless forecheckers to help us:

Scott Surgent, author of *The Complete Historical and Statistical Reference to the World Hockey Association*, for his support during the course of this project.

David Stewart-Candy, the first person to chronicle all the standings for all the known leagues, for researching the Vancouver newspapers, for giving us great input, and for being a great guy. David's *Professional and International Ice Hockey Almanac* is available for viewing at the Hockey Hall of Fame in Toronto.

Michel Vigneault, a walking encyclopedia of early Franco-Quebec hockey, for translating the work of the French-Canadian historian Gilles Janson, whose biography of George Kendall is the most comprehensive ever created. Michel was putting the finishing touches on a doctoral dissertation, which he shared with us, and he delineated quite clearly the fine distinctions between French and English Montreal. We owe Professor Michel a giant *merci*.

Stu McMurray, for his help and direction, and for his research into the undying question, "What was the name of the 1918 Stanley Cup–winning team?" For the answer — or if you're a diehard Toronto Maple Leafs fan — see Stu's Web site at www.leafstats.8m.com.

Len Kotylo, a member of the Society of International Hockey Research, for his assistance with obtaining some of the many lawsuits filed by Eddie Livingstone.

Marc Foster, Tex Liebmann and the Hockey History Internet mailing list. Without this newsgroup, the two authors — one based forty minutes north of Mexico and the other a ten-minute subway ride from the Hockey Hall of Fame in downtown Toronto — would never have met.

Kirk Howard, Barry Jowett and the hard-working staff at Dundurn Press, who took a chance when all the other publishers said, "Great project, but we don't believe there is a market for this."

Lloyd Davis, copy editor extraordinaire, for his guidance and support, which went above and beyond the call of duty. A four-hour meet-

ing at the King Edward Hotel in Toronto was particularly memorable —
and hopefully, now that this book has been published, all three of our
wives will forgive us.

Brian Dobbs of Haileybury, Ontario. We have never before seen a
team picture of the Toronto Tecumsehs, and now we know why. Brian
had them.

Patrick Houda, Swedish journalist extraordinaire, for letting us
bounce ideas off him to formulate the direction we chose to follow. And
Joe Pelletier, for contributing contacts and research. Pat and Joe have co-
authored a book on the Canada/World Cup entitled *The World Cup of
Hockey: A History of Hockey's Greatest Tournament*, slated to be published
by Warwick Publishing in 2002.

Stephen Anderson, for research on his hometown of Cleveland, a
city whose rich hockey heritage is widely overlooked.

Dr. John Wong, for sharing his University of Maryland dissertation,
which was in progress while we worked on this project.

Don Reddick, author of the hockey novels *Dawson City Seven* and
Killing Frank McGee, for information he provided during the research
phase of his two books.

Dave Clamen, for spurring us on to question the way Eddie
Livingstone was treated.

Other authors and researchers who gave us support, including
Murray Greig (*Big Bucks and Blue Pucks*), Kevin Shea (*A Fan for All
Seasons*), Mike Porter, Paul O'Neill and Duff McFadden.

Paul Whiteside, for background information, clues and cues on Percy
Quinn and Charles Querrie.

Ken McAuley for information on his famous relative, Ken Randall.

The staff at Toronto's Mount Pleasant Cemetery for their assistance.

Carolyn Marr at the Museum of History and Industry in Seattle for
her assistance in tracking down Pete Muldoon.

The children of hockey players can be a great resource to help us
verify our information, and we are indebted to Ed Druxman (son of
Nate) and Gordon Keats Jr. (son of Duke) for their time and memory.

Fannie Witherspoon of the Kansas City *Star* for her assistance. There
were many other research librarians who have helped us, include a number of "nameless" faces who were "just doing their jobs." We would like
to thank the following libraries for hiring such wonderful, helpful people to work in their microform and interlibrary loan departments. In
Alberta: the Glenbow Museum in Calgary. In Arizona: the Phoenix
Public Library. In British Columbia: the Vancouver Public Library and
Victoria Public Library. In California: the Aliso Viejo Public Library;

Escondido Public Library; Garden Grove Public Library; San Diego Public Library; California State University San Marcos Library; San Diego State University Library; University of California, Irvine Library; and the Young Research Library at the University of California, Los Angeles. In Illinois: the Chicago branch of the National Archives and Records Administration. In Michigan: the Detroit Public Library. In Nevada: Lied Library at the University of Nevada, Las Vegas. In Nova Scotia: the Halifax Public Library and the Public Archives of Nova Scotia. In Ontario: the London Life Resource Centre at the Hockey Hall of Fame; the National Archives of Canada; the Archives of Ontario; the Haileybury Public Library; the Scott Library at York University; the Robarts Library at the University of Toronto; and the Toronto Public Library. In Quebec: *la bibliothèque nationale du Québec*. In Washington: the Tacoma Public Library and the Suzzallo Reference Library at the University of Washington.

We owe thanks to the Office of the Registrar General of Ontario for helping us figure out where Eddie Livingstone is today. Turns out he's just a few blocks from the Hockey Hall of Fame — which is where he was all along, and nobody ever knew it.

Morey also wishes to thank his very supportive wife Annette, daughter Camille, and son Cameron, for allowing Daddy to skip family time to work on this project.

Joseph also wishes to thank his very supportive and hockey-tolerant wife Annemarie, and Christopher, who came into his life during the writing of this book. Also, a thank you to his parents and his late "uncle" Andrew for the chance for Joseph to see his first hockey game, a Pittsburgh Penguins–Boston Bruins contest in the early 1970s. Boston won.

Since Joseph mentioned it, Morey also wants to thank his dad for buying the TV that allowed him to see his very first game — between the Detroit Red Wings and Chicago Blackhawks, played on the night in 1971 that Gordie Howe's jersey was retired — and for taking him to the first of many nights at the Olympia, a Rangers–Red Wings tilt in 1973. New York won, 6–3.

They just don't make hockey buildings like the Olympia any more.

But the good news is they don't run the game the way they used to, either.

Chapter 1

Birth of the Legend

Writing ability, first, of course. But you've got to be a hero-wor-
shipper, someone who gets a kick hob-nobbing with the great.[9]
— Elmer Ferguson, on what it takes
to be a great sportswriter

*A*pril 1972. *Flowers bloomed. Birds* chirped. The frozen rivers, ponds
and lakes where children played hockey day after day were starting
to resemble the swimming and fishing holes they would become. The
long, cold winter receded into memory, taking with it another National
Hockey League regular-season schedule, and the annual tournament to
crown a new Stanley Cup champion began anew.

But this would be no ordinary spring. A couple of months before, a
group of men fed up with the National Hockey League and its management felt the time was ripe to create a competitor. Meeting in
Anaheim, California — birthplace of Disneyland, but no NHL superstars
— this group of men launched the World Hockey Association. Soon they
would engage in active pursuit of one of hockey's greatest drawing cards:
the world-renowned Golden Jet, Bobby Hull.

Meanwhile, Bobby Orr's agent, Alan Eagleson, was among a group
negotiating with the Soviet Union to bring the Cold War to the ice.
Most of the experts believed the eight-game "Super Summit," as it was
to be called, would be a walk in the park for the brash NHL superstars.
Canada would easily sweep all eight from the hated Russians, they said.
In fact, Canadians would learn soon enough that other nations had not
only picked up their great game of hockey, they had mastered it. The
NHL's best would win by the narrowest of margins, and in the process a

Toronto Maple Leafs winger of average ability by the name of Paul Henderson would be vaulted into immortality. But that classic series was still a summer away.

While the hockey world, as Canadians had come to know it, was on the verge of collapsing, the spring of 1972 was also marked by the passing of one of those who had been there at the very beginning.

On April 26, Elmer Ferguson, the dean of Canadian sportswriters — the dean of *all* sportswriters, for that matter — died in Montreal's St. Mary's Hospital at the age of eighty-seven. The native of Charlottetown, Prince Edward Island, had spent more than seventy years in the newspaper business, starting as a newsboy selling papers on a railway platform. When he was an infant, Ferguson's family moved to Moncton, New Brunswick, and in 1902 — with the benefit of a ninth-grade education and a business course — he joined the Moncton *Transcript*. He moved on to flings in Boston and New York before settling in Montreal. His stint at the Montreal *Witness* lasted anywhere from an hour to a full day when he discovered his new bosses did not like professional sport. The next day, Ferguson appeared at the *Herald* which, like the *Witness*, had long since gone out of business by the time Ferguson died.[10]

Ferguson is held in such high esteem by the hockey establishment that, since 1984, the Hockey Hall of Fame has presented an award named after him to those who are inducted into the Hall's media wing. But Canada lost more than a storied sportswriter — who was initially disappointed at having to switch from drama critic to the "toy department" — when the august Maritimer died. It had lost the last survivor of the meeting at which the National Hockey League was founded.

The howling winds of change blew on that dreary, cold November day in 1917 as the lords of hockey met at the Windsor Hotel, in the heart of English Montreal, and formed the National Hockey League.

Strangely, the new league's president and secretary, Frank Calder, kept few minutes of the proceedings, so for many years it fell to Ferguson to relate what had happened. One version of his account, written in 1965, appeared in a Toronto Maple Leaf program:

> There's only a few of us left, to borrow a slightly melancholy passing phrase in sport. We would have borrowed a phrase of more accuracy, could we locate such. For so far as concerns the founding of the National Hockey League, now the greatest international professional sports body in

the world, there's not a few, but only one of us left. That's the writer of these paragraphs.

The National Hockey League was founded the afternoon and early evening of November 22, 1917, and the only reporter remaining on the scene when the magnates of the day emerged from their session, was this observer.

For professional hockey hadn't achieved anything remotely resembling its present stature. In these piping times, when the National League convenes, there's half a hundred reporters, feature writers, news-hounds of all types patrolling the scene. There's a press room. Back in 1917, when the new sports body was launched into war-torn space, the National League didn't even have an office to call its own. Much less a press room. And why no press room? Few reporters, not more than one or two, ever attended the sessions. For that was the stature of and the eminence of hockey in those times.

The National League was born in a room in Montreal's Windsor Hotel, a plain and simple room rented for the occasion. And we doubt if any one of the small group which launched the National League that afternoon had any idea of the future of the league, even of the game itself.

Certainly Frank Calder didn't have any such perceptivity. The redheaded Britisher who had come to Canada to play professional soccer, and as a sports writer fell in love with hockey, was no soothsayer.

He came out of the meeting-room, and, having toiled in the old Montreal *Herald* with Frank and having, in fact, succeeded him as a sports editor, I called over: "Hey, Frank, what happened?" "Nothing much," said Frank, briefly, striding to the nearest elevator. He was a modest man, too modest to say he had just been named president of a new hockey league, figuring, perhaps, it was just a small job, of little importance or future. He was keeping right on with his advertising business, anyway. And he was a hungry man, too, hastening home to a late dinner. In those days, the hockey magnates weren't tossing any of the luscious parties which have come to be an interesting part of the game's conduct.

The late George Kennedy emerged, smiling a bit triumphantly. George was owner then of the Canadien team which he had in late 1910 purchased for $7,500, a deal which many financial critics of the time gravely assessed as a wild gamble. George was smiling, because the formation of the National League meant the ousting from major hockey of Eddie Livingstone, of Toronto, who held a franchise in the National Association, which preceded the NHL and had a week before met an unexpected death, when all its members except Livingstone resigned.

George Kennedy and Livingstone didn't get along, personally. They almost came to blows on a few occasions, at meetings of the National Association. George Kennedy was a jovial and friendly man, one of the gaudy, florid type of sports folk who kept the sports wheels turning in the Gay Nineties [1890s], and around the turn of the century. George had been a wrestler, under the name of George Kennedy. His real name was Kendall. He took on the other tag because his folks didn't look kindly on wrestling. George was a colourful personality, a free spender, wore a huge diamond in his tie, another glittering rock of three carats or so on his finger.

So we asked George what had been going on. "Well," he said, "let us go down to the bar and I'll tell you what happened."

So we did, and he did. "We formed a new hockey league," said George. "It is called the National League, and it's just about the same thing as the NHA, with one exception," he added, grinning mischievously.

We guessed: "You haven't invited Eddie Livingstone into the new group?"

"No," said George thoughtfully, "We haven't. I guess we forgot. Anyway, he is still a member of the National Association, and has a franchise in that fine body. Of course he may have a little difficulty getting a place to play, and any teams to play against. Because the rest of us just resigned from the Association and formed this new league. Eddie still has his team and Association franchise. Good luck to him. Now, what about a drink?"

"It's strictly legal," the late Sam Lichtenhein, owner of the Wanderers, dropped by and assured us. "We didn't throw Eddie Livingstone out. Perish the thought. That would have been illegal and unfair. Also, it wouldn't have been sporting. We just resigned, and wished him a fine future with his National Association franchise."

Tommy Gorman, representing the Ottawa club, chortled happily, as was his wont. "Great day for hockey," he said. "Livingstone was always arguing. No place for arguing in hockey. Let's make money instead." And, chuckling happily, Tommy Gorman dashed off to catch the Ottawa train.

Mike Quinn had represented Quebec at this meeting. His mighty Bulldogs, with the peerless Joe Malone scoring 30 goals or so in each of the brief seasons of the time, had been Stanley Cup winners, but Quebec couldn't support a professional team then, and Mike, a handsome, debonair chap, always dressed and kid-gloved in the height of fashion, decided not to operate that first year, and drifted off to the Quebec train.

William Northey, manager of the major rink in Montreal, the Westmount Arena where Wanderers played, had represented Toronto. When Quebec dropped out, the Toronto Arenas came in. The Westmount Arena burned down, Wanderers were homeless, and they dropped out. So, in its first year, the NHL operated with three teams, Canadiens, Ottawa and Toronto, and employed a playoff system by dividing the season into two halves, an idea which was borrowed from the National Association. And Toronto won the title.

Every person mentioned in the above bit of reminiscence has since passed away. Last to go was William Northey, a fine constructive sportsman who was responsible for building the Montreal Forum, among other accomplishments. Frank Calder died quietly, after being stricken with a heart attack. He was in his Montreal hospital bed, the League books spread around him one morning. He was ready to carry on the business of the league, when death tapped him on the shoulder. When Canadiens and Seattle engaged in their Stanley Cup series the spring of 1919, the Black 'flu, sweeping the continent, forced cessation of the series, unfinished. Joe Hall, famed defence star, died. George

Kennedy was stricken, failed steadily in health, and died in 1921. His widow sold the club to the combination of Joe Cattarinich, Leo Dandurand and Louis Letourneau for $11,500.

Laughing Tommy Gorman died at his Ottawa home. Millionaire Sam Lichtenhein died in Montreal. We always thought that after his son Phillip passed away, Sam wasn't much interested in living any longer. But in the era when he owned the Wanderers, and the Montreal Royals baseball team, Sam Lichtenhein was a remarkable and unpredictable character. When, in 1911, it was proposed to move from the cumbersome 7-man game to six players, Sam stood stolidly against it. "We'll offend everybody in Canada," he declared. "'Hockey is a 7-man game, everybody in Canada knows it. We can't buck tradition."

Without a complete agreement, the National League couldn't adopt six-man hockey. William Northey solved the problem. "Did it ever occur to you, Sam," he asked the Wanderer owner, "that with six-man hockey you would have one less salary to pay?"

"I never thought of that," said Sam. "By George, this is a great idea, this six-man hockey. I'm for it."

And so it came into being.

Eddie Livingstone didn't stop fighting. He posted a couple of retainers in the old Jubilee rink, the shabby east-side natural ice rink where Canadiens were born. His idea was to seize the rink, and prevent Canadiens from playing there. George Kennedy laughed tolerantly. One autumn afternoon he sent a squad of a dozen rugged chaps, wrestlers and such, and the Livingstone forces, out-numbered, fled in disorder, while George laughed and bought a dinner for the boys.

Then Eddie went into the courts, but got nowhere. As the boys declared, it was all quite legal. They didn't throw Eddie out. They just resigned, left him a one-team league of his own, complete with franchise. All very legal. Pretty shrewd, too. So there's not "only a few of us left" from that meeting 48 years ago. Just one. Your faithful observer.[11]

Ferguson's words are the sole remaining legacy of that meeting. It must be pointed out that, not only was Ferguson "the only reporter remaining on the scene," but he was well known to the "magnates of the day." The *Herald's* sports editor often made a few extra bucks officiating National Hockey Association games, and Frank Calder would appoint him the fledgling NHL's first official statistician.

It was not uncommon for the press to have such a cozy relationship with hockey's powers that be. A former journalist himself, Calder often enlisted the help of reporters to spread the good word about the NHL; in exchange, he would frequently find room for them on the league's payroll as a referee, or an arena employee, or on the staff of the member teams. The clubs might also take it upon themselves to support the Fourth Estate. In 1925, Frank Ahearn bought the Ottawa Senators from Tommy Gorman, and immediately the team became a target of Gorman's former employer, the Ottawa *Citizen*. After the paper alleged that the Senators had rigged some games, Ahearn, with Calder's support, sued the *Citizen* for $45,000. Under oath, Ahearn said that the team had paid $1,000 for display advertising — and for write-ups in the *Citizen's* sports pages! He even produced a contract to that effect.[12]

Ferguson's tale of the NHL's formation has always been the official account. As the version above appeared nearly half a century after the fact, one might be willing to forgive the sportswriter if his memory of the events strayed a little from the facts. But Ferguson is so inaccurate that the disservice he has done the sport survives into the present day.

And Fergie was wrong on one important count.

The NHL didn't exactly rid itself of Eddie Livingstone on that November day in 1917.

Chapter 2

Frank Calder's Beginnings

"Certainly Frank Calder didn't have any such perceptivity. The redheaded Britisher who had come to Canada to play professional soccer, and as a sports writer fell in love with hockey, was no soothsayer."

— Elmer Ferguson, 1965

*F*rank Calder was born to Scottish parents in Bristol, England, on November 17, 1877. The redheaded aspiring soccer player with the round face and square jaw immigrated to Canada in 1900 and began teaching at the Abingdon School, an English-language private school that

Courtesy of the Hockey Hall of Fame

no longer exists. After abandoning an athletic career, Calder fell in love with and married a fellow teacher, Amelia Cole. While his parents had never needed to worry where tomorrow's dinner was coming from, Calder discovered he was going to have to work hard to meet the demands associated with being a newly-wed with a daughter on the way. Three sons soon followed.

Frank Calder

Rugged, with a stocky physique, Calder by nature was reticent, reserved and generally self-contained. He preferred to use three words rather than three sentences if he thought he could get away with it. His eyes were grey, his gaze steady and direct. His mouth was almost always fixed in a tight-lipped expression that made him look grim at times, but his friends consistently described his nature as kindly and charitable.

His reputation for honesty was beyond reproach. Were Frank Calder so inclined as to sell you Montreal's grand Nôtre-Dame Basilica, chances are you'd pay cash and allow him to deliver the title deed at his convenience.

Although rarely sentimental, the British expatriate always had presence of mind to remember a favour or to loan money to a down-on-his-luck former sportsman. He was meticulous to a fault — it was said that no detail was too small to be overseen by Frank Calder. These days he might be described as a control freak — and it's true that during Calder's twenty-five-year reign as president of the National Hockey League, he employed exactly two people to work in the head office. One was a stenographer, taken on at the suggestion of the New York Rangers owner Tex Rickard after an instance when Calder was unable to provide adequate minutes of a piece of business transacted at a meeting of the NHL board of governors. The other was a secretary to answer the phone during his frequent absences: Calder travelled so much on league business that American Airlines fêted him as its first passenger to fly more than 100,000 miles. Calder wrote, typed and approved every item, letter, note and press release that left the NHL's Montreal head office. Through the years, he kept himself physically fit by playing a daily game of handball.

The young Calders moved around at first, changing addresses no fewer than four times between 1905 and 1913. Initially they lived in the Westmount district, which to this day is predominantly English-speaking; in 1907, they moved east and across the river to Longueuil, a community where little English is spoken. Also in 1907, Frank Calder left his position as assistant master of the Abingdon School to become the sports editor of the Montreal *Witness*.

From the *Witness*, Calder jumped to the Montreal *Herald and Daily Telegraph*, again as sports editor. A couple of years later he hired a young journalist from Moncton, New Brunswick, by the name of Elmer Ferguson. "Ferg," as Calder called him, proved every bit as forthright as his mentor. One day, Calder assigned him to cover a boxing exhibition at the old Readoscope Theatre on Nôtre-Dame Street East. The advertised match was between two noted welterweights of the era, the Dixie

Kid and Bill Hurley. Ferguson, who had seen both fighters before, took his seat in the packed house and found that he didn't recognize one of the combatants. "He was an impostor," Ferguson wrote, "who hardly knew how to put on his gloves, and was knocked out in the first round."

Calder asked Ferg if he was sure of his facts. Ferguson replied in the affirmative.

"Nice work," Calder said.

Calder later confirmed the impersonation and he and Ferguson were on their way to a lifelong friendship.

One of Calder's last stories for the *Herald* involved an investigation of racetracks and gambling. A group of gamblers and race fixers, having exhausted the Montreal venues, had leased a small track in Valleyfield, Quebec — about twenty miles southwest — and started a series. Calder denounced the meeting as a travesty: the track was deep in mud; horses fell and were put down; jockeys were injured. Calder campaigned tirelessly against the race promoters, who responded to his efforts by offering him a job. He turned it down. Next they offered him hush money. Calder sneered, then campaigned so bitterly in the press that the promoters were forced to shut down their operation.

According to Ferguson, out of sheer admiration for Calder's trenchant pen and for the way he had fought them, the racetrack consortium sent him an expensive pair of diamond-set platinum cuff links. These were returned by the next mail, with a letter that should have been written on asbestos.

Leaving the sports reporting to the capable "Ferg," Calder moved on to the financial editor's chair, which covered what was then Canada's largest market, the Montreal Stock Exchange. Still, he did not abandon the sports world — far from it. He is named as a founder of the Montreal School Rugby League, and he served as secretary of the Montreal and District Football League, a soccer league that evolved into the Province of Quebec Football Association — with Calder as treasurer. Thus his leap into professional hockey management was not without precedent.

Whether driven by his noble upbringing, or his self-imposed duty to right the ills of the world, Calder made a name for himself with the publication of a piece called "The Wrestling Trust." Written for a weekly publication after he had left the *Herald* in 1912, "The Wrestling Trust" was an exposé of corruption within the Montreal pro wrestling circuit. Calder charged that four men — George Kennedy, Jack Curley, Jack Herman and Jim Coffee — were engaged in fixing the bouts. It was one of the first attacks on the sport.

Asked his opinion of the story, George Kennedy said, "I don't like it, but you've got to admit the guy has plenty of guts to write it."

In an odd turn of events, it would be Kennedy who, a few years later, recommended to NHA president Emmett Quinn that Calder be hired as the league's secretary and treasurer.

Like Calder, Kennedy had enjoyed all the advantages of being raised in a prosperous family. He was born George Washington Kendall in Montreal on December 29, 1881. His father, also named George, had been a merchant seaman before he married. With a child on the way, George senior came ashore for good and went into business for himself. In time the younger Kendall, a stocky man with a round, expressive face that was usually topped by a bowler hat, would join his father's compa-

ny as a bookkeeper. By that time, the firm had changed its name from G. H. Kendall and Company to the Montreal Carpet Boating Company.

The hard-working father did not always see eye to eye with his athletic young son, who after a short time left the company's employ. In 1901, Kendall began boxing and wrestling competitively, a choice that did not sit well with his father. Legend has it that George senior so disapproved of his son's involvement in wrestling that he kicked him out of his firm *and* his house. As if to further emphasize his estrangement from the family, George Washington Kendall began fighting under the name George Kennedy.

He became the amateur boxing champion of Canada in his weight

George Kendall, who took the surname "Kennedy" after becoming estranged from his family during his wrestling career

class, but a 1903 loss to Eugene Tremblay in a wrestling match convinced Kennedy he wasn't going to make it as a professional athlete. Instead he turned to sports promotion, and his first such venture was to find matches for Tremblay. His most notorious moment came on May 8, 1904, when he staged a "Bull Wrestling Match" on the National Lacrosse Grounds. The afternoon spectacle devolved into a farce when the bull decided that the grass of the lacrosse grounds was far more interesting than Neromus, the bullfighter. Poor Neromus tried to wrestle the bull, but had to be rescued when the bull held him against the grandstand fence. A year later Kennedy joined forces with J. P. Gadbois to found the *Club Athlétique Canadien*, which was incorporated in 1908.

Hardheaded to a fault, Kennedy tried his hand as a furrier and tailor for a few years, and even made an ill-fated attempt as a plumber. Despite the apparent lack of direction, Kennedy was able to make a comfortable home in Montreal's better English neighbourhoods for himself and his wife, the former Myrtle Agnes Pagels, whom he married on June 1, 1907. The couple had two daughters, one of whom died before her first birthday.

The *Club Athlétique Canadien* flourished, promoting boxing and wrestling — not only in Montreal, but all over North America — as well as hockey, baseball, lacrosse and even bowling. In 1912, a clubhouse was built at the corner of Ste-Catherine and St-André streets. Perhaps the pivotal date in the club's history came in 1910 when, as part of an out-of-court settlement, it became the owner of the Montreal Canadiens of the National Hockey Association.

According to Frank Cosentino's book *The Renfrew Millionaires*, the story of how George Kennedy's *Club Athlétique Canadien* came to own the Canadiens hockey team begins a year earlier — and about two hundred miles to the northwest.

In November 1909, Ambrose O'Brien set off for Montreal to petition the Stanley Cup's trustees to allow his team from Renfrew, in Ontario's Ottawa River Valley, to compete for the trophy. While Renfrew could not exactly be considered a hockey capital, as recently as January 1907 a team from the tiny northwestern Ontario community of Kenora had upset the powerful Montreal Wanderers to claim the national title. In addition, the smallish right winger was no ordinary hockey operator: his father was the railroad and mining magnate M. J. O'Brien, and so he had access to virtually unlimited capital. The Cup trustees refused his request; undaunted, O'Brien approached the Cup champion Ottawa Hockey Club to propose an exhibition game. Again, he was rebuffed.

O'Brien was not one to be easily discouraged. He concluded that if he could gain membership in the Eastern Canada Hockey Association — the league that effectively controlled the Stanley Cup — he could realize his dream of bringing the trophy home to Renfrew. Influenced by the defending champions from Ottawa, the ECHA refused to admit O'Brien's team into the circuit. But another piece of league business would seal Ambrose O'Brien's place in hockey history.

As it turned out, the ECHA had a problem in Montreal, where the Wanderers' new owner, P. J. Doran, had decided to move his team from the Montreal Arena to the much smaller Jubilee Rink — which he happened to own. It was a change that threatened to cut the visiting teams' share of the gate receipts by more than half. On November 25, 1909, the other owners responded by voting to dissolve the ECHA and form a new league: the Canadian Hockey Association. The Wanderers were out, their place taken by a pair of Montreal teams: *le National*, owned by and stocked with French-Canadians, and All-Montreal, led by the star defenceman Art Ross.

Jimmy Gardner, the Wanderers' left winger and manager, was attending the league meetings on Doran's behalf. While the bosses of the newly minted CHA met in Room 135 of the Windsor Hotel, Gardner held discussions with O'Brien down the hall in Room 129. A week later the pair announced that they had organized a rival league, the *National* Hockey Association, which would also include teams from the Ontario mining communities of Haileybury and Cobalt. Both of these teams had been playing in the Temiskaming league — and not coincidentally, both were owned by the O'Brien family.

Almost immediately, and as somewhat of an afterthought, a fifth team was created from scratch: *les Canadiens*. Two strong motives drove this decision. On the one hand, a fifth team would give the NHA the same number as the CHA — and therefore, O'Brien hoped, a similar measure of credibility with the Cup trustees. On the other, Gardner had convinced O'Brien that an intra-city rivalry in Montreal, the cradle of hockey, would be good for the league, especially if the enmity between English and French could be worked into the picture. O'Brien agreed to finance the Canadiens for one year, in hopes that French-Canadian interests would take the team off his hands after the 1909–10 season. Toronto's Eddie McCafferty was also granted a franchise, with the understanding the team could begin play once it had an arena built.[13]

The NHA would compete with the CHA for players — scoring a major coup by enticing the Ottawa star Fred "Cyclone" Taylor to sign with Renfrew — and for fans, at least in oversaturated Montreal. Between the two leagues, there were five teams slated to play out of the city's two rinks in 1909–10. Games would often be staggered to start at 7:00 and 9:00 P.M. to accommodate the teams.

About two weeks into the schedule, the two-league arrangement had proven to be an economic disaster, and the NHA and CHA merged — in a manner of speaking. The NHA agreed to take on only Ottawa and the Montreal Shamrocks. *Le National*, All-Montreal and the Quebec City team were cast adrift. At the time of the amalgamation, O'Brien thought he had made a deal to sell *les Canadiens* to their all-French CHA counterparts, *le National*. The following article from the *Gazette* shows just how close we came to revering the Montreal Nationals as hockey's most successful franchise.

> Nationals definitely decided today not to take over the franchise of the Canadian club in the National Hockey Association. The hitch came principally in the matter of rinks. Canadians insisted that the transfer of the franchise must bring with it the obligation of the Canadian club to play in the Jubilee rink. Nationals were bound by contract to the Arena, but the Arena management expressed a willingness to waive their claims on the club if suitable arrangements could be made with Canadian owners in other respects. However, for one thing, Nationals could not figure how they could make any even break in their finances unless they played in the larger rink. Finally a compromise of three games in the Jubilee and three games in the Arena was suggested by the Nationals, but Canadians declined, and with this negotiations were broken off. It was reported tonight that it would have cost the Nationals $9,000 to assume the season obligations of the Canadians. Possibly when the franchise would be purchased the Nationals would find difficulties with their players and other costly problems might arise.
>
> In any event, after two meetings of the directors of the Nationals today, it was announced that Nationals would take over the obligation of the Canadian club only on condition that they play their games at the Arena. As Canadians refused negotiations were broken off. In the evening Mr. Nap Dorval stated that his club would stick to the Canadian association and would ask tomorrow that a meeting of that body be called at once so that the clubs could find out where they stood.[14]

It was easily the worst business decision Dorval ever made.

The 1910 season was a rough one for Amby O'Brien. He'd paid out some outrageous salaries in an attempt to make his Renfrew Creamery Kings a Stanley Cup contender. As a result, the team is widely known as the Renfrew Millionaires. But they finished third behind the Wanderers — the only charter member of the NHA that O'Brien didn't own — and Ottawa, the very team that Renfrew had raided to acquire Cyclone Taylor. As league champions, it was the Wanderers who would go on to claim the Stanley Cup by defeating a challenger from Berlin (now Kitchener), Ontario.

At the other end of the spectrum, *les Canadiens* struggled on the ice — their record of 2 wins and 10 losses placing them at the bottom of the seven-team NHA — and at the box office. The team's financial losses made it all the more urgent for O'Brien to find local, French-Canadian ownership for the NHA's second season. Fate intervened, in the form of a lawsuit filed by George Kennedy of the *Club Athlétique Canadien*, who felt the name "*les Canadiens*" infringed on his wrestling club's trademark. O'Brien sensed an opportunity.

While he would have preferred to pocket some cash by selling the Canadiens, O'Brien was relieved to find a French-Canadian who was interested in his league. In what has to be the easiest out-of-court settlement in hockey's history, O'Brien agreed to give Kennedy the hockey club in exchange for the withdrawal of the suit. On November 12, 1910, Kennedy promptly changed the official name from *les Canadiens* to *Club Athlétique Canadien*, although most Montrealers still referred to the team as the Canadiens. For the next three seasons the team's sweaters would bear a maple leaf crest, superimposed with the initials CAC.

Dorval, through his friendship with Kennedy, later redeemed himself by taking a small position in the hockey club. He retained the shares until 1921.

If Kennedy thought he had one-upped O'Brien and got something for nothing, an unpleasant surprise awaited him.

During the 1909–10 season, the Canadiens had loaned the superstar centre Edouard "Newsy" Lalonde to Renfrew for four games. It would be considered a remarkable transaction had O'Brien not owned both teams. O'Brien promised the Cornwall, Ontario–born francophone that the transfer was only temporary, and that he would be returned to Montreal at season's end. Apparently, Amby had a change of heart. On December 15, 1910, Lalonde skated onto the ice for the Canadiens' first practice under Kennedy's ownership. At the end of the session, he was greeted by O'Brien and his partner, George Martel. They informed him that Renfrew had not released him, and that they still considered the NHA's leading scorer of 1909–10 to be their property. By hook or by crook, O'Brien meant to get some quid pro quo for his former franchise, and the best way to do that was to tie up the rights to the league's marquee player.

When reporters asked whether a deal couldn't be made to allow Lalonde to stay in Montreal, Martel replied that it was all up to the Canadiens. In the end, Kennedy settled by paying O'Brien $7,500 for the rights to Lalonde. Newsy would repay Kennedy by locking horns with him every year over his salary — proving, if nothing else, that time marches on, yet time stands still.

O'Brien may have won that battle, but retribution awaited the upstart from Renfrew. Sportsmen in Montreal, the first city the Cup called home, had long considered the trophy to be their birthright — and so far, Ottawa had proven to be the only consistently successful rival to their dominance of the game. By founding the NHA, O'Brien had hoped to break the Ottawa-Montreal compact, but thanks to the CHA merger his adversaries had become his business partners. His fellow owners envisioned an all-powerful league that would give them control of the Stanley Cup in perpetuity. And those plans would not include J. Ambrose O'Brien or his Renfrew Creamery Kings.

Chapter 3

The Trash King and Yarn Spinner

"Tommy Gorman, representing the Ottawa club, chortled happily, as was his wont."

— Elmer Ferguson, 1965

*F*rank Calder was tiring of the newspaper business. His reports about the Wrestling Trust had not only garnered him job offers and jewellery — which he characteristically turned down or returned to their senders — but they had yielded threats to himself and his family. It was about this time that he became fascinated with the winter sport of hockey and struck up friendships with the Ottawa reporter Tommy Gorman and the Montreal sports baron Sam Lichtenhein.

The contrast between Calder — the stoic, reticent straight shooter — and these two men could not have been more pronounced, yet Calder and Gorman almost always saw eye-to-eye. Calder and Lichtenhein also developed a strong friendship; almost anytime Lichtenhein wanted something, Calder provided it willingly, and vice versa.

Samuel E. Lichtenhein, owner of the Montreal Wanderers

Courtesy of The Ottawa Citizen

Gorman, or "T.P." as he was known around the newsroom, was a loquacious storyteller about whom the Hall of Fame centre Frank Boucher once said, "He was an excellent writer, even if he wasn't always accurate. He always had an angle. My brother George used to say that he never wrote anything without a purpose, and that you had to try to figure out what that purpose was."[15]

Tommy Gorman attended the Montreal Canadiens' first game at Renfrew in his capacity as a reporter. The match featured an altercation between Newsy Lalonde and the normally mild-mannered Lester Patrick. Gorman reported that "Lester Patrick and 'Newsy' Lalonde were each banished three times, the rival captains clashing on several occasions. In the second half Patrick cut Lalonde's head open with a swing and as soon as the Renfrew leader had got back in play, Lalonde got to him with a wicked cross check that sent the famous rover into the air as though shot from a cannon."[16]

It is difficult to gauge how serious these "assaults" truly were, but Gorman is almost definitely embellishing. For their transgressions, Patrick and Lalonde were each assessed no more than a two-minute penalty. They tell us the hockey was rougher in the old days, but surely being "shot from a cannon" was worthy of more than a couple of minutes on the fence. Even then. And we can't imagine anyone being crosschecked so severely and not needing a breather. But as Gorman himself goes on to report, "Gilmour and Millaire were the only players forced to retire, Referee Eddie Phillips and Judge of Play Bouse Hutton handling everything to perfection."

But that was Gorman.

One of Gorman's most legendary flights of journalistic fancy, a tale that has been handed down as part of hockey lore for more than ninety years, deals with Cyclone Taylor's famed backwards goal.

In February 1910, Cyclone's Renfrew Creamery Kings were scheduled to play Ottawa in what was his return to the nation's capital. Gorman wrote that the superstar had vowed — albeit in jest and with his former teammate, the goaltender Percy LeSueur, in the room — that he would score a goal while skating backwards through the entire Ottawa team. A crowd of 6,800 — the largest to attend a hockey game in Ottawa to that date — packed into the arena, with fans lining the standing-room areas three and four deep.

The game was a classic, with the score tied 5–5 at the end of regulation time. In those days, overtime consisted of a pair of five-minute periods — there being no sudden death — and Ottawa scored three times to win 8–5 and effectively laid to rest Renfrew's Stanley Cup dreams. Taylor was effective, and managed to win over the hostile crowd, but was held off the scoresheet. As Gorman reported, eleven minutes into the second half, "The one and only Taylor, the cyncosure of all eyes, eventually carried the puck through to Whitcroft who, amidst a wild demonstration on the parts of the Renfrew backers, tied the score."[17] The wire services said that, "The crowd towards the close were unable to retain a demonstration in favour of Taylor. When he carried the rubber down and gave it over to Whitcroft, who tied the score, nearly every one in the rink broke into cheers. Nine out of ten people expect Taylor to go up in the air, but, on the contrary, he was as cool as an iceberg."[18]

Like the Millionaires' Cup hopes, Taylor's promise to score a goal backwards went unfulfilled.

The teams would face off again a few weeks later in Renfrew. By that time, what had been projected as a showdown between the two pre-season Cup favourites had become a meaningless game; the Montreal Wanderers had surprised everyone by clinching the league championship. In those days of Cup challenges, a Stanley Cup champion that lost its league's title the following year surrendered to the new league champs the right to defend the trophy. So it was that the Wanderers captured the Stanley Cup from the Ottawa Senators.

With nothing to prove, Ottawa played a listless game while Renfrew came out with all its guns blazing and romped to a 17–2 rout. The Millionaires' newest addition, Newsy Lalonde, scored nine of the team's seventeen goals — and he wasn't even the star of the game. That honour belonged to Cyclone Taylor, who scored three goals against his former team — including the one mythic tally that is still talked about in hockey circles.

Twenty-five minutes into the second half, Taylor made good on his promise. He had lots of room in which to work: each team had three men on the penalty bench, leaving either side with only three skaters plus a goaltender. As Tommy Gorman wrote in the Ottawa *Citizen* under the headline "Taylor Scores Backward":

> For five minutes there were only four men on each side. [Percy] LeSueur, [Walter] Smaill, [Marty] Walsh and [Bruce] Ridpath [for Ottawa] playing against [Bert] Lindsay, [Bobby] Rowe, [Cyclone] Taylor and Frank Patrick. Rowe was penalized and Renfrew for a minute had only two men, they scored after Lester Patrick had resumed. Taylor got this goal, and it was actually shot while the Listowell Cyclone was skating

backwards, LeSueur missing a swift side shot by an inch or two.[19]

The Renfrew *Journal's* article also featured the subheading "Taylor scores backward." Without reading the complete story, it would be easy to conclude from these accounts that Taylor skated the length of the ice backwards, showboating through a full complement of Ottawa players and scoring a meaningful goal. In *The Renfrew Millionaires*, Frank Cosentino writes:

> Taylor picked up the puck in his own end and raced towards the boards, sharply cutting up ice. He isolated the point men with a feint inside and moved around them. In just a few strides he was alone in on LeSueur. He pivoted around, his back to the goalie and while continuing backwards, lifted the puck past the startled Ottawa net-minder! [20]

Which might suggest a goal scored on Taylor's backhand more than it would a goal scored while skating backwards. Taylor, for his part, was canny enough to know that Gorman's version was a cornerstone upon which his legend had been built, and he was not about to explode any myths. Until finally, more than sixty years later, he felt the time had come to set the record straight.

In 1973, the legendary Toronto *Star* sportswriter Frank Orr was preparing to interview Cyclone at the Pacific Coliseum in Vancouver. Noticing the old guy in the fedora skating on the ice, he asked the Hall of Fame defenceman Babe Pratt who it was. Pratt pointed out that it was Taylor. Orr asked Pratt how many goals he thought Taylor would score in the expanded, sixteen-team NHL.

"Sixteen to eighteen," Pratt replied.

Orr was incredulous. "Sixteen to eighteen? Is that it? He was one of the all-time greats."

"Yeah, well," Pratt replied, "you'd have to remember he's eighty-nine years old."

Then Orr asked Taylor about the backwards goal. Cyclone testified that he could not recall scoring one backwards, "not unless one went in off my rear."[21]

However much the product of his imagination, the story of the goal provided the foundation for Gorman's career as well as Taylor's. According to a 1999 article in the *Citizen*, the account helped earn Gorman a promotion to sports editor, a position from which he was eventually able to take over ownership of the Ottawa Senators.

Samuel Lichtenhein viewed life as though he was a monarch and his employees were serfs — even though he had literally achieved his station in life from the proceeds of his father's trash.

Edward Lichtenhein operated the Montreal Cotton & Wood Waste Company, and as a result young Sammy was born with a silver spoon and raised in the finest neighbourhoods in Westmount. In time, the junior Lichtenhein was appointed the company's manager, and after Edward's death in 1915 he took over the family business. His first foray into professional sports came in 1908, when he purchased the Montreal Royals of baseball's Eastern League, and the hockey Wanderers were added to his portfolio in December 1910.

True to his character, Lichtenhein burst onto the Montreal sporting scene with a flair that would have been more at home in Hollywood. His first target was the press, which at that time included one Francis Calder.

"It is easy to get good advice from people who know more about your [sporting] venture than you do yourself," Lichtenhein said, "… but the same men are never around when there is any chance that they will have to break into their wads to help things along. For the last month there have been interviews in the papers with men 'prominent in hockey circles' in which they were stated that 'such and such' should be done, but where are they tonight?"[22]

Furthermore, he sneered that the business of the Wanderers should be handed over to the newspapers to run, because "they will run our business anyway."[23] Little could Lichtenhein have suspected that he would one day invite a newspaperman, none other than Calder, to join his hockey league's executive committee.

Chapter 4

The Western Raiders and an Ottawa Power Play

Without a complete agreement, the National League could-
n't adopt six-man hockey. William Northey solved the prob-
lem. "Did it ever occur to you, Sam," he asked the Wanderer
owner, "that with six-man hockey you would have one less
salary to pay?"

"I never thought of that," said Sam. "By George, this is
a great idea, this six-man hockey. I'm for it."

And so it came into being.

— Elmer Ferguson, 1965

*I*n *1907, Joe Patrick sold* his lumber business in Quebec and moved west to start up another one. His destination was the new (incorporated in 1897) community of Nelson, British Columbia, located on an arm of Kootenay Lake about 150 miles north of Spokane, Washington. He was accompanied by his eldest son, Lester, who at the age of twenty-three had already been a standout player for two Stanley Cup–winning teams, the Montreal Wanderers of 1906 and 1907. A second son, Frank, who was two years Lester's junior, remained in Montreal to attend McGill University — and to play defence for the school's hockey team. After spending the 1907–08 campaign with the Montreal Victorias, Frank followed his family to B.C.

While both sons had moved west to help their father run his business, it soon became clear that their appetite for competition would not go unsated, as they both played for the local side in Nelson. In December 1908, Lester accepted an invitation to join an Edmonton squad that made an unsuccessful bid to dethrone his old team, the Wanderers, as

Stanley Cup champions. They may have been thousands of miles away, but the eastern hockey establishment did not forget the Patrick boys. In 1909, when Ambrose O'Brien of the newly formed National Hockey Association was stacking his Renfrew Creamery Kings with a lineup designed to win the Cup, he sought out and signed Frank and Lester.

In 1910–11, the NHA dropped the Montreal Shamrocks as well as its teams in Cobalt and Haileybury. Also absent from the league were the Patricks, who had returned to Nelson. By this time, Joe Patrick was again ready to sell his lumber operation, and his sons convinced him to invest some of the proceeds in an idea of theirs: the Pacific Coast Hockey Association.

The PCHA was a revolutionary concept in that Frank and Lester planned to own and operate the league, it teams, *and* its arenas. Unlike their eastern brethren, the brothers proposed to make hockey their sole business activity and source of income. As a concession to the mild Pacific coast climate, the rinks — built in Vancouver and Victoria, with a third scheduled for New Westminster on B.C.'s Lower Mainland — were also state of the art: they were the first in Canada to feature artificial ice. Another way in which the Patricks departed from the status quo: while they cultivated members of the press and were well aware of the promotional value their coverage would yield, they did not hire reporters as league officials.

The brothers drew up a schedule for the coming winter, 1911–12, and to stock the new league with players they called upon many of their old teammates and friends in the east. There was a surplus of players available: the Renfrew Creamery Kings had disbanded after their second NHA season when Ambrose O'Brien balked at the — expensive — prospect of travelling from Renfrew to Toronto, a city into which the NHA planned to expand. The Toronto expansion was put on hold pending completion of the city's Arena Gardens, prompting O'Brien to make overtures to be allowed to play one more season, but he was rebuffed.

The owners of the four remaining NHA teams picked at the Millionaires' carcass by holding a dispersal draft of the team's players. Cyclone Taylor, Renfrew's star rover and arguably one of the top ten players of all time, was claimed by the Montreal Wanderers, as was Donald Smith. Montreal owner Sam Lichtenhein thought he had taken a giant step towards regaining the NHA title and the Stanley Cup, but the Patricks would foil his plans in short order. Jimmy Gardner, the man who had been instrumental in the creation of the Wanderers' intra-city rivals the Canadiens, joined the New Westminster Royals, becoming one of the first NHA players to flee to the coast. He brought defensive stalwarts Ernie "Moose" Johnson and forward Harry Hyland with him to the

Royal City. Defenceman Walter Smaill became a Victoria Senator, as did forward Don Smith, who had signed with Montreal but hadn't skated a shift as a Wanderer.

The Patricks committed their greatest act of larceny against Sam Lichtenhein, however, with the acquisition in 1912 of Cyclone Taylor, who by this time had not only emerged as the game's first national superstar, but was used to being the focus of controversy.

The Montreal Wanderers owned Taylor's NHA playing rights, a fact that didn't jibe with his career plans. He had a comfortable off-ice job with the federal government in the Interior Department, and he was not terribly interested in leaving the nation's capital. Taylor went so far as to say that he would quit the game altogether rather than sacrifice his job. Furthermore, he was keen on returning to his old team in Ottawa and believed that he ought to have been given the chance to purchase his release from the Renfrew team.

Ottawa management tried to make a deal to pry Taylor loose. The Senators actually owned a player on the Montreal roster: Gord Roberts, an outstanding left winger. In 1910 Roberts announced his intention to study medicine at McGill University, a move the Senators facilitated by loaning him to the Wanderers until his studies were completed. With this in mind, Ottawa proposed a one-for-one trade: Taylor for Roberts. Lichtenhein demurred; Roberts was a very good player — in fact he was named to the Hockey Hall of Fame in 1971 — but he was no Taylor. He asked Ottawa to throw in their right winger, Albert "Dubbie" Kerr, and a sum of cash. The Senators had no problem with the money, but refused to part with Kerr, so trade talks broke down.

Taylor could only sit and watch — and grow increasingly fed up with Lichtenhein's antics. "It looks as if I won't play hockey at all this winter," he told the Citizen's sports editor, Tommy Gorman.

"Are you not going down to play for Wanderers?" a *Citizen* man asked.

"No, I am not," was the emphatic reply.

"Haven't they fixed things up yet?"

"No, there isn't any fixing to do. I do not intend to go to Montreal to play for Wanderers or any other team. If I don't play with Ottawa I shall certainly remain out of hockey.

"No, I do not intend to go to the Coast, either," concluded Taylor. "I'd like to play this winter, but it does not look as though I would do so."[24] Instead, he spent the winter working out at the Rideau rink with the Dominion Methodist Church Sunday School team.

An angry Lichtenhein told the Ottawa *Journal*, "You can take this final word from me, Taylor will play for me or he will sit on a bench all winter. I won't release him. I won't sell him, nor will I trade him to Ottawa or anyone else." The Wanderers owner added that he had everything fixed with the Cyclone, and that all that was needed was the necessary leave of absence from the Interior Department.

"If he could get off to play for Ottawa, he could get off to play for the Wanderers," Lichtenhein said. "The government should have no favourite hockey team." He also intimated that he feared Ottawa might be tampering with his star puck chaser. "I am coming up to Ottawa soon and if I find the Ottawa club have been approaching Taylor there will be big trouble. There is a $500 to $1,000 fine provided for that sort of thing. I need Taylor because I have promised the public I was going to have him. If some of our present team get hurt they would say I was trying to run things on the cheap by selling all my good men after the public had bought their season tickets."[25]

Lichtenhein's tantrum forced Emmett Quinn, the president of the NHA, to call an emergency meeting. In the days leading up to that conference, Lichtenhein continued his tirade against the Ottawa owners, reminding the public of the long-running feud between the Wanderers and Senators, which dated back to a 1904 Stanley Cup challenge from which the Wanderers walked away after tying the first game 5–5. Back then, the Wanderers found fault with the refereeing and turned down subsequent attempts to replay the match. It was a dispute that prompted the Stanley Cup's trustees to accept a challenge from Joe Boyle of the Yukon in the hopes of restoring public confidence in the Cup. An article in the Ottawa *Journal* suggests that Lichtenhein still saw favouritism displayed towards the Senators:

> Mr. Sam Lichtenhein, of the Wanderers, said that Ottawa was the "spoiled child in the N.H.A. family," and claimed that it had been a one-team league for these many moons. This is all to be changed now, and Ottawa is to have its wings clipped — or trimmed off altogether. In future we must take our directions from Montreal. Toronto also claim that they will be pre-eminent in the hockey world next season. 'Tis evident that we will have to serve many masters in the near future.[26]

While Lichtenhein aimed to lay down the law where Ottawa was concerned, Phil Ross — the publisher of the *Journal* and one of the

Stanley Cup's trustees — was planning to do likewise to Lichtenhein. "If the Wanderers president thinks he is doing the 'Cyclone' any good by keeping him out of hockey, he is welcome to his opinion," Ross wrote, "but it is certain that such antics will injure the game far more than boosting it, and in the end it would not be surprising if the Montreal club suffered most."[27]

The overheated rhetoric in the sports pages makes it hard to determine whether such a trade was actually discussed, but the Ottawa papers reported that Lichtenhein had asked for Kerr and Skene Ronan in exchange for Taylor, then left the matter with the Senators to accept or decline as they thought fit.

"The Ottawa Hockey Club will not consider any of the propositions which Mr. Lichtenhein made," said team treasurer N. C. Sparks. "His offers were preposterous. None of our players are for sale."[28]

The next day Lichtenhein stepped up his threats, giving Ottawa one day to accept his offer or not get Taylor at all.

The *Journal* opined that the meeting was "a raw deal" and that

> Mr. Lichtenhein is bringing baseball methods into hockey and reasons that a hockey player is as much the property of the club as a baseball player is of the club to which he belongs, forgetting that one man is doing nothing else but playing baseball, while the hockey player has other interests and only plays hockey for a couple of months. It might also be pointed out that a hockey player does not get anywhere near the salary that a major league ball player receives, and yet, by the last decision and the Taylor case, he seems to be expected to allow himself to be tied hand and foot in much the same fashion. There is some sentiment left in hockey, even if these new magnates care to admit it or not, and the public will do well to demand that what little there is left be retained.
>
> We don't want to have the game reduced to the baseball standard, where not a single member of a team hails from the town for which he is playing.[29]

The *Journal*'s staff were apparently no fans of the summer sport, as a week later they were still using the sport to take cheap shots at Lichtenhein, who also owned the Montreal Royals of minor-league baseball. "The Montreal Baseball club are having an awful lot of trouble with their franchise just at present," read one article. "There were threats of selling the franchise and taking organized ball out of Montreal. Perhaps the baseball club is suffering from an overdose of management as the N.H.A. has been for the last three weeks or more."[30]

Frank Patrick monitored the stories of the squabbling back east, then sent the following friendly, albeit short, telegram to Cyclone Taylor:

> Dear Fred,
> Wish you were here. Having a great time.
> Frank.[31]

The Senators did not take Lichtenhein's threats too seriously. When they travelled north to face the Redbands on January 24, 1912, the word was even leaked to the media that a certain famed cover point might be among the travelling party. President Emmett Quinn stated that Taylor's status was still unaltered and that, as far as he was concerned, if Cyclone played for Ottawa before being released by the Wanderers, the Senators would lose a protest.

Ottawa management defied Quinn and started Taylor at defence. The Cyclone was out of shape and out of practice and looked horrible in the first period as the Wanderers took a 4–1 lead. In the second period, Ottawa manager Alfie Smith replaced Taylor with Fred Lake, and the Sens came back to win the game, 10–6.

Wrote Tommy Gorman in the *Citizen*:

> The "Cyclone" played for Ottawa for the first period of the match and if he had remained on the ice it is not at all improbable that the locals would have walked away with the victory in almost as easy way as Ottawa actually did. Taylor was at cover point when the game started, with [Hamby] Shore at point, and the result of the change from Lake to Taylor was the complete disorganization of the defence of the champions and it was a wise move that pulled him from the game and put Lake back at his old position at the beginning of the second half, for with the old lineup working smoothly, the champions fairly swamped the Wanderers, and after pulling down the two point lead Wanderers had gained in the

first period, travelled right ahead, piling up the points, allowing the locals through only once more for a tally.[32]

The *Journal* was a bit more generous in its appraisal of Taylor's play:

> ... although his rushes were as brilliant and sensational as of yore, he was not efficient at repelling the Wanderers' attacks, and it was through this that Wanderers were actually able to go into the second period with a 5 to 3 lead. Taylor showed the result of being kept on the fence up to this time, and while he was just as good when he had the puck as ever, he was not there when it came to working with Shore on the defence.

As if to further muddy the waters, the *Journal* also accused Lichtenhein of additional brinkmanship in the matter of Cyclone Taylor's playing rights.

> The trouble over Taylor playing did not delay the game. Mr. Lichtenhein had informed President Quinn in the morning that he would release Taylor for a cash consideration under the understanding that Taylor would not be used in last night's game, nor in the game on Saturday in Ottawa. The Ottawas were quite willing to leave it at this and did not intend to play the "Cyclone," but the Wanderer magnate when he arrived at the rink denied any such offer and demanded three men in exchange for Taylor. The Ottawas then put Taylor on the ice, and the crowd cheered when they recognized the former Renfrew star.[33]

Afterwards, Lichtenhein was furious at the Ottawa stunt and protested the game. Furthermore, according to Gorman, the Montreal owner vowed to do all he could to have the Senators suspended. In his reportage, T.P. Gorman demonstrates that he knew well which side his bread was buttered on: "Of course Wanderers protested the game. All efforts to compromise made by the Ottawa club failed." He went on to point out that Ottawa had filed a counterprotest, this one regarding Gordon Roberts's presence in the Redbands lineup.

According to Gorman, the Senators had notified the Wanderers prior to the game that the loan of Roberts was revoked immediately.

The Wanderers "replied that the release, when given, stated explicitly that it would be in force as long as Roberts was a resident of Montreal and [they] would not be frightened into not playing the defence man. Consequently the childish tit for tat has been submitted to President Quinn for judication."[34]

Although Taylor had made no impact in the game — except perhaps a psychological one — Lichtenhein was not about to wait for Quinn to make a decision. The rivals were scheduled to meet again three days later in Ottawa. The Senators followed through with their protest of Montreal's use of Roberts, while the Wanderers threatened to skip the game altogether. According to the Montreal *Gazette*, the threat of a $300 fine from the NHA gave Lichtenhein a strong inducement to reconsider his position. Money spoke loudly to the waste wood and cotton king of Montreal.[35]

The Senators braintrust, meanwhile, were feeling their oats. According to the *Gazette*, the team received a letter from Quinn, demanding to know why it had insisted on violating the league's constitution by using a player who belonged to another team. Club spokesman Llewellyn Bate told the *Gazette* it was none of the league's business. "You may inform Quinn, through the medium of the press, that if wise he will say no more about Taylor. The Ottawa Club is out to fight the N.H.A., and Quinn had better let a sleeping dog lie." As defending Stanley Cup champions, the Senators apparently had no use for the NHA and would be content to play exhibition games and Stanley Cup challenge matches for the rest of the season. Teams in New York and Boston, as well as the Maritime and Pacific Coast league champions, were waiting their turns. And Ottawa would continue to use Taylor, whether Quinn and Lichtenhein liked it or not.

Bate, having worked up a head of steam by now, stated boldly that the Ottawa team would even decide how the game should be played, and would ignore the NHA's decision (made prior to the 1911–12 season) to switch from seven-man hockey to the six-man format we know today. "The six-man game is farcical," Bate declared, "and Mr. Lichtenhein had better bring up seven players. We will use Taylor on the defence and Walsh, Darragh, Ronan and Kerr on the line. The seven-man will be back inside of a week and we will probably take the first step in that direction by using seven men tomorrow night. The NHA and Mr. Lichtenhein don't seem to have comprehended the fact that the Ottawa Club has all along held the key to the professional situation." Other members of Senators management chimed in, vowing that the team would refuse to take the ice with anything less than a seven-man lineup.[36]

NHA president Emmett Quinn upheld the Wanderers' protest and declared that Ottawa had forfeited the game to Montreal, with the stipulation that if the decision had an impact on the championship race it would be replayed at the end of the season. To add insult to Ottawa's injury, the Stanley Cup trustees ruled that any team that accepted a challenge from outside Canada would forfeit the celebrated trophy. "Defending teams may play for the silverware in any rink or in any city they may choose," said trustee William Foran, "but not in the United States. The cup was donated for the championship of Canada, and we will certainly oppose any move to play for it outside the Dominion. In the event of there being no ice in the East in time for the games against the Pacific Coast champions, consequently the Easterners may go West and play for the mug at the Vancouver Arena."[37]

Quinn chimed in that if the Senators accepted a challenge from the Patricks' "renegade" league, they might as well consider themselves outlaws. "I have only the constitution to go on," he told the *Gazette*. "It says that no club in the N.H.A. shall compete with any other club playing men who have been suspended from the association. If the Western challengers have such men on their line-up, why, our teams cannot play them, that is all there is to it."[38]

Ottawa was suddenly faced with losing its hold on the Stanley Cup, as well as its membership in the league that effectively controlled the Cup. The Senators braintrust reconsidered their stance, got back into line, put Cyclone Taylor back into mothballs, and concentrated on winning the NHA title — they still held a slim lead in the standings over Quebec.

Meanwhile, Foran announced that the NHA champion would have to meet the winners of the PCHA, but only if the Patricks' west coast league announced a champion quickly. The *Gazette* quoted him as saying, "If they do not wind up their series by March 15, as scheduled, it will be impossible to give them a chance for the championship this winter."[39]

The Patricks received the message but couldn't rearrange their league's schedule to meet Quinn's deadline. The New Westminster Royals won the PCHA's inaugural title, but there was no time for Jimmy Gardner and his squad to head east. The Patricks rescinded their Cup challenge.

There would be no lack of drama in the 1912 Stanley Cup race, however. The Senators hit a wall, while Quebec's Bulldogs embarked on a winning streak that would leave the teams tied at the season's end. The deadlock necessitated a replay of the Senators–Wanderers game of January 24. If the Senators won this time, the tie in the standings would be upheld and Ottawa would have to play Quebec to determine the league, and Stanley Cup, champion. A victory for the Wanderers, however, meant Quebec won the league title outright — and the Ancient Capital would celebrate its first Cup win.

Even the Ottawa *Journal* could afford to be sentimental about a perennial league doormat taking home the cherished chalice:

> And won't it cause joy in old Quebec should the Wanderers triumph and the Stanley Cup rest in Quebec! Victory after all these weary years of waiting will taste all the sweeter. Just think of how Paddy Moran and Joe Hall will swagger up and down those hills, telling how the famous deed was done! And a framed portrait of Mike Quinn will form one of the decorations of the City Hall, wearing the smile that won't come off.[40]

The Wanderers upset the Senators, 5–2, and the *Citizen*'s Tommy Gorman seemed almost inconsolable. "For the first time in its tempestuous career," he wrote, "the far famed Stanley Cup goes to Quebec."

> The stormiest league season in the annals of professional hockey in Eastern Canada came to an ignominious conclusion at the Westmount Arena when Wanderers defeated Ottawa by 5 goals to 2, and thus presented to the city made famous by Wolfe, Montcalm, Hon. L. P. Pelletier, Joe Hall, and others of equal prominence, the professional supremacy of the world. Yes, the dear old Stanley Cup, which for over a year has adorned the window of a Sparks street jewellery firm, has passed, temporarily at least, into the hands of the blue and white. Ottawa failed, in other words, to effect a "comeback" in the replay of their protested match against the "red bands" and that which on many occasions has been the pride of the red, white and black, must once again part company. Ottawa fought hard to retain the silverware in a sensational struggle against their old rivals, but fate, luck, goal umpires and everything else appeared against them, and Wanderers eliminated Pete Green's team from the championship running. No home and home series against Quebec; no more "capacity house" at the Laurier Avenue arena; no Russell House banquet and no worry about dates for Stanley Cup matches.[41]

Despite the moral victory over Ottawa, Lichtenhein would not let the Taylor issue drop. The Cyclone would play for the Wanderers or for no one at all. When the teams travelled to New York and Boston for a series of exhibition games, Taylor was told to suit up for Montreal or else forget about playing. When the Senators tried to host a benefit all-star game for former player Bruce Ridpath, who had been injured severely in an automobile accident and could not pay his medical bills, Lichtenhein refused to release Taylor to suit up for Ottawa. Taylor defied his would-be boss by paying his way into the game, buying tickets for the Boy Scout troop he led, and then officiating the game for free. When Taylor told the Redbands owner that he would never play for the Wanderers, Lichtenhein announced to the world that Taylor had retired.

> There is little chance, however, that Fred will be with the Wanderers next season, as both he and Kerr have stated they intended to retire from hockey altogether this season, the two, in fact, having a bet with each other of a considerable sum that they would never appear in a uniform again.[42]

After the 1911–12 season, Frank Patrick arranged a three-game all-star series between his league's top players and the elite of the NHA. In the spacious, modern Vancouver arena, the west romped to a 10–4 victory in the first game. In Victoria, the PCHA stars won 8–2. Finally, the eastern squad was able to eke out a meaningless 6–5 victory in game three.

The PCHA lineup featured a number of faces familiar to the fans in eastern Canada: New Westminster's Hugh Lehman, formerly of the Berlin (Ontario) Pros, starred in goal; his teammate, the ex-Wanderer Harry Hyland, had a four-goal game; and Newsy Lalonde scored four goals in the series. Perhaps more importantly, the series demonstrated that western Canada was capable of developing top-notch players of its own. Tommy Dunderdale of the Victoria Aristocrats, born in Australia and raised in Winnipeg, scored four goals in game two. Except for a year's tour of duty with each of the Montreal Shamrocks and Quebec Bulldogs, Dunderdale's whole career was played west of the Manitoba-Ontario border.

Starring for the eastern side, meanwhile, was Cyclone Taylor. But the east would not be able to claim him much longer. Within six months, he had a new job with the Immigration Department in Vancouver, and a new team: the Vancouver Millionaires. He would be joined in the latter capacity by his fellow retiree, Dubbie Kerr.

Chapter 5

Livingstone, We Presume

The formation of the National League meant the ousting from major hockey of Eddie Livingstone, of Toronto, who held a franchise in the National Association, which preceded the NHL, and had a week before met an unexpected death, when all its members, except Livingstone, resigned.

— Elmer Ferguson, 1965

*I**n 1912, the National Hockey** Association finally made its move into what was then Canada's "Second City," awarding, in a move guaranteed to ease the other teams' travel budgets, not one but two franchises to Toronto. In the years to come, one local sportsman, Eddie Livingstone, would gain — and then lose — control of both teams.

Born in Toronto on September 12, 1884, Edward James Livingstone was the youngest of David and Rita Livingstone's three children. Like Calder's father, David Livingstone was a Scottish émigré. He was a printer by trade, and his Arcade Printing Company was successful enough to afford Eddie, sister Helen and older brother Harry a comfortable life in a residential neighbourhood far from the city's downtown

Eddie Livingstone

core. Livingstone's mother, the former Rita Conde Hurst, was an American. She and her sister Emma had moved to Beamsville, Ontario, halfway between Hamilton and Niagara Falls, while they were still children. After David and Rita married, they made their home on Delaware Avenue in a quiet, middle-class west end neigh-bourhood about a fifteen-minute walk west along Bloor Street from the University of Toronto campus.

Harry, not Eddie, was David's favoured son. He would grow up to be extremely successful in the newsprint business, and would become one of the founders of the Ontario Club, a private club that still thrives today. Young Eddie was always being compared to his older brother, and when he found that he couldn't keep up in other endeavours, he turned to sports, playing rugby, cricket and hockey.

The Livingstone household was one of the first to have a hockey rink in the back yard; Livingstone recalled that he grew up playing "with remnants of once real hockey sticks."[43] He loved to depict himself as a self-made man, one who paid his own club dues, bought his own equip-ment and arranged for his own transportation.

As a young hockey player, "Livvy" made up with tenacity what he lacked in size. "He didn't weigh more than the law allows and he was handicapped by weak eye sight," commented the Toronto *Daily News*, "but he was game and willing and his perseverance earned him a spot on the team. Better players were passed up because they lacked the stick-to-itiveness of the slender youth. 'Livvy' was nothing more than a plugger, but he would be depended upon to battle to the finish."[44]

Eddie was hardheaded and stubborn enough that he refused to give in on any decision if he felt he was in the right, but he also believed in the amateur ideal of sport that ruled Toronto in that day. In 1901 he scrapped his way right onto the roster of the St. George's junior hockey team that played in the Ontario Hockey Association, the organization that ruled amateur hockey in that province in the late 1890s and early years of the twentieth century. In the team's opening game, Eddie accounted for four of his team's seven goals. He notched another goal that season and helped his team finish second in its group with a 2–2 record. His performance was enough to earn him a promotion to the intermediate squad the following season.

Unfortunately, his talents weren't enough to keep St. George's from finishing winless in its group. The low point for Livingstone came on January 31, 1902, when his team played the Wellington intermediates. Eddie engaged in a set-to with a player by the name of Moffatt, com-plete with swinging sticks and fists. Referee F. D. Woodworth ruled the pair off the ice, and the two continued their dispute in the dressing room, with Livingstone emerging as the loser. He played his last game for St. George's four nights later.

Arguably, Livingstone realized his greatest sporting success as a cricket player. He was a member of the Rosedale team, which played out of the upscale Toronto neighbourhood of the same name, and with this club he played against visiting teams from the U.S. in 1902, 1904 and 1905.

Young Eddie was only twenty years old when he witnessed his first hockey controversy. After Joe Boyle's famed Yukon Hockey Club, now known popularly as the Dawson City Nuggets, lost to the Ottawa Silver Seven in the most storied of all Stanley Cup challenge series, the team took off on a barnstorming tour to raise money for the trip home. This did not sit well with Dr. Peacock, the St. George's manager, who expressed fierce opposition to the idea of professional athletics. Boyle got so riled up that he offered "to play St. George's at any time, any place, for free."

The game was never played, and the Yukon team made its way through the United States before heading home by way of Manitoba.

It was a broken collarbone that eventually forced Livingstone to retire as a hockey player. "Finally one night he bumped into somebody bigger than himself," reported the Toronto *Daily News* some years later, "and when he came to, he discovered that, in addition to a bruised cranium he had a broken collarbone and right then and there he decided he would confine his attentions to the executive end of the game and let the more robust fellows chase the puck."[45] In 1908 he joined the Toronto *Mail and Empire* in the role of assistant sports editor, and he maintained an affiliation with the newspaper until 1913, when he became the manager of the Railway Contractors Supply Company for a short time.

The newspaper job meshed well with a sports-related sideline, as Eddie refereed the occasional OHA game. After each match Livingstone sent a "Special to the *Mail and Empire*" in which he summarized the proceedings. As a game official, the bespectacled Livvy was no pushover. During one game in Cobourg, Livingstone penalized four hometown players for rough play, temporarily leaving the team with only three skaters and a goaltender.

The games gave Livingstone a chance to become familiar with the young players in the junior and intermediate ranks, knowledge that would come in handy when he was running his own teams years later. One such example: at a game in Port Perry, Eddie first laid eyes on a talented right winger named Ken Randall. Thanks to Livingstone's tutelage, Randall enjoyed a lengthy playing career in the NHA and later the NHL.

Livingstone's interests extended to other sports. In 1909 he was named secretary of the Ontario Rugby Football Union, a post he retained until he entered professional hockey. A short time later he also assumed the role of treasurer.

Livvy was also one of the prime movers when the Toronto Amateur Athletic Club was organized, representing the club on the cricket pitch after TAAC took over the Rosedale field. Later, when there was a split within the TAAC ranks, Livingstone formed the Toronto Rugby and Athletic Association and managed the new club's hockey and football teams. Under his able direction the Black and White forces won most of their games in both sports.

The tenacity Livingstone had displayed as an athlete served him well when he joined the management ranks. He refused to back down from a battle with any other owner, no matter how underfinanced he was or how flush with cash his opponents might have been. Another hallmark of Livingstone's management style was his belief in treating people fairly and in striving to make the ethical decision. His manner could not fail to earn him enemies, as is evidenced by a decision he made in the course of his ORFU duties to suspended a Grey Cup–winning team from the league — a verdict he delivered with the best interests of the league at heart.

In 1912, Livingstone's TR&AA team played, and lost, a match against the Hamilton Alerts. Toronto protested the game, pointing to a penalty call that affected the outcome of the game. The ORFU upheld the protest and ruled that the game be replayed. The date chosen for the replay conflicted with a scheduled match between the Alerts and their intra-city rivals, the Hamilton Tigers, so they elected not to field a full squad for the Toronto replay. The result was an easy 39–7 victory for TR&AA. The Tigers also won their game with the semi-Alerts, 12–8, but neither loss seemed to matter much, as the Hamilton Alerts went on to defeat the Toronto Argonauts, 14–7, in the 1912 Grey Cup game.

The Alerts also had designs on forming a new league, but these plans fell through. There were calls to expel the Alerts, but Livingstone took a more moderate — if no less forthright — tack: "I may say that the matter of the notice of motion of expulsion, like all matters of the union, dealt with what will be taken up in accordance with the requirements of the constitution. The fact that the Alerts have demonstrated their ability to play clean football, as illustrated by their last three games, will undoubtedly weigh in their favour. However, you may be sure that intimidation will have no more influence on the union next Saturday than it has had in the past. The union will do as it has always done — what it considers right.

"The fact that plans were laid for the formation of the union was known to us. Likewise, we are aware that the revolters have met with no encouragement, and that the project had fallen flat. We intend going along as we have for years: fighting an uphill fight, doing what we can in the best interests of the Ontario Rugby Football Union, and treating — and I say this advisedly — every club with absolute fairness."[46]

The Toronto *Daily News* opined, however, that Livingstone was not beyond reproach. "In Hamilton, it was said Livingstone would do anything, even commit arson or murder, to gain his ends. There is no doubting the fact that 'Eddie' likes to win, and that he never overlooks a trick on the board when he is after a championship, but his worst enemy cannot say that he has ever violated the rules or unwritten laws of any game in which he has been a participant."[47] In other words, Livvy might never have broken a rule, but in the Toronto sporting society of the 1910s, with its heavy British influence and sense of fair play, it was as important to conform to the *spirit* as much as the letter of the law.

In the end, the Alerts were suspended from ORFU competition. They applied for reinstatement under a new name, the East Hamilton Athletic Association, but were turned down. In 1914 the Alerts merged with the Hamilton Tigers, a team that still plays today as the Tiger-Cats.

Livingstone was equally adept at managing his own teams. In 1915, he led his TR&AA squad to the Grey Cup game, where they were beaten, 13–7, by the Hamilton Tigers. The defeat would have been hard to take for the normally reserved, mild-mannered Livingstone, who bristled at losing.

The opening of the 1912–13 hockey season gave Livingstone, who was no longer an active player, a chance to start from the ground up as the TR&AA's senior team was admitted to the Ontario Hockey Association. Livingstone responded to the challenge by recruiting many of the players he had encountered in his sporting travels. An earlier hint of the team's power came during a match against Stewarton. The OHA finalists from the year before were completely outclassed by Livingstone's crew.

The TR&AA surprised everyone by winning the OHA senior title in its first year. A crowd of 6,411 — the largest to view a hockey game in Toronto to that date — packed the brand new Arena Gardens on Mutual Street to watch as the John Ross Robertson Trophy was presented to Eddie Livingstone's team. TR&AA added to this triumph by winning the Pellatt Cup, emblematic of the championship of eastern Ontario. The trophy had been donated by Sir Henry Pellatt, the financier and civic leader known for building the Arena Gardens and his famous mansion, Casa Loma. Although the club played an exhibition series against the defending Allan Cup champions, the Winnipeg Victorias — losing both games by 3–1 scores — Livingstone's side did not challenge for the national championship of senior hockey. Livvy and the Allan Cup trustee William Northey could not come to an agreement over the terms under which a challenge series would be played. It would not be the last time that Livingstone and Northey lined up on opposite sides of an issue.

The Arena Gardens (also known as the Mutual Street Arena)

While Livingstone enjoyed success in the OHA, the pro game — in the form of the National Hockey Association — was also setting up shop in the barn near the corner of Mutual and Shuter. The Toronto Hockey Club, known as the Blueshirts because of their plain blue sweaters emblazoned with a white T, were led by hometown hero Bruce Ridpath, the Ottawa Senators star who had recently been struck by an automobile in the streets of Toronto and almost lost his life. It was the benefit game for Ridpath, and the fiasco triggered by the Montreal Wanderers owner Sam Lichtenhein, that prompted Cyclone Taylor finally to make the decision to jump to Vancouver. Ridpath was also at the core of a dispute involving his former team when the Senators demanded a cash payment in return for Toronto's use of Ridpath. The dispute blew over, but the resulting ill will likely scuttled Ridpath's attempt to trade for Ottawa's backup goaltender, Clint Benedict.

The Toronto Hockey Club was owned by Frank Robinson and Percy Quinn, with the latter serving as team manager. In short order the pair assembled a winning outfit, made up of players from Ontario and the west, from scratch.

The Blueshirts enjoyed their first taste of champagne from the Cup in 1914 — in only their second season. The city's other team did not enjoy as auspicious a start.

The Toronto Ontarios began life as the Tecumseh Hockey Club, and its players were selected from manager Charlie Querrie's lacrosse team, which bore the same moniker. It became clear as early as the winter of 1911, when the Toronto and Tecumseh lacrosse squads played an exhibition game of ice hockey, that this was a doomed strategy: a bunch of converted lacrosse players could not compare with the genuine article. Querrie stepped aside, turning the Tecumsehs over to Billy Nicholson; under his guidance, the team racked up a 7–13 record and finished in last place in its maiden season. They were also a financial disaster, as the team lost $2,500 on club operations and declared bankruptcy. (The Torontos, by comparison, finished with a $300 deficit.)[48]

There would be a change in ownership as well as a new nickname when the team took the ice for the 1913–14 campaign. Tom Wall, manager of the Spalding Company's Canadian operation, took over the club from W. J. Bellingham, then recruited Jimmy Murphy, with whom he had various business connections, to operate the team. The renamed Ontarios fared worse than the Tecumsehs — a dismal 4–16 — and were again last in the six-team NHA.

Meanwhile, Livingstone had spurred his TR&AA team to win the John Ross Robertson and Pellatt cups for the second year in a row. The club was a hit at the box office as well, breaking its own attendance record when 7,127 people turned out to see the TR&AA win the OHA title of 1914.

After just one season Tom Wall was looking to dump the Ontarios. At the NHA's executive meeting prior to the 1914–15 season, team president Jimmy Murphy announced that his club was for sale. The owners from Montreal, George Kennedy and Sam Lichtenhein, as well as Quebec's Mike Quinn, keeping one eye firmly fixed on their travel costs to Ontario, dearly hoped the team would stay in Toronto — or at least move no farther west than nearby Hamilton.

The newspapers featured Livingstone's name prominently as a potential buyer, and why not? Who better among Toronto's sports impresarios to reverse the Ontarios' fortunes than the man who seemed to have the Midas touch where his TR&AA football and hockey squads were concerned?

However, unlike hockey's other promoters, who were outspoken and craved the limelight, Livvy used the media only to express his complaints or to try and generate publicity for his team — based on its own merits. On December 1, 1914, the reluctant suitor was quoted in the Ottawa *Journal* as saying he was approached about the team, but was uninterested.[49] Still, the NHA's owners seemed convinced that the slight, short, and sometimes short-tempered Torontonian would be an asset to the professional ranks. Just three days later, the Toronto *Mail and Empire* reported the league was very much interested in Livingstone.

> It is understood here that an effort is being made by the N.H.A. magnates to have E. J. Livingstone, of the T. R. and A. A. Club, of Toronto, purchase the Ontario franchise in the N.H.A., the latter body realizing that with him in charge of the Ontarios they would be represented by a good team, owing to his ability in picking out successful hockey players.[50]

On December 8, 1914, Livingstone finally made the plunge into NHA ownership. He was about to embark on a journey that would test even his noted resourcefulness.

The immediate challenge was to rebuild a team whose roster was laden with aging players. And time was at a premium: the Ontarios' first game was scheduled for December 26, just eighteen days away. Blistering speed and the ability to work consistently at a fast pace once set were the hallmarks of Livingstone-managed hockey teams. Now the same standard would have to be applied to Livingstone himself.

Three days after gaining ownership, Livingstone had his introduction to the team he had purchased. The McNamara brothers, George and Howard, were the first to arrive, from Sault Ste. Marie. Then Sammy Hebert, the goalie from Ottawa, dropped in, accompanied by Corb Denneny,[51] a husky lad from Cornwall who was trying for one of the forward positions. Tommy Smith — who was the NHA's leading scorer in 1913–14 and had been secured from Quebec in a trade for Jack MacDonald — and Wilber Beatty came down from Midland. Tom Molyneaux, of Sherbrooke, arrived the next day, while Alf Skinner, two-sport star Andy Kyle, and Ken Randall, all three local boys, were also to be given a chance. Livingstone was also trying to finesse a deal to secure Percy LeSueur, the crack netminder from Ottawa.

The 33-year-old LeSueur had been Ottawa's goalie for the past eight seasons, and was the last remaining member of the powerhouse teams of 1909 and 1911 that had captured the Stanley Cup. But the Senators also owned a hot young prospect by the name of Clint Benedict, who at the tender age of twenty-two had already split the goaltending duties with LeSueur over the previous two seasons. Benedict was already somewhat of a legend in Ottawa senior hockey circles after he scored a goal during the 1912 playoffs.

At Ottawa's 1914 training camp, Benedict was matching LeSueur save for save. This was no doubt happy news for Senators management, as Clint represented a younger, and cheaper, netminding option. Just as fortunately for the team, the local fans had taken to blaming LeSueur — and not the club's anemic offence — for the close losses the team had suffered en route to a fourth-place finish in 1913–14.

While Livingstone kept trying to pry LeSueur loose, NHA president Emmett Quinn added to his distractions by scheduling a charity game to be played in Toronto on December 19. Livingstone was to manage an all-star team made up of Ottawa and Ontarios players against the champion Blueshirts. On the same evening in Montreal the runner-up Canadiens would face off against a combination of Quebec and Wanderers stars. The proceeds of the games were distributed among the poor in Toronto and Montreal.

Less than a week after taking control of the Ontarios, Livingstone pulled off his first trade, sending the aging defenceman Fred Lake and $300 east to Ottawa in exchange for LeSueur. On the surface, the deal looks like a hands-down win for Livingstone: Percy LeSueur would backstop Toronto for the next two seasons, while Lake only played two games in a Senators red, white and black striped sweater. But Ottawa benefited, too, by opening a spot for Clint Benedict, the future Hall of Famer who would lead the Senators to three more Stanley Cup championships over the next decade. Along the way, the innovative Benedict changed the face of goal-tending by sprawling across the ice to make saves.

For the charity game against the Torontos, the Senators sent Eddie Gerard, Harry "Punch" Broadbent and Leth Graham, while Livingstone contributed LeSueur, Sammy Hebert and George and Howard McNamara. Livingstone also used the game as an opportunity to try out some of his newcomers, including Tom Molyneaux and Corb Denneny. The latter player upstaged the veterans by scoring half his team's goals in a 6–6 tie.

Now that the charity work, which raised $700 for the poor, was out of the way it was time for Livvy to get back to assembling a team. In goal the Ontarios would be well served by Percy LeSueur, while on defence

George McNamara   ***Howard McNamara***

there were the Dynamite Twins, Howard and George McNamara. The forward line would feature rookies Corb Denneny and Alf Skinner. The substitute players on the roster were mostly youngsters that Livingstone had recruited during training camp.

As opening night neared, however, there remained a significant hole in the Ontarios lineup.

Eddie Livingstone had owned the Toronto Ontarios for only a week, but he was already in trouble with Frank Patrick, the president of the Pacific Coast Hockey Association.

The rhubarb involved Tommy Smith, the scoring ace who was slated to be the cornerstone of Toronto's forward line. Tom Wall, the previous owner of the Ontarios, had traded for Smith in October 1914, before selling the franchise to Livingstone. There was just one hitch: the Patricks believed they now owned Smith's rights.

Under an agreement between the two leagues, the PCHA was entitled to draft one player from each of three selected NHA squads. The teams in question in 1914 were Ottawa, Montreal Wanderers, and Quebec, and the three players were Skene Ronan of Ottawa, George O'Grady of the Wanderers, and Tommy Smith of — well, there was the rub. The Patricks believed Smith to be Quebec property, and therefore eligible to be drafted, while Livingstone was honestly under the impression that the player belonged fair and square to his Ontarios — indeed, the purchase price he paid for the team took this assumption into account.[52]

Ronan was also causing some headaches for the Patricks because he claimed the westerners had not tendered him a contract. He therefore refused to travel to the coast. The disputes over Ronan and Smith were both turned over to the National Hockey Commission, a body headed by Toronto Blueshirts manager Percy Quinn, whose brother was NHA president Emmett Quinn. Percy turned the files over to a respected arbitrator by the name of James A. Taylor, and the players' status would remain up in the air while the cases were adjudicated.

Livingstone's immediate concern was to sign Smith to a contract. According to the player, it would be easier said than done. "There is a big margin between us. I'll play here or in Mexico if the money is strong enough. I don't care where I play."[53] But after trying to negotiate with Livingstone, Smith might have felt he was indeed fated to play *la hockey sobre en Acapulco*.

The former Quebec star was at home in Ottawa when training camp opened. He objected to the terms Livingstone offered and was told to take a few hours to think things over. He did so — and missed practice in the process. When Smith finally turned up, Livingstone informed him that he, too, had been "thinking it over," and that he now considered his original proposition to have been a trifle generous — that said, Smith could either take the offer or leave it. Livingstone added that Tommy was being fined $100 for failing to live up to the rules of training camp.[54]

The Ottawa *Journal* seemed confident that Smith would be brought back into the fold. "It was stated when Smith returned to Ottawa that he jumped the Ontarios because Livingstone threatened to fine him $100 for missing a morning practice. It is true that Livingstone did say this, but it was more of a joke than anything else. At all events, Smith will return to the Ontarios and play with them this winter in the event of the Patricks not being awarded his services."[55]

As Smith mulled things over in the nation's capital, the Toronto *Telegram* couldn't help but take the opportunity to have some fun at the expense of the rival city and its population of civil servants:

> Tommy Smith, of Ontarios, has gone back to Ottawa. All of which shows how remarkably strong is the homing instinct. Most people go to Ottawa only

when they are paid salaries, and then they get leave of absences as often as possible.⁵⁶

Given the choice of being blacklisted, marooned on the west coast, or reporting to Livingstone, Tommy Smith ultimately chose the latter course. He would not be wintering in Puerto Vallarta after all.

Meanwhile, arbitrator Taylor ruled on the Skene Ronan case. After weighing evidence supplied by the Patrick brothers and the Senators, he concluded that Ronan was the property of the latter because the PCHA had not paid the requisite $500 draft price to the Senators.⁵⁷

Taylor also issued a ruling on Tommy Smith in which he stated that the NHA's leading scorer was indeed subject to the draft by the coast league, validating its claim to his services. By this time the question seemed academic, however, as the western circuit seemed no longer to have any need of him. "With the teams nicely balanced and with their lineups complete for the season, the magnates at the Coast are pretty well equipped for material," the Vancouver *Sun* reported, "and it is practically assured that Smith will be allowed to play out the season with the Quebec club, to whom he is awarded in case the Patricks do not use their draft privilege."⁵⁸

As far as Emmett Quinn was concerned, the *Sun* could report all it wanted that Smith belonged to Quebec; in his opinion, while the arbitrator held sway over east-west disputes, the affairs of the National Hockey Association were *his* business. And so, for the time being at least, Smith remained the property of the Ontarios.

The Ronan decision had no sooner been issued than Livingstone was working on a trade for the erstwhile Senator. Although Ronan had led the NHA in scoring in 1912, his position on the Ottawa roster was now being filled ably by Eddie Gerard, and he was therefore considered surplus. The Sens' lineup did have one glaring weakness, however, in that they were not carrying a spare goalie to back up Clint Benedict. It just so happened that Toronto had an extra netminder, Sammy Hebert, and he was available in exchange for Ronan.

Ottawa accepted the deal, and at last all seemed ready for the Toronto Ontarios' debut under the management of E. J. Livingstone.

The first opponent that Livingstone's Ontarios would face was Sam Lichtenhein's Montreal Wanderers. After his club fell to an 11–6 defeat on home ice, Eddie Livingstone may have had cause to ponder the wisdom of his decision to buy a professional hockey team.

The main culprit for the loss was the haste with which the team had been assembled. Rookies Corb Denneny and Alf Skinner, while both clearly talented, were accustomed to the seven-man game that was still common in the amateur ranks at that time. They had yet to adjust to the six-man system. The McNamara brothers were also below par in this first game and frequently found themselves behind the play. Skene Ronan served only briefly as a substitute because, having missed training camp, he was not in full game shape. Even Percy LeSueur had an off night as he was chased from the Ontarios' net after the first period.

The players would soon find out that being out of shape was not an excuse their stormy new boss would accept. If the new coach didn't say anything in the locker room, the players could read it in the pages of the Toronto *Telegram*:

> Livvy's Ontarios didn't win their first game. But what of that? You can hear Eddie whistling "It's a Long Way to Tipperary," with an occasional pause to tell his players where they'll spend the rest of the winter if they don't get busy and play the kind of hockey that wins championships.[59]

To get as much as he could out of his poorly conditioned charges, Livingstone resorted in subsequent games to a series of rapid line changes which helped the Ontarios get off to a successful, surprising start, despite the initial cobwebs.

Chapter 6

Livingstone's Battles Begin

Lester Patrick is sore over the Smith deal and in a letter to Montreal has threatened to raid the eastern teams next winter as they did not stand behind him in the trade. Wanderers are the only team that Lester promises not to wreck, they having been in favour of shipping Tommy to the coast.
— Toronto *Telegram*, January 12, 1915

A s *December 1914 drew to* a close, Tommy Smith and the rest of the Toronto Ontarios were playing much better. On Vancouver Island, meanwhile, Lester Patrick and his Victoria Aristocrats were off to a miserable start. The time had come to seek out reinforcements, and the battle for Tommy Smith was joined anew. "Lester is downcast over the showing of last year's champions and he is eager to bolster up the scoring division," the Vancouver *Sun* said. "In their four starts to date the Victoria team has been forced to take defeat on each occasion, and the dose is becoming nauseous to the Capital city magnate."[60]

NHA president Emmett Quinn responded to the Patricks' entreaties on January 2, 1915, with a letter whose tone could charitably be called exasperating. Quinn argued that, as Smith had not yet been tendered a PCHA contract and the NHA had not received payment, the Patricks' claim that their draft rights had been violated was "arbitrary."

> … You were aware that the Quebec Club were making trade with Ontario, Quebec advised you in March of this fact, and you were apparently satisfied. Smith never has been subject to draft as Quebec Club distinctly stat-

ed when deal was made with Ontario that if deal was not allowed they would reserve Smith....

You no doubt have overlooked the fact that when you were present at our meeting in Montreal in March last, Mike Quinn mentioned in the presence of Mr. T. J. Wall of the proposed trade of players, and you were apparently satisfied to allow negotiations to proceed.[61]

Quinn then accused the Patricks of dragging their heels:

At that meeting you completed arrangements with Wanderers and Ottawa to draft [George] O'Grady and [Skene] Ronan, but allowed matters to drift until late November before you tendered Ronan an offer, and in so far as O'Grady is concerned, I have not heard whether he was even tendered an offer....

If you draft a player, and do not tender him a contract or pay a club for him, to whom does he belong? The club from whom he is drafted has no control over him and gets nothing in return for him. However, if no contract is forwarded to him before the 15th of October he will become a free agent and can sign with any other club.

If I remember you rightly, you distinctly stated yourself when the agreement was drafted that it was hardly likely that you would draft a player, pay $500 for him, and not have him report. You intimated that when drafting you would first have the consent of the player to go to the coast, otherwise you would be out $500. However, in drafting up revised agreement, some clause will have to be embodied to cover same, and Secretary Calder is now preparing a new draft and will submit same to you for approval.

I fail to see that you can claim Smith, as he was not reserved by Quebec last year. You could have drafted any player from Quebec other than [Harry] Mummery, [Joe] Hall and [Joe] Malone, and this you failed to do.

It is unfortunate that matters have become complicated, but I can assure you that we have endeavoured to live up to the agreement in every respect.[62]

Looking ahead to the 1915 draft, in which the PCHA would be allowed to claim one player each from the Toronto Blueshirts and Ontarios and the Montreal Canadiens, Quinn offered a compromise: the NHA would also allow the PCHA to draft a player from the Quebec roster. "This will give you the right to four players instead of three," Quinn concluded, "and you would then have your player from Quebec, whom you would have had this year had the draft been made in the regular way."[63]

The Patricks wanted no part of Quinn's "compromise." If the NHA wanted to play dirty, they would be happy to reciprocate. On January 5 the Vancouver *Sun* reported "a strong possibility that the National Hockey Commission will be broken up by the P.C.H.A. unless the N.H.A. decides to send Tommy Smith to the Coast." The *Sun* sounded an ominous note when it added that "[s]hould the commission be 'busted', the Coast league will hardly be able to secure any player this season because of the fact that the N.H.A. stars are under contract, but next year they will be able to pick and choose."[64]

The threats from the west coast were taken seriously in the eastern media. The Toronto *Telegram* of January 12 noted that "Lester Patrick is sore over the Smith deal and in a letter to Montreal has threatened to raid the eastern teams next winter as they did not stand behind him in the trade. Wanderers are the only team that Lester promises not to wreck, they having been in favour of shipping Tommy to the coast."[65]

There was a reason why the Wanderers were aligning themselves with the Patricks: barely a month into his tenure as an NHA owner, Eddie Livingstone had already made an enemy of Montreal's Sam Lichtenhein. Just before he traded Sammy Hebert to the Senators for Skene Ronan, Livvy had been trying to peddle the goalie to the Wanderers. Then, abruptly, Livingstone cut the negotiations short.

Like Livingstone, Lichtenhein was a small man with a broad stubborn streak. The two men seemed destined to clash, and NHA observers felt it was only a question of when — not *if* — the fireworks would begin. When Livvy announced his plan to purchase the Ontarios, the Toronto *Telegram*, perhaps a trifle miffed that he had broken the story to the *Daily News* instead of his former — and less widely read — employer, said, "Now that Livvy has jumped to the pro-ranks, why not arrange a fight to the finish between him and Sammy Lichtenhein?"[66]

The question that dogged the other NHA owners was which one to support should push come to shove. Lichtenhein certainly had more money, and seemed to need the league much less than it needed him. Or so he made it appear. And he seemed to have an on-again, off-again ally in the Montreal Canadiens owner George Kennedy.

Culturally, Lichtenhein and Kennedy were polar opposites, representing in microcosm the divide that still exists within their hometown. Lichtenhein was an English-speaking Jew of German descent who had been raised in Westmount; the French-speaking Protestant Kennedy — *né* Kendall — was a product of the city's francophone east end. (To this day, residents of Montreal rarely venture too far beyond St-Denis Boulevard, the city's east-west dividing line and the unofficial boundary between English and French Montreal.)

On the other hand, the two owners were about the same age, were sons of successful businessmen, and were colourful characters. And either man could be accused — although usually in fun — of being a bit of a schemer. There was mutual respect between Lichtenhein and Kennedy, even if they sometimes did not like one another.

Stories of sports promoters being involved in gambling were nothing new in the hockey world, and the two Montrealers were apparently not above a friendly wager to make things a little more interesting when their teams took the ice. One such instance did not escape the notice of Cup trustee Phil Ross, who commented in the February 1, 1912, edition of the Ottawa *Journal* that

> Mr. Lichtenhein, of the Wanderers, bet George Kennedy $25 that the Wanderers would take a fall out of the Canadiens last night. And Wanderers did take a fall out of the Canadiens, so that Mr. Lichtenhein is $25 richer today, that is, if he collected. Just think of the awful example to the players, though. An owner betting on his team![67]

Lichtenhein did not enjoy such harmonious relations with his other fellow owners. His inflexibility over the Cyclone Taylor affair had rendered the NHA inferior to the Patricks' league. The team that had hoped to secure Taylor's services, the Ottawa Senators, certainly wouldn't call Sammy a friend. In fact, the perception in the nation's capital was that Lichtenhein enjoyed throwing his weight around — ironic, since the hometown Senators had never hesitated to flex their muscles in the various leagues they had belonged to over the years. The *Journal* took a humorous look at hockey ten years into the future with the Wanderers' owner in control:

Montreal, Dec. 13, 1923 — A few minor changes to the rules were drafted at this afternoon's meeting of the I.N.H.A. at Montreal. Seven clubs were represented at the meeting, the following organizations sending delegates: Boston, New York, Canadiens, Wanderers, Ottawa, Quebec and the two Toronto clubs.

Possibly the most important ruling made was on the question of the number of men on the ice. At the motion of Mr. Lichtenhein, the teams will now consist of two men, the three-man team having been found cumbersome as well as expensive. Besides, they littered up the rink, and made the game slow and uninteresting. The goal keeper will not be allowed to wear pads, as it was found they impeded his progress up the ice and tended to spoil the combination. This rule was passed, although the Ottawa representative made a feeble protest.

Again the popular and talented Mr. Lichtenhein came to the fore with another suggestion. This was to do away with the loose system of looking after the players. Last season the men were allowed to roam at large, and this was found to have developed a spirit of Independence, which went a long way towards retarding the managers at their work. At the suggestion of Mr. Lichtenhein, they will now be kept in quarters attached to the arenas, and will not be allowed out unless accompanied by a guard. Salaries were fixed at $10 a week.

The penalty system was also improved upon. In future a man must receive a written warning from the master of ceremonies, and he does not have to regard the message as official unless written over the signature of at least three officers of both clubs. Files will be placed at frequent intervals along the side of the rink, on which the players can hang these warnings, and there will be no difficulty for a player to tell when he must pay a fine.

On the motion of the two Toronto clubs, the Quebec team were dropped from the league. As the Quebec team did not make the same amount of money for the other teams in the league, it was felt that their remaining in the league would lower the high ideal of sport maintained by the association. The Quebec representative nearly caused a riot when he suggested that the public might not like this move. The wins and losses on the schedule were then arranged.[68]

As January wore on, Smith continued to play for the Ontarios, whose lineup gained more cohesion with every game. An overtime victory over Quebec was followed by a relatively easy 5–3 win against the Senators, vaulting the Ontarios into fourth place among the NHA's six teams — ahead of the defending Cup champs the Toronto Blueshirts.

The Ontarios' tying goal in the Quebec game found Livingstone at the height of his managerial powers and earned him plaudits from the Toronto *Daily News* columnist Charlie Querrie:

> Few of the hockey fans noticed the desperate chance that Owner Livingstone took in the last few minutes. With the score standing 2 to 1 for Quebec, and a couple of minutes to play, the Ontario man showed his real ability as a manager of a hockey team.
>
> He called Howard McNamara to the side-lines and sent in four forwards instead of the regulation three, and his move proved a wise one. It got his sextette the tieing goal, and while it may have been a desperate play, it was the only chance to win the game.
>
> At that it nearly proved disastrous when Quebec broke away and only had George McNamara to beat, but LeSueur saved the day with a good stop, and going away fast, Smith, Ronan, Skinner and Bawlf went up and through for the tieing goal.[69]

The Ontarios cleared the .500 barrier when they beat the Canadiens, 3–1, for their first road victory. In recognition of their fine play, Livingstone acceded to a players' demand that, given the tenor of the times, seems positively radical.

Toronto in 1915 was not only a very British city, it was a very *Orange* one: the Orange Lodge, that bastion of Irish Protestantism and unqualified support for the monarchy, was as influential as ever in the city known as "the Belfast of Canada." It was still impossible to become mayor of Toronto without being an Orangeman, and the battle for Home Rule that had recently been waged in the British Parliament did not help the Catholic cause.

Against this backdrop, Livingstone abandoned the Ontarios' orange sweaters in favour of green ones, and renamed his team the Shamrock Hockey Club. That decision made the front page of the *Daily News*:

> For some time the McNamara triplets, "Skene" Ronan, "Tommy" Smith and one or two others have been agitating that such a change be made and matters came to a head at Montreal after the victory over the Canadiens. It irked the Irish members of the contingent that they should be called upon to flaunt a parti-coloured orange sweater and they petitioned Mr. Livingstone to not only make a switch in name but in the club's colours, and on Wednesday night they will appear in brand new sweaters in which green will predominate.[70]

Said Livingstone, "If the departure will make the team play faster or add to its drawing power I am satisfied. The boys have acquitted themselves in great style lately and they are entitled to anything they want."[71]

The newly renamed Shamrocks won only one game the rest of the way. So much for the luck of the Irish.

The inter-league dispute over Tommy Smith's playing rights continued to percolate. In mid January Emmett Quinn, the NHA president, claimed not to have heard from the Patricks regarding the olive branch he had proffered two weeks earlier.

> I have twice communicated with the Patricks over the Smith case and have had no answer. If President Patrick had any announcement to make concerning the agreement naturally he would come to me. But I have not heard a word officially and until I do I must decline to discuss the merits of the case. We have our grounds, however, for keeping Smith here.
>
> It was late in the season when the matter was settled, the Patricks had their teams aligned and we could not afford to lose any players. The claim by the Patricks that Quebec made the Smith deal with Ontarios to protect Smith in the draft is absurd. The deal was made in good faith, as the fact that he is now playing with Ontarios shows.[72]

In his haste to adopt a conciliatory tone, Quinn forgot to mention that the arbitrator had ruled the Quebec-Ontarios trade invalid based in part on evidence supplied by the NHA itself.

A few days later, Quinn would have his answer from Frank Patrick. "We put it up to the arbitrator, with the consent of all parties, and under the agreement were expected to accept his award. The NHA violated the agreement when they refused to part with Smith, and the coast league will stick by its guns and conduct its own affairs in future."[73]

The threat of another hockey war prompted the NHA to hold a special meeting on January 17. The result was another letter to Patrick repeating the NHA's position. If anything, it bought the league a bit of time.

On January 26, the moguls of the PCHA held a meeting of their own. "It looks like a fight to the end between the National Hockey Association and the P.C.H.A.," the Victoria *Colonist* reported. "At a special meeting of the Coast League, which was held in Vancouver yesterday, it was intimated that the P.C.H.A. will refuse to consider any dealings with the N.H.A. as long as the latter allows Tommy Smith to play with the Shamrocks."[74]

For Emmett Quinn, the solution was quite simple: have Smith shipped back to Quebec. Earlier in the month, Livingstone had been trying to deal Smith to Ottawa, the forward's hometown. Quinn stepped in and barred the negotiations, naming Quebec as the only team with whom he would permit the Shamrocks to make a deal. On January 29, Tommy Smith returned to the Ancient Capital in exchange for cash. According to the Vancouver *Sun*, the deal was to be consummated at the end of the season, but Quebec had an immediate need for a player to replace the injured "Phantom" Joe Malone.[75] Given the circumstances, Livingstone did about as well as he could have expected.

In a further attempt to mollify the Patricks, Quinn gave them the right to draft a player each from five of the six NHA teams. For the time being, the Patricks relented. There was a Stanley Cup series to consider — one that the PCHA was scheduled to host for the first time ever — and the Patricks did not want to forgo that series over the draft issue. Word was sent that a new agreement for the PCHA to sign should accompany the NHA champions on their trip west in March.

At the same time as Livingstone was being forced to trade Tommy Smith, Corbett Denneny's younger brother came to the Shamrocks owner's attention. In 1953, Cy Denneny would recall the way he broke into professional hockey.

> Manager Livingstone had a unique method of discovering
> whether or not a youngster competing for a place on his

squad had "what it takes." ... Livingstone merely ordered the team's two giant defencemen, the McNamara twins, George and Howard, to give a rookie "the works" in practice sessions and so test his ability.

The McNamaras, famous as the "Dynamite Twins," weighed about 225 pounds each. I used to come in flitting from left wing with my insignificant 145 pounds, and be given a McNamara sandwich with the beef on the outside and me in the middle!

There was nothing underhanded about it, and no foul high-stick by the husky brothers. I was never cut or actually injured. But they slammed me down at every opportunity, knocked the wind out of me, and I afterward had to be helped off the ice for a breather. I was really given "the business."

Then one day after a practice, the McNamaras took me aside and good-naturedly explained what they had been instructed to do. Then they said that in their opinion I had passed the test and they would recommend that Livingstone sign me up.

I might add that I found out later, as did everyone else in pro hockey, that the hefty McNamaras were genial, good-natured and kind men. But when they body checked a player in a hockey game, he knew he had been hit![76]

Livingstone concurred with the McNamara's assessment that the 23-year-old Denneny had passed the test, and signed him to replace Smith in the Toronto lineup. Ironically, Smith, the pre-season holdout who vowed to play in Mexico if the money was right, had grown fond of Livvy's Shamrocks team and was reluctant to leave. Upon his departure, the itinerant left winger who had played for twelve teams over the previous ten seasons told the *Mail and Empire*, "Shamrocks are the first club that I played with that I really wanted to stay with."[77]

No sooner had the Smith trade been made than the Shamrocks suffered more bad luck.

Early in the season, the team's three McNamara brothers — George, Harold and Howard — received word from Sault Ste. Marie that their father Andrew, who owned a construction company, had fallen dangerously ill. The trio began journeying to the Soo on days off to spend time with him. The day after the Smith trade brought news that Andrew

McNamara was near death, and the brothers were urged home at once. They departed on the nine o'clock train for Sault Ste. Marie, and Livingstone immediately contacted Emmett Quinn.

A couple of weeks earlier, when it looked as if the McNamaras would not return in time for a game against the Blueshirts, the NHA agreed that it should be postponed. It was also understood that, should such a problem crop up again later in the season, games would also be rescheduled. But this time Sam Lichtenhein, whose Wanderers were scheduled to play the Shamrocks next, refused to agree to a postponement.

Livingstone told Quinn that to play the game was out of the question and that under no circumstances would he ice a team. Nor *could* he put a suitable team on the ice: NHA rules required each team to dress a minimum of nine men, but with the McNamaras away, the Shamrocks had only five skaters, plus Percy LeSueur and a spare goalkeeper, and there was no time to recruit any fill-ins.

Livvy argued that the McNamaras' absence could not have been foreseen, and stated that if the NHA refused the postponement he would default the Wanderers contest. This was no small consideration: under the NHA's constitution, a franchise that defaulted a game was subject to a $300 fine, payable to the opponent; in those days, that sort of money could retain the services of a decent professional hockey player for half a season.

Livingstone seems to have enjoyed the support of Stanley Cup trustee Phil Ross, whose Ottawa *Journal* commented, "If (the league) gives the game to Wanderers by default, and the latter accept, it will show that neither the NHA moguls nor the Wanderers care for human nature.[78]

Charlie Querrie, the manager of the Arena Gardens and columnist for the Toronto *Daily News*, also sided with the Shamrocks owner. "The action of the Wanderers in trying to force the Ontario-Shamrock team to play with a team that would only make a farce out of the contest, is not very good sportsmanship on the part of Mr. Lichtenhein.... The Ontario magnate absolutely refused to fool the public and declined to play with a weakened team."[79]

The battle lines were drawn. Sam Lichtenhein had fired the first shot, and if Edward James Livingstone had learned anything in his life it was never to back down from a challenge.

Lichtenhein did make a minor concession in that he offered to play a man short if the Shamrocks suffered an injury; this, however, did not make up for Toronto's lack of a full complement of players. In a telegram, Livingstone instructed Emmett Quinn, "Make it absolutely clear to Wanderers no game here and not to come, so as to prevent Wanderers incurring expenses. Impossible to play, and I do not consider game is being defaulted under the circumstances existing. Feeling regarding McNamara matter was unanimously concurred in at league meeting previous to Toronto-Ontario game. Objection by Wanderers absurd and inhuman."[80]

It is hard to guess which was harder to take: being called "inhuman" or missing out on a chance to pocket an easy $300.

The battle royal was about to begin. And it had taken all of three months.

"Sammy Lichtenhein and 'Eddie' Livingstone have at last 'hooked up,'" reported the Toronto *Daily News*, "and now look out for squalls." The reporter went on to observe that "It would be absurd in any event to stack a make-shift outfit against the speedy Wanderers, and Mr. Lichtenhein's sportsmanship will be called seriously into question if he insists upon the fixture being paid.[81]

Lichtenhein did indeed claim the default, even though his team did not appear for the game in Toronto. Abiding by a strict reading of the NHA constitution, Quinn ruled that the game had been forfeited despite Livingstone's request for a postponement. And Livingstone was on the hook to pay the $300 compensation to the Wanderers, despite the warning to Lichtenhein not to travel to Toronto. The Wanderers were also awarded a victory for the forfeited game — we think. The language Quinn used was so confusing that even Livingstone was not quite sure, but if Quinn was declaring the game a forfeit, the Toronto owner was threatening a stunt worthy of Lichtenhein himself.

"If you persist in counting the unplayed game as a default," Livingstone told Quinn, "I will default all games during the remainder of the season. Call a meeting of the league immediately, as my team will not go to Quebec to play Saturday unless your decision is rescinded. This is final."[82]

A league meeting was scheduled for February 6, prompting Livingstone to drop his threat. He conceded to a Toronto *Star* reporter that the circumstances were unusual, and sounded an optimistic note: "I know that I will get what I am entitled to — a fair deal."[83]

Livingstone's idea of a "fair deal" was the farthest thing from Sam Lichtenhein's mind. His team was in a dogfight with Ottawa for the NHA championship, and he needed the win. What he didn't need was to risk first place by a make-up game. He refused to budge.

The February 6 meeting saw the league split along the Ottawa River: the Shamrocks, Torontos and Ottawa were on one side of the issue, while the Wanderers, Quebec and Canadiens weighed in on the other. Emmett Quinn was left with the deciding vote and could scarcely contradict his previous ruling. To save face, Lichtenhein repeated an offer made prior to the meeting to play the Shamrocks at the end of the schedule. All parties agreed, and the following motion was made:

> That the decision of the President be sustained, and that the fixture between the Wanderers and Shamrocks, scheduled for February, be considered as defaulted by Shamrocks, but that a game be played on Saturday, March 6.[84]

The PCHA issue was also discussed at the meeting, and the owners agreed to submit another peace proposal to the Patricks. This time they offered to allow the PCHA to draft one player from all six of the NHA teams. Once more a letter was sent west and the proposal was accepted.

The next day, Livingstone decided he wasn't satisfied that he understood the motion that had been passed regarding the game with Montreal. Another letter to Quinn followed, hoping to avoid "the ambiguousness that was allowed to remain in the McNamara affair when dealt with at the directors meeting of January 17" and "to preclude any possibility of a repetition of unpleasantness."[85] The question on his mind: Would the March 6 game between the Wanderers and Shamrocks count in the standings?

Quinn's reply was cryptic: "The Wanderer-Shamrock game which was awarded to the Wanderers by default and later agreed between the club representatives to be played over at a later date."[86]

Livvy took that as a yes, then took matters into his own hands by penning a letter to the *Mail and Empire*:

> In view of certain statements and insinuations which have been made regarding the announcement that the unplayed game between the Wanderers and Shamrocks, which was postponed in consequence of the three McNamaras' absence at their father's death bed, will take place later in the season, I desire to make clear the actual situation.
>
> The game will be played on March 6th, and as a league fixture, counting in the official standings. At the meeting of the directors of the National Hockey Association, which I attended, it was decided that according to the constitution the non-playing of the game in question was technically a default; but the unfair side of this appealed so strongly to Mr. Lichtenhein, as well as the other directors, that his — Mr. Lichtenhein's — good

sportsmanship made itself evident, and he declined to accept the game. Thus it was arranged between the Wanderers and Shamrock Clubs, and endorsed officially by the executive, that the game be played as a championship contest on March 6th, in Toronto.

It is not my intention to publish details as to this matter, but in fairness to myself, Mr. Lichtenhein and the N.H.A. Executive, I deem it advisable to present the facts.[87]

Livingstone clearly knew that, by publicizing the terms under which the game was to be replayed, he was putting Lichtenhein and Quinn in an untenable position: if they went back on their word, the hockey world would know of their deceit.

And it soon did.

Lichtenhein was fuming. He claimed that he had attached a condition to his offer stipulating that *he* would be the one to announce the arrangement. Now that Livingstone had let the cat out of the bag, Lichtenhein proclaimed that he was having second thoughts. "Now I do not think I will play the game at all," said Lichtenhein. "Manager Livingstone has failed to keep his part of the agreement, and I don't see why I should keep mine. The association awarded the game to me, and it is quite likely I will let it go at that."[88]

Given the opportunity of taking the high road, Lichtenhein had chosen to take a victory at the expense of the McNamaras' tragedy. But the cheerleaders who masqueraded as reporters wrote not a word in the Montreal papers — English or French — to point out that Lichtenhein was behaving like a spoiled 11-year-old.

Despite their slow start and a spate of injuries, the Shamrocks were a better team under Eddie Livingstone's stewardship. Their record — 7–13, compared with 4–16 in 1913–14 — only hinted at the progress that had been made. Goal scoring was up, from 61 to 76, while the addition of Percy LeSueur had trimmed goals against from 118 to 96 — better than a goal a game. As a result of the improved play, combined with the excitement Livingstone was generating, the team almost broke even financially — a vast improvement over its economic performance in its first three seasons.

The Wanderers, meanwhile, still entertained hopes of winning the NHA championship as the season wound down. They were neck and neck with the Ottawa Senators, and the prospect of losing the title by playing the Shamrocks was not an enticing one for Sam Lichtenhein, who resumed his demands that the February 3 default count as a Montreal win.

The Toronto media had a field day.

Charlie Good, in his *Daily News* column, wrote: "The game makes no material difference but Owner Lichtenhein evidently does not intend to keep his plighted word. The whole thing shows him up in rather a poor light. If the Red Bands decline the issue and refuse to meet the Irish team, Mr. Lichtenhein's status as a sportsman will be settled for good and all."[89]

The *Star* put it even more bluntly: "Sammy Lichtenhein exercises a woman's privilege to change his mind."[90]

Faced with the prospect of losing a gate, and convinced that public opinion was on his side, Livingstone wrote Emmett Quinn, requesting that he think carefully about his decision:

> "[S]hould the Wanderers' stand be backed up by your-
> self, the only view the public could possibly take would
> be that Mr. Lichtenhein does absolutely as he pleases.
> Your supporting our just position in this matter would
> not mean that you were going back on any former deci-
> sion. It would mean that you have the uprightness and
> backbone necessary to uphold an agreement made
> before and ratified by the directors of the association and
> yourself. There is no reason why I should be made to
> suffer as a consequence of Mr. Lichtenhein's unsports-
> manlike tactics."[91]

Livingstone then attacked Lichtenhein in his own back yard by speaking to the Montreal *Gazette*:

> It is reported that the Wanderers intend defaulting
> their league game with Shamrocks, scheduled to be
> played Saturday … I have requested President Quinn
> to call a meeting without delay so as to prevent, if pos-
> sible, this occurring, or if Mr. Lichtenhein persists in
> defaulting, to have the championship awarded to the
> Ottawa Hockey Club.…
>
> Understanding that Mr. Lichtenhein has stated that
> I gave my promise not to make public the fact that the
> postponed Wanderer-Shamrock game to be played on
> March 6, would count as a league fixture, I wish to

emphatically deny that I gave any promise in this direction, though I have no doubt that it may have been intimated that he [Mr. Lichtenhein] would be allowed to make it public first. This Mr. Lichtenhein did not do.[92]

Livingstone accused Lichtenhein of wiring Lol Solman of the Arena Gardens to inform him that there would be no game, thus placing the availability of home ice in jeopardy. The Shamrocks owner therefore stated his willingness to meet the Wanderers in Ottawa, even though to him it seemed most "unfair and absurd that the whims of Mr. Lichtenhein should be considered when [they are] to the detriment of the Ottawa Club, as well as to myself, and in spite of an arrangement officially made by the association. To me it means a financial loss on the season, to the Ottawa Club their right to have the Wanderers fight their way to the championship by winning on the ice."[93]

Lichtenhein was fit to be tied. The loose cannon put on a display that would have captured first place in the International Fireworks Competition if it had been running in Montreal back then.

How dare Livingstone, a newcomer to the professional game, act as if he were an equal in the league when everyone *knew* the real power was in Montreal? (Even the Toronto Blueshirts were owned by a Montreal native, Frank Robinson, and Arena Gardens on Mutual Street was owned by Montreal interests.) As far as Lichtenhein was concerned, it was time to put this upstart in his place. He pleaded his case in an open letter to Emmett Quinn, which was published in the *Gazette*:

> I am getting disgusted with the way President Livingstone is trying to use this league, and will try and be brief as possible and outline the facts as they are, not as President Livingstone has endeavoured to distort them.
>
> First and foremost, President Livingstone wilfully defaulted his game with us in Toronto on February 3, according to the constitution, and you saw fit to allow an appeal on your ruling to this effect.… [T]he delegation there present declared that the game of February 3 was defaulted, and counted as a win for the Wanderer Club. Mr. Livingstone, however, appealed to me from a sentimental standpoint and asked me to give him a game to help on his receipts, and I consented to play a game on March 6th only, however, on the understanding that he would not make this public until after I had done so …

Mr. Livingstone is trying to pose as a very much abused individual, and endeavouring to make me butt of his martyrism, therefore it is about time that this league as a body say whether this should continue, and as this is not the first time that Mr. Livingstone has attacked me publicly, I assure you I intend making it the last. Sport has no room for gentleman like Mr. Livingstone … Therefore, I must resent this attack on his part, and I will go further by saying that he must be removed from this league, and the sooner he is removed and men like him, the sooner the league will have the confidence of the public in every city in which it performs.

In order that there be no misunderstanding between us, I am forwarding copies of this letter to one or more of the papers in every city in our league, with a request to the sporting editor of such paper to publish.

Mr. Livingstone has also saved his penalty of $300 or more, as the directors decided, for defaulting his game on February 3. I personally waived my claim to this $300, because he claims he had been losing so heavily. This shows you the class of man that is attacking me, and I cannot continue to allow him to vilify me without submitting the true facts to the public in every city in this league.[94]

There was no question in Emmett Quinn's mind as to the correct course of action. A tie in the standings would require a playoff between the Senators and Wanderers — which would generate a couple of lucrative dates, all of the proceeds of which would go directly into the league's coffers. A Wanderers loss in a league game against Toronto would upset that plan.

The Toronto press knew which way the wind blew. The *Daily News* alleged that "President Quinn is doing his level best to add a little more weight to the argument that the NHA professional hockey league is a Montreal institution solely and exclusively [run] by 'Sammy' Lichtenhein, the leader of the Wanderers, and that Mr. Quinn is only his acting representative.

"There has been a strong feeling in Toronto on several occasions that the local teams never were given a square deal from the Eastern magnates and the latest developments would only seem to bear out the contention."[95]

As expected, the league meeting on March 4 afforded Lichtenhein the opportunity to wriggle out of his commitment to play a rematch against the Shamrocks. The league directors simply rewrote the prior motion so that the Wanderers were off the hook. Siding with the Shamrocks were the Senators and Torontos, while Quinn again cast the deciding vote in Lichtenhein's favour. As a salve to Livingstone, the league voted to refund his $300. The way had now been paved for the Wanderers to take part in a playoff for the league title and the right to play for the Stanley Cup on the west coast.

The meeting then turned its attention to the question of who would participate in a series of postseason exhibition games in the United States. The Shamrocks were not invited to take part. Instead, Quebec and the Canadiens, accompanied by the loser of the league championship series, would represent the NHA in New York and Boston.

It was no skin off Livingstone's nose. He made arrangements for a three-game series of his own, to be played against the Torontos in Cleveland, a city with which Livingstone was familiar from his OHA senior days. But first, he attended the NHA playoff series and likely cheered silently as the Senators won the right to meet Vancouver in the Stanley Cup finals. The Wanderers would have to make do with the consolation prize: a trip to New York and Boston.

In Cleveland, the Torontos won two of the three games over the Shamrocks in a hard-fought series. The Cleveland *Plain Dealer*'s Henry Edwards raved over the fast pace of the NHA pros, which stood in contrast to the amateur brand of hockey to which the Forest City was accustomed. After watching game one, in which the Shamrocks prevailed 7–5, he wrote, "Clevelanders can understand why it is that many of the Canadian pros are going to Europe to engage in the war," Edwards wrote. "They are going merely to keep in condition for next winter's battles on ice."[96]

The games may have been exhibitions, but they were definitely not non-contact affairs. Edwards wrote that the second game, a 9–5 victory for the Torontos, featured "high dives, head spins, hammerlocks, and toe holds … interspersed with hooking, tripping and chopping." He also recounted an episode in which "little Harold McNamara, who weighs only 190 pounds, became involved in an altercation with Foyston of the Torontos. Just about as they were going to discard the N.H.A. rules and settle it according to the Marquis of Queensbury and Killarney fair code, up skated little Harold's big brothers and the dispute was settled by arbitration."[97]

Edwards also applauded Livingstone's managing in the third game. "Last night's 8 to 3 victory for the Toronto pros over the Shamrocks, also of Toronto, at the Elysium introduced to the Cleveland public a system of pacification which should be adopted by Kaiser Wilhelm, King George, Czar Nicholas and other combatants across the seas," Edwards enthused.

> Ed Livingstone, manager of the invading exhibitionaries, was the formulator of the system. To go back a little, it may be remembered that in the first game between the Torontos and Shamrocks at the Elysium Thursday night, Cyril Denneny slashed Cully Wilson across the face with his stick, loosening three teeth and inflicting cuts that required sewing up. Wilson then threatened to get even, but when Friday night's contest passed into history without his making much effort it was thought he had forgiven his enemy.
>
> He had merely declared a truce, however. The second period of last night's contest was still young when he got his chance. Embracing opportunities is Wilson's long suit and he gave this one a most decided hug, hooking Denneny in such a manner as to gouge a chunk out of his chin and cause him to retire to the dressing room for extensive repairs. Wilson was banished for the remainder of the period, twelve minutes in all.
>
> "I am willing to call it even now," said Wilson as he watched his adversary go to the hospital.
>
> "He may think it is evened up," said Denneny when he came back, after being sewed up, "but just watch me in the last period. They will have to call an ambulance for Wilson."
>
> News of the threat made by Denneny reached Manager Livingstone, who diplomatically manipulated his players so that whenever Wilson was on the ice, Denneny was on the bench, and when Denneny was in the game, Wilson was on the bench. Just imagine what a bloodless warfare the affair in Europe would be if the Livingstone system was placed in operation.[98]

At the end of March 1915, the NHA teams submitted their lists of players they intended to protect from the PCHA draft. The Torontos had reserved Jack Walker, Cully Wilson and Frank Foyston, while the Shamrocks protected Skene Ronan and the Denneny brothers, Cy and Corb, from the Patrick teams.

The only problem was that there was in fact no draft agreement between the eastern and western leagues. When Frank Shaughnessy arrived on the west coast with his Ottawa Senators to play the Stanley Cup games, he did so without an agreement in hand — or the authority to negotiate one. Shaughnessy seemed not even to know that he was supposed to be the courier who delivered the peace treaty.

Once again, Emmett Quinn and his compadres had slighted the Patricks.

Chapter 7

The War of 1915:
Real or Imagined?

Back in 1917, when the new sports body was launched into war-torn space, the National League didn't even have an office to call its own. Much less a press room. And why no press room? Few reporters, not more than one or two, ever attended the sessions. For that was the stature of and the eminence of hockey in those times.
— Elmer Ferguson, 1965

The **summer of 1915 should** have been a time of celebration on the west coast. The champions of the Pacific Coast Hockey Association, Frank Patrick's Vancouver Millionaires, had made short work of the Ottawa Senators, defeating them 6–2, 8–3, and 12–3 to claim the Stanley Cup. Cyclone Taylor scored seven times in the three games against his former club, while Frank Nighbor and Mickey MacKay also starred.

But a pair of oversights on the part of Ottawa's Frank Shaughnessy served to rain on the Patricks' parade. Not only had Shaughnessy arrived without the paperwork pertaining to the draft, but he had neglected to bring the Cup itself. It would be autumn — a full six months after the series — before the Millionaires took possession of the trophy.

Frank Patrick was furious over Emmett Quinn's apparent decision to renege on the NHA–PCHA agreement, but there was a larger problem, one that threatened his league's very survival. As part of the British Empire, Canada was automatically involved in the First World War, its commitments intensifying with every passing day. And the word was out that the Canadian Army had designs on commandeering the Victoria arena to use as a recruitment depot for the duration.

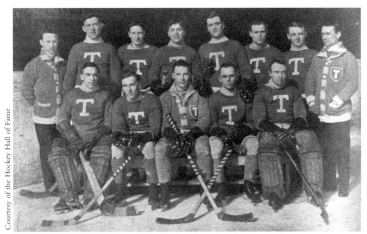

Courtesy of the Hockey Hall of Fame

The Toronto Blueshirts, Stanley Cup winning 1913–14 team.
Top Row — (l to r) Dick Carroll (trainer), Con. Corbeau, C. Roy McGiffin, Jack
C. Marshall (manager), George McNamara, Jack Walker, C.W. "Cully" Wilson,
Frank Carrol (trainer). Bottom Row — Claude Wilson, Frank C. Foyston,
Alan M. Davidson, Harry Cameron, Harry Holmes.

A contingency plan was devised. At the PCHA's annual meeting —
held at Frank Patrick's house on October 12 — Patrick announced that
the league would be moving into Seattle. The city of roughly a quarter-
million had a new arena, was near enough to Vancouver and — pending
their decision to play — Victoria, and would provide a rival for the team
in Portland, Oregon (to which New Westminster had relocated for the
1914–15 season). Pete Muldoon, who had guided the Portland Rosebuds
the year before, would manage the new club.

With that bit of business out of the way, Lester Patrick spoke up:
Victoria would play the 1915–16 season after all. Which introduced the
problem of where to find enough players to stock the Seattle team.
Western Canada had not yet begun to produce high-quality players in sufficient numbers, so the only solution was — as it had been in 1911 — to
look east. The most likely target seemed to be the Toronto Blueshirts who,
only a year after their own Stanley Cup triumph, had fallen into disarray.

In the space of a year, the Blueshirts had fallen from first to fourth place
in the NHA standings, finishing only two points ahead of the
Ontarios/Shamrocks. The onset of the Great War had cost the league players and, more importantly, fans. The Torontos' indifferent play also put the
brakes on gate receipts. Owner Frank Robinson's decision to volunteer for
the Canadian forces seemed to be the club's death knell.

The Blueshirts had already lost their architect, Percy Quinn, after the 1914 season. It took Quinn, the brother of NHA president Emmett, only two seasons to build a championship team from the ground up — an impressive feat in any era. Citing increased business responsibilities, the insurance company manager withdrew, turning over the decision making to Robinson and player/manager Jack Marshall. While the Ontarios rebuilt under Eddie Livingstone, the Torontos chose to stand pat with a lineup that included such veterans as Minnie McGiffin, a goon who would make Marty McSorley or Donald Brashear look like a model citizen.

Robinson's absence meant he would not be able to run the Blueshirts, so he decided to put the club up for sale. He received two offers: from Livingstone and from the McNamara brothers, who had inherited a considerable sum after the death of their father. With cash in hand, the boys were looking to buy their way into hockey management.

The choice between the two suitors was a difficult one. The McNamaras seemed the logical choice, since Livingstone already owned the Shamrocks. This was not because it might be considered unethical for an owner to operate more than one club — at one point, Ambrose O'Brien controlled four teams. It was simply that the other governors would never approve of Eddie Livingstone having two votes in the league boardroom. There was no way of knowing which way the Senators would swing, but the Quebec owners could be counted on to vote as a bloc, and Sam Lichtenhein was sure to turn thumbs down on the idea.

The problem with the McNamara bid, however, was that the brothers were offering less money than Livvy, and the NHA had expressed a preference for Toronto-based ownership — the McNamaras called Sault Ste. Marie home. After Livingstone arranged to buy three of Robinson's best players — Harry Cameron, Cully Wilson and Frank Foyston — the McNamaras withdrew their bid.

Frank Patrick's expansion plans would provide a solution that appealed to both Robinson and Livingstone.

When the owners of the other four NHA teams started to hear rumblings that Frank Patrick was interested in transplanting players to the shores of Puget Sound, and had been making inquiries with that goal in mind, it was no longer a case of "all quiet on the eastern front."

George Kennedy's Montreal Canadiens had been raided before, when the PCHA plucked Newsy Lalonde, Didier Pitre and George "Skinner" Poulin off his roster, and he wasn't about to let it happen again. As a pre-emptive strike, he announced that he was finally paying

— after three years — the $750 transfer fee that Frank Patrick had asked for when Lalonde returned to the Canadiens. Kennedy set the money aside with the provision that it be paid when there was peace between the leagues. The money never did make its way west: Kennedy froze the transaction, claiming that there was no peace treaty in place. It is more likely that by reneging he aimed to hold the transfer fee hostage and thus deter a raid. And it is even more plausible that Kennedy was balking at the prospect of paying twice for Lalonde's rights — once to Ambrose O'Brien in 1910 and again, now, to the Patricks.

Wanderers owner Sam Lichtenhein called Kennedy's bluff, siding with the PCHA. "The statement that Lalonde was bought subject to a new peace agreement is incorrect," Lichtenhein asserted. "Lalonde was purchased at the beginning of last season outright, and the price agreed on was $750. There was no contingent clause, and the Canadien club owes the Patricks that money.

"I regard it as detrimental to the interests of the league that Mr. Kennedy should now refuse to pay that purchase money, war or no war, and I think the NHA would be better off without Mr. Kennedy at the helm of the Canadiens. So strongly do I feel about this that I intend to ask the league at its next meeting to demand Mr. Kennedy's resignation and to place the Canadiens franchise into other hands."[99]

Frank Patrick took Lichtenhein's comments to heart, and immediately sent word that the Wanderers players would not be touched.

George Kennedy, on the other hand, went ballistic. "I will demand at the next meeting of the N.H.A. that all of Lichtenhein's correspondence with the Patricks be shown, not only that relating to the new agreement, but other correspondence which I have reason to believe he had. I think he is handing the N.H.A. a fine double cross and throwing down all his partners."[100]

In Toronto, Robinson and Livingstone were oddly unconcerned by the prospects of a raid.

Said Livingstone, "I have none of my players signed up yet, but have had assurances from the majority of them that they will be with me again, providing they receive a fair salary. I think the players, after they find out the cost of living, etc., in the West, will be content to remain in the East, especially when they find that they can make as much money playing in the N.H.A."[101]

The Ottawa Senators' ownership group looked on in concern. They entertained hopes of bringing Cyclone Taylor back from Vancouver, but Lichtenhein held the player's NHA rights. If he prevailed, there would be absolutely no chance of the Cyclone ever again being seen in a Senators sweater. Ottawa therefore felt it had no choice but to support Kennedy. The others backed Lichtenhein cautiously because he had the one thing they needed: the exclusive rights to operate a professional hockey team out of the Westmount Arena, the largest and finest facility in the east.

As it turned out, Kennedy needn't have worried about a raid on his team, as the Patricks had apparently found another target. On November 5, 1915, the Vancouver *Province* reported, "The entire Toronto hockey team has been secured by President Frank Patrick of the P.C.H.A. for Seattle, according to an official announcement made by the Coast league magnate when he arrived back in the city from Seattle this morning. Frank's pockets were overloaded with telegrams from prominent Eastern players wanting to come to the Coast, and while he has secured the services of at least ten men for the P.C.H.A., he would only admit that the entire Toronto team had been secured."[102]

The *Province* added that ex-Blueshirts Harry Holmes, Eddie Carpenter, Jack Walker, Frank Foyston and Cully Wilson were to line up with the Seattle team, while Harry Cameron, one of the top defencemen of the day, would play for Lester Patrick's Victoria squad.[103] The only Toronto regular the western league declined to take was Roy "Minnie" McGiffin, a thug who, despite having scored the Cup-winning goal for the Blueshirts in 1914, had racked up 131 minutes in penalties in 18 games in 1914–15. To make room for Cameron, Bobby Rowe — who had played alongside the Patricks in Renfrew — was transferred from Victoria to Seattle. The plan, designed to bolster the Aristocrats' defence and improve the league's competitive balance, backfired when Cameron was persuaded to stay in Toronto for 1915–16.

Patrick took advantage of the confusion among the eastern owners to zero in on Emmett Quinn. He was still upset with the NHA president over his handling of the Tommy Smith affair, and he repeated that the west would not deal with the NHA as long as Quinn was in charge.

> I would have much preferred a peaceful settlement of the differences between the two sections, but the N.H.A. and its officials have made that impossible. We are out to build up a team for Seattle and to strengthen the other teams in the Coast Association wherever we think it necessary. We have entered on the war with a very definite idea as to just what we are going to do, and have not gone into it blindly. We realize that it is going to cost something to bring our plans to fullest fruition, but having entered into the conflict, we are not going to

be deterred by anything until our plans are carried out to their last detail.

The real trouble with the N.H.A. has been the weakness of its government. When Arbitrator Taylor, who was the choice of the N.H.A., awarded Tommy Smith to the Coast Association, Quinn wired me begging that Smith be permitted to remain in the East. I replied that under no circumstances would I sanction his playing with any other club than a Coast club, but, nevertheless, he was played in Toronto that winter. When the Ottawas went to Toronto they refused to play if Smith were included in the line-up, and I was assured by the Ottawa management and players that they were advised by Quinn that I had waived claim on Smith and was agreeable to his appearance in the N.H.A. No such permission was ever given by me, as president of the Coast association, nor by anyone else, but it was only one of the bold wanderings from the path of verity chargeable to the N.H.A. executive head.

For two years past Quinn has been going to send out the draft of a new agreement, but with Quinn's superior talent for procrastination dominating his actions, none appeared until after the meeting of the N.H.A. about six weeks ago, when we heard from them in respect to the new agreement. It was such an absurd proposition that came to us that we paid absolutely no attention to it, and no attention will be paid to the East until they get someone at the head of their organization who has regard for the truth and the obligations which the East may assume in regard to the West."[104]

Patrick's statement is interesting in that he admits to the reason for the raid on the Torontos — to stock the Seattle team — and that there was a plan in place to do just that.

One day after Patrick's "raid," Livingstone dropped a bombshell of his own.

"It may surprise you to know that I have bought the Toronto franchise outright from Frank Robinson," he told the *Mail and Empire*. "This is no conversation statement, but an absolute fact. I also own, or rather owned till Saturday night, the Shamrock franchise as well. I had several offers for the Shamrocks, and as I could not very well be connected with two clubs at the same time, I decided to accept the best offer. Who the purchaser is will not be made public for a few days."[105]

Livingstone vowed that the war with the Patricks would not deter him from icing a winning team. "I have indisputable information to the effect that the players I most desire to keep will stick to me. These alone, with my ex-Shamrock players and the several crack amateurs I have on my reserve list, will make an aggregation quite strong enough to suit the most fastidious fan." He also threatened to use the courts against any player who jumped to the rival league,

> and even the knowledge that they will have to return their option money should be sufficient to deter the possibly decided "jumper" from going West, as in many cases it amounts to $400 or more.
>
> In connection with the Shamrock players, I think this is an opportune time to express my personal appreciation of their attitude toward myself. Many received offers, but not one man even considered deserting the team. More than that, two of the players signed the temporary contract that called for no specific salary and left their salaries entirely up to me. These two were among the best men in the league last winter. Others offered to sign, but were told to wait until a definite salary was put up to them.
>
> Naturally I should prefer to see the present complications straightened out amicably, and the Coast League, if they have been given the worst of anything, compensated therefore, but if the Patricks persist in their present dictatorial attitude I shall certainly not advocate peace measures at the N.H.A. meeting. The wrongs cannot be all on one side."[106]

When the dust had settled, Frank Patrick had obtained the players he needed for his league's new Seattle franchise, while the guise of a "raid" helped him advance his vendetta against Emmett Quinn. Frank Robinson was able to unburden himself of his team, escape with money in his pocket — and save face. After all, he might point out, he hadn't sold his team; it had been stolen from him by those raiders from out west. Eddie Livingstone acquired the Torontos' name and Stanley Cup–winning heritage without the added expense of the players' contracts. *And* he had the Toronto market to himself.

Conventional wisdom has told us that the Seattle PCHA club initiated a raid on the NHA, hollowing out the Toronto Blueshirts roster and wreaking havoc on eastern hockey. In fact, aside from those Blueshirts who were Seattle-bound, not a single NHA player went west for the 1915–16 season. Meanwhile, the NHA declared open season on PCHA rosters.

George Kennedy opened his wallet wide to lure a couple of his ex-Canadiens players back east. "Skinner Poulin and George Rochon, I know, are anxious to come back east for hockey," he told the Montreal *Herald*. "Judging by the offers which have been made my players, the salaries which are being paid on the Coast are much lower than those in the East. The contracts which I have offered these players aggregate $10,000. Rochon could not reach a salary settlement last season, and was out of the game. Poulin's heart has always been in the East, and with the shorter season here, he is very likely to return."[107]

In Toronto, meanwhile, reaction to the "raids" was virtually nonexistent. "I do not think we need to worry very much about this war talk," Frank Robinson said, before adding, "It will, however, be well for any player belonging to the N.H.A., and particularly those who have received advances on their salaries for next season, to realize that if they go west, they will surely be arrested on criminal charges."[108]

Robinson did not elaborate on how he or the NHA proposed to effect criminal charges against a player who jumped his contract — especially one who chose to take up residence on the west coast and perhaps even in the United States, in the days before air travel. Such a task would certainly have tested the most savvy of legal minds.

And despite all the bluster he offered for public consumption, Livingstone's activities hint strongly at a backroom deal between Robinson, Patrick and himself. For although the "raid" on his Blueshirts gave him apparent cause to do so, and he certainly had the fan and media support — not to mention the temperament — to retaliate against the coast league, he never did. During his entire tenure as an NHA owner, he never once raided a PCHA roster.

As far as the Patricks were concerned, they had made the deal the NHA deserved. Two owners were very happy, while the remaining partners were left wondering where the knives in their back had come from.

Chapter 8

Two to One in Toronto

George Kennedy and Livingstone didn't get along, personally.
They almost came to blows on a few occasions, at meetings of
the National Association.

— Elmer Ferguson, 1965

*I*n the days leading up to the NHA's meeting of November 9, 1915, rumours were swirling as to who would be the new owner of the Toronto Shamrocks. The Toronto *Star* insisted that the McNamara brothers had finally reached an agreement for the team.[109] But the smart money seemed to favour Lol Solman of the Arena Gardens — who also happened to be bankrolling Charlie Querrie's Tecumseh lacrosse team — and James McCaffery, the owner of the Toronto Maple Leafs baseball club. A third scenario, put forth by the Toronto *Daily News*, had Livingstone planning to merge the Torontos and Shamrocks if he didn't receive the support of the league.[110]

As it was, the Toronto question remained on the back burner — for the time being, at least — after Livingstone asserted that he could not afford to reveal the new owner's identity until after the deal had closed. Meanwhile, the escalating war of words between George Kennedy and Sam Lichtenhein was defused once Lichtenhein presented his correspondence with the Patrick brothers and Kennedy found it to be to his satisfaction. With the Canadiens owner appeased, Lichtenhein went after Emmett Quinn, criticizing his abilities as league president and nominating himself for that office. The other directors, expressing their undivided support for Quinn, turned him down.[111]

Livingstone, meanwhile, had not only managed to avoid a show-down over his Toronto purchase, but he also returned from Montreal with Harry Cameron's name on a contract.

"I've won the first round of the fight with the Patricks, if I never win another," Livingstone enthused. "I have signed up one of the men the Patricks claim — Harry Cameron. I met him in Montreal yesterday, and he signed a contract. I have also signed up a crack goalkeeper who will replace Harry Holmes. I have made no effort to retain either Holmes or Cully Wilson. If they have signed up with the Patricks, let them go to the coast. I will have plenty of players and a good team."[112]

The "crack goaltender" turned out to be Percy LeSueur of Livvy's other team, the Shamrocks. Shortly afterwards, Skene Ronan was also transferred to the Torontos, as were the Denneny brothers. The quiet attrition of the Shamrock team — to the benefit of the Blueshirts — could not escape the league's attention, and another NHA meeting was called for November 13. An ultimatum appeared in the Montreal *Gazette*:

> Should Livingstone not dispose of the Shamrock franchise before next Saturday [November 20] the league will deal with the matter and sell the club over his head. At the present time there are one or two bidders for the club, but the N.H.A. decided that it would be fairer to give Livingstone the first chance to get rid of the franchise.
>
> With the players to be reserved by Livingstone in his transfer of the club, there will be few left for the new owners to start out with this season.[113]

If Livingstone expected to enlist Ottawa's support, he was mistaken. Tommy Gorman, speaking on behalf of the Senators, said, "It would be better, should the sixth club fail to materialize, to drop the Torontos and have the four clubs in the East, playing a triple schedule. The Ottawas were never enthusiastic about Toronto, because it is a hotbed of O.H.A. enthusiasm and newspapers there have never given the professional promoters a fair show."[114]

In other words, because the Toronto media had the audacity to question the NHA's moves and motives — and even had the time of day for the amateur game — the city didn't deserve *any* NHA teams.

"Ottawa has all she can do to look after one team," Livingstone retorted, "and Montreal will find two teams plenty. I think the best plan is to let Toronto have one good team this year and it will be royally supported. Two teams of only ordinary calibre will hurt the pro game in Toronto, not help it."[115]

Watching gleefully from the sidelines were the members of the sporting fraternity in Hamilton, where there was no love lost for Eddie Livingstone. Grudges were still held as a result of Livingstone's decision to suspend the Alerts football team back in 1912. So, when Emmett Quinn visited the "Ambitious City" on November 16 and 19 to inspect the arena, and promised that Hamilton would get eight players if the Shamrocks were moved there, the news was well received. Sadly, it was the beginning of a long game in which the NHA, and later the NHL, would use Hamilton as a pawn.

Just before the November 20 deadline, the management of the Arena Gardens, thought to be on the Torontos' side, abruptly turned on Livingstone during lease negotiations. The Arena later claimed that Livingstone wanted a guarantee of $14,000 while Eddie insisted he merely wanted a bigger share of gate receipts. Lol Solman countered with a proposal that would give his company control of the team, which Livvy naturally rejected, and talks broke down. Left without a place to play, Livingstone wired Emmett Quinn to say that he might be forced to move both Toronto franchises to Boston if relations with the Arena Gardens management didn't improve. Quinn met with Solman and convinced him to hammer out an agreement with Livingstone. Professional hockey would remain in Toronto.

On November 20, Quinn seized control of the Shamrocks, as threatened. The McNamara brothers were still interested buyers, but they couldn't arrange financing — besides which, Quinn had already blocked one bid from the boys from the Soo, and the proud president made a habit of sticking to his guns. The Hamilton group was also found wanting, as the arena was dismissed as too small for the professional game. They also lacked players. On December 2, despite a last-ditch effort by the McNamaras, a five-team league schedule was issued.

At around this time, the Stanley Cup trustees, William Foran and Phil Ross, had a significant change of heart: competition for the Cup, originally commissioned to be awarded to the champions of the Dominion of Canada, would now be open to American teams, as long as they were affiliated with a Canadian league.

"The Stanley Cup is not emblematic of the Canadian honours," Foran proclaimed, "but of the hockey championship of the world. Hence, if Portland and Seattle were to win and carry out the usual arrangement with regard to the recognition of the rules and the production of a bond for its safekeeping, they would be allowed to retain the trophy the customary length of time."[116]

It was only a few years earlier that Ottawa had threatened to take the Stanley Cup and play challenge series against teams in Boston and New York City. If one reads between the lines, the message that Foran and Ross were sending was clear: the Stanley Cup playoffs were not to be held hostage by a squabble between the two leagues. The Cup was the property of the PCHA until the next series was played.

Skene Ronan had no problem with the new arrangement in Toronto, expressing his wholehearted support for his employer. "He is the best man I have ever played under. And it will be a great surprise to me if he does not produce a winner this season. I know, in any event, it will not be the fault of the players if he does not do so. We will work our hardest for 'Livvy.'"[117]

Livingstone devoted the next couple of weeks to preparing his Blueshirts for the coming season. George McNamara, apparently bearing no grudge at being shut out of NHA ownership, signed on for another tour of duty with Livingstone. The Meeking brothers, Gordon and Harry, both got tryouts, with the latter making the squad.

Still, the 1915–16 season did not begin as the Toronto owner had hoped. Corbett Denneny was missing from the lineup due to illness. The Blueshirts missed his scoring touch, as they opened with five straight losses. On three of these occasions, they were limited to a single goal (their opponents ganged up to score twenty-five times in those three games).

For Sam Lichtenhein, conversely, the new season couldn't be off to a better start. The Wanderers had won six of their first seven games and appeared to be running away with the title — until their clash with the Blueshirts on January 19, 1916. Ken Randall of Toronto and Sprague Cleghorn, the Redbands' star defenceman and tough guy, both rushed for the puck near the end of the rink. The players collided and plunged into the boards, Cleghorn striking them feet first. The impact left Cleghorn with a sprained ankle, while he was cut in the face and neck by Randall's skate as the Toronto player rolled over at the same time as Cleghorn tried to get up. The gash in the neck required two stitches, while the other cut was not as serious.[118]

After the game, X-rays showed that Cleghorn's ankle was fractured and ligaments were torn. He would miss the rest of the season. Cleghorn's injuries had a devastating effect on Lichtenhein's team: although they beat

Toronto, 7–4, they went on to win only three of the sixteen games that remained to be played. Real or imagined, Sam Lichtenhein had yet another reason to hate Eddie Livingstone.

The Torontos were also, indirectly, the source of a problem for Montreal's other team, when Skene Ronan was traded to the Canadiens. One of the conditions under which the Canadiens franchise was required to operate was that it could carry no more than two English-speaking players on its roster — the rest had to be francophones. The addition of Ronan put the Canadiens over the limit. On the same day that Cleghorn was injured, Kennedy used Ronan in a game against Quebec, apparently without permission of the other clubs, and consequently Mike Quinn, the Bulldogs manager, filed a protest with league president Emmett Quinn — the two men were not related — demanding that the game be replayed.[119]

The NHA president fined Kennedy $100 for the infraction and ruled that the game would be replayed at the end of the season if it affected the standings. If this didn't have Kennedy questioning the wisdom of trading for Ronan, the game in Toronto a few days later would.

The Canadiens-Blueshirts game was marred by considerably rough play in the final fifteen minutes. At one point, Alf Skinner of Toronto was skating down the boards, trying to get at the Canadiens puck carrier. Ronan hooked Skinner over the eye with his stick, temporarily knocking the Blueshirt unconscious. Skinner sustained a cut over the eye, but returned to the game after a few minutes' delay. As the fans called for his blood, Ronan was ejected. He was arrested and charged with aggravated assault, then was released on $200 bail — which Kennedy, of course, would have to pay. In his defence, Ronan stated that he intended to hook Skinner's stick, which may well have been true, since the two men had been good friends when they were still teammates.

The Ronan arrest was the start of a police crackdown on rough play in the NHA. Only a week before, Gordie Roberts had sucker punched a goal judge in Ottawa without facing any real consequence. President Quinn merely fined Roberts and ordered him to write an apology to the official. The arrest of Ronan sent a signal that the game was not above the law — a mantra oft-repeated today.

Fortunately for Ronan, he would not have to face the police court magistrate in his January 31 trial. Colonel George Taylor Denison made it clear that if he tried the case the sentence would be no mere slap on the wrist. "If I can stop this kind of rowdyism, I'll do so. In future cases like this the charge will be common assault, not aggravated assault, and there will be no fines."[120]

George Kennedy was still seething over the $100 fine he faced for playing Ronan in the Quebec game. Only a couple of months after rising to the president's defence in the face of Lichtenhein's attempted coup, the Canadiens owner was now the one calling for Emmett Quinn's removal. Kennedy claimed that the NHA president not only knew before the game that Canadiens were going to play Ronan, but had actually advised him to pursue the ex-Toronto star. Calling Quinn's decision "absurd," Kennedy refused to pay the fine.[121]

On January 31, Kennedy and Ronan made the trip to Toronto for the latter's trial. Fortunately for the centre, he did not have to rely solely upon his boss's testimony.

The referee got him off the hook.

As he had been in a better position than anyone else in the rink to see what actually occurred, referee Lou Marsh's account carried a great deal of weight with Judge Winchester. The judge made it plain, however, that in future the police would have the power to stop games that in their opinion were too rough, and that players could expect judges to mete out something more substantial than a couple of minutes on the sidelines.[122]

(Too bad the judge didn't question Marsh about who was paying his salary during the game in question — the Toronto *Star* or the National Hockey Association. According to records, he was working for both!)

Despite Winchester's warning, the rough play went on unabated. When Toronto travelled to Ottawa on February 19, the game was halted while the Ottawa police conferred with referee Cooper Smeaton about the chippiness. The game was allowed to finish, with the Senators coming out on top, 5–2. After the game Smeaton wrote a report for Emmett Quinn in which he asserted that Ken Randall of the Blueshirts had threatened him in the course of the game. Quinn immediately suspended the Toronto defenceman. The only problem was that he didn't notify the Blueshirts. "I was not aware that there had been the slightest trouble between Randall and Referee Smeaton till I read it in the papers," Livingstone told the *Mail and Empire*. "If Randall acted as he is said to have, I have no sympathy in his direction, because that kind of thing will not be tolerated by me. However, in any event the punishment meted out is too severe on the club and out of proportion to penalties that have been inflicted in the past for similar offences. We will be severely handicapped if Randall is not available for the game with Ottawa this Saturday, and I have wired President Quinn for confirmation and will protest strenuously if the penalty mentioned has really been inflicted."[123]

Quinn confirmed the suspension and set the terms for Randall's return: an apology to Smeaton and the payment of a $25 fine. That punishment did not sit well with the Senators. Nor did the fact that Randall, due to a break in the schedule, missed no games during his suspension. The final insult came when the Blueshirts visited the capital and rolled to a 9–2 victory. A well-rested Randall scored Toronto's first two goals.

As the season wound down, thoughts turned to postseason exhibition games. Emmett Quinn and Sam Lichtenhein made the trip to Boston to negotiate a series in that city. Perhaps remembering Livingstone's earlier threat to relocate there, the two magnates deliberately excluded the Torontos from the series. Livingstone again responded by arranging a postseason trip to Cleveland; this time the Torontos would line up against an all-star unit headed by Frank Nighbor.

But there was still a season to finish. The Torontos had reeled off seven straight home victories leading up to the final game of the season — against the Montreal Canadiens, who had clinched the NHA title. The game meant little to the Habs, but bragging rights were at stake for Livingstone: a win would vault the Blueshirts ahead of Sam Lichtenhein's Wanderers into fourth place in the five-team league.

As always, Livingstone was looking for an edge, and he found one. Prior to the 1915–16 season, the NHA had not declared the former Blueshirts who had been scooped up by Seattle to be outlaws, which meant that they were technically still eligible to play in the east. And it just so happened that the PCHA wrapped up its schedule before the NHA's was done. It crossed Livingstone's mind that he could insert ex-Blueshirts Frank Foyston and Harry Holmes into the lineup for the game against the Canadiens.

His decision raises an important question: if we are to believe that Livingstone's Blueshirts were truly "raided" by the Seattle Metropolitans, why would Livvy consider asking the "traitors" to suit up in their old colours and play a game for him now? Furthermore, PCHA president Frank Patrick expressed no opposition to the idea — more circumstantial evidence that he was not at war with the Toronto team after all.

Foyston and Holmes had returned from the west four days before the Montreal game. They would have arrived sooner, but their services were needed for a series of warm-up games against the PCHA champs, the Portland Rosebuds, before that team made its own trip east to play the Canadiens for the Cup.

Despite the reinforcements, the Blueshirts went down to defeat, 6–4, leaving them in the NHA basement, one point behind the Wanderers.

Although Elmer Ferguson of the Montreal *Herald*, for one, argued that Livingstone was entitled to use the players since they were still his proper-

The Wanderers in action against Ottawa. This was the first flash photo ever taken at a hockey game, taken by the United Photographic Stores on January 24, 1912. It appeared in the Ottawa **Evening Journal** *on February 28, 1912.*

ty, Emmett Quinn didn't see it that way: at the next meeting of the league's board, held during the Stanley Cup series, Livingstone was censured.

Livingstone assembled a star-studded cast to play against his Blueshirts in the Cleveland series: Harry Holmes, Harry Cameron, Odie Cleghorn, Rusty Crawford, Frank Foyston, Billy Bell and Frank Nighbor.[124] All but Bell, Cleghorn and Crawford had played for Toronto at some point, and all but Bell and Cleghorn are in the Hall of Fame. Whether the NHA players had been granted permission from their respective teams to perform in the series is unknown, although Ottawa newspapers suggest that the Senators had no objection to Nighbor playing in Cleveland. After the Cleveland exhibitions, the hockey world concentrated on the main event, the Stanley Cup series. It was a unique situation this year: for the first time, the team from the east was cast in the role of challengers, and that team was the NHA's longtime doormats, the Montreal Canadiens.

As PCHA champions, the Portland Rosebuds took over stewardship of the Stanley Cup from the 1915 winners, the Vancouver Millionaires. Team manager Ed Savage dutifully engraved his team's name on the coveted bowl:

> PORTLAND, ORE.
> P.C.H.A. CHAMPIONS
> 1915–16[125]

thus solidifying the City of Roses' claim as the first U.S.–based club to win the Cup. (This practice ended after the 1916 series; thereafter, a team

Courtesy of the Hockey Hall of Fame

could only be recognized as Cup champs if it won the Stanley Cup series. Reference sources therefore consistently name the 1917 Seattle Metropolitans as the first champions from south of the border.)

The Rosebuds would not get to keep the Cup for long, however. Georges Vezina starred in leading the Montreal Canadiens to their first Stanley Cup championship, as they beat Portland three games to two.

After the season, NHA president T. Emmett Quinn, tired of being verbally abused by the NHA owners, announced his resignation.

The proverbial final nail in the coffin was the cancellation of the Boston tournament. Only two games were played, to sparse crowds, before the folks at the Boston Arena pulled the plug. Not even a last-minute plea by league secretary Frank Calder — who was already being touted for the presidency — could rescue the matches.

Another bit of business changed the complexion of hockey forever. Eddie Livingstone of Toronto observed that it seemed unfair, under the current system, that a team beset by injuries might miss out on its chance at a championship — as happened to the Wanderers in the season just past. For those teams that fell out of the running early, it was equally hard for players and spectators to keep up their interest as the season wore on.

Livingstone proposed that the season be split into two segments. At the midway point, every team would start anew with a record of no wins, no losses and no ties. The league leader at the halfway mark would then play for the league title against the best team during the second half of the schedule.

Livvy had been trying for a year to convince his fellow owners of the plan's merits, and even now Ted Dey of Ottawa took some convincing. Tommy Gorman of the Ottawa *Citizen* was present at the meeting, and he reported that the proposal was adopted "after a lengthy dispute." However, after "Livingstone pointed out that it would help to maintain the interest and encourage good hockey on the teams that ordinarily might be put hopelessly out of the race in the first half," the two Montreal owners, George Kennedy and Sam Lichtenhein, took a shine to the plan. It passed unanimously.[126]

There can be no doubt that what made the idea palatable to the Montreal owners was the prospect that the playoff gate receipts would not have to be split with the players. It also meant clubs might not have to rely on the year-end exhibition games in Boston or New York to break even.

The owners agreed to the change, and hockey's first official playoff system was born.

Chapter 9

Eddie Livingstone Goes to War

"We didn't throw Eddie Livingstone out. Perish the thought.
That would have been illegal and unfair. Also, it wouldn't have
been sporting."
— Sam Lichtenhein, 1917

*A*t the beginning of 1916 Sam Hughes, the Canadian minister for the militia, pledged to raise an army of 500,000 to fight the Great War in Europe. It was an ambitious promise for a country of just over 7 million, whose standing army numbered only a few thousand before the outbreak of hostilities. Recruitment was brisk early in the year, but by summer the stream of willing young men had dwindled. As major campaigns were waged the numbers of casualties and soldiers missing in action had grown to alarming proportions, and losses touched an ever-growing number of Canadian families. Young men were less and less willing to volunteer to die, and there were already rumours that the government might have to resort to conscripting able-bodied men into armed service.

In Toronto, as in other Canadian cities, the military tried to present a comforting face to the public. Numerous sports teams, made up of enlisted men and officers alike, competed in city and provincial leagues in almost any game imaginable. Over the summer of 1916 the military was able to recruit some of the country's best hockey players, and by December a single unit, the 228th Infantry Battalion — also known as the Northern Fusiliers — would have enough hockey players to fill an OHA senior team, a junior squad, three teams in Toronto's Beaches league, and a team in the National Hockey Association. In all, the 228th could claim sixty-three players.[127]

The McNamara brothers from the Soo headed that list, and it was in fact Lieutenant George McNamara who approached the NHA at the end of August to ask Emmett Quinn if the pro league would admit the 228th Battalion for the upcoming season.

Within a couple of days the word leaked out to the press through Goldie Prodgers, who was confined to the base hospital in Toronto and had passed the information along to a reporter. The story was then picked up by the Canadian Press wire service for nationwide distribution.[128] Lieutenant-Colonel Archie Earchman immediately wrote the NHA members, hoping to ease their concerns over the team's ability to complete the season by stating, "I might add this Battalion is not very old; we will probably not go Overseas until next spring."[129]

At about the same time Earchman sent his letter, a rumour began making the rounds that the military was set to take over the Arena Gardens for the duration. This did not sit well with the rink's owners, who had only to consider the situation in Victoria, where Lester Patrick's arena had been "occupied" by the army — a move that forced him to move his team to Spokane, Washington — to appreciate what fate might be in store.

While the 228th was hoping to be admitted to the NHA, the Ottawa Senators were looking to withdraw, as money had grown tight in the nation's capital, thanks to the uncertainty of the wartime economy. The NHA refused this request, and by the league meeting of September 30 the issue appeared settled. The manager of the arena in Ottawa, Ted Dey, would operate the club on behalf of the Ottawa Hockey Association. Tommy Gorman, the sports editor of the *Citizen* who doubled as manager of a lacrosse team during the summer months, was brought in as an assistant after Dey had trouble recruiting enough players for the new season.

The eastern circuit also had to deal with the resignation of league president Emmett Quinn, who had held the job since the NHA's formation in 1910. So that the application of the 228th Battalion could

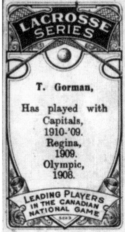

A rare card from Tommy Gorman's lacrosse days

be considered without interruption or distraction, Quinn agreed to postpone his resignation until the October league meeting.

The Fusiliers' bid to join the NHA seemed to be good news for Eddie Livingstone and his Toronto Blueshirts. The owners from the province of Quebec — Mike Quinn of the Bulldogs, George Kennedy of the Montreal Canadiens and Sam Lichtenhein of the Wanderers — had been grumbling for some time about having to travel to Toronto to play only one team during the 1915–16 season. Lichtenhein had gone as far as to suggest at league meetings that Toronto be dropped as a cost-cutting measure — and more likely to force his arch-enemy, Livingstone, into selling his team. The 228th's proposal restored the complement of Toronto teams to two, eliminating the excuse that Toronto's presence in the league put undue pressure on travel budgets.

A league whose gate receipts had been suffering of late could hardly afford to turn down an interested applicant, and so, despite the possibility the team could be called overseas at any time, president Emmett Quinn approved the Battalion's application. As every other team was required to do, the 228th had to post a $3,000 bond with the Ocean Accident and Guarantee Corporation to ensure that they would finish the season. In order to prevent the 228th from raiding other NHA squads, a further condition was imposed: the Battalion was prohibited from signing up any members of the established teams after the league's September meeting. This was made clear in the minutes of that meeting:

> It was moved by S. E. Lichtenhein and seconded by M. J. Quinn that this Association allow the 228th Battalion to operate at their own expense the franchise of the Ontario Hockey Club, which franchise the Association loans them gratis for the season 1916–17, the list of their players as furnished under date of September 27th to be accepted. All N.H.A. players playing for this club have the permission of this Association after the season 1916–17 to revert to their respective clubs when the season is over or at any time if not required on their military duties. The 228th Battalion Hockey Club, after being admitted as members of this Association, must conform in every way to the laws and constitution and all agreements of the membership in this Association. Carried unanimously.[130]

Notice that the 228th were to run the former Ontarios/Shamrocks franchise. In a nutshell, Sam Lichtenhein had taken over one of Livingstone's teams, and there was nothing Livvy could do about it.

The league's other major order of business was to replace Emmett Quinn. Prior to the league's October meeting, the Ottawa *Citizen* identified Frank Calder, the NHA's secretary, as the Senators' choice for the top job, with the former Ottawa star Harvey Pulford and Major Frank Robinson — the former owner of the Torontos — also in the running.[131]

A pair of owners, Sam Lichtenhein and Mike Quinn, also threw their hats into the ring, but in the end it was Robinson who got the nod. He had "won" the responsibility for overseeing a mob of argumentative owners and a league with a team that might withdraw at any moment.

It was also decided that Emmett Quinn, in recognition of all his years of service, would be given a silver tea service.[132]

The job of managing the 228th Battalion team fell to Leon W. Reade and Colonel Earchman. Reade, a railroad contractor by trade, was noted in Toronto hockey circles for managing the Toronto Victorias, stocked with many of Livingstone's old TR&AA players, to the Ontario Hockey Association championship in 1915.

The formation of the army team angered the Patricks who, earlier in the summer, had voluntarily given up the Victoria Arena to aid the war effort and — at great financial loss — moved the PCHA's Aristocrats to Spokane. And when former PCHA players such as Art Duncan started to show up in Toronto, playing for the Northern Fusiliers — in the NHA — the brothers felt their patriotism was being taken for granted. The biggest insult came when Eddie Oatman, the Portland Rosebuds' star right winger, appeared in a khaki sweater. Portland owner Ed Savage sent word to the 228th that Oatman was under suspension and therefore ineligible to play for the military team.[133] After the presidents of both leagues got involved, it was resolved that Oatman could indeed play in the NHA. Savage would have to grin and bear it.

Meanwhile, Eddie Livingstone spent the early days of October 1916 patching together a team weakened by military recruitment. His Blueshirts would have to do without Harry Cameron, George McNamara and goaltender Percy LeSueur. It was the loss of LeSueur that was most damaging, as Toronto would have to scramble to find a competent replacement. For the moment, the team's projected netminder was Claude Wilson, the club's longtime spare goalie. Livingstone could fill Cameron's spot by moving Ken Randall, perhaps the best two-way player on the team, back to defence. A couple of OHA products, Reg Noble and Archie Briden, would pick up the slack on the forward line.

Noble, born in Collingwood, Ontario, was locally trained, having started out with the St. Michael's College team before joining the Toronto Riversides. He led both teams in scoring. Briden, a native of Renfrew, had been discovered during the 1916 exhibition tour in Cleveland, where he was playing with the Cleveland Indians.

Like the Blueshirts, the Montreal Canadiens were affected by the 228th Battalion's arrival on the scene, as they lost the services of Amos Arbour, Goldie Prodgers and Howard McNamara to the military team. In fact, the Montreal Wanderers and Quebec Bulldogs were the only teams whose rosters were untouched.

But it was Livingstone with whom the Fusiliers clashed almost immediately. Duke Keats, who had scored 22 goals as a rookie for the Blueshirts in 1915–16, had recently volunteered for the army. The problem was that, although Keats was now a soldier, the 228th had traded his playing rights back to the Torontos in exchange for the right to use Percy LeSueur. LeSueur practised with the Battalion but never did play for the team — he preferred the job of training new recruits and elected to stay with the unit to which he had been assigned.

Earchman and Reade, thinking they might put one over on Livingstone, insisted that Keats would still have to play for the 228th. Clearly, the military men had underestimated the determination of the Blueshirts owner. Livingstone didn't care how much of a drawing card the military team would be; he was not about to be steamrollered by that popularity.

One can imagine the outrage that would have erupted had the Senators lost Clint Benedict to the Battalion, or if Newsy Lalonde of the Canadiens or Quebec's Joe Malone had been raided. And those clubs weren't even being forced to share their market with the 228th. Yet Livingstone's fellow owners shared the opinion that he should be grateful for the inconveniences — after all, they hadn't kicked him out of the league. Undaunted, Livingstone took his grievance straight to the new league president, Major Frank Robinson.

The 228th had amassed such an impressive array of talent that it should have been easy for them to proceed without Duke Keats. But instead of negotiating with Livingstone, the Battalion's managers threatened to withdraw their team from the league were Keats not permitted to play for them.

On November 14, the new president ruled on the matter.

> When the 228th Hockey Club came into the associa-
> tion, it was agreed that they would be awarded a
> reserve list of all military players. This included Keats.
> Afterwards, in my presence, Capt. Reade, manager of
> the 228th, and Manager Livingstone of Toronto agreed
> on the trade of Keats for LeSueur, the former going to
> Toronto, and the latter to Reade. Now, from Toronto
> reports, it looks as if the colonel of the 228th is trying
> to compel Keats to get back to the 228th the best way
> he can, thereby naturally breaking his arrangement
> with Livingstone.[134]

Earchman grudgingly accepted the verdict. "We are in the hockey
game because we believe that a little sport and recreation helps the men,
and gives the ones in the regiment who do not play something to keep
together and cheer for," the colonel said. "We also think that it will
attract recruits to our battalion, and in spite of the fact that Keats cannot
play with his own regiment we will 'carry on' just the same.… [O]ur
battalion are ready to stay with us to the finish, and we will play the best
we can at all times, and try and win the championship with or without
the services of Keats."[135]

Keats would wear the blue sweater of the Toronto Hockey Club,
although his fellow members of the 228th would make life difficult for
the young star.

"When the two teams [Toronto and the 228th] faced each other on
the ice, Keats was often missing because of 'extra Army duties,'" recalled
Babe Donnelly, a former soldier — and defenceman. "On the day of the
important final game, he was put in the 'clink,' but got out just in time
to get into that night's game.

"All that didn't make matters any easier for Keats when the battalion went overseas. Nearly every time the Duke happened to get a real
cushy Army duty, some officer or sergeant-major would make it a point
to find some tough duty for him to do. Keats did more latrine duty than
any dozen other men."[136]

As the controversy raged over which team Duke Keats rightfully belonged
to, Eddie Livingstone of the Toronto Blueshirts was having problems retain-
ing another of his superstars: Cyril "Cy" Denneny. Between them, Keats

and Denneny had accounted for 46 of the last-place team's 97 goals in 1915–16, so to lose one or both would be catastrophic.

Denneny was a stubborn holdout who had reached an impasse with an equally determined club owner. The left winger claimed to have a job lined up in Ottawa and would therefore need a far more generous offer than Livingstone was prepared to make if he were expected to pick up stakes and move back to Toronto. The problem was that owners throughout the NHA were trying to reduce salaries, and this was especially true for Livingstone, who would again be sharing the Arena Gardens ice, and the Toronto market, with a second team — in this case, the 228th Battalion.

In late October, Denneny told an Ottawa *Journal* reporter that he had received a telegram from Livingstone informing him that he faced suspension if he didn't report to Toronto. Denneny responded by demanding a trade to Ottawa. Furthermore, he informed Livingstone, if no trade materialized he was fully prepared to sit out the entire 1916–17 season.[137]

Still, the *Journal* seemed confident that the Senators would land Denneny. "[T]he Ottawas are almost sure to land Cy Denneny of the Torontos. They think there shall be little trouble in arranging a deal with Eddie Livingstone for him."[138]

Determined to get full value for his reluctant star, Livingstone offered Denneny to Ottawa's new manager, Ted Dey, in exchange for Frank Nighbor.

Dey telegraphed his sarcastic reply: "Don't be so generous. You will break up the league."[139] Dey conveniently overlooked the circumstances under which Ottawa had obtained Nighbor, who got his start as an original member of the Blueshirts before being lured to Frank Patrick's Vancouver Millionaires in 1913. Two years later, the Pembroke Peach rejoined the NHA, becoming a Senator, and Ottawa never compensated Livingstone — nor does it appear that Livvy ever demanded any payment.

Gorman, now a member of the Senators executive, used his newspaper to advance his team's cause. "Livingstone must be joking," he wrote. "The Ottawa Club is not worrying as to Denneny. The lacrosse club brought him here and we have had no dealings with him. Denneny himself suggested some time ago that we might be able to get his release, so that he would be able to play again. It is immaterial to us whether he does so or not. I know that Mr. Dey would not entertain any transaction involving Nighbor. We were told that Denneny was permanently established in Ottawa and on this account we suggested a trade. Livingstone then refused it and allowed the matter to drop."[140]

Gorman neglected to make full disclosure when he expressed this opinion. For not only was he affiliated with the Senators, but *he* was the manager of the lacrosse team that had brought Denneny to Ottawa!

A few weeks later, Gorman made sport of Livingstone's trade demands:"Eddie Livingstone and Ted Dey will talk business next Saturday at the NHA meeting concerning Cyril Denneny. However, the Ottawa manager denies the report that he will offer Boucher, Hebert, Gerard, Nighbor, his rink, the Langevin Block and the present contents of the O.A.A.C. building in exchange for the Cornwall product."[141]

Boucher, Gerard and Nighbor are all members of the Hockey Hall of Fame. Incidentally, the OAAC building and the Langevin Block (a federal government office building) are not.

By November 8, Livingstone had modified his proposition: he was willing to accept Nighbor or $1,800 cash for Denneny.[142] Again Dey refused.

In his column, Charlie Querrie of the Toronto *Daily News* fired a shot at Gorman and the Senators:

> Down in Ottawa the small town press are making quite a holler over the fact that E. J. Livingstone, the manager of the Toronto Hockey Club, insists that his star forward, Cyril Dennenay, either plays in Toronto or the Ottawa Hockey Club comes across with the cash equivalent for his services. Seeing as Mr. Livingstone developed this player from the bush leagues and made him into a star, there is no reason why he should not play here or else recompense the Toronto magnate for his loss. If Tyrus Cobb, the Detroit baseball star, wanted to play in New York the general public would think the baseball magnates had gone crazy if he were allowed to go without the comment of his club. Cyril Denneny secured his chance to make good with the Torontos and under Mr. Livingstone's methods he improved every game. If Ottawa wanted his services, they saw him play in Cornwall long before he was signed by the Torontos. He belongs to the "blueshirts" and the Ottawa magnates should answer to the N.H.A. authorities if they are trying to persuade him to stay in the Capital.[143]

Querrie had good reason to back Livingstone. As manager of hockey operations for the Arena Gardens, he might be out of a job were the pro game not played in Toronto.

The Ottawa *Journal* countered by branding Livvy as "the best comedian in pro hockey":

> He has pulled some funny ones since he broke into the N.H.A., but his latest stunt has them all beaten. He wants $1,800 for the release of Cy Denneny, or he might, if given time to think it over, take Frank Nighbor in exchange. Really, Livvy, you should not make us laugh. Suffering from cracked lips, you know.[144]

The *Journal* went on to toe the company line that the Sens were not interested in Denneny and did not dispute Livingstone's claim to Denneny's playing rights. Besides, the newspaper protested, the Senators didn't need any help. "They will have plenty of players," the *Journal* promised.[145]

At the November league meeting, the Canadiens and Wanderers expressed some interest in acquiring Cy Denneny, but no firm offers were forthcoming. Shortly thereafter, Livingstone mailed Denneny a contract for the coming season, and the winger sent back word that he refused to report to the Toronto Hockey Club. Livingstone saw no option but to suspend his forward — a technique first used by Sam Lichtenhein of the Wanderers against Cyclone Taylor in 1911. "You are being badly misled in Ottawa," Livvy warned Denneny. "Your job is only temporary, etc. However, letter received, and you are now under indefinite suspension. If you wish to remain out, even for life, the Toronto Club will offer no objection."[146]

Livingstone told the *Mail and Empire* that he felt sorry for Denneny, whose brother Corb was still a member of the Blueshirts. "Mr. Livingstone … knows that it is not the boy's fault," the newspaper reported. "He has apparently been influenced adversely without his being aware that 'scare' stuff was being used on him. His job in Ottawa is a very ordinary one, and temporary at that…. Mr. Livingstone believes Cy will soon realize that he is being made a 'goof.'"[147]

Lest there be any doubt as to the identity of the "adverse influence," Livingstone was explicit: "Cyril Denneny plays lacrosse with Tommy Gorman, who is interested in the Ottawa Hockey Club. In addition, he works side by side with [Senators star] Eddie Gerard. No, he's not being influenced. It's only Cyril's welfare they have at heart."[148]

Gorman, of course refused to bite at this piece of "hockey gossip." Instead, he painted a heartwarming picture of a man more sinned against than sinning.

Denneny received notice of his suspension yesterday. He states that he had hoped to play hockey this winter, but not at the sacrifice of his position, and his chances of promotion. Denneny takes a sensible view of the situation, saying that he has done his share of knocking about and that he has decided to settle down. He has taken up house in Ottawa with his wife and baby, and is putting one of his younger sisters to school here. His position is better and more promising than the one Torontos were able to get him, and he feels if he resigned and went to Toronto again, he would not be treating fairly the Ottawa Lacrosse club, which went to a lot of trouble last spring to bring him here. In the first place, he could not pay expenses for the winter on the terms Owner Livingstone suggested. However, since being suspended he has been able to take three squares a day and sleep in comfort. He has started training with a view to playing hockey…[149]

The next day, Gorman went a step further, attacking the Toronto owner. "Livingstone, undoubtedly, has the power, if he refuses to sell or trade him, to keep Denneny out of the game, but it would be the poorest piece of sportsmanship in the annals of Canadian hockey and would only serve to multiply his unpopularity at Toronto and elsewhere."[150]

Strong words indeed. It may be instructive to point out that Gorman did not venture an opinion as to whether it was "a poor piece of sportsmanship" to tamper with another team's player — as his Senators seem to have been doing with Denneny. Had the *Citizen*, or any other Ottawa newspaper, even bothered to look critically at the Ottawa Hockey Club's machinations over the previous twenty years, so many incidents of "poor sportsmanship" could have been turned up that Livingstone's punishment of Denneny would not even crack the top ten.

A closer look at "the annals of Canadian hockey" yielded the following incidents which, in Gorman's mind at least, are nowhere near as serious than the Denneny affair — each of which has been documented earlier in this book:

- the drafting and suspension of Cyclone Taylor for refusing to report to the Montreal Wanderers in 1911;
- the Montreal Canadiens' refusal for more than two years to pay the PCHA the agreed-upon price of $750 for the rights to Newsy Lalonde;

- the gamesmanship behind the Ottawa Senators' failure to ship the Stanley Cup to its rightful holders, the Vancouver Millionaires, until six months after the western team won it in 1915;
- the Quebec Bulldogs' appointing themselves the World Champions of 1913, even though they were clobbered by the Victoria Aristocrats in three straight exhibition games;
- the Wanderers' decision to renege on an agreement to reschedule a game with the Toronto Shamrocks after three of that team's nine players were grieving the death of their father.

Tommy Gorman is an honoured member of the Hockey Hall of Fame for his achievements as a builder of the game. It would seem evident that integrity and ethics are not prerequisites for admission to that elite circle.

And just why was it so important for Cy Denneny to play in Ottawa? The answer comes, not from Gorman or the Ottawa papers, but from the Montreal *Gazette*. It seems that T. P. Gorman, who as a boy was a Parliamentary page, used political connections to arrange a new job for Denneny within the Seed Grain branch of the Interior department. This job started three weeks after the erstwhile Blueshirt's holdout began. Gorman's intention all along had been to embarrass Livingstone.[151]

But Livvy hadn't given up yet. Adopting a more conciliatory tone, he wired Cy: "Your brother, Corbett, says you are sincere regarding position, so intend giving you chance to prove it. Will lift suspension providing you sign contract permitting you to live in Ottawa and will only be required to play the scheduled games."[152]

He was effectively calling Denneny's bluff on whether he was in Ottawa for family reasons (and the government job) or to play with the Senators. Denneny again refused to sign with Toronto.

Chapter 10

Toronto:
Shipped Out and Drummed Out

Eddie still has his team and Association franchise. Good luck to him.

— George Kennedy, 1917

As the opening of the National Hockey Association's 1916–17 season neared, Lieutenant-Colonel Archie Earchman of the 228th Battalion team made another play for Duke Keats, who had been named the captain of the Torontos.

In the wake of Percy LeSueur's refusal to turn out for the team, the colonel was of the opinion that the previous agreement with Eddie Livingstone should be voided. The Battalion brought in Howard Lockhart to cover their net, but when it became clear that Livvy wouldn't renegotiate the deal to the military team's liking, the 228th threatened to withdraw from the league.[153]

"We expect to decide to-morrow whether or not the battalion will be represented in the N.H.A.," said Captain Leon Reade, the 228th's manager. "Secretary Calder of the league was notified by wire tonight that a definite statement might be expected tomorrow. Lieut.-Col. Earchman says that Keats will not play with the Torontos. That is final."[154]

The Montreal owners, while loath to lose the 228th, made sure that Livingstone knew his team was hanging by a thread. Both Kennedy and Lichtenhein made public pronouncements that if the Battalion withdrew, the Blueshirts would be dropped from the league.

The following day the 228th made a statement: the team would stay in the league and Keats would be allowed to play with Toronto until his status could be determined. For a brief time, there was peace between the

The 228th Battalion Hockey Team
Bottom row (l to r): Amos Arbour, Archie Earchman, Donaldson, Art Duncan.
Top row (l to r): Leon Reade, Harry Meeking, Eddie Oatman, George
McNamara, Howard McNamara, unidentified, unidentified, Goldie Prodgers.

two clubs; Livingstone even coached an NHA All-Star team made up of members of the Torontos, Montreal Canadiens and Ottawa Senators in an exhibition match against the 228th, losing to the team in khaki by a 10–3 score.[155] The Wanderers' Lichtenhein was still so incensed at Livingstone that he refused to let his players participate in the game. Quebec's Quinn claimed not to be enchanted with the idea of his players missing several days' worth of practice and followed Lichtenhein's lead.

So much for patriotism.

While a tentative peace reigned with the 228th, the Torontos' relations with Ottawa were not so good, as the negotiations over Cy Denneny remained at an impasse. For a time it looked like the Senators, now being managed by Martin Rosenthal, would give up goaltender Clint Benedict for the rights to the holdout winger. The talks can be followed through a series of telegrams reprinted in the *Citizen*.

> Livingstone: Understand our conversation
>   consummated the Denneny-Benedict
>   trade. What about it?
> Rosenthal: I told you in our conversation
>   that the Benedict-Denneny trade was

> subject to the approval of our directors.
> They consented, but Benedict states that
> he will not go to Toronto.
>
> Livingstone: Explanation received. Consider
> Benedict-Denneny deal off, but will
> give you Denneny for Frank Nighbor,
> providing Nighbor will accept terms
> we offer him. Will also let you have
> Harry Meeking.
>
> Rosenthal: Your generosity is beyond all
> conception. Our directors will consider
> proposition. Meanwhile I will offer you
> Sammy Hebert and Hank Stavenau for
> Denneny, if you hurl in Harry Meeking
> to clinch the bargain.[156]

Although they kept the telegraph operators busy, the talks were fruit-less and Denneny remained under suspension. Gorman once more tried to tug at the heartstrings of Ottawa's hockey faithful, writing in the *Citizen*, "Cy Denneny, who will likely be out of hockey this winter, watched the practice. Shame to keep a good boy like him out of the game."[157]

We can almost imagine Denneny's tears freezing on the frozen sur-face of the rink at Dey's Arena.

On January 3, 1917, the two Toronto rivals met for the first time. More than 5,000 fans filed into the Arena Gardens to watch the Northern Fusiliers shut out the Blueshirts, 4–0. Livingstone used a tight-checking system to hold the soldiers to a 1–0 score through two periods, but the soldiers drew on their superior experience to dominate the third.[158] "Eddie Livingstone took his defeat in good part," the Toronto *Daily News* reported. "He was so well satisfied with his team that he took them all out to supper and even extended an invitation to the referee."[159]

As 1917 began, the Senators were itching to get Cy Denneny into their lineup. Rosenthal appealed to the president of the NHA, Major Frank Robinson, to act on what he characterized as an epidemic of idle play-ers. Although he was only interested in the fate of one player, Rosenthal had to couch the issue so as to make it appear as though there were a league-wide problem, so he cited the examples of LeSueur, who was not reporting to the 228th; Tommy Smith, who had not reached terms with the Canadiens; and Harry Hyland, who had not accepted a contract from the Wanderers.

Robinson did not intervene, and so Tommy Gorman continued to serve up generous helpings of bathos in the *Citizen*:

> Eddie Livingstone has been absolutely ridiculous in his suggested terms for Cy Dennenay, whom he values at $3,000, which is nearly three times as much as the drafting rate set two years ago by the Pacific Coast for the pick of the Eastern players. He has evidently forgotten that Dennenay has a wife and baby to support and that if he went to Toronto play for the sum he offers — $500 — he would be out of a position and right up against it at the close of the season.[160]

The next day found Denneny in worse shape, if the *Citizen* was to be believed:

> Livingstone seems to be determined to keep the boy out of the game, though Cy needs the money badly.[161]

On January 6, when the Blueshirts made their first trip of the new season to the capital, Livingstone issued his latest demand: Denneny for Benedict or $2,000. He also informed Ottawa that if they didn't want to deal, the Wanderers and Quebec were waiting in the wings.[162]

Gorman's account of the behind-the-scenes activity suggested that Cy would never again wear the blue and white of Toronto:

> Later in the afternoon, Denneny himself blew in to pay respects to his brother Corbett and other members of his former team. "Livvy" also corralled him and had a long interview, during which he offered "Cy" the handsome sum of $600 to throw up his position in Ottawa and to finish out the season with Toronto. In fact, he wanted Cyril to put on a suit and play with Toronto Saturday night. Denneny, who was all dolled up in his glad clothes and who looked prosperity itself, refused the Toronto manager's pleas.
>
> "You know I can't get away to play for Toronto," he said. "Trade me to the Wanderers or Canadiens if you

won't let Ottawa have me." Livingstone added that he had done much for Denneny in previous seasons and considered that the Cornwall boy was showing ingratitude. However, the deadlock refused to break and Denneny witnessed the game from the press box. Needless to say, he was feeling far from pleasant.[163]

The Toronto-228th rematch on January 20 rekindled the fires between the two teams. From start to finish the game was a rough, close-checking affair, with the soldiers again winning, 8–6. The Blueshirts' 37-year-old netminder, Billy Nicholson, was particularly bad on two long shots he let in.[164]

According to the *Daily News*, more trouble awaited the Toronto club after the game. Colonel Earchman informed Livingstone that, on account of the roughness of the game, he would not permit Archie Briden or Duke Keats to play for the Blueshirts any longer. "It is hard to believe that the sporting commander of the Fusiliers would take such drastic action," the *News* said. "Saturday's match was strenuous, but not more so than any other game, and this excuse will hardly stand muster."[165]

After another confrontation with Eddie Livingstone, the military team retreated for a third time. However, an item in the January 26 edition of the *Mail and Empire* hinted that a greater battle for Livingstone lay on the horizon.

> It was learned last night that the 228th Battalion will be unable to finish out their hockey schedule in either the N.H.A. or the O.H.A. Their inability to do so will be regretted by the local fans.[166]

Where the paper was getting its information is unclear, for NHA Secretary Frank Calder would later testify in court that neither he nor anyone else in the league had any knowledge that the Northern Fusiliers would not finish the season.[167]

Meanwhile, the Blueshirts' goaltending situation continued to worsen. Nicholson was pulled from the game — an extremely rare event in those days — during an 8–2 loss to the Wanderers, to be replaced for the remainder of the match by Duke Keats. After this game the goalie was handed his unconditional release.[168]

As January drew to a close, Sam Lichtenhein made a play for Cy Denneny, sending the Wanderers' coach, Dickie Boon, to Ottawa with the purpose of recruiting the forward. "It is understood that Denneny did not sign the regulation N.H.A. contract," the *Gazette* pointed out, "but that he attached his signature to an agreement stating that he would play with Wanderers for the sum stipulated and providing he could arrange leave of absence. The latter has yet to be looked after. If [Denneny is] unable to do so, the deal is off altogether. Denneny will take the matter up today and is hopeful that he will be on the Wanderer forward line for Wednesday's game against Quebec."[169]

Livingstone was not amused with Lichtenhein's bit of tampering. According to the Ottawa *Journal*, "Last night Livingstone called up Denneny and admonished him for signing any papers with Wanderers, and informed him the only club he could play with would be Toronto. Cy said he couldn't get away from Ottawa [anyway], and the stuff [with the Wanderers] was therefore off as far as he was concerned."[170]

On January 30, Livingstone finally traded Denneny to Ottawa for Sammy Hebert and $750. Hebert, the former Ontarios goalkeeper who wasn't even playing for the Senators, was a far cry from the front-line players Livvy had been demanding. There was no chance he would report to Toronto, which was just as well — he was playing more like Billy Nicholson than Clint Benedict.

The next night the Senators rushed Denneny into their lineup for a game against the 228th. In so doing, Ottawa defied an order issued by NHA secretary Frank Calder not to play the winger.

The reason for that edict? Incredibly, Calder believed that Denneny's rights belonged to the *Wanderers*, with whom Cy had illegally signed an agreement. Not coincidentally, Wanderers owner Sam Lichtenhein was a good friend of Calder's. No explanation exists as to why Calder, and not the president of the league, Frank Robinson, issued the ruling.

In the pages of the Ottawa *Citizen*, Gorman's spin-doctoring continued.

> "This seems the limit," exclaimed one of the Ottawa Hockey Club officers. "We have been put to a great deal of trouble over Denneny this season and Livingstone has succeeded in keeping one of hockey's brightest stars on the bench for half the season. Now that we have finally bought him at a record price, Sammy Lichtenhein steps in and claims him. I for one am certainly in favour of playing him and fighting it out afterwards. There is no doubt in our minds as to where Denneny will wind up. He is the property of the Ottawas. Verbal agreements are

not binding. He is anxious to play here and it would be a shame to keep him out of it longer."[171]

So hard done by was the unnamed Ottawa official that he neglected to mention the reason the Senators were in such a hurry to have Denneny suit up. The PCHA–NHA agreement contained a clause that set a cutoff date for Stanley Cup eligibility. Players who weren't on a club's roster by January 31 would not be allowed to take part in the finals. The date of Denneny's Ottawa debut? January 31.

A brief recap of the Cy Denneny affair puts the brinkmanship into clearer focus.

Tommy Gorman used his Ottawa *Citizen* pulpit to advance his own business interests by agitating for Denneny to be traded — for next to nothing — to the Senators, of which he was a part owner.

To be fair, Gorman at least acknowledged that Denneny's previous contract bound him to the Toronto Blueshirts; Sam Lichtenhein observed no such courtesy when he boldly signed the player to a letter of intent.

Meanwhile, Frank Calder, that pillar of integrity who exposed the Wrestling Trust, ignored the terms of his league's own player contracts and ruled that Denneny's rights belonged to the Wanderers — even though, as the league's secretary-treasurer, Calder had neither the right nor the authority to make such a call.

Eddie Livingstone tried to negotiate in good faith with his young star, offering a salary of $600 for the season. But Denneny, under Gorman's influence, would not budge.

In his later years, Denneny recalled the contract he signed with the Senators after the trade. It paid him $600. "That was good pay," he pointed out.[172]

But apparently not good enough to play for Livingstone.

On the same day that the Denneny trade was reported, the Toronto *Globe* contained another item that boded ill for Livingstone:

> The 228th Battalion N.H.A. team left last night for Ottawa to fulfill their scheduled engagement with the Senators. The Soldiers propose to go ahead without regard to the fact that their last leave has expired and that orders are momentarily expected, which will bring about their

removal from Toronto to a point at which they will be unable to play further games in the N.H.A. The outlook in the pro league is, therefore, somewhat indefinite.[173]

The Toronto team owners were summoned to Montreal for a league meeting on February 1. The military brass were made to state definitively whether the Fusiliers expected to finish the season. According to the Toronto *Daily News*, "Capt. Reade, manager of the 228th Battalion, assured the league that the soldier team would remain in the series until the end of the schedule."[174] The league seemed to accept this assurance.

Most of the meeting was taken up by the Denneny debacle. Lichtenhein claimed he had three witnesses who had heard Livingstone give him permission to sign Denneny. Martin Rosenthal countered by reminding the Wanderers owner that, under the NHA constitution, *written* permission was needed, and since Lichtenhein could not produce any paperwork there was no deal. In the end, league president Frank Robinson deferred a decision, permitting the Senators to continue using Denneny.

To say the meeting was stormy would be an understatement. The Denneny affair served mainly to bring up all the old grievances between Lichtenhein and Livingstone. Stories about the ill will between the two men made their way into the papers over the next few days. "Lichtenhein and Livingstone not only had a verbal battle," the *Daily News* reported, "but the former tried to have the Toronto owner expelled from the league. The end is not yet."[175]

The Ottawa *Journal* added that it had been told Lichtenhein offered Livingstone $3,000 to walk away from his team. And on other fronts, "Livingstone and Capt. Reade were near blows on two occasions, and [Livingstone once] started to take a wallop at George Kennedy, but thought better of it."[176]

A few days later, the *Daily News* repeated the story of Lichtenhein's buyout attempt, adding that Livvy had made a counter-offer of $5,000 for the Wanderers, "and when the latter said 'no,' Edward J. Livingstone politely told him that if the Montreal club's holdings were worth more than $5,000, ten times that amount wouldn't buy the Toronto club."[177]

By the first week of February, Livingstone had had his fill of the Fusiliers and their ways. The 228th were once again making an issue of whether Duke Keats and spare player Archie Briden should be allowed to suit up for the Blueshirts' game against the soldiers on February 7. Seething, Livingstone threatened to skip the game.

He might also have been concerned about whether the military squad would even show up for the game. On the morning of the 7th, the newspapers reported that the 228th's senior team had withdrawn from the OHA.[178] That evening, NHA president Frank Robinson sent a telegram to Livingstone ordering him to put his team on the ice no matter what.[179] As game time neared, Colonel Earchman refused to give any assurances to Livingstone about Keats or Briden, going as far as to predict that neither player would be available to Toronto for the remainder of the season.[180]

In the third meeting between the Torontos and the 228th, Livingstone did get some measure of satisfaction as his team overcame a 3–1 Battalion lead to come back and win 4–3.

It was clear that the military command was tiring of the professional game as practised under Reade and Earchman. The great attempt to lure hockey fans into the army was flagging badly. Charlie Good of the Toronto *Daily News* quoted an anonymous commander as saying, "You can make this as emphatic as you like. We are thoroughly disgusted with the notoriety we have been subjected to in connection with hockey, and even the players are willing to quit. There has been too much bickering over Keats and Briden. They may be good hockey players, but they are not good soldiers, and I am of the opinion that it would have been better for everybody if the 228th had not engaged in sports at all."[181]

On February 8, 1917, Militia Headquarters in Ottawa ordered the 228th Battalion overseas. The Fusiliers had a scheduled game in Quebec on February 10, and Reade tried to talk the brass into letting the team play a final farewell game, but this request was turned down.

The response from the players came quickly. Tommy Gorman quoted the Senators' Eddie Lowrey as saying, "They should never have allowed the Soldiers in. They've been threatening to quit ever since the league race got under way." Cy Denneny chimed in that the league "should have thrown Toronto [Blueshirts] out. Livingstone has been kicking ever since he entered the league."[182]

Harsh words indeed for the man who gave Denneny and his brother their start in pro hockey. It is hard to fathom how Denneny felt qualified to comment on his ex-boss's behaviour since he wasn't even in the league when Livingstone took over the Ontarios in 1914. It is more likely that Gorman fabricated the quote and attributed it to Denneny. If the left winger had any problem with words being put into his mouth, his performance in Ottawa — only three goals and an assist to show for ten games — hardly put him in a strong position to object.

Meanwhile, the walls were closing in on Eddie Livingstone. A league meeting was called to take place on February 11 in Montreal. The Montreal papers were making it clear that, if the 228th did withdraw from the NHA, Kennedy and Lichtenhein aimed to drop Livingstone's team as well. In Toronto, the *Daily News* scoffed at the suggestion:

> In regard to reports from Montreal that the eastern clubs will pass up the Toronto club in the event of the soldiers withdrawing and form a four club league, this is all buncombe and evidently inspired by parties who have little love for Manager Livingstone. The Ottawa club would never agree to a "freeze out" such as the one proposed and Mike Quinn of Quebec would hardly be foolish enough to ally himself with the Lichtenhein-Kennedy combination. Then there is the matter of the bond to be considered. Each club in the league is liable to the extent of $3,000 to finish the season and the Toronto club could exact this amount from each club if another union was formed with the blueshirts on the outside.[183]

Prior to the Montreal meeting, Livingstone twice contacted Major Robinson about the proposed agenda. In a telephone call, Livingstone informed the league president that he would not be attending the meeting — he would later claim that a painful boil on his neck contributed to his absence and that the Major had consented to represent him. A telegram followed up their conversation with the suggestion that Toronto would accept a five-team schedule to finish the season.[184]

On February 11, 1917, the two Montreal teams, supported by Quebec's Mike Quinn and Ottawa's Martin Rosenthal, kicked Eddie Livingstone out of the National Hockey Association and moved to finish the season without him or his Blueshirts franchise. League secretary Frank Calder oversaw what the *Mail and Empire* characterized as a raid of the Toronto players. The Wanderers claimed Harry Cameron, Ken Randall and Alf Skinner; the Canadiens took Reg Noble and Arthur Brooks; Corb Denneny, accompanied by Andy Kyle and Gerry Coughlin, was to be reunited with his brother in Ottawa. Quebec reclaimed Sammy Hebert, who had returned to Toronto for one game. "Robinson could only look on as the teams under his presidency kicked out his former franchise and stole Livingstone's players," the *Mail and Empire* said. "The only thing the major could offer in Livingstone's defence was the telegram he had received, and even that was used against the Toronto magnate."[185]

Livingstone fired off an angry letter to Frank Robinson demanding an explanation. "I do not understand by what right somebody at the N.H.A. meeting opened my personal telegram to yourself in which it was outlined what was desired by the Toronto club, and I intend going into the matter very fully. What made this most unfortunate was that the telegraph company, in taking the message from me over the phone, used the word league in place of schedule. This mistake could be construed by prejudiced persons to give the impression that unless a five-club schedule was drawn up the club would drop out of the N.H.A., which was far from correct."[186]

Livingstone's faith in Frank Robinson's ability to represent Toronto's interests had been sadly misplaced. The league president was in no position to help Livingstone because he, too, was under attack. Sam Lichtenhein, still fuming over the Cy Denneny decision, had sought Robinson's resignation only a week before. Robinson reminded the Wanderers owner that the NHA had recruited him for the position with a promise to abide by his decisions.

But Tommy Gorman reported that Robinson *would* resign. "He also insinuated that he would prefer to step down and out. Frank Calder, secretary of the league, is slated to succeed him. President Robinson's resignation would be regretted as he is a splendid sportsman and has evidently endeavoured to conduct things in a fair, dignified manner."[187]

The minutes of the meeting carried this resolution:

> Moved by Wanderer's Hockey Club and seconded by the Quebec Hockey Club:
> That in view of the impossibility of carrying out the request of the Toronto Hockey Club as contained in its telegram of the 10th instant that this Board do not make a demand on the bond of the Toronto Hockey Club, to wit:
> The Toronto Hockey Club franchise stand suspended with instructions to President Livingstone to dispose of said franchise on or before June 1, 1917, but not before April 1, 1917. On his failure to dispose of the said franchise and players this Association shall dispose of the same to the best possible advantage and turn over the entire proceeds to E. J. Livingstone.
> Also that Article 21 of the Constitution shall be suspended, making the Toronto Hockey Club's players eligible for the balance of the season to play with any other club in the National Hockey Association of Canada Limited. All such players shall constitute part of

the Toronto franchise when sold and shall be turned back to the owner of the Toronto franchise at the end of this season.

All players taken over by the National Hockey Association clubs for the balance of the season shall receive their pro rata salaries as paid by the Toronto Hockey Club beginning from date February 12th, 1917.

Also the Toronto Hockey Club shall not be compensated this season for the loan of any of its players to its clubs in the National Hockey Association desiring their services.[188]

Nothing like making up the rules as you go along.

Livingstone was sent an official copy of the minutes of the meeting — not by Robinson, who refused to do the owners' dirty work, but by league secretary Frank Calder.[189]

Gorman was exultant. "Naval experts declare that the good ship E. J. Livingstone was torpedoed without warning," he wrote in the *Citizen*.[190]

The Ottawa *Journal* put the case against Livingstone to its readers:

Last year he [Livingstone] used the jumping players, [Frank] Foyston and [Harry] Holmes, in straight defiance of League orders. If T. Emmett Quinn, president at the time, had been given his way, Livingstone would have been obliged to pay a fat fine or quit. As it was, the directors allowed the fine to remain suspended on future good behaviour — and the latter has been lacking. First there was the tangle over the Denneny trade, and then the reported refusal of the management to put the team on the ice Wednesday night against the Soldiers. It was the latter team's gate, and the receipts were seriously affected no doubt through the uncertainty aroused by the Toronto management's threat.[191]

It was a rather one-sided account that the *Journal* presented. The paper chose not to mention, for instance, that the league gave the Toronto team no notice of its expulsion, and offered no compensation, or that Lichtenhein and Kennedy had been pulling similar stunts for years. Or, most importantly, that the Denneny debacle had been ignited by the sports editor of the Ottawa *Citizen*, who was neither censured nor punished by the league, the team or the newspaper. And while it is true that Livingstone may have caused some brief discomfort by threatening not to play the game against the 228th, it was the military's constant interference with Duke Keats that triggered the situation.

It is interesting to speculate as to why the various parties sided with Lichtenhein. In Quebec's case, the possibility of collecting the league-mandated $300 penalty for the cancelled game would have been attractive, while the savings the league's easternmost team would realize by not having to travel to Toronto for a single match were also considerable. For Ottawa, the prospect of the Wanderers' dropping their claim to Cy Denneny must have held considerable sway. Assuming that Lichtenhein's play for Denneny was made in earnest, and not merely to vex Livingstone, his desire to be rid of the Toronto owner was so great that he would put his own franchise in jeopardy by relinquishing any stake — no matter how wrongly acquired — in Cy Denneny's playing rights. The Canadiens, of course, were already in league with Lichtenhein.

Hardly any time passed before the league turned its attention towards the 228th Battalion. The four remaining clubs eyed greedily the $3,000 bond that the military team had put up. Under the NHA constitution the league could fine a club $300 for any games it defaulted, up to the full amount of the bond. Without going through any process to warn the Northern Fusiliers that they had violated this rule, however, the league fined the 228th the full $3,000.

The reaction to this decision was overwhelmingly negative. In the Toronto *Daily News*, Charlie Querrie voiced his displeasure:

> If the National Hockey Association persist in their reported action to collect the $3,000 bond from the 228th Battalion, it is just as well they have no teams representing their association in this city. There have been many petty and small actions in sport both in this country and others, but we have yet to hear of one as small as that reported by the supposed to be big hockey association of Canada. The 228th Battalion made the N.H.A. in the early part of the season, and they tried their best to continue in the game, but were needed to play their part in the greatest of all present games. They had to default the rest of their engagements, and the N.H.A. moguls would be better advised if they would call a meeting and move a vote of thanks for the Battalion for what they did in the league. If the N.H.A. carry out their action and try

to collect the bond from the soldiers they should be rend out of any sport that is played.[192]

Querrie seems to display a short memory, forgetting why the military team was yanked in the first place: squabbling over personnel who belonged to another team was not a good way to build the troops' morale — or support for the war effort, for that matter.

The next day, Querrie continued to berate the Montreal compact of Lichtenhein, Kennedy, Calder, and Calder's friend Elmer Ferguson.

> Mr. Ferguson, of the Montreal *Herald*, is out with a long screed to the effect the N.H.A. is quite justified in collecting the $3,000 bond from the 228th, and points out that the soldier team were let into the association without the necessary expense of buying a franchise and paying for players, etc., and that they had good gates, and a lot more bunk to the same effect. We don't care how much the soldiers made, but we do know they were let into the association by the "wise men of the east" for the express purpose of helping along a league that was really up against it. The soldiers practically placed professional hockey in the limelight again when it looked like a tough session, and helped draw big gates for the other clubs. If the khaki lads made money, so much the better. They were forced to stop playing by military necessity, and any bunch of moguls who collect a forfeit from a team that placed them on their feet does not deserve to be classed as sporting men.[193]

An additional bit of ammunition that Querrie didn't use: Ferguson, who had defended the NHA's cash grab, was also on the league's payroll as the official statistician.

On February 17, the *Mail and Empire* suggested something else might be rotten in the league office.

> It is hinted in Eastern quarters that the $3,000 bond which the N.H.A. declared that the 228th had defaulted, may be given over to the Quebec Club to recompense them for the loss they sustained when the 228th defaulted their game at Quebec without giving them any notice. There is also something

funny about Quebec not drawing any of the Toronto players in the shuffle.[194]

Toronto-based detractors of the NHA got more ammunition when Eddie Oatman and Gordon Meeking spoke to reporters about their experiences as members of the 228th Battalion. Oatman's tale, told "in a frank manner that leaves little doubt he is telling the truth," was recounted in the *Daily News*.

> Early this winter, while at his home in Tillsonburg, he was making preparations to go to the coast to play hockey with Portland at a much larger salary than $1,200, when Captain George McNamara and Sergeant [Goldie] Prodgers came up to see if he would not join the soldier team. He was told that the hockey team was being run entirely distinct from the battalion, but they wanted every man to enlist; that salaries would be paid the same as usual. Oatman decided it was up to him to get in khaki and he turned down the coast offer and signed a contract (which, by the way, he has with him) calling for a salary of $1,200 for the season and enlisted, and was prepared to go overseas with the battalion.
>
> During the season he received $400 and after the Toronto game here [in Montreal] made inquiries about the rest of his salary and was assured by Captain Reade and [team] captain Howard McNamara that he would receive it. When the soldiers left for St. John, he went along and trouble started right away. He asked for his money and was told that it would all be settled up on Thursday, but at a meeting of the officers held last Friday, they declined to pay the amount, although ... Howard McNamara agreed to give him $200 that he had received during the hockey season. Oatman accepted $25 in cash and a cheque for $175 and the next morning it appeared in the company orders that he had been discharged under the heading "special circumstances."
>
> Oatman left then for Montreal and interviewed President Robinson of the N.H.A., who claimed that his contract had been filed with the association, but it

called for [a salary of] only one dollar. Oatman, on his arrival here, visited the bank to cash the cheque given him by McNamara and found out that the latter had wired from the east not to pay it. This is Oatman's story and he feels that he has been badly treated. He enlisted in good faith, and had no desire to get out of "doing his bit" but was simply fired out of the battalion under the "special circumstances" clause.[195]

Gordon Meeking attested that he had been temporarily attached to the 228th and promised a commission as a lieutenant in exchange for his services. During recruiting efforts on behalf of the battalion he even wore an officer's uniform. As with Oatman, he was released when the battalion reached Saint John. As reported in the Ottawa *Citizen*:

Meeking stated that, at a meeting of the officers of the battalion and hockey players, it was agreed to divide the surplus from the hockey at the conclusion of the season. At this meeting he says that he agreed to play without receiving anything for his services other than the commission for which he had qualified. On the Friday on which the battalion was given moving orders, Meeking was informed that his appointment had not been made and was ordered to get into a private's uniform. This he was unable to do, as the clothing had been packed and shipped. He says he informed the commanding officer of this and was advised to remain over in Toronto and follow the battalion at a later date, which he did. To his surprise, on his arrival at St. John, he was handed his discharge as being medically unfit, and he claims that he was not given transportation back to his home in Toronto.[196]

Speaking of the hockey season, Meeking said that the club's share of the gate receipts had amounted to nearly $7,000 for their five home games played at Toronto, while he estimated that the club's expenses could not have exceeded $2,000.[197]

When these reports were published, the NHA's supporters saw them as full justification for claiming the $3,000 bond. Tommy Gorman wrote in the Ottawa *Citizen* that, if Oatman had not enlisted with the 228th, he was never eligible to play for the team — after all, Frank Patrick had approved his transfer under the understanding he was serving as an active member of the Battalion. In view of this deception, "his days in the Eastern League should be considered over."[198]

Oatman would indeed return to Portland for the 1917–18 season, and would finish his career in the west. History does not record whether he was ever paid the $700 he claimed the Battalion owed him.

Now that Oatman and Meeking's revelations were public knowledge, Eddie Livingstone's complaints against the team in khaki gained credence. "The exposé of the methods of the 228th Battalion is a complete vindication of the Toronto Hockey Club and myself," Livingstone told the *Mail and Empire*.

> Their tactics from the moment of their admittance to the N.H.A. [were] wholly responsible for all the trouble. They early boasted that they would break up the Toronto team or so weaken it as to render it incapable of being a stumbling block to their aspirations, financial and championship. This they endeavoured to carry out, and forced me into the unenviable position of protecting the club's vital interests by fighting back against an organization that used a blanket of patriotism to cover selfish plans. It put me in the wrong with the public, as well as with the N.H.A., both of whom, not knowing or not believing the facts and that the situation was simply intolerable, passed judgment without foundation therefore.

Livvy couldn't resist prodding his old partners.

> While the public may well be excused for their attitude, not so the N.H.A. This body was well posted as to the true state of affairs long before the climax was reached, but instead of taking proper action [the league] preferred to use the nasty complication that existed as a club with which to inflict undeserved punishment on the Torontos by way of aiding the material interests of Wanderers, Canadiens, and Quebec. I do not exempt Secretary Calder from blame either, but in fairness to President Robinson and Ottawa must state that no stigma attaches to them.[199]

With that statement, correct as it might have been, Livingstone might as well have signed his own death certificate where the quiet, vindictive Calder and his loud, obnoxious comrade Sam Lichtenhein were concerned.

Frank Patrick kept an attentive eye on the reports from back east, but told the Vancouver *Sun* he would reserve comment until he received a letter from NHA president Frank Robinson. He would admit only that the PCHA was under the impression that Eddie Oatman was a legitimate member of the 228th Battalion when it granted him the right to play in the NHA. The *Sun* went on to warn that:

> If it develops that the N.H.A. moguls knew of the manner in which the 228th Battalion team was handled on the money basis, as it now apparently appears, and further if it develops that they sanctioned the idea, there is an excellent possibility that war may break out again between the eastern and western hockey bodies. A great deal depends on the action that President Frank Patrick decides upon after he receives the letter from President Robinson of the N.H.A.[200]

The NHA was in a bind. The only way for Robinson's letter to seem genuine would be to discredit Livingstone's statement to the *Mail and Empire*. In the short term, that meant that Calder's reputation would have to take a small hit. On February 21, the following item appeared in the Ottawa *Journal*:

> Owner Livingstone of the Toronto Hockey Club now comes out with the statement that he had known for some time the way the 228th Battalion was handling things and also that Secretary Calder, of the N.H.A., was aware of the situation. No doubt both concealed the facts thinking that they were doing it for the good of the game. They were not, however.[201]

A laughable piece of shoddy journalism when one considers that Livingstone had been complaining about the 228th since the beginning of the season, only to have his beefs fall upon deaf ears in Ottawa. And now the newspaper published by Phil Ross, a Stanley Cup trustee, was accusing Livvy of abetting Earchman's scam. Still, a lack of facts failed to stop the *Journal* from continuing its malicious attack:

> When such scandals as the Oatman case are kept under
> cover, the longer they stay there the more the unpleasant
> odour they give out when they do reach the public ears.
> If Livingstone and Calder knew all about the 228th's
> method of conducting its hockey team they should have
> spilled the facts and let the N.H.A. deal with the soldier
> outfit. Instead of helping the game they were in fair way
> to hurt it, and it will be hard to keep the public from
> thinking that perhaps the N.H.A. knew of the whole
> inner workings of the 228th club almost from the first.[202]

Whether the *Journal's* article had an effect on Frank Patrick is not known, but he did accept his NHA counterpart's pleas of innocence. A potential crisis had been averted.[203]

As for the 228th, it did ship out to England and, minus Oatman and Meeking, continued to play exhibition hockey matches well into May 1917 at Prince's Rink in London.

Meanwhile, the Ottawa *Citizen* held out hope that Livingstone would also fade from the scene. "In the event of the Toronto franchise being sold next year, players now on their list revert back. Should [the team] not be operated, the players will be placed on the market and prices placed upon them. It is not likely that Eddie Livingstone will ever again control the Blue Shirted combination."[204]

The withdrawal of the 228th Battalion Hockey Club from the NHA unleashed a series of legal actions that would last more than thirteen years — four times as long as Eddie Livingstone held membership in the National Hockey Association. The resolve of the Toronto owner had clearly been underestimated.

Chapter 11

The Litigious Era Begins

*Eddie Livingstone, the Toronto magnate, no more gets back in the
National Hockey Association than he wants someone fired out.
This time he is after Sammy Lichtenhein, and the battle between
them should be a royal one.*

— Charlie Querrie, 1917

If the remaining National Hockey Association team owners thought
the departure of the 228th Battalion would net them a quick cash
windfall, they would be proven wrong. Led by the league's secretary and
treasurer, Frank Calder, the merry men charged into a lawsuit against the
Ocean Accident and Guarantee Corporation in an attempt to get their
hands on the $3,000 bond the military had put up as assurance that they
would complete the 1916–17 schedule. However, the case would take a
year and a half to come to trial before Chief Justice Sir Glenholme
Falconbridge in Toronto. It fell to Calder — who by this time was president of the fledgling National Hockey League — to testify as to why
the 228th's bond should be turned over to the NHA, which had suspended operations. Under the questioning of Ocean Accident's lawyer
G. H. Sedgewick, Calder fell down on the job.

> Sedgewick:Under what powers in your
> constitution did you proceed when
> you fined the 228th Battalion Hockey
> Club $3,000?
> Calder:Well, there is a clause in our consti-
> tution, section 19 of our constitution as

brought up to 1914, which is identical with 1912, the second clause: "Any club, for any reason defaulting any scheduled game shall pay the sum of $300, for any and all games defaulted, to the opposing Club and such further compensation as shall be decided by the Board of Directors."

Sedgewick:Now, is that what you found yourself on? That does not give you the power to suspend a franchise?

Calder:We can suspend a franchise or terminate membership under Section 15: "The membership of any club may be terminated by disbandment of its organization or team during the championship season, failing or refusing to fulfill its contractual obligations."[205]

With those words, Calder admitted under oath that it had been against the league's constitution to kick out Eddie Livingstone's Blueshirts, as Livingstone had fulfilled all of his contractual obligations to the league.

Sedgewick:Well, that might suspend, but is it suspended without action, or do you have to take action to suspend it?

Calder:No, it wasn't necessary for the Association to take any action in this case. The 228th Battalion had taken the action itself subject to greater force. They were in a position where they couldn't help it, they had to go overseas.[206]

The last two lines of Calder's examination would prove crucial when it came time for Mr. Justice Falconbridge to release his verdict. Yet it was another exchange between Sedgewick and Calder that reveal much about the NHA's motivation for launching this lawsuit:

Sedgewick:Then may I ask you this: was it intended or is it intended that the

Sedgewick:$3,000, when you get it, will go to the
Quebec Hockey Club?
Calder:Oh, no.
Sedgewick:Well, who else has lost every-
thing?
Calder:Well, it will go to the National
Hockey Association and it will be dis-
tributed among the sufferers as the
National Hockey Association will see fit.
Sedgewick:Only among sufferers?
Calder:Well, non-sufferers would hardly
expect to benefit.
Sedgewick:I suppose there were some clubs
that had made money out of them and
did not incur any loss, were there not?
Calder:Well, one club in particular had ful-
filled all its obligations to the 228th
Battalion and therefore would not have
any more contracts.
Sedgewick:And therefore this $3,000 would
be a fund to recoup the famine sufferers?
Calder:Exactly. That is right.[207]

The only club to "fulfill its obligations" where the 228th was concerned was Eddie Livingstone's Toronto Blueshirts — and only because
the other owners had kicked the Blueshirts out of the league.
Meanwhile, given the chance to do the honourable thing by repaying
Gord Meeking for his transportation home, Calder was looking for
ways to line his own pockets and those of the owners. It was a pattern
that he would follow over and over.

It would appear that, aside from Quebec, the other "sufferers" for
whom the money would have been earmarked included the Ottawa
Senators syndicate, Sam Lichtenhein and George Kennedy of Montreal
— and Calder himself. There was no one else to consider, except for
maybe the Montreal-based owners of the Toronto Arena.

On October 10, 1918, Falconbridge issued his long-awaited verdict. He
ruled that the 228th had a higher duty to perform than to play hockey, and
that the war dissolved the team's contract with the NHA. Falconbridge also
held that it was debatable whether the Battalion was ever legally a member
of the association, and that the very nature of the contract suggested to him
that the parties must have known from the beginning that it could not have

been fulfilled. The action was dismissed, with the NHA held responsible for Ocean Accident's court costs. The dormant league did not appeal the case, but paid Ocean Accident $317.70 to cover legal expenses.[208]

Falconbridge's decision would appear to have given Eddie Livingstone grounds to pursue a case against the NHA for its members' "borrowing" his suspended Toronto Shamrocks franchise. Whether he declined to further this cause as a peacekeeping mission, or was just unaware of the situation, Livvy passed on the opportunity.

He did sue the Arena Gardens, however, just to get paid for the last home game the Blueshirts played, since in those days the arena received the admissions and paid the tenant club after its own expenses were deducted. Livingstone told the *Daily News*, "We were told the Arena had a bad season, and therefore in view of the 228th going away they considered the receipts were theirs. After waiting four months, we were compelled to take legal action, with the result the Arena was forced to settle."[209] Could the Arena's unwillingness to pay Livingstone have had anything to do with the fact that its owners were based in Montreal and were friends of Frank Calder?

Days after he was expelled from the league, Livingstone suggested to Torontonians that, for the good of hockey in Toronto, it might be time for him to step aside.

> For some time past I had decided that this year would be my last in hockey in Toronto. It was my ambition to continue until I had succeeded in building up the team into a first-class aggregation and placing the club on a successful financial footing. This I have done, thanks to the younger players developing materially and to the splendid support of the Toronto hockey public. Now I am through and will shortly sell the controlling interest in the Toronto club.
>
> In addition to the raw treatment meted out to the club, the public, and myself by the National Hockey Association during the past three seasons, there is another and as equally important a reason for my decision. I am associated with the placing of arenas in two American cities, and have been invited to connect myself with a third. All three will be in operation by

next winter, which with the addition of already completed plants in certain other cities will compose a
stable and well-financed circuit. My interests in this
direction will naturally make it impossible for me to
spare the requisite time locally. It is not my intention
to run the new league in any manner antagonistic to
the N.H.A., however.

Livvy's statement featured a verbatim transcript of the league's resolution regarding the Blueshirts, and he concluded by lamenting the fact
that his communication to president Robinson had been intercepted.

That a personal and private wire should be opened
and read by parties for whom it was not intended, was
apparently not sufficient offence against all decency
and convention that to it had to be added the further
flagrant breach of constitutional procedure of con-
demning the Toronto Hockey Club by virtue of a
non-official and private document, the public can
judge for itself.[210]

Livingstone indicated that he had found his fallback position. The
possibility of tapping the rich American markets had tantalized hockey
promoters throughout the years (indeed, many would argue it continues
to bedevil the National Hockey League's leadership to this day).
Livingstone, whose mother had emigrated from the United States, was a
man with close ties to several American groups that could be convinced
to organize a league. His frequent barnstorming trips to Cleveland, for
instance, had built considerable goodwill in that city. If Livingstone could
put the pieces into place, nothing the NHA did to him would matter:
he would have obtained the bigger prize.

Unfortunately for Livvy, factors beyond his control would scotch his
plans, at least in the short term.

The manpower shortage the Canadian military was facing by the
middle of 1917 would force the federal government to consider drafting
civilians into the military. In anticipation of this event, cross-border travel was restricted so as to prevent draft-eligible Canadian men from seeking residence in the United States, which was still neutral. It would be
virtually impossible to recruit talent to move south when players faced
being turned back at the border, or even arrested. It would also prevent
a league with U.S. teams from challenging clubs in Canada. If there was

an advantage to this situation it was that the other owners faced the same problem if they tried to expand southward.

Before doing anything else, though, Livingstone sought to gain re-entry into the NHA — or, if denied, to wreck the league. On February 26, 1917, Livingstone sent another letter to president Frank Robinson with his grievances, one of which charged that the meeting had conflicted with Ontario's blue laws:

1. That the meeting was held on a Sunday, which makes any and all actions of the directors illegal, unconstitutional and void.
2. That the whole affair was framed up by the Quebec, Wanderer and Canadiens clubs and was cut and dried before the meeting was held.
3. That an effort is being made to keep the Toronto club from sharing the forfeited 228th bond, despite the fact that the Toronto club was the only club that gave the 228th Battalion team a home game in the second series.
4. That the directors at their meeting wilfully used for the basis of their resolution affecting the Toronto club the contents of a personal telegram sent the presumptive representative of the club and which had no connection whatsoever with the N.H.A. This wire was unwarrantably taken official cognizance of and deliberately misconstrued.
5. That through the non-acting of Major Robinson to whom, with his permission, proxy of the Toronto club was sent, the club was unrepresented at the meeting.
6. That I have good reason to believe that the directors, being fully aware that they acted illegally and unconstitutionally, intend, should the [Toronto] club take legal measures, to throw the National Hockey Association Ltd. into liquidation and form a new league for the purpose of evading the responsibilities and penalties which they are liable for.
7. That through their illegal actions they have, unless the substantiability of franchises and property rights of clubs are upheld, depreciated greatly the value

and status of all franchises in the association, that of the Toronto club in particular.

8. That the actions of the Wanderer, Canadien and Quebec clubs have been most detrimental to the interests of the association; so much so that it is necessary to expel, with the least possible delay, all three clubs.

9. No comment was asked or obtained from the Toronto club that the meeting of February 11 be held on a Sunday.[211]

The NHA magnates were not prepared to let things lie. Sam Lichtenhein got into the act by having Harry Cameron, Alf Skinner and Ken Randall parade before Frank Robinson and claim that Livingstone had not paid them bonus money that was allegedly owed them.

The claims were dismissed.

On March 7, Robinson wrote Livingstone to inform him that he was being reinstated as a member in good standing of the National Hockey Association. This relieved Livingstone of the fear of having his franchise sold from under him. On all other matters, Major Robinson remained silent.

Livingstone, perhaps emboldened, responded with another attack on Lichtenhein.

The owner of the Wanderers had tried to convince his ex-Blueshirts to remain in Montreal, even though the league moguls had promised to return the Toronto players to Livingstone at the season's end. In a nutshell, the Wanderers owner was trying to pull the same stunt that the Ottawas had used so successfully with Cy Denneny.

Said Livingstone:

> It has come to my knowledge that the Wanderer Club is again tampering with the players of the Toronto Hockey Club. The previous time was, as I notified you, when the president of the Wanderers endeavoured to have Players Randall, Skinner and Cameron put in a claim to the league for a bonus, for which there was no foundation in fact. This was grave enough, but the latest offence is even a thousand fold more serious.
>
> I charge unhesitatingly that the president of the Wanderer Club is and has been attempting to secure players illegally and unconstitutionally from the Toronto Club for his next winter's team through the medium of

offering to obtain positions for those players in the City of Montreal, and that he has plainly made his intention known to the said players. All of this has been done without the sanction of the Toronto Club, the penalty for which, and the penalty I hereby demand, is the expulsion of the offender from the National Hockey Association of Canada, Ltd., and the forfeiture of the franchise of the Wanderer Hockey Club, Ltd. I name players Randall and Skinner. Conclusive evidence is in my possession, and is at the disposal of the league.

It has been stated by certain partisan and hypocritical parties during the recent 228th Battalion fiasco that a house cleaning of the league was essential, and that I as the guilty party must go. I think you will bear me out that I have been proven to be innocent of wrongdoing. The guilt has been demonstrated to be in an entirely different quarter. Now, I agree that a house cleaning is a necessity, but with this alteration that I propose to be the one to inaugurate the house cleaning, and to see to it, as far as lies in my power, that those who have created the troubles of the NHA are punished in accordance with the extreme gravity of their offences. I have only started.

The league must be placed on the basis to which it is entitled, the game must be protected from the wrong kind of people, and confidence in both restored to the public.[212]

Lichtenhein responded immediately with an ultimatum, demanding that Livingstone either prove or retract his allegations within the next ten days,

and if he fails to do this I will have him arrested for criminal libel if possible, and if not, civil libel, the first time he comes into the Province of Quebec, and will also try to have it done in Ontario if the law permits me. This man has been bluffing long enough. He says he has a lot of evidence and other foolish rot, now let him produce it.

There is nothing illegal or unconstitutional, nor is it tampering with players by helping them to get work, and I will try and get every player work if I possibly can, irrespective of what club he belongs to. Tampering with players means offering them a contract or salary to play.

Such has not been done and the players will so testify. I do not think that Mr. Livingstone knows what the word "tampering" in the English language means. I sent the ex-Toronto players to President Robinson and asked him to hear their story, regarding their claim for a bonus. I also told the players at the time that they had no bonus coming to them, as there was no agreement in their contracts for a bonus, it being only a verbal agreement with Mr. Livingstone. I did not even go with the players to President Robinson....

My attorneys will deal with the matter on March 19th unless Mr. Livingstone's remarks are retracted or proof of his statements made in writing to Major Frank Robinson.[213]

Lichtenhein's deadline of March 19 would pass without comment. The Wanderers owner would wait nearly two more months before filing a civil libel suit against Livingstone in Montreal, seeking damages of $5,000. The case went nowhere.

Eddie Livingstone was not without his supporters. Charlie Querrie, the hockey manager of the Arena Gardens, knew how much professional hockey meant to his facility. In his Toronto *Daily News* column, Querrie wrote: "Eddie Livingstone, the Toronto magnate, no more gets back in the National Hockey Association than he wants someone fired out. This time he is after Sammy Lichtenhein, and the battle between them should be a royal one. The Toronto leader accuses the Eastern magnate of tampering with Randall and Skinner, two of his leading lights, by promising them positions in Montreal for the summer, with an idea of keeping them for next winter. Whether it is right or not remains to be seen, but it is besides the point. The NHA is a discredited organization in this portion of the world, and unless the magnates get together and elect a regular 'Ban' Johnson style of president with absolute power to act as he sees fit, they will never have the confidence of the sporting world. The present leader of the association, Major Frank Robinson, no doubt has the ability to conduct the affairs of the professional hockey league, but at present he is just an outsider, or a chairman who sits at a meeting and counts the votes. Give Major Robinson absolute control for a couple of years and pass up the Board of Directors is our advice to the professional hockey magnates if they have any desire to again retain any of the lost prestige among the people who pay the money to make the league possible."[214]

But as much as Querrie threw his support behind Livingstone in the press, his other employer, the Arena Gardens, was withholding gate receipts from the Torontos' February 10 match against Ottawa. Querrie might have criticized the NHA in his newspaper column, but he never mentioned or offered reasons why the Arena was not paying Livingstone what he was owed.

Livingstone, feeling that Sam Lichtenhein had forced the issue with his threats of legal action, believed he had no other choice. Having been stripped of his contracted players without compensation, denied the Toronto Hockey Club's share of the gate for its last home game, and left to pay the rent and other expenses for three unplayed games at the Mutual Street arena, Livingstone filed suit against the members of the NHA on March 9, 1917.

He claimed that the resolution that suspended his team from further participation in the NHA, cancelled the contracts between the Blueshirts and its players, and forfeited his franchise were invalid. He also asked for an order directing the officers and directors of the NHA to rescind the minutes of the meeting and to reinstate the Toronto club; an injunction restraining any of the other clubs from employing any of Livingstone's players in any capacity; and an injunction restraining the NHA's members from releasing players so as to permit the owners to form a new league and render his franchise worthless.

Livingstone claimed damages for the forfeiture of the bonds entered into by the five defendant clubs, each for $5,000.

In support of the application, Livingstone filed an affidavit stating that the Toronto club was not represented at the meeting at Montreal, and that by reason of the action taken there, the Toronto club was deprived of the proceeds of the unplayed home games, which would have netted the club $2,500, in Livvy's estimation. He also complained that the Arena Gardens' decision to withhold the proceeds of the February 10 game — amounting to more than $700 — was the result of the NHA's actions.[215]

Livingstone went to Ottawa for the NHA finals between the Ottawa Senators and Montreal Canadiens. His interest was not in see-ing the Canadiens win the two-game, total-goals series, 7–6. Writs needed to be served to his fellow NHA owners, and the big game in Ottawa was just the place to find them. He also tried to serve George Kennedy and Sammy Lichtenhein with an injunction to prevent their teams, the Canadiens and Wanderers, from using his players in exhibi-tion games. Kennedy accepted the paperwork when it was handed to him, but stowed it in his pocket without so much as glancing at it. He didn't know what it was until he had been informed that Livvy had also tried to hand the Wanderers owner a copy. Sammy refused to accept the papers and demanded to know if the Toronto owner was a bailiff. Lichtenhein also told Livvy that he could see him at his office in Montreal, but that he did not care to be accosted in public. Livvy tossed the papers at Sammy.[216]

The serving of legal papers did not distract Lichtenhein from his earlier threat of libel action. He sent a telegram to Livingstone saying as much.

The management of the Ottawa Senators did not take Livingstone seriously at first. Tommy Gorman reported the story in the Ottawa *Citizen*.

> During the heat of the excitement over the Ottawa-Canadien game at the Arena last Saturday, Eddie Livingstone stepped up to Secretary Rosenthal of the Ottawas, handing him a bulky envelope and saying: "Look these over, Martin, when you get the chance."
>
> Mr. Rosenthal threw the documents into the locker of the Ottawa room and the envelope lay there until yesterday. Meanwhile, Secretary Calder, of the N.H.A., telephoned Mr. Rosenthal and inquired if he had been served with a notice of action.
>
> "Livingstone gave me something Saturday night, but I was too busy to examine it," replied the Ottawa director.
>
> "Better look it over," advised the N.H.A. secretary. Accordingly, Mr. Rosenthal put Trainer "Cozy" Dolan on the trail and the latter resurrected the soiled papers, returning them to Mr. Rosenthal, who ascertained that they represented writs for action for damages against the N.H.A. and the Ottawa Club.
>
> Secretary Rosenthal was naturally surprised when he discovered that the Ottawa notices had lain in the dressing room since Saturday. The Ottawa officers say that Livingstone has no grounds for action and expect to see all his suits dismissed.
>
> Had Livingstone remained silent he might have had some chance to force the N.H.A. to backwater, but in view of his charges, his case would now appear hopeless. Counter actions are certain and it is likely that he would be glad to call things off. It is understood last week that the Toronto club had been reinstated, but the

latest upheaval is said to have been due to the fact that President Robinson gave Livvy notice to sell out, quietly intimating that his company was no longer desired by the professional hockey magnates.[217]

Again, we see the hand of Frank Calder, rather than league president Frank Robinson. There can only be one reason: Calder was protecting Kennedy's and Lichtenhein's interests.

Gorman clearly did not understand Eddie Livingstone's character. Livvy was not one to sit back when his rights were threatened, as they definitely were in this case. There was absolutely no guarantee that his team would be allowed back into the league. One day Frank Robinson indicates Toronto is back and, practically the next day, Lichtenhein orders Livingstone to sell the team. Yet, given how the other owners had debased the name of the NHA, how would Livingstone expect to get a fair return on his investment?

Livingstone explained to the *Daily News* why he filed the lawsuit. "We have reacted throughout with respect for the laws of the land. We, I repeat, pay for what we get. We do not attempt to 'bolshevik' the property of others.

"To sum it all up, when things that 'simply can't be done' are done, one's redress is forced to come from the courts. You may hold a royal flush which cannot be beaten, but five of a kind with a gun to your head will take the pot in spite of it."[218]

Incredibly, the defendants denied ever passing the motion to kick the Blueshirts out of the league. In their statement of defence, the NHA owners said the resolution was "a nullity and of no binding effect upon the parties to this action" and that "any uses made by any of the defendants of any of the players belonging to the Plaintiffs had ceased to exist long prior to the bringing of this action."[219]

Well, not exactly. Reg Noble, for instance, did not suit up for the Canadiens in the Stanley Cup series — having not been on the Canadiens roster by January 31 — but he did accompany the Canadiens to Seattle. Perhaps feeling that peace with the Patricks would mean an end to player raids, the Canadiens and Metropolitans played a three-game series in San Francisco after the conclusion of the Stanley Cup finals. Frank Patrick had an eye on the California city as a potential site for an arena and a PCHA team. Starting at left wing for Montreal in the first two games was none other than Reg Noble. The San Francisco series started March 31, 1917, and concluded on April 4 — well after Livingstone had served Kennedy with the injunction.[220]

Because of the dearth of press coverage, Livingstone probably never found out about this series. A small report at the bottom of page 8 of the *Mail and Empire* contained the only mention — aside from accounts in the San Francisco *Chronicle* — of the Canadiens' using Noble in this series, which no other hockey publication has ever acknowledged.

Noble played in the first game, a 5–4 Montreal victory. Newsy Lalonde and Didier Pitre each scored a pair of goals while Bert Corbeau tossed in three assists.[221] Seattle tied the series in the second game with a 5–2 victory, with Cully Wilson scoring three goals and Bernie Morris adding the other two for the Mets.[222] In the series tiebreaker played on April 4, Noble took over for Pitre. The native of Collingwood, Ontario, was kept off the scoresheet, but the Canadiens took the series with an easy 6–2 victory.

Chapter 12

The Penny Drops

It's strictly legal. We didn't throw Eddie Livingstone out. Perish the thought. That would have been illegal and unfair. Also, it wouldn't have been sporting. We just resigned, and wished him a fine future with his National Association franchise.
— Sam Lichtenhein, 1917

If Eddie Livingstone thought that the long, hot summer of 1917 would soften the resolve of the Montreal magnates, he might as well have been living in a dream world, as his lawsuit hung over the league and its teams like the sword of Damocles. The promised return of Livingstone's players gave him control over his most valuable assets — and in a league where the player base was shrinking, the value of Livingstone's players was appreciating rapidly.

There were three factors that drove the player shortage. The most obvious was the war. As the summer of '17 wore on, the Canadian government drew closer to passing legislation that would allow it to address the shortage of military manpower by "conscripting," or drafting, men into armed service. The greatest worry confronting any owner of a hockey team was that his players might be drafted into service and sent to another part of the country — or overseas. After the debacle of the 228th Battalion, neither the government nor the public would support a hockey team keeping soldiers at home.

Regulations allowed those who could demonstrate they were contributing to the war effort — by taking a job in a munitions plant, for instance, or working a farm — to earn an exemption from the draft. Some NHA players, such as Odie Cleghorn, took advantage of this exemption, but in doing so they were barred from playing professional hockey.

The third factor was in no way related to the war: most teams had simply failed to recruit new players over the past few years. The Wanderers, Canadiens and Quebec were especially hard hit by this lack of foresight. Where Livingstone had actively introduced new talent, Sam Lichtenhein, George Kennedy and Mike Quinn relied upon the players who had served so faithfully over the years. Eastern owners got a taste of what an infusion of new talent could do for their teams after they raided the Torontos in the wake of the withdrawal of the 228th Battalion team. Unfortunately, neither Lichtenhein nor Quinn could keep their Toronto booty and so would have to figure out their own solutions for the 1917–18 season.

Mike Quinn's approach was to attempt a merger with Quebec City's top senior team, the Sons of Ireland. A sticking point seemed to be whether the latter club's players would relinquish their amateur status. In the end, the Sons did not accept the merger invitation.

In Montreal, Sam Lichtenhein had a more radical solution to his problem, one that would also rid him of a particularly annoying thorn in his side. Lichtenhein felt the only way to revive the Wanderers quickly would be to raid the Toronto team again. This solution, like Quinn's, had its flaws: for one thing, there was the lawsuit pending against the Wanderers and the National Hockey Association. Nor could Lichtenhein count upon NHA president Frank Robinson to go along with his plan.

For his part, Robinson decided he'd had enough of the backbiting and dishonesty between the owners just as his predecessor, Emmett Quinn, had done. He particularly did not approve of the way the owners had disposed of Livingstone. Robinson may not have been Livingstone's friend, but the president's integrity was sufficient for the Toronto owner to ask him to represent the team at the ill-starred February 1917 meeting. Livingstone would have never made such a request of the league's secretary, Frank Calder, whose every move seemed to be for the benefit of Sam Lichtenhein, George Kennedy or the Montreal arena magnate William Northey, who owned the Arena Gardens.

The NHA president knew he lacked the power to protect Livingstone if the other governors turned against him again. The honourable thing to do, he decided, was to resign and not be tarred by what was about to happen. At the NHA's annual general meeting, held on September 29, 1917, Frank Robinson formally announced his resignation from the association. Unfortunately, the Ottawa Senators — a team that had developed a reputation for dithering on the eve of each season as to whether they would even play — did not send a delegate to Montreal for the meeting. The AGM was held over until October 20.

(At the rescheduled meeting, Frank Robinson's luck would be no better. He sent a letter to the delegates informing them he would not be available as president for the coming season, but the owners turned around and voted him president for another term.)[223]

Eddie Livingstone of Toronto was also absent. In his place he sent John Boland, the lawyer who was representing him in his suit against the NHA and its teams, to speak for the Toronto Hockey Club. Boland informed the magnates that Toronto intended to operate its franchise in 1917–18 and he suggested that Jimmy Murphy, the one-time manager of the Toronto Ontarios, would run the club.[224]

Livingstone later told the Toronto *Daily News* he had refused to attend the meeting, and would continue to do so until the other owners were replaced. He also served notice that he was not about to fold his tent and go: "My holdings in the Toronto club will be retained by me until such time as I desire to dispose of them, which, I may say, will be the first moment an acceptable offer is submitted, and not till then."[225]

Livingstone kept his word, refusing to attend the league meeting on October 20. This time his representative Donald Barclay, despite an invitation from Frank Calder, was forbidden to take part in any of the discussions. Lichtenhein and — oddly enough — Calder took pains to lecture the Toronto representative on how the Toronto owner was not welcome in their company. Barclay was sent away with instructions to deliver an ultimatum to Livingstone, ordering him to sell his franchise within five days.[226]

Even Charlie Querrie — who, through his association with the Arena Gardens, was an employee of William Northey of the "Montreal Mafia" — saw what was going on. "While we do not always agree with Eddie Livingstone, the Toronto hockey magnate," he wrote in the *Daily News*, "there is one thing certain about the latest move of the eastern wing of the National Hockey Association, and that is they are simply trying to grab a number of good hockey players without paying for their release. Mr. Livingstone, as manager of a professional hockey club, is open to criticism, and has received it on many occasions, but he deserves the support of all local hockey enthusiasts in his fight to give this city the best brand of the winter pastime."[227]

Livingstone, predictably, rejected the "request" of his fellow owners. As he had predicted, the end of the National Hockey Association was now in sight.

"The National Hockey Association have practically admitted that they cannot go ahead under the same name and exclude the Torontos," reported the *Daily News*,

> so it is more than likely they will try the ancient scheme of going out of business and organizing a new league, including the Wanderers, Canadiens, Ottawa and Quebec, but while this looks like a "foxy" move on the part of Eastern clubs, there are many difficulties in the way of such a procedure. In the first place, they will have a legal battle on their hands with the Torontos, who will not let go without a struggle, but it is also likely to cause a lot of trouble with the Pacific Coast League, who have a peace agreement with the N.H.A. at present, but if the latter disband and try and form a new association the Western magnates, who are badly in need of players, may consider this a good opportunity to make another raid on the clubs in the East. At present the Western magnates have very little use for the N.H.A., and this would give them a loophole to crawl out of their arrangement.[228]

The *Mail and Empire* blamed the league's troubles on the Wanderers owner, Sam Lichtenhein, who also owned the Montreal Royals baseball club.

> The N.H.A. as usual have started squabbling, and very brazenly have "requested" the Torontos not to play this season. This request should have been handed to the Wanderers instead of the blue shirts and, with the moguls so anxious to only have a four-club league, the Wanderers' stepping out would have balanced the circuit. Torontos are in better shape to-day, despite the fact that they have lost a couple men, than any of the other N.H.A. clubs, and when it comes to a drawing card, why, they have it over the Wanderers like a tent. It has been said that the year Wanderers finished tie with Ottawa for the leadership, and the Canadiens were tailenders, the latter club were the team to make money and not the leaders. The Wanderers are like the Montreal Ball Club, a poor drawing card in Montreal or elsewhere, and if the citizens of that city fail to patron-

ize either club there surely is something wrong, and the answer is not hard to guess.[229]

In late October, Lichtenhein decided it was time to pay Eddie Livingstone a visit. He wanted to tell his — and presumably the league's — side of the story: that the NHA directors had given the Toronto management since March to dispose of their holdings, and that they had informed the Toronto delegate that, if control of the club passed into other hands, it would be allowed to play. Furthermore, under these circumstances, the Wanderers and Canadiens would have amalgamated, making the NHA a four-team league. "This had not been done, and it was now too late," Lichtenhein later told the *Daily News*, adding that the NHA — or a new league — would go ahead without the Torontos.[230]

As usual, Livingstone refused to see Lichtenhein, appointing John Boland to meet with him instead. This deliberate snub would surely have further enraged Lichtenhein, who promptly started hatching yet another plan to remove Livingstone from professional hockey. The first step was to visit the offices of the Toronto *Daily News* and sports columnist Charlie Querrie.

Querrie acknowledged Lichtenhein's visit in his column but was vague about its purpose. It is reasonable to assume that the topic of Livingstone's ownership of the Toronto Hockey Club was discussed, since Querrie was the man who booked hockey events at the Arena Gardens. It was public knowledge that the Arena had suggested that Livingstone sell it the Toronto franchise before, when Livingstone wanted help in fighting the PCHA "raid," but the Toronto Hockey Club owner had rejected the idea. A possibility existed this time, however, that Livingstone might listen to such an idea, given the case that Lichtenhein had presented to Boland.

Querrie took the proposal back to his boss at the Arena, Lol Solman, who was probably the leading figure in Toronto professional sports.[231] Solman recognized that, without the revenue that professional hockey generated, the Arena's finances would be bleak during the winter of 1917–18. The possibility of getting the hockey club at a bargain price had obvious appeal, and Solman, in turn, contacted the Montreal shareholders — which included William Northey — to recommend that negotiations be opened.

Upon his return to Montreal, Sam Lichtenhein had another bit of league business to conduct. If a new league was to be formed, it would need the tacit approval of the Pacific Coast Hockey Association. A telegram was sent to Frank Patrick asking if his league would extend the NHA–PCHA agreement to cover the proposed new league.

Patrick replied that as long as the new league consisted solely of NHA clubs, he would not object; nor would he have a problem if the new eastern league consisted of four teams rather than five — in fact, it was preferable.[232] The failure of the Spokane Canaries left the coast league — now a three-team circuit — looking shaky. The PCHA would save face if the eastern league were also shrinking. One less team in the east also meant there would be less chance of the player raids being renewed: each league would have plenty of surplus players to distribute among its surviving clubs.

The response in Toronto was, predictably, heated. "This is a fine boost for professional hockey," Charlie Querrie wrote, "when four clubs of the supposed to be strongest circuit in the world have to sit down and wait for assistance to try and beat one other club out of their rights and privileges. This fine piece of work would not be tolerated in any other sport, and if the Patrick brothers, of the Pacific Coast League, become a party to their action, then professional hockey in Canada is in poor hands."[233]

In early November 1917, Livingstone went to Montreal to see the owners of the Arena Gardens and offered them a lease proposal, which they accepted, for the 1917–18 season. It is likely that they also discussed the Montreal hockey situation. Merger talks between the Canadiens and Wanderers, which Lichtenhein had let slip during his Toronto visit, had led nowhere. Lichtenhein's Wanderers seemed ripe to be pushed into such an arrangement: they were a poor draw and were facing significant player losses leading into the 1917–18 season.

George Kennedy was the fly in the ointment. His team was basically intact and making money. The only way Kennedy might be willing to deal was if he had the upper hand in running the merged club. And he was not about to honour Lichtenhein's request to split any profits down the middle.[234]

Amidst all this manoeuvring, the rush to create a new league continued. The telegram from Frank Patrick had removed a barrier that hindered the eastern owners' quest to oust Livingstone. On November 3, 1917, a week before the NHA was to meet again, the Ottawa *Citizen* laid out the blueprint for what we now know as the National Hockey League, but which remained unnamed at that point.

> Following the advice of their counsel, the Wanderers, Canadiens, Quebec and Ottawa clubs have decided upon their first move in the National Hockey Association turmoil. For the first time since Eddie Livingstone, acting on behalf of the Toronto club, endeavoured to butt into the N.H.A. series against the wishes of the other four clubs at

the annual meeting held in Montreal, matters in Eastern hockey circles started to take definite form yesterday, and it is intimated that before the end of next week the four clubs will have arranged their plan of campaign for the coming season.

Secretary Martin Rosenthal, of the Ottawa club, stated yesterday that after being in communication with one of the other clubs, it was definitely announced that the Quebec club would be in the race this year.... Secretary Frank Calder of the National Association retained counsel in the matter and yesterday he was advised that the Wanderer, Quebec, Canadien and Ottawa clubs would be perfectly within their rights in [seceding] from the N.H.A. and forming a new body. Thereupon it was decided to make this move and, at a meeting of the four clubs to be held next week in Montreal, the required action will be taken in the matter. The books and communications of the League will be turned over to Mr. Livingstone and the Toronto club as the only remaining member, while the other four clubs go ahead and draw up their schedule....

Apparently the stage is set for the exit of Mr. Eddie Livingstone of Toronto. Eddie has had his little joke and it is now up to him to move off. There is a report emanating from Montreal to the effect that the stormy petrel of the N.H.A. will attempt to make the Eastern N.H.A. clubs sell out to him at a fixed price per club or make the clubs in question buy him out at the same price. It is rumoured that the Toronto magnate could secure sufficient backing to pull this, providing the purchase price were paid partly in cash and partly in notes. However, it is not likely that the [seceding] clubs will countenance any such a proposition, but that hockey will be played as usual this winter only under a different head and without Mr. Livingstone.[235]

Another purpose for Livingstone's Montreal sojourn was to visit outgoing NHA president Frank Robinson. Robinson suggested that Livingstone try to sell his players to the other teams and follow his lead by getting out of the game. Otherwise, Robinson warned, he could be sure his players would again be stolen from him, as had happened in February. When the other owners' plans to go through with their new league were publicized, Livingstone vowed to make sure he would not lose his players a second time.

"I really want to get out of hockey, particularly the National Hockey Association," Livingstone told the Ottawa *Citizen*. "They are no more anxious to get rid of the Toronto club than I am to cut away. But I don't propose to tolerate any so-called 'freeze out' process. I have instructed my lawyer, Mr. Boland, to continue the action started some time ago, and he will represent me at the next meeting of the league. The Toronto club has all Toronto behind it and it would appear unjust to crowd it out when we have an excellent team. We have Hebert and Brooks for the nets, with Randall, Kyle and Cameron for the defence, while as forwards we have Corbett Denneny, Reg Noble, Alf Skinner, Jerry Coughlin, Gordon Meeking, Harry Meeking, and two or three good amateurs. It is evident that Wanderers and Quebec will be weak and their scheme to leave Toronto out is evidently based on their desire to corral Toronto's players. However, they will not get them.

"I have lost money since I entered the N.H.A., and I am prepared to spend more, if necessary, to see this thing through. If forced to do so, I will sign all my players and pay them their salaries for the season. We can play exhibition games in many American cities, and I would not be afraid to bet that my team will be as strong as any in the game."[236]

Livingstone's statement sent the other owners into panic mode. Their grand plan to rid themselves of the Toronto magnate had hit a snag. Ottawa was in a precarious position because the team operated in Ontario and would be more adversely affected by legal action than the Quebec-based teams. Once more the clubs went back to their solicitors.

On November 10, 1917, the NHA held its fourth meeting of the fall. Once more, John Boland represented Livingstone. The meeting, chaired by Frank Calder in Frank Robinson's absence, was the briefest in the history of the league. Boland announced that Toronto intended to continue as an equal member in the NHA — if the league operated. Should the league reopen under a new name, he said, Livingstone had indicated a willingness to step aside and let the Arena Gardens manage the Toronto team.

Livingstone had forced the issue, and so the other owners suspended the operation of the National Hockey Association. Leaving Boland behind, they withdrew to discuss their options with Calder. It was agreed that they should reconvene several days later.

As for Frank Robinson, his absence from the November 10 meeting underlined his unwillingness to participate in the "freeze-out" of Livingstone. The dirty work was left to Frank Calder, who by now was displaying a real talent for such machinations.

Chapter 13

Quebec Bows Out

"Hey, Frank, what happened?"

"Nothing much," said Frank Calder, briefly, striding to the nearest elevator. He was a modest man, too modest to say he had just been named president of a new hockey league, figuring, perhaps, it was just a small job, of little importance or future.
— Elmer Ferguson, 1965

Much that Elmer Ferguson didn't tell his readers in later years can be found in his report of the November 10, 1917, meeting which appeared in the Montreal *Herald*:

> The action of the N.H.A. is an excellent exhibition of camouflage. The suspension is merely a strategic move to cover the formation of a new and Livingstoneless league. The action taken at Saturday night's meeting was exactly as forecasted in the *Herald* more than a week before, this paper giving exclusively the plans to circumvent legal action by the Toronto club, and at the same time rid the league of a troublesome factor.
>
> Canadiens, Wanderers, Ottawa, and *either* Toronto or Quebec will form the new league, although officials of the N.H.A. to-day made solemn assertions that they knew nothing about it — their fingers probably being crossed at the time, however.
>
> It leaks out from Saturday night's meeting that the condition in Quebec is a trifle shaky. The resignation of

Mike Quinn as manager is the trouble, for no one seems to wish to take up the burden where he left it off, and matters are at a dead-lock in that connection, without any great hope, apparently, of being placed on a firmer basis.

On the other hand, with Eddie Livingstone out of any new league, there would be no further objection to the entry of a Toronto team. The report was current to-day in usually well-informed circles that steps were already being taken to have Toronto represented, with the Arena controlling the team directly. The Arena interests have been anxious throughout to have Toronto in professional hockey, but the presence of Livingstone was the stumbling block. Under the decision of Saturday night, Livingstone's franchise, like all the others in the N.H.A., will not be operative this winter. And Edward will certainly find no "welcome" on the mat if he tries to horn in on the new league. He would be as welcome as the Liberty Loan news is to the Kaiser.

When the new league is formed this week, it will be necessary to cast about for a new President. Major Frank Robinson, who was elected President of the N.H.A. at an earlier meeting this year, declared to-day that he had no intention of accepting, and would not become head of a proposed new organization, even if asked to do so.

In deciding to suspend for the season at Saturday's meeting, the directors reiterated their former reason "that it was considered impossible to run with five clubs, owing to the scarcity of players." All five clubs were represented, but none showed any willingness to withdraw. One of the delegates proposed that the five names be placed in a hat, and the club withdrawn should discontinue operations for the winter. This proposition was not seriously received, for four of the clubs were solid in the stand not to work with a Toronto club which was operated by Eddie Livingstone. The Toronto club was represented by J. E. Boland, who was instructed to inform the delegates that if the Association operated, then his club wished to retain equal rights with the others.

Frank Calder, secretary of the N.H.A., presided at Saturday night's meeting. If the new league is formed, it would not be surprising if Frank was made the

President, since Major Frank Robinson asserts he will not act. Incidentally, Saturday's meeting was one of the most orderly and briefest ever held by the delegates.[237]

After the meeting, Calder and the other four teams held a private conference without Boland. "Everybody knew that the old league was going to suspend, to force Eddie Livingstone out, and to side-track his law suits," Ferguson wrote. "But the spectacle of George Kennedy and Sam Lichtenhein maintaining their gravity while admitting under pressure that there may be a new league, and that they're going to talk it over with the other clubs, makes us think that the stage lost a couple of likely recruits when these two esteemed friends went into sport."[238]

Funny, but Ferg found nothing unethical about the decision to lift Livingstone's franchise from him, even though just a few years earlier he was the type to write an exposé of a boxer operating under false pretences. Perhaps his moral compass got recalibrated when he was named the NHA's head statistician.

To maintain peace with the Patricks, the NHL decided to try to operate as a four-team circuit. The only question was whether to give Quebec or Toronto the boot. Both teams were located on the fringe of the Ottawa-Montreal axis, so travel to either city represented a financial burden. Although Mike Quinn insisted the Bulldogs were still planning on operating during the 1917–18 season, the proposition seemed like a pipe dream. Their bid to merge with the Sons of Ireland had not panned out, and the team was also hurt by Quinn's decision not to stay on as team president. Meanwhile, the prospect of the Arena Gardens, under William Northey of the Westmount Arena, controlling the Blueshirts made that club seem all the more attractive. And Northey was good friends with Frank Calder, who was taking it upon himself to expel Livingstone from professional hockey in eastern Canada.

"I suppose many hockey fans were getting tired of seeing the same old faces of the management and players," Quinn said by way of farewell, "and I think it is just as well to give somebody else a chance. Quebec is a great hockey town, and I'm sure with a completely re-organized outfit, interest would be revived in the professional game here."[239]

Just as the NHA had done with Robinson, the Quebec Hockey Club refused to consider their manager's resignation until the NHA made a decision about the coming season. The league, on the other hand, gave the club one week to decide whether it was definitely in on the new league.

The next couple of days saw more meetings, as Quinn offered his players for sale but found no takers. For public consumption he protested that he was still committed to trying to make hockey work in Quebec City. The league's November 17 deadline passed without any comment from Quebec. Two days later, Quinn requested a meeting with Frank Calder. As usual, Elmer Ferguson heard first-hand the request from the Ancient Capital.

> The Quebec Hockey Club, so it was announced to-day, has written a letter to Secretary Calder of the National Hockey Association asking that a special meeting be called the middle of the week to which the delegates of the Canadiens, Wanderers, Ottawa and Quebec Clubs will be invited to attend. Just what the plans of the Quebecers are is not stated, but developments recently have made it urgent that action be taken. The Quebec club's attitude will be known at this meeting.
>
> From present indications, Quebec will be ready to retire, and may definitely announce this decision to the meeting. Plans are already on foot to divide up the Quebec players if the Ancient City club drops out. It is understood that the Ottawa Club has secured first call on Dave Ritchie, and that it is also negotiating for another defence man. Sammy Hebert goes to Toronto, while Wanderers and Canadiens will likely divide up others, Crawford, Mummery, McDonald, Malone, Hall and Carey included. Torontos state that they will not require any players.
>
> Mike Quinn has wired the Ottawa, Canadien and Wanderer clubs inquiring if they desired to buy some of the Quebec players. Something likely lies behind such action and it appears to be this: The Quebec Club is endeavouring to keep the other clubs in the dark as to their intentions to quit this season and at the same time get rid of their players in exchange for some real money. Mike Quinn and the directors of the Quebec Club know that if they announce they intend to drop that the other clubs will simply grab their players and pool them around.[240]

On November 20, the Ottawa *Citizen* sports editor and Senators co-owner Tommy Gorman let the world know the name of the proposed new league. "The successor to the N.H.A. will likely be known as the National Hockey League instead of the Eastern Hockey League," he wrote. "The former name is favoured and it is understood that the substitution of the league for association will overcome any legal difficulties that may arise from the similarity of names. The N.H.A. is, of course, incorporated. There will not be any trouble on this score."[241]

Despite the new name, one thing had not changed: five clubs wanted into a league that had set itself a four-team limit. And the solutions remained the same: merge the Montreal teams, or drop one of Toronto or Quebec.

The arena magnates in Montreal were getting very concerned about the time the hockey moguls were taking to settle matters, and decided to take a more active role in league affairs. They made up their minds to attend a league meeting that had been called for November 22 to clear up whether Quebec wanted the fourth franchise.

Elmer Ferguson of the *Herald* expected the sparks to fly at this gathering.

> Professional hockey officials are getting ready for a long and stormy session tonight, when the eastern circuit for the coming season will be lined up, with either Quebec or Toronto coming in to form a four-club league, along with Canadiens, Wanderers and Ottawa. Whether Quebec or Toronto will be the fourth club was still said to-day to be problematic, as at any time during the past three weeks, the matter hinging entirely on whether the Quebec club will be able to operate. It was stated that, if Quebec decided not to run, matters were all in shape to have Toronto enter a team owned and controlled by the Arena of that city, and managed by Charlie Querrie.
>
> The battle to-night is expected to wage around the question of what recompense Quebec will get for its players, providing the Ancient City decides not to operate.
>
> The suspicion among the other directors, based on the general tenor of previous Quebec offers, is that Mike Quinn and Co. will want a cash price for players and franchise. On the other hand, the local officials want to know how Quebec can ask for a cash price for a franchise which practically does not exist, and for players who became free

agents when it was decoded to suspend operations of the National Hockey Association.

This is the situation which may arise, however, and if it does, there are prospects for a very lengthy pow-wow tonight. The hockey magnates are very careless about the flight of time when they start talking dollars.

Both local clubs were unanimous today in stating that they were determined not to play in a league containing an odd number of teams, nor in a league where Eddie Livingstone was present.

It is said that the Toronto Arena Company was prepared two weeks ago to take over the Toronto players from E. J. Livingstone and all arrangements were completed that were satisfactory to the Toronto magnate, but the deal is still hanging fire until after tonight's meeting.[242]

Ferguson's comment that about the NHA owners being "very careless about the flight of time" is an apt one. For although many sources state that the NHL was born at the November 22 meeting, the Toronto *Mail and Empire* pointed out two days later that little was actually accomplished.

On Thursday evening, which was declared unto the world at large as the final and decisive meeting, the representatives littered the ozone and the Windsor Hotel for four hours with many precocious statements, but the upshot of the whole thing was that President Mike Quinn arose in his majesty and moved that the meeting adjourn until tonight. Here's hoping that the same magnates will not waste more valuable time.[243]

Quinn had reason to be upset with his NHA brethren. His Quebec Bulldogs had been kicked out of the Canadian Hockey Association in 1910, after that league's "merger" with the Ambrose O'Brien–controlled NHA. The lateness of the amalgamation, which took place on January 15, made it impossible to iron out the scheduling glitches that the Quebec team posed. Quinn agreed to sit out 1910, and was welcomed back with open arms the following season.

Ever since, Quinn had had to deal with the possibility that his fellow owners might turn on him and his club again. As such, he refused to commit to the NHL, even though he was involved in all the meetings and welcomed to join at any time. The owners even tried to placate

Quinn by offering him the presidency of the new league and to recognize the Bulldogs' NHA reserve list if the team dropped out.

The first reports out of the NHL formation meetings paint the picture that Quinn needed to sit back and think about operating for a few days. But behind the scenes, Quinn was manoeuvring to get out of the hockey business. The November 24 meeting was postponed to November 26.

"The Quebec hockey club seems to have replaced Old Man Procrastination as the well-known thief of time," Elmer Ferguson cracked. "The Quebec hockey club is taking more time to make up its mind than it takes Mike Quinn to arrange his high-class sartorial effects."[244]

"Things have taken a new turn," the Toronto *Globe* reported on the 26th, "and it is now practically assured that Toronto will have the fourth franchise in the new league, and that Quebec will drop out. Quebec have been negotiating with the promoters of the league for the sale of the players on the club's reserve list, and, as the Montreal promoters, who control the Toronto Arena, have guaranteed to pay for them, they will likely be given a franchise and included in this season's schedule.

"There is a local feeling that it would be better to keep Quebec in the league, with Canadiens, Ottawa and Toronto, and drop the Wanderers, who have lost practically all of their players, and more particularly since Odie Cleghorn has been denied the privilege of playing this season and Harry Hyland can hardly play in the face of getting an exemption [from military service] for no apparent reason."[245]

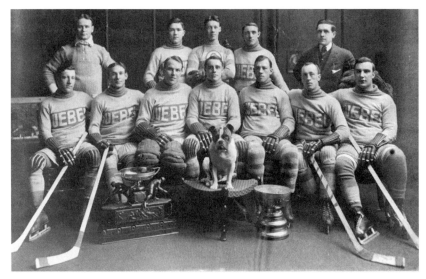

Mike Quinn's 1912 Stanley Cup Champion Quebec Bulldogs.
Quinn is in the back row, far right.

Ferguson's expectations of the November 26 meeting were not as lofty as those of the *Globe*'s man. "If there is a meeting tonight, it will be slimly attended," he wrote, "for Sam Lichtenhein of the Wanderers is on a jaunt in Virginia, and Ottawa will be represented through Frank Calder."[246]

Ferguson also reported that Calder was the one who called the meeting, although the league secretary did not keep minutes, so this cannot be confirmed. He went on to report that:

> The new professional hockey league is in process of formation in Montreal to-day, and by to-night the circuit will probably have been definitely formed.
>
> As indicated by the developments of several days past, Toronto will be in and Quebec out, the new circuit consisting of Torontos, Ottawas, Wanderers and Canadiens. A representative of the new Toronto club is expected in the city today. He will confer with Frank Calder, the secretary of the N.H.A., and general Pooh Bah of the new league, after which there will be a pow-wow tonight, at which the schedule will be drawn up and officers elected, with Calder probably then being elected president.[247]

George Kennedy was present — the same George Kennedy whom Calder had labelled as crooked in a wrestling exposé just four years earlier, *and* the same George Kennedy who recommended Calder for the job of secretary-treasurer. As Calder held the proxies of the Wanderers and Ottawa, it was a simple decision as to who the president of the new league was going to be.

Frank Calder elected himself president, as well as secretary-treasurer, of the National Hockey League, and did such an outstanding job on his first day that he failed to keep detailed minutes of the meeting.

The establishment of the NHL meant that Frank Robinson, who essentially walked away from the job in September, was finally free of professional hockey. And Toronto would continue to have a hockey club, as long as Eddie Livingstone was not involved with its operation.

In the end it was Quebec that wound up on the outside looking in. Mike Quinn's efforts to turn the reins of leadership over to someone else had failed. None of the city's well-heeled men — English or French — was willing to accept responsibility for the team.

A little over five years before, the Ancient Capital had celebrated a Stanley Cup championship. The events leading up to November 26, 1917, did much to ensure that the city would never win another.

Chapter 14

Lichtenhein Loses the War

*The Westmount Arena burned down, Wanderers were homeless,
and they dropped out. So, in its first year, the NHL operated
with three teams.*

— Elmer Ferguson, 1965

*I*n *the wake of the* National Hockey League's formation, the Toronto
Globe suggested that "the professional hockey league tangle was finally
straightened out."[248] All five clubs that had competed in the now-defunct
National Hockey Association were represented on the new league's board
of directors — including Toronto, *sans* Eddie Livingstone, and Quebec, who
retained their seat even though the club did not plan to compete in
1917–18. Frank Calder, of course, was president and secretary, while
Quebec's Mike Quinn was given the title of "honorary president."

As for the management of the Blueshirts, representatives of the
Arena Gardens were said to be negotiating "with one of the best-known
and most popular sportsmen in Toronto. The new owners and new
manager will be thoroughly acceptable to the other clubs of the
league."[249] The *Globe* said that Jimmy Murphy was considering an offer
to take over the reins.

According to the French-language newspaper *La Patrie*, Quinn had
demanded $2,000 to sit idle for the winter. The other teams realized that
the Quebec manager would be a very valuable asset if he sided with
Livingstone, so it was not only worth their while to pay for Quinn's
ongoing co-operation, it was essential. The directors settled on a plan
whereby the four active clubs would draft the former Bulldogs and pay
Quinn a fee of $200 a head to lease them for the season.

The Montreal Wanderers claimed Jack McDonald, Dave Ritchie, George Carey and Jack Marks; Joe Malone, Joe Hall and Walter Mummery went to the Canadiens; Rusty Crawford became an Ottawa Senator; and the Torontos picked up Harry Mummery and Skull Johnson.

The *Globe* also weighed in with its criticism of the antics of the NHL's Montreal ringleaders.

> The announcement was sent out from Montreal that the Toronto franchise in the National Hockey League would belong to a syndicate of Toronto sportsmen. That is a most desirable — even an essential — condition, but it is not demonstrated by the journey of the prospective manager, Mr. Murphy, to Montreal to close whatever arrangement he may make with the owners. The prevalence of camouflage in connection with professional hockey hereabouts has been the chief obstacle to its success, and if the false-face business is to be continued there is no reason to expect a revival of real interest on the part of the public.[250]

The "false-face business" continued when Calder and company blatantly lied to the media about the winding down of the NHA. Under the Canadian corporate laws of the day, the NHA could not be dissolved unless it wanted its lawsuit against the Ocean Accident and Guarantee Corporation dismissed, despite Ferguson's comments to the contrary.

On May 9, 1917, the NHA sued the Ocean Accident and Guarantee Corporation Limited for payment of the $3,000 bond the 228th had been ordered to post. There was much behind-the-scenes dickering, as Calder and Stewart Leitch, who was superintendent of guarantees at Ocean Accident, exchanged at least thirty-one documents.

Calder chose some interesting words to open his affidavit filed on March 15, 1918:

> "I, Frank Calder, journalist of the City of Montreal make oath and say:
> 1. I am the Secretary-Treasurer..."[251]

Interesting for what he didn't say: that he was also the NHA's self-appointed president after Major Frank Robinson resigned from the hockey boardroom — in part because he was fed up with Calder's power plays — and that he was the current president of the National Hockey League.

Meanwhile, the new NHL's teams set about readying themselves for the new season. Each club would have to address the task of integrating their "loaned" Quebec players into their lineups. Sam Lichtenhein thought the infusion of new talent would solve his team's problems, but things started almost immediately to go horribly wrong. On November 27, 1917, the Toronto *Mail and Empire* reported that

> Sprague Cleghorn, the most brilliant defence player in professional hockey, will not play the game this Winter. Cleghorn is in the General Hospital to-day with his right leg broken, the result of a fall on St. Catherine Street last night. The leg is fractured above the ankle and the accident will keep him out of hockey all Winter. Cleghorn slipped on the icy sidewalk and his ankle snapped like a pipe stem. He will take action against the city for $10,000 as the accident has probably wrecked his hockey career."[252]

Lichtenhein knew only too well how valuable Cleghorn was to his team. When Cleghorn went down in a heap with Ken Randall of the Blueshirts a couple seasons before, so did the Wanderers' hopes of playing for the Stanley Cup. The Redbands went from being the class of the league to fighting for last place within weeks of the injury. This time around, Sprague's absence would be compounded by the loss of Odie Cleghorn, who had gained an exemption from the military draft on the condition that he not play hockey.

The Wanderers defence now rested on the broad shoulders of ex–Quebec Bulldog Dave Ritchie, who had posted similar statistics to Sprague Cleghorn but had nowhere near the mean streak of the injured defenceman. Odie Cleghorn's 28 goals in 1916–17 would be even harder to replace, given that Montreal's new forwards, Carey, Marks and McDonald, had combined for only 22 the year before.

As late as December 7, none of the ex-Bulldogs had been signed to Wanderers contracts, according to the Montreal *Gazette*. The situation prompted the club's manager, Art Ross, to travel to Quebec City to close the deals.[253] He returned empty-handed.

In time, Jack McDonald, a good scorer but hardly an adequate replacement for Odie Cleghorn, reported, followed a few days later by Ritchie. But Jack Marks, who made it clear he didn't want to play for Lichtenhein, remained in Toronto, practising at the Arena Gardens. The situation triggered what would be the first crisis of Frank Calder's young presidency.

Speaking from New York, where he was attending the baseball meetings, Lichtenhein threatened to pull out of the NHL. "You may say for me, and make it as emphatic as you can, that unless the Wanderers get some players from some of the other clubs of the National Hockey League the Red Bands will not have a team this season," he told the Quebec *Chronicle*. "And that is not all, either; unless I have favourable replies from the other clubs by the time I arrive home on Saturday night next, I will immediately withdraw from the pro league. The time is too short to permit any haggling over players now. Under existing conditions I don't care whether the Wanderers play or not."[254]

Back in Montreal, Art Ross was singing from the same hymn book. "When the draw was made we were satisfied, as we had the two Cleghorns," he told the *Gazette*, "but since that time the Cleghorns have become lost to us, while two of the four players we secured from Quebec did not report to us. Carey is unable to come to Montreal, while Marks says that he will not play in Montreal this winter. Without those men all we have is [Harry] Hyland, [Jack] McDonald, Billy Bell and [Phil] Stephens, to build up a team from which would be impossible this winter."[255]

When no help was forthcoming from the other league owners, Lichtenhein demanded that *all* of the Quebec players be turned over to him. "Unless the other clubs hand us over players at once," Ross complained, "the Wanderers will not think of operating this season. We have lots of amateur material out with us, but this will not make us strong enough to cope with the other teams.… I have just notified President Calder of the facts, and it will now depend upon his action as to whether there will be a Wanderer team or not this season. Canadiens should be made to hand us over Malone and Hall, Ottawa should give us Crawford, and Toronto Johnson and Mummery."[256]

"Coming but ten days from the opening of the N.H.L. schedule, the statement caused a sensation in professional hockey ranks," Elmer Ferguson wrote in the Montreal *Herald*.[257] Less than two weeks after Tommy Gorman crowed that the hockey owners "have never been so united," the fledgling league seemed on the verge of falling apart.

Frank Calder expressed shock at Lichtenhein's threats. "I am greatly surprised at hearing Sam Lichtenhein use the word 'quit,'" he told the *Herald*. "In all the years I have been associated with him in sport, I've never before heard him talk quit. On the contrary, he was the gamest sticker we had.

"I don't know what will be the outcome, but I doubt if the other teams will care to be held up at the last minute, when all their arrangements for the coming season have been made. I will consult with the other teams to-day in an effort to untangle the latest trouble."[258]

George Kennedy of the Canadiens told the Quebec *Chronicle* he would gladly keep Montreal to himself. "Let the Wanderers get out," he said. "Who cares? I have friends in Quebec who will be glad to jump right in now and furnish a good team in Wanderers' place. The time to complain about scarcity of players was before the schedule was made up, not now."[259]

Kennedy also attacked Lichtenhein for the benefit of the hometown fans, telling Elmer Ferguson: "I signed Malone up only today, but not before Wanderers had caused me a good deal of difficulty with this player. If Ross had gone about it in a right way, he could have made a deal with me for Malone, or almost any other player. As it is now, I won't stand for being held up, and so far as I am concerned, the sooner the Wanderers quit the better. Wanderers have taken a high-handed position, and I don't think any club-owner will stand to be shaken down in this way."[260]

Calder met with Ross on December 11 to serve the Wanderers manager an ultimatum of his own. Ross was told he would not be getting the players he sought, but that Kennedy would turn over Tommy Smith and Walter Mummery if Ross could sign them. Calder also suggested that Ross trade Marks for Harry Mummery, a Toronto holdout. The Wanderers were given twenty-four hours to accept the proposal.[261]

"I want it understood that I have not received any official information about this 24-hour clause issued by the president," Ross said. "I have been trying to get one of the men Mr. Kennedy has offered us, and I think I will be able to close with him shortly. I have one other man in view, a man who does not belong to any other club in the NHL. If I can get these two men I think I will be justified in keeping our team in the league as a team likely to give others a fair run for their money. Before this I was unable to show anything but a team much weaker than the others. At the same time, I cannot make any definite announcement till I receive a communication from my president, who is in the United States, but with whom I expect to connect some time to-day."[262]

When Ross called Toronto's management they told him they were not interested in the Marks-for-Mummery trade Calder had suggested. After that, Ross and Lichtenhein — surprisingly — kept their mouths shut for the rest of the preseason. They even permitted the team to take part in a benefit game to raise money for the Halifax Explosion relief effort. The Maritime city had been decimated by the explosion of a munitions ship in the harbour, killing nearly 2,000. The game combined the Canadiens and Wanderers into two outfits: Team #1 had the Canadiens' offence and Wanderers' defence; on Team #2 the roles were reversed. Team #1 won the game by a score of 10–2.

It would not have been a surprise to see the Wanderers play a benefit game on their own behalf. Sam Lichtenhein's operation was starved for cash, and he was not one to accept losses — financially or on the ice. However, his threats to pull his team out of the league were falling on deaf ears. Lichtenhein had no friends in Toronto, he had few in Ottawa, and his friendship with the Canadiens' George Kennedy was shaky at best.

Left to his own devices, Lichtenhein tried to use patriotism as a means of drumming up support for opening night. On December 18, the day before the Wanderers were to meet the Torontos, this notice appeared in the *Herald*: "President Lichtenhein of the Wanderers and the Arena management have extended an invitation to all returned invalided soldiers to be their guests at the opening game in the National Hockey League tomorrow night at the Arena, when the Toronto club will meet the red bands. The soldiers will be in charge of their respective officers."[263]

As usual, there was a catch: the freebies were offered to soldiers who had been wounded in action in the Great War, as long as they were accompanied by an officer. In what would be the highlight of the Redbands' season, Montreal defeated the Blueshirts 10–9 before a crowd of — seven hundred. No record exists of how many of those admissions were compliments of Lichtenhein, but if there was one free ticket handed out it would be a shock. Dave Ritchie scored the new league's first goal, while Harry Hyland led the way with five scores. The Redbands had started the season with a bang, even if the community seemed indifferent. But the opening-night victory would be the only one the Wanderers recorded in the NHL.

(There has been some debate amongst hockey fans over the years as to whether it was Ritchie, or Joe Malone of the Canadiens, who scored the NHL's first goal, but upon reviewing the newspaper reports we feel it is clear that the former deserves the honour. The Ottawa-Canadiens game was delayed due to a dispute between players and Senators management. Hamby Shore and Jack Darragh were irked that the league was requiring them to play two more regular-season games than the NHA had played a year before, without an appropriate raise in salary. This was a theme that would be replayed a few years later in Toronto and Hamilton. While the Ottawa players stalled, the Toronto-Wanderers game started on time and Ritchie notched a goal a minute into the action.)

It was clear, however, that the Wanderers could not hope to outscore every opponent. Toronto, at that point, was weak in goal, but the Canadiens, with Georges Vezina, and the Senators, who had Clint Benedict, were far more formidable. The other teams had more potent offences to contend with as well. To remedy his club's ills, Lichtenhein decided it was time to try something that would have been unthinkable only a few years before: to appeal for help from the Pacific Coast Hockey Association.

PCHA president Frank Patrick's attitude towards Sam Lichtenhein had softened in the years since the western raids on the Wanderers. Lichtenhein had even sided with Frank Patrick a couple seasons ago when the NHA refused to enforce the draft rules between the leagues. With the closing down of the Spokane franchise, Frank Patrick had to find somewhere for his extra players to ply their trade; the Wanderers seemed the safest bet. He was further convinced after Lichtenhein divulged that he was willing to waive his claim on Gordie Roberts and permit him to play in the west. "According to the latest advices," the Toronto *Mail and Empire* said, "the Wanderers have secured a working agreement with the Pacific Coast League and will have the services of any of their players in the East. This includes [Frank] Foyston, [Eddie] Oatman, [Jack] Walker, [Eddie] Carpenter and [Cully] Wilson."[264]

The Wanderers also gained the rights to Harry Holmes, a goaltender the Torontos coveted. Lichtenhein and Ross immediately offered a trade of Holmes for Reg Noble. Toronto turned that offer down but kept in the hunt for the netminder. The negotiations were still ongoing as of January 2, 1918, when catastrophe struck the Montreal Wanderers, almost closing down professional hockey in the east and very nearly striking down the NHL less than six weeks after it had been formed.

The story bumped news of the war off the front page of the Montreal *Herald*:

> With losses that will reach nearly a half of a million dollars, the Montreal Arena, for nearly a quarter of a century Montreal's hockey headquarters, was reduced to wreckage at noon today by a series of fire and explosions.
>
> Fire, which started from an unknown cause in a cellar beneath the offices, swept through the woodwork, exploding the acids and boilers in the artificial ice plant, and within a half an hour from the start the brick walls had crashed in, leaving the big plant a heap of twisted metal.
>
> The fire spread to the bleacher seats of the Montreal Baseball Park [which adjoined the arena] and the tremen-

dous heat ignited residences across Wood Avenue, where incipient blazes were quickly extinguished.

There were no casualties, but the family of caretaker McKeen, residing in the rear of the Arena building, barely managed to escape in their house clothes, saving none of their household effects.[265]

The *Herald* called the blaze one of the most spectacular the city had seen in years, and before long it had become too much for the Westmount fire department to handle on its own. Reinforcements from Montreal were called in, but even so the flames proved hard to extinguish. "So intense was the heat," the *Herald* said, "that it was feared the residences on Tupper street, over one hundred yards away, would be ignited."

"So far as could be ascertained in the confusion, only a few of the books were rescued from the offices," the *Herald* article continued,

> while in the rink itself, everything was destroyed, including the equipment of the Wanderers and Canadiens … and teams of the City League, the well-known local amateur body which stages its games at the Arena.
>
> The big artificial ice plant, the only one of its kind in Montreal, installed only a few years ago at a cost of about $100,000, is practically ruined, with nothing left but the walls of the plant and the extensive piping beneath the ice a mass of ruins. It was in the plant that the explosions occurred, in acid vats and then one of the boilers exploding, sending wreckage flying from seventy-five to one hundred feet.
>
> The walls of the plant, being of a recent construction, withstood the strain but the older building toppled, and one by one the walls crashed down. In one corner, a telephone pole collapsed and several by-standers narrowly escaped injury.…
>
> The Arena was one of the most famous sporting headquarters in eastern Canada. The games of the professional hockey league have been played there for years, and previous to that the famous amateur teams of bygone days staged spectacular struggles. The Arena was built in 1897, and in pre-war days, was the scene of not only hockey matches, but horse shows, automobile shows, motor-boat displays, concerts and bazaars. Some

of the world's greatest entertainers, including famous musical organizations have performed within it spacious walls and political gatherings have been addressed there from time to time by famous speakers.[266]

As it turned out, the Canadiens did not lose all of their equipment — six pairs of skates had been sent out for sharpening in preparation for that evening's game against the Wanderers. But the rest did indeed go up in flames, along with William Northey's Buick automobile. The *Herald* reported that the Canadiens would meet the Ottawa Senators three nights later in new skates, stockings, pants — and caps, which for many players were an integral part of the hockey uniform in the 1910s. There was no time to commission a new set of sweaters, so the team would take the ice in the colours of the Hochelaga seniors. The paper estimated the Canadiens' losses at $1,000 — which, as the team carried no insurance, would have to be covered out of George Kennedy's pocket — and concluded that the "Wanderers may consider playing at the Victoria rink, which was in bygone years a great hockey centre," noting that "The City League has already made arrangements for playing its games at this rink."[267]

The owners of the Westmount Arena immediately declared that they would not rebuild. E. D. Sheppard of the Montreal Arena Corporation said, "A new building will cost us at least $150,000." Besides, the land at the corner of Ste-Catherine Street and Wood Avenue, which had cost eighty cents per square foot when the Arena was built, was now worth two dollars.[268]

The Jubilee rink wasn't the only facility to offer ice to the Montreal teams. The Quebec *Chronicle* reported that Leopold Dessault of the Quebec Arena Company had made an offer to the Montreal teams to use his rink.[269] His kindness would be rewarded later in the season — an exhibition game was played in the provincial capital on February 21, and a regular league game took place there on February 27.

The league held an emergency meeting after the fire, which Lichtenhein tried to use as leverage to strengthen his team. Immediately before the meeting, he threatened — once again — to quit the NHL. "There is little use of Wanderers continuing under present circumstances," he told the *Herald*. "At this afternoon's meeting, I will ask the other teams to sell me three players — two seasoned players and one defence player. Our object is to purchase [the] players at a fair price, but if they are not forthcoming then there is no use in our continuing. The club is not strong enough to reach contention, and with our games being staged in a locality so far distant as the Jubilee rink is from our following, we would not pay the players' car fare. With three good players, we could make a show-ing in the race. Any action I take, however, will be for the benefit of the league rather than for the benefit of the Wanderer club alone."[270]

Still, no matter what happened, Lichtenhein pledged that the Wanderers would take part in their next game.

The next day, Elmer Ferguson wrote that the NHL had decided to continue operations, but as a three-team circuit.

> As was intimated exclusively in the *Herald* yesterday, Wanderers resigned when the other teams in the League refused to make any sales of players in response to the demands of the red hooped team … This morning, President Lichtenhein, before leaving for Toronto, announced that the club have been disbanded, all the players having received their outright releases, and that no more games will be participated in by the Wanderer club this season. This means, of course, that Wanderers will not go to Toronto Saturday night, but the Ottawa club will come here to fill its engagement with the Canadiens at Jubilee rink.[271]

Lichtenhein's terse letter of resignation read as follows:

> Dear Sir,
>
> Owing to this club being unable to obtain playing material to compare with the calibre of this league, we respectfully desire to withdraw from this league for this season, or for as long as this League wishes us to do so. Wishing the League every success.
>
> Yours very truly,
>
> SAM E. LICHTENHEIN,
> President[272]

The league did not accept the Wanderers' resignation immediately, electing to wait and see whether the team showed up for its scheduled match in Toronto on Saturday, January 5. Ferguson predicted that, if the Wanderers defaulted, the Torontos would take legal action, while the NHL would seek the $3,000 bond the Wanderers had put up at the beginning of the season. (As the NHA had done, with no success to this date, when the 228th Battalion dropped out.) Ferguson did mention that contingency plans were being made, however: "A new schedule for the balance of the season will be drawn up by President Calder, and in the standing the games which the Wanderers have already played will be counted."[273]

The deadline did expire, and the once-powerful team that had been known as the Little Men of Iron was thrown onto the scrap heap of hockey history. The Wanderers' scheduled games of January 2 and 5 were officially recorded in the standings as victories for their respective opponents, the Canadiens and Torontos.[274]

Long forgotten were the prophetic words that the Stanley Cup trustee Phil Ross had written in his newspaper, the Ottawa *Journal*, in 1912 after Lichtenhein effectively kept Cyclone Taylor out of hockey and eventually forced his move to Vancouver:

> If the Wanderers president thinks he is doing the "Cyclone" any good by keeping him out of hockey, he is welcome to his opinion, but it is certain that such antics will injure the game far more than boosting it, and in the end it would not be surprising if the Montreal club suffered most.[275]

The Wanderers never again captured the Stanley Cup after the Taylor debacle.

The fight to the finish between Sam Lichtenhein and Eddie Livingstone, which had been predicted in 1914, had claimed them both. Both had seen their most valuable assets — player contracts — go to others. The winners were Ottawa, the Canadiens, the owners of Toronto's Arena Gardens, and Frank Calder. It was now up to them to turn a fragile league, born out of a clash of personalities, into the most powerful force in hockey.

Chapter 15

Dey's Deceptions

Tommy Gorman, representing the Ottawa club, chortled happily, as was his wont. "Great day for hockey," he said. "Livingstone was always arguing. No place for arguing in hockey. Let's make money instead."

— Elmer Ferguson, 1965

***B**y 1918, the management of* the Ottawa Hockey Club had rested for some time in the hands of three men: Martin Rosenthal, Tommy Gorman and Edwin P. "Ted" Dey.

Both images: Courtesy of the Hockey Hall of Fame

Tommy Gorman   **Ted Dey**

All three men were equal partners in the running of the hockey club. Rosenthal's involvement with the club dated back to 1901; for most of that time he was the team's secretary-treasurer, which meant the club's finances were under his thumb. Gorman doubled as the sports editor for the Ottawa *Citizen* and had only been a member of the Senators management for a couple of seasons. Still, his influence was growing rapidly. Dey was a member of the Ottawa family known for its arena and its boat-building facilities. It was through his arena connection that Ted gained his shares.

Gorman and Rosenthal were also shareholders in the Ottawa Hockey Association, a corporation that oversaw hockey matters within the city of Ottawa and, having owned the Senators through to the 1917–18 season, was one of the defendants in the first lawsuit Eddie Livingstone filed in 1917. The other shareholders in this group included Llewellyn Bate, C. A. Irwin, Paddy Baskerville, P. M. Butler and D'Arcy McGee.[276]

Rosenthal had acquired a track record over the years for suggesting any number of changes to the way hockey was played. One proposal was that points be awarded for combination work. Under this scheme, the number of goals a team scored would become less important than the way they were scored.[277] That proposal was, thankfully, never passed. One can only shudder if one tries to imagine what the game would be like today if a row of judges, like those found in figure skating, were seated at rinkside, grading the action. And the implications for international hockey — given the allegations and scandals around sports like Olympic diving or figure skating — would have been monstrous!

As the 1918–19 season neared, however, the Ottawa partnership was not a happy group. Ted Dey had heard, through the newspapers and the grapevine, of the profits being made in Toronto, where the owners of Arena Gardens now owned the hockey team. The idea of doing the same in Ottawa would have set dollar signs flashing in Dey's eyes. It would also eliminate the annual, time-consuming dickering over lease terms between club and arena. All that was needed was a way to get Rosenthal out of the picture.

The instrument by which Dey hoped to accomplish his plan was Percy Quinn, the one-time manager of the Toronto Blueshirts of the NHA.

When Quinn walked away from the Blueshirts in 1914, he was only thirty-six years old, but he had already spent a lifetime in hockey. Orphaned at the age of thirteen, the Montreal native sold newspapers to support himself and his brothers — one of whom, Emmett, became the National Hockey Association's first president. At age fourteen he began working for the Queen Insurance Company, which was later acquired by the Royal Insurance Company. Percy grew into a standout goalie for the Montreal Shamrocks in both hockey and lacrosse, leading his team to a world championship in the latter sport in 1896. After his employers transferred Quinn to Winnipeg in 1902, his playing career came to an abrupt halt — but a brief one: it wasn't long before the insurance manager was moonlighting as a hockey referee and helping to found a lacrosse team. He also had an impact on hockey's rule book; in 1903, he was officiating a Stanley Cup challenge game that was tied after sixty minutes. To the chagrin of Stanley Cup trustee Phil Ross, Quinn announced he had been paid for only sixty minutes, and there was no concrete rule requiring him to officiate further. As a result, sudden-death overtime was introduced.

After four years in Winnipeg, Quinn was again transferred — this time to Toronto, where he became the insurance company's local manager. The Blueshirts were the second team whose managerial reins Quinn had taken over. He had also run the Toronto Argonauts, a professional club in the Trolley League for which Newsy Lalonde had played.[278] In 1912, the busy Quinn was elected president of the Dominion Lacrosse Union, a league also known as the DLU or Big Four. It was a choice that sparked some snide comments in the Ottawa *Journal* — published by Phil Ross, whom Quinn had put on the spot years before.

> The election of Percy Quinn to the presidency of the D. L. U. is causing comment, and the comment is that R. J. Fleming, manager of the Toronto Street Railway Co., is the man who put him there. This fact has caused even the Toronto people to take alarm over the future of lacrosse. With the men now running the game, lacrosse had better die quickly and be done with it.[279]

By 1914, Quinn, with the aid of old pro Jack Marshall, had built the Toronto Blueshirts into a powerful team, one that defeated the Montreal Canadiens in a two-game, total-goals NHA playoff series by a 6–2 score to win the Stanley Cup. A few days later, Lester Patrick's Victoria Aristocrats arrived to play a best-of-five series. Patrick had failed to submit a challenge, an oversight that seemed to bother no one other than the Cup trustees, Phil Ross and Bill Foran. Most everyone in Toronto considered this series to be the *real* Stanley Cup showdown, and the Blueshirts did not disappoint, sweeping the series in three straight, including a thrilling 6–5 overtime win in game two, which was played under western rules.[280] Frank Foyston became an instant hero in Toronto with three goals in the series, including the series winner in game three.

Quinn's association with Eddie Livingstone, his intra-city rival, dated back to lacrosse and amateur hockey days. While Quinn had as many enemies as friends, Livingstone's foes *outnumbered* his allies.

In a nutshell, the two men were cut from the same cloth.

On June 11, 1918, Percy Quinn reached an agreement with Mike Quinn (no relation) to purchase the inactive Quebec Bulldogs franchise for $4,000, of which Percy paid $600 upon signing the purchase agreement.[281] The reaction to the sale was less than warm. Toronto manager Charlie Querrie commented: "It seems to us that the hockey season is opening a little early. Percy Quinn had better put his Quebec franchise in cold storage until October at least, and give the summer games a chance."[282]

The status of the Quebec team — which the new owner had renamed the Shamrocks — was taken up at the National Hockey Association's meeting on September 28. (Despite reports by Elmer Ferguson and Tommy Gorman to the contrary, the NHA had not yet been wound down completely. Calder and the other club owners were still trying to collect the bond of the 228th Battalion.) All the leading figures from the old NHA were present: Eddie Livingstone, George Kennedy, Tommy Gorman, Ted Dey, and Percy and Mike Quinn. Even Sam Lichtenhein, whose Wanderers had abandoned the NHL one year earlier, and Tom Wall, who represented the old Toronto Tecumseh franchise that had lost its standing when Livingstone was forced to merge the two teams, attended.

The sparks flew from the moment the meeting was called to order. Livingstone started the ball rolling by moving that Harvey Pulford replace Frank Calder as league president. He dropped his next bombshell when he announced he would drop his lawsuits if he were allowed to operate in a revived NHA. Lichtenhein and Kennedy both came to Calder's defence, renewing their vow never to work with Livingstone — which in Lichtenhein's case was academic, as he would never again operate a hockey team. Other nominees for the NHA post were put forth, but none could garner unanimous support.[283] Strangely, even though he was present and active at the meeting, Tommy Gorman did not report in the Ottawa *Citizen* on this attempted coup, so it is unclear what position the Senators took. And as was often the case, Secretary Calder failed to keep minutes.

In any event, Calder had survived this round.

The next issue on the agenda was the transfer of the Quebec franchise from Mike to Percy Quinn. The NHL owners were suspicious of Percy

Quinn's motives, and his connection with Eddie Livingstone, but could find no cause to deny the transfer. Still, as if hedging their bets, they confirmed Quinn's purchase of a franchise in the NHA — but not the NHL. He would have to apply for NHL membership at a later date.[284]

The final piece of new business involved whether the NHA should continue to exist. On this topic, Gorman did report:

> After the reading of the minutes and the presentation of the financial statement, Mr. Lichtenhein brought up the question of resuming operations. He made it clear that Wanderers were prepared to go ahead if other clubs were willing, but referred to general conditions, including the lack of a suitable rink at Montreal, and finally moved that the National Hockey Association suspend operations. George Kennedy of the Canadiens seconded this. Torontos and Shamrocks fought against the plan and thought that the N.H.A. should continue. Difficulties in connection with the legal actions taken against the N.H.A. by E. Livingstone, the Toronto club owner, were explained and ultimately it was decided by a vote of three to two to suspend. Ottawa voted in favour of the motion and the meeting was declared adjourned. Naturally, the move came as a surprise, though it had been reported that neither of the Montreal clubs favoured a resumption of play. Ottawas were thought to have been favourable to a return to the National Hockey Association, but after getting a "close-up" of the actual situation, the Ottawa delegates were in accord that it would not be in the interests of the N.H.A. to resume immediately.[285]

After the NHA meeting was adjourned, the Ottawa and Montreal delegates reassembled to quiz Percy Quinn in greater depth about his intentions for the Quebec franchise. Ted Dey excused himself from this session, while Gorman stayed.

Livingstone, meanwhile, approached Dey. He figured that Ottawa would be the weak link in the NHL chain since, as far as he knew, the Senators had not signed a lease with Dey's Arena for the coming season. And Dey admitted that the two sides had a verbal agreement but nothing on paper. Livingstone then asked if *he* might lease Dey's rink for the 1918–19 season. Dey didn't respond definitively, but left the door open for further negotiation — open so wide, in fact, that

Dey travelled to Toronto on October 1 to meet with Livingstone and Percy Quinn.[286]

Back in the nation's capital, Rosenthal thought *he* had a pact for the 1918–19 season. Even Gorman, who was surely in a position to know otherwise, reported that "The Ottawa Club is not worrying over threats of the Toronto millionaire [Percy Quinn] to lease the Ottawa Arena, as Secretary Rosenthal closed on Friday last with Mr. E. P. Dey for the usual privileges at the local rink during the season of 1918–19. Mr. Dey is part-owner of the Ottawa Club, so the Senators would appear to hold the whip hand as far as the local ice situation is concerned."[287]

Rosenthal was soon to learn his agreement with Dey was worthless. Tommy Gorman kicked things off by writing in the *Citizen* that all was sweetness and light between Dey and Livingstone.

> Mr. Dey declared that there were no hard feelings toward "Eddie" Livingstone, as far as Ottawa was concerned. In fact, he intimated that the Ottawas would like to see the "stormy petrel" of hockey in the game again. Mr. Dey expressed regret that it was impossible to restore harmony in the N.H.A., but emphasized the fact that under existing conditions, it was not practicable to operate the N.H.A. He said that Percy Quinn and his associates had made a splendid impression and he predicted, if things turn out as expected, that the Shamrocks would prove a decided acquisition to the proposed circuit.
>
> It was reported that the two Toronto clubs planned an entirely new circuit, that Ottawa had been invited to enter and that a big offer had been made to Mr. Dey to operate a team here, independent of the Ottawa club, the N.H.A. and the N.H.L. The Ottawa Arena owner said he was not in a position to confirm these.[288]

A day later, Gorman added fuel to the fire, reporting that Dey was confirming he had been offered $6,000 for the use of his arena by a proposed new hockey league, and that "a Toronto magnate had offered him $12,000" in the event that Ottawa ended up hosting *two* teams in the new circuit.

> "I was approached in the Windsor Hotel after Saturday's meeting, and the proposals were then made to me," said Mr. Dey. "Eddie Livingstone made it quite clear that he

intended to remain in hockey despite the suspension of
the N.H.A., and another Toronto gentleman assured me
that they would have sufficient capital to finance a new
league, if it were necessary to launch one. The proposition involved the operation of both teams by the league
executive.... They did not inform me who would be
behind the league, but I think R. J. Fleming's name was
mentioned, and I know Eddie Livingstone said he
would sign his Toronto players immediately and operate
in it. They said steps towards the organization of a new
league would be made this week."[289]

Dey had two objectives for his visit to Toronto in 1918. The first was
to get Livingstone or Quinn to take out an option on the Ottawa arena.
The second was to be seen in the company of the two NHA exiles so
that tongues would start wagging back in Ottawa. The Toronto *Daily
News* unwittingly obliged Dey on this aspect by reporting, "There is a
chance that a new league will be formed to buck the N.H.L. That a project of that sort is brewing is deduced from the fact that Edward [sic] Dey,
the Ottawa rink owner, was in the city conferring with Percy Quinn, the
local double-barrelled magnate."[290] Quinn did his part at the National
Club by scrawling his terms on a menu card and having Livingstone witness the arrangement. The contract, signed by Dey, Quinn and
Livingstone, was as follows:

> I hereby agree and undertake to grant an option for ice
> accommodation to Percy J. Quinn to play and operate
> two (2) hockey clubs in the rink known as Dey's Arena
> at Ottawa, Ontario, in consideration for which he is to
> pay the sum of at least $500.00 a night for each game.
> Details of same to be arranged later and option to
> read for a period of 30 days.[291]

It was understood that when Dey returned to Ottawa he would talk
to his lawyer and draft a formal document for the parties to sign.[292] Dey
did not do this. Instead, he took the hastily made agreement back to
Ottawa that night, October 2, and used it to lock the hockey club out of
his facility.

The next morning, Percy Quinn, realizing he had not given Dey a
deposit, sent the Ottawa rink owner a cheque for $25. Dey set the
cheque aside for the next month and a half.

On October 4, Gorman chronicled his business partner's actions to put the next phase of his scheme into play:

> Mr. E. P. Dey, owner of the Ottawa Arena, and a third owner of the Ottawa Hockey Club, returned yesterday from Toronto and announced he had thrown in his lot with Percy Quinn, Eddie Livingstone and the other western magnates who fought against the suspension of the N.H.A. Mr. Dey stated he had gone to Toronto at the invitation of the Queen City hockey men and that, while there, he had been convinced that it would be better were a change brought about in the general situation. Hence he notified his confreres in the Ottawa Hockey Club that he would not go through with the agreement entered into last week, by which they were to have had the exclusive privileges at the Laurier Avenue rink during the coming winter.
>
> Mr. Dey explained that while he had accepted the terms of the Ottawa Club, and though he had represented the club at the N.H.A. meeting, being in accord with their decision to vote against the resumption of the N.H.A., he had changed his mind and had decided not to honour the agreement. He did not care to discuss the situation more fully, but admitted he had given an option on his rink to the Toronto men, who are supposed to be backing the new league.
>
> Later in the day it was learned that the Ottawa Arena owner had made an offer to President Bate for the franchise of the Ottawa Hockey Association under which the Ottawa Hockey Club operated. Two of the Ottawa Hockey Club owners are shareholders in the Ottawa Hockey Association, which still has control of the stock. Mr. Dey said he wished to secure control of the Ottawa Association and Club and made a cash offer for the stock, franchise and players. President Bate confirmed the announcement that he had received an offer for his stock and said he understood each individual director had also been approached by Mr. Dey.[293]

The statement put Rosenthal in a tough position. Dey's Arena was the largest covered rink in Ottawa. The Rideau Rink, having been converted into a parking garage, was no longer an option. There remained one other alternative. On October 4, the club issued a declaration to the local newspapers: "We intend to apply immediately for permission to use one of the big buildings at Lansdowne Park as an arena during the coming winter. We will make application to the Board of Control at the earliest possible moment, and will suggest that the rink be run on a co-operative plan between the Hockey Club and the city. We transformed the Aberdeen Pavilion in 1902 into one of the finest hockey rinks in the Dominion, and could repeat on this occasion."[294]

Putting a brave face on the situation, Rosenthal said, "The Ottawa Hockey Club will carry on as usual and we don't propose to submit to any hold-up on the part of the arena owner here. Mr. Dey has no further connection with the Ottawa Club. His offer to purchase the association was, as we suspected, a bluff, probably engineered by Percy Quinn, Eddie Livingstone and company."[295]

Back in Toronto, Quinn and Livingstone took the goings-on as a sign that Dey was still on board with their plans for a new league, to be called the Canadian Hockey Association, and so they acted accordingly. "The hockey war is still progressing merrily," Charlie Good wrote in his *Daily News* column.

> Percy says one thing, Querrie another. Dey of Ottawa is apparently straddling the fence, and Kennedy for a change is keeping silent. According to reports from the east, the Montreal owners of the Toronto Arena have instructed their local representative manager, Charlie Querrie, not to have any dealings with Percy Quinn unless he is prepared to place a team in the National Hockey League. They seem to be suspicious of the bona fides of the Shamrock magnate, evidently believing he is working in "cahoots" with "Eddy" Livingstone. Apparently the latter is not very popular with the Arena outfit. Quinn, however, professes that he is not worrying over any action that the outside dictators of Toronto pro-hockey may take, and he is busily engaged at present organizing a new league, which will not include the Canadiens or "Tommy" Gorman's Senators.[296]

Livingstone was "not very popular with the arena outfit" because he was involved in a pair of lawsuits against its Montreal-based owners.

NHL President Calder was keeping a low profile during these gyrations, surfacing occasionally to say that he expected the NHL to prevail. His statement of October 7 was typical: "October is a good month to hatch a new hockey league because there will be plenty of time to let it die before there is real hockey weather."[297]

On the same day, the Ottawa Hockey Club's prospects brightened somewhat, courtesy of Stewart McClenaghan, president of the Central Canada Exhibition Association. "It will, of course, be a matter for the board and council to decide, but if the plan can be worked, I don't think there will be any objection from the Exhibition Association. It was done a few years ago and there is no reason why the city should not receive some revenue from the [Aberdeen Pavilion], which is practically in use only one week of the year."[298]

Martin Rosenthal would still have to convince the Ottawa board of control and city council on the merits of the Aberdeen plan.

On October 10, the Montreal *Gazette* revealed that NHL players were starting to receive CHA contract offers. "When asked regarding a dispatch from Toronto which stated that a new hockey league had been formed and that an offer of $1,800 had been made to him by the promoters, 'Newsy' Lalonde, the star of the Canadiens for the past two years, stated that he had received the offer and that the message requested him to secure the services of [Didier] Pitre, [Georges] Vezina and [Bert] Corbeau, of the Canadiens of last season, and Sprague Cleghorn, who played with the Wanderers until he met with an accident."[299]

A few days later, George Kennedy of the Canadiens — in Toronto for the NHA's court case concerning the 228th's bond — provided a hint as to how the NHL might deal with Percy Quinn. "If Percy Quinn cuts loose from E. J. Livingstone and shows us that he is free, he may be allowed by the N.H.L. to transfer his franchise from Quebec to Toronto — and he will get ice here on the same conditions. We would like to see a second team in Toronto and, for my part, I would welcome Percy Quinn, but all Quinn will have is the Quebec players he purchases with that club when he completes his option [the players Mike Quinn had loaned to the other NHL teams, at $250 each, for the 1917–18 season, when he chose to sit out the 1917–18 season]. You know all he has is an option on the Quebec club," Kennedy said, as much for Quinn's benefit as the reporter's. "He hasn't completed the purchase yet."[300]

Dey resumed his quest to control professional hockey in Ottawa by taking a run at cornering the stock of the Ottawa Hockey Association. With this goal in mind he approached two Association shareholders, D'Arcy McGee and H. P. Butler, in early October 1918.[301] Shortly after those meetings the Ottawa Hockey Association seemed open to offers for its control over the territory and its hockey teams.

By October 18, in fact, the association had three bids to consider. The first was from an unnamed local hockey magnate who wished to purchase the entire organization and operate out of the Aberdeen Pavilion. The second was from Dey, who offered $2,500 for the use of the pro club in the NHL. The third proposal, and the one that was accepted, came from the Ottawa Hockey Club itself. Under the deal, the Hockey Club would, over time, acquire the Association's assets.[302]

That the hockey situation in the capital was up in the air is reflected by the fact that Ottawa sent no delegates to an NHL meeting held on October 19. "It was evident that the representatives appointed by the Ottawa club were ill and that they had requested a postponement," the *Citizen* reported, "but in reverse there was a rumour to the effect that the Ottawas had not yet been able to complete their rink arrangements and that L. N. Bate and his confreres might be obliged to suspend. There has been trouble between the Ottawas and Owner Dey over the Arena, and evidently the Ottawas have not yet succeeded in completing their plans for the use of Aberdeen Pavilion at Lansdowne Park."[303]

The league meeting proceeded in the Ottawa club's absence, with Frank Calder appointing himself the team's proxy. Similarly, Percy Quinn was not present, but the league did ratify his takeover of the Quebec franchise. No move was made on Quinn's proposed move to Toronto, but that city would be guaranteed at least one NHL team in 1918–19, as the league directors accepted a franchise application brought by Charlie Querrie. This brought the complement of active clubs to three: Toronto, Ottawa and the Canadiens.[304]

Three days later, the Ottawa board of control brought down its decision on the Aberdeen Pavilion. James Devitt, the superintendent of Lansdowne Park, delivered the bad news: "It would cost a small fortune to convert Aberdeen Pavilion into an arena. It would, no doubt, make an ideal rink, but since it was [last] used by the Ottawa club many of the stands have been permanently installed. The electrical fixtures are worth thousands of dollars and there would be an immense amount of work attached to their removal and their restoration. Aberdeen Pavilion is out of the question."[305]

In spite of this announcement, there were signs that the Senators had not been dealt a death blow. First of all, word leaked out that the hockey club was sending out renewal notices to its players. Then, two days later, the Toronto *World* — claiming to have spoken both to Dey and Rosenthal — scooped the Ottawa papers with a report that the hockey club and arena had worked out an exclusive five-year lease. "This kills the rumour artists' one place of refuge," the *World* said.[306]

The next morning, however, Dey denied the *World*'s report. It is possible he realized the potential trouble such a pact might cause if Quinn's option came to a court's attention. It is also likely that Dey had been advised to delay signing the five-year pact until after the option expired.

October 28 brought the realization of part of Dey's plan. Martin Rosenthal resigned, after seventeen years, from the Ottawa Hockey Club, the Ottawa Hockey Association, and the NHL's board of directors. For this reason the Ottawa team requested that the scheduled NHL meeting be postponed.

The Sens' next order of business was to neutralize Eddie Livingstone's CHA. For the upstart league to work, Livingstone needed ice time at the Arena Gardens, but the owners — who now had an NHL franchise of their own — were not about to budge. Nonetheless, as late as the end of October there remained a faint hope that the two sides might come together on a deal that would allow Livingstone to return to professional hockey. That flicker was extinguished after Tommy Gorman visited Toronto. He met with Querrie and Livingstone under the pretence that he would act as a mediator, but Charlie Good of the *Daily News* hinted that he had an ulterior motive.

> There wouldn't be any hockey difficulty if the Toronto Arena Company would come to time. A week or so ago the Montreal owners of the local ice palace were apparently inclined to "listen to reason," but after entering into negotiations with Mr. Livingstone they abruptly changed their tune. Their switch in tactics coincided with "Tommy" Gorman's visit here. The latter said he came here as a "peace" agent but evidently he was camouflaging.[307]

At this meeting, Livingstone offered his NHA franchise — and the rights to his players — to the management of the Arena for $15,000. The Arena declined; it is not clear whether they lacked interest or — considering the losses the Westmount Arena fire had caused — cash.

On November 2, Quinn's option on Dey's Arena expired. Still, the CHA insisted the option had been exercised and that Percy Quinn — not the Ottawa Senators — had the right to use the rink. When the NHL's Ottawa faction seemed to ignore the CHA's claim, Livingstone and Quinn retaliated by beginning to make offers to the Senators players.

At the NHL meeting a week later, Dey tabled the paperwork to confirm to the other owners that his Senators were locked into a five-year deal for exclusive use of the Ottawa ice. Furthermore, the Senators would not be joining any league but the NHL. George Kennedy, upon seeing Quinn's uncashed cheque, suggested it "be framed as a memorial to the Canadian Hockey Association."[308]

Dey and Gorman had brought two more documents with them. The first was an agreement to recognize the NHL as the only governing body in Canada for professional hockey — even though the older Pacific Coast Hockey Association was still going strong. The second was a contract that would bind the current member clubs to play together for the next five years. The Ottawa delegates insisted they would not remain with the league unless the latter agreement — which was clearly aimed at keeping a certain Toronto owner out of the National Hockey League — was signed by the others. All three franchises signed the papers without hesitation.

"We are stronger now than ever before," George Kennedy of the Canadiens told the Ottawa *Journal*. "Livingstone has made us a real league. We were more or less disjointed but now we are solid. We owe Eddie Livingstone a vote of thanks for what he has done for us. He has created a lot of newspaper talk as well, which will not do any harm."[309]

The league addressed the issue of Percy Quinn and his Quebec franchise by voting to issue an ultimatum: either declare his intentions regarding the franchise within forty-eight hours or be left out of the league. It was also hinted that his ownership of the Quebec franchise would be revoked.

The Montreal *Star* took a wry view of the situation. "They have given Percy Quinn short shrift. Shorter than the Allies gave the German High Command to accept Armistice terms," it said on November 11, 1918. "The latter had seventy-two hours; Quinn only got forty-eight and it is announced on the authority of Frank Calder, President of the National Hockey League, that unless he announces his decision by this evening, he will be 'a dead cock in the pit' as far as professional Hockey is concerned this year, and he will lose the six hundred dollars he has put up as part payment for the Quebec franchise."[310]

"It is to laugh," Livingstone snorted in reply. "The N.H.L. meeting Saturday was no exception to their rule. A lot of fabrication for the benefit of the players, the fooling of the public, and the 'scaring' of Mr. Quinn." He added that, as far as he was concerned, nothing had changed. Quinn still had control over who would and would not play at Dey's

Arena, while the CHA also lay claim to the Jubilee rink in Montreal, "and Quebec is no doubt still open to the highest bidder." He boasted that he and Quinn held the rights to enough players to stock two teams, and that they had the wherewithal to outbid the NHL for any players who were not under contract.[311]

Livingstone also expressed confidence in Quinn: "Now, strange to say, in fact unbelievably so, they expect Mr. Quinn to doublecross me, and in that possibility they are placing all their hope. The only way I can account for this is that they are judging Mr. Quinn by [their own track record]. However, they are grasping at the proverbial drowning man's straw, for any person who has had the privilege of being associated with the president of the Shamrock Club in business or in sports knows his integrity."[312]

Speaking for himself, Quinn, who had missed the last two NHL meetings, saw the shell game Dey was playing with the Ottawa arena as a betrayal. And to add insult to injury, Calder — wearing his president's hat — had been the one to issue the NHL's ultimatum against him. The only problem was that Calder — acting as league secretary — had not sent Quinn a formal notice after the meeting, an omission that Quinn pointed out to the press: "I have seen or heard nothing about the N.H.L. proposition except what I have read in the papers, and I have not decided what I will do or whether or not I will do anything."[313]

Word leaked to the press on November 11 that Quinn might seek an injunction against Dey in an attempt to block the NHL from playing in Ottawa until his case could be judged.

To reduce the chances of a ruling against him, Dey returned Quinn's uncashed deposit cheque. As for the question of the timing of the conflicting contracts, Tommy Gorman was there to make everything perfectly clear in the pages of the Ottawa *Citizen*:

> The Ottawa Hockey Club's agreement to play at the Laurier Avenue Arena was, according to its officers, drawn up and signed on November 4, two days after the expiration of Percy Quinn's option. Quinn had sent Mr. Dey a cheque for $25 to bind his option, but Mr. Dey has never cashed the cheque and will, though he has the legal right to retain it, return it to the Shamrock president. Mr. Dey states that when Quinn drew up the option, the Canadian Leaguers led him to believe that they would get ice at Toronto and place two teams in Ottawa. After that they made no move and Percy Quinn's option automatically lapsed.[314]

Quinn gave Dey one last chance to reverse his position in a telegram sent on November 14:

> Ottawa Press dispatch says you would welcome any legal action I care to take to test validity of our agreement, which you know full well is authentic; is this true? If so, no use my going to Ottawa to see you in regard to same. Please wire me reply at once, and failing to hear from you, you will understand I will be obliged to take immediate action to protect my own interests.[315]

There was no reply, which left Quinn no choice but to follow through on his threat. A writ of summons was issued by Quinn's solicitors, MacDonell & Boland, the next day. And, as had been hinted a few days earlier, Quinn tried to have the courts restrain Dey from leasing his arena until the court could decide whether his option had been exercised.[316]

There were two reactions to the news of the lawsuit. The first came from Frank Calder.

"Sorry you cannot be here Saturday," he wired. "In view of the association of your name with another league, of which I have seen proof, I advise you to state immediately what you intend to do regarding your franchise in the National Hockey League."[317]

This time it was Quinn who did not answer, and the Quebec franchise was suspended for the NHL's 1918–19 season. Calder telegraphed as much to Quinn at the Royal Insurance Company the next day. What he failed to mention was that Quinn could appeal to the league's board of directors to overturn the franchise suspension. Quinn had to get that advice from the newspapers.

He replied the same day: "Wire received. Responsibility yours. If your associates had the proper conception of what honour means you would not be placed in your present serious predicament. I am always open to deal with people in an above-board way, but no other."[318]

Ted Dey's response to the lawsuit was more cutting. After Quinn's Shamrocks were suspended, he fired off a letter to President Calder calling for the Quebec players to be redistributed among the three remaining NHL clubs.[319] If Quinn needed any further evidence that he had been played, this was it. Calder obliged, allowing all of the Quebec players who were loaned in 1917–18 to remain on the same team for 1918–19. This time, no one from Quebec was compensated. It marked the second time in two years that Calder had orchestrated the theft of players' contracts from an antagonist, while rewarding those teams that were loyal to him.

Simply put, it was the tactic of a bully — of power and fear, of reward versus punishment, of tossing integrity and ethics to the wind.

As a result, Calder's power base was strengthened.

Such was the glorious beginning of the National Hockey League.

The CHA side suffered another blow two days later when the first appellate court in Toronto dismissed the case of *Toronto Hockey Club v. Ottawa Hockey Association et al.*[320] Calder took the court's ruling as another opportunity to split the Livingstone-Quinn compact. "True, his franchise was suspended by me last Saturday," Calder told the *Mail and Empire*, "but the suspension will be lifted if he asks for it within a reasonable time and comes to us without an [encumbrance]."[321]

Again, Quinn was silent.

As November 1918 drew to a close, the options for Quinn and Livingstone were dwindling rapidly. They were not welcome at the Ottawa or Toronto arenas, Livingstone's court case had reached a dead end, and Quinn had been shut out of the NHL. Three avenues remained open to the duo. The first was exploited when they served Ted Dey with an order to appear in court. The second would become available to them on December 1, when the Jubilee rink lease would be thrown open to bidders. And finally, Livingstone felt certain that there was something fishy about the votes cast by George Kennedy, the owner of the Montreal Canadiens, at NHA meetings.

To raise money, Kennedy had sold twelve of his fifty shares in the National Hockey Association to the Brunswick-Balke-Collender Company, the manufacturer of billiard tables and bowling equipment. Since that deal, made two years beforehand, Kennedy had continued to vote the full fifty shares at NHA meetings without declaring that some were being cast by proxy. Livingstone and Quinn demanded a meeting of the National Hockey Association to have all of those votes in which Kennedy had participated declared *ultra vires*, or "outside the law."

The pair were able to force one last National Hockey Association meeting, which was held on December 11, 1918. It did not go well for the CHA promoters. The Brunswick company sided with George Kennedy, which placed the defunct league's votes beyond reproach.

W. M. Gladish reported on the rest of the meeting in the Ottawa *Journal*:

> There are absolutely no new developments in connection with the holding of the burlesque session of the National Hockey Association in Montreal on Wednesday, according to information secured at the Ottawa Hockey

Club yesterday. The meeting became a true "wake" over the remains of the dead Association. Like a true wake, there was many a scrap. The hockey moguls got rid of a lot of loose words — but not one definite action was taken during the meeting, it is reported. The only "result" of the confab was that Livingstone & Company discovered that they did not control the pro hockey world and that they could not reach the National Hockey League through the N.H.A.[322]

In the meantime, the battle of the Jubilee rink in Montreal was also coming to an unsatisfying end. Lucien Riopel, who had arranged for Kennedy to use the Jubilee in the 1917–18 season after the Westmount Arena burned down, was refusing to surrender control of the rink to its new leaseholder, Albert Allard. Allard had negotiated a lease with the Jubilee board, then talked with Livingstone and Quinn about having them bid for ice time once he took possession. Not so fast, Riopel warned, claiming he had signed a new lease with the Jubilee's accountant *before* the Allard agreement was signed.[323]

The problem for Riopel was that the Jubilee's board of directors argued the accountant was not authorized to make the deal. Riopel, through his occupation of the rink, was able to keep Allard out of the Jubilee for the entire 1918–19 hockey season. George Kennedy's Canadiens were thereby able to play there under this illegal arrangement.

The Quebec courts later sided with Allard's claim and ordered Riopel to pay rent for the time he occupied the Jubilee past his lease's expiration.[324] Curiously, Allard expressed concern that Kennedy might do "an injury to the rink" and sought advice from his lawyer.[325] Just over four months later, the Jubilee burned down — the second Montreal arena to be engulfed in flames within two years.

(Just in time for the 1919–20 season, the Canadiens moved into a brand new facility in the community of Mount Royal.)

After the December 11 meeting, Frank Calder sought a wind-up order for the National Hockey Association.[326] Never again would the old NHA be a tool to be used against the new league. (Calder never got around to closing the NHA's bank account, however: court documents from 1922 show that cheques were still being made payable to him as the NHA's president.)

Livingstone kept a low profile, saying little and still trying to work things out behind closed doors. When he finally broke his silence, it was to once again praise Quinn.

Ever since the seeming victory of the Arena crowd and
their confederates in high-hockey there has been a del-
uge of requests for an explanation of the whole situation.
More than that, my many friends have urged that the
motives of Mr. Percy Quinn and myself in this unfortunate fight be truthfully set forth, and the incidents that
have led to the existing deplorable conditions which spell
the death knell of professional hockey hereabouts, be
outlined. Mr. Quinn's motives are easily accounted for.
They are actuated by love of fair play; good sportsmanship in its truest sense; the inability to sit back and
become an accessory to anything mean or small; the
belief in the future of hockey, properly conducted, professional or amateur. I know that these are Mr. Quinn's
ideals. In my own case one can only say I hope my ideals
are similar to his. What Mr. Quinn has unselfishly done
for me constitutes a debt that can never be repaid; what,
too, he is endeavouring to do for hockey places a heavy
obligation on the whole sporting public."[327]

The last hope for the 1918–19 season, as far as Livingstone and
Quinn were concerned, was the action against Ted Dey. Livingstone
defended his decision to file the suit, in the Toronto *Daily News*.

"Why take sporting matters into the courts?" you may
ask. Just this: There is no other way of protecting our
rights to valuable property against people who hit
below the belt. Canadiens are using our ice in Montreal,
Ottawas our ice in Ottawa. The Toronto Arena has
appropriated our Toronto Hockey Club players, while
Mr. Quinn's men have been divided up as has best suited our opponents. Surely, there is nothing in the breaking of written agreements in the violation of iron-
bound contracts to be condoned. Had we condescend-
ed to stoop to similar methods the C.H.A. would be in
operation today."[328]

The first phase of the case took place in Ottawa on December 23;
Dey, Clint Benedict and Eddie Gerard were called to testify. The latter
two would not add anything of substance to the case, except to deny that
Dey had talked to them about Mr. Quinn.

Dey, on the other hand, would admit to a number of things under oath. Chief among those was that he had signed an agreement with Quinn on October 2. John Boland, Livingstone's attorney, cross-examined Dey and drew more out of the Ottawa rink owner. Dey, for instance, admitted that the deal for Rosenthal's shares was reached before the Quinn option expired, and that Tommy Gorman was his scheming partner:

> Boland: How many were in the syndicate 1917 and 1918?
>
> Dey: Three of us.
>
> Boland: Yourself, Mr. Gorman and Mr. Rosenthal.
>
> Dey: Yes.
>
> Boland: And today I believe the syndicate is composed of Mr. Gorman and yourself?
>
> Dey: Yes.
>
> Boland: Mr. Rosenthal transferred his interest to you?
>
> Dey: I bought it out.
>
> Boland: So you control two-thirds and Mr. Gorman one-third?
>
> Dey: No, each one-half.
>
> Boland: What was your interest in the 1917 and 1918 season?
>
> Dey: One-third.
>
> Boland: And Mr. Rosenthal had one-third?
>
> Dey: And Mr. Gorman one-third in 1917 and 1918.
>
> Boland: Notwithstanding you acquired all Mr. Rosenthal's interest, you made a new arrangement with Mr. Gorman and he and you have a half interest?
>
> Dey: Yes.
>
> Boland: When was this arrangement made whereby you acquired Mr. Rosenthal's interest?
>
> Dey: About the 4th of December.
>
> Boland: Not before the 4th of December?
>
> Dey: No.

Boland: When did Mr. Rosenthal resign from the Ottawa Hockey Club?

Dey: I would not be able to say in regard to that.

Boland: I think I can tell you.

Dey: I didn't pay any attention to that. I think it was in the paper.

Boland: I think I can tell you, it was the last Saturday in October — October 26th. I believe that was the date Mr. Rosenthal published in the paper the statement he was resigning from office in the Ottawa Hockey Club and had transferred his interest.

Dey: Yes, that was in the Ottawa Hockey Club.

Boland: But that date he didn't transfer his interest in the syndicate of three?

Dey: Yes.

Boland: To whom did he transfer his interest?

Dey: To Mr. Gorman and myself, in equal shares.

Boland: So we can say [that] Mr. Rosenthal, on October 26th, would have no interest in the Ottawa Hockey Club?

Dey: The stock had not been handed over.

Boland: But apparently it was agreed then that Mr. Rosenthal should transfer his interest in the syndicate of the Ottawa Hockey Club to Mr. Gorman and yourself?

Dey: Yes...[329]

Boland: In the letter produced as Exhibit 6, there is reference to an arrangement with the Royal Bank for an accommodation [that] you apparently desired. What was this for, Mr. Dey?

Dey: I didn't speak to Mr. Quinn about that.

Boland: You say you did not discuss any arrangement with Mr. Quinn?

Dey: Not about that.

Boland:To what does he make reference?

Dey:I could not tell you.

Boland:You don't know?

Dey:No.

Boland:Were you at the time negotiating for the purchase of the Ottawa Hockey syndicate?

Dey:Yes.[330]

On December 26, the scheduled date of the Ottawa Senators' first home game of 1918–19, Mr. Justice Robert Franklin Sutherland turned down Percy Quinn's request for an injunction and moved to have the case held over for a further hearing on January 14.[331] Gorman and Dey subsequently announced they would waive their exclusive rights to Dey's Arena.[332] It was an empty gesture, given that Quinn and Livingstone's players had been stripped from them by the NHL teams, and signed to year-long contracts.

In order for the CHA to operate, Quinn and Livvy would have to raid players already under contract, or else sign amateurs. The latter plan would saddle the duo with an inferior league to the NHL, while the former would court legal action.

When the next hearing of *Quinn v. Dey* convened, Quinn was on the stand. The Quebec Shamrocks owner refuted Dey's testimony that he had not talked about arranging a loan with the Royal Bank of Canada.

Quinn:I was to obtain him a loan of money of $2,400 to see if he couldn't get control of the Ottawa Hockey Club and [then] combine them in with this league I was going to form. It was for that reason that he was so extremely friendly with me.[333]

The most telling part of Quinn's testimony came when he was asked why he had been dealing with Dey. Dey's lawyer, C. J. R. Bethune, questioned Quinn.

Bethune:What was your idea in securing the exclusive use of the Arena Rink at Ottawa?

Quinn:That was the idea, a new hockey league.

Bethune:In point of fact have you got up
such a club?

Quinn:No, not so far. We were prevented
owing to Mr. Dey's action in this matter.

Bethune:You mean Mr. Dey entering into
this agreement with the Ottawa Club?

Quinn:Blocked us entirely.

Bethune:Had it not been for that, would
you, do you think, have been able to
get together a club?

Quinn:We certainly would have gone
through with it, positively."[334]

Quinn's case was dismissed the following week. The court ruled that the agreement, as written, was vague and would not meet the criteria necessary to prove a fraud had occurred. It was also determined that the option had expired without a contract being signed.[335] Unfortunately for Quinn, the court could not rule on Dey's ethics, merely whether he broke a law or committed a tort.

Quinn and Livingstone would make other attempts to launch the CHA, but this was the closest the pair would come to succeeding.

By 1925, Quinn had decided he'd had enough of pro hockey, and he took up a new career representing those victimized by society. As a member of Toronto city council, even Quinn's most vociferous critics admitted he stood up first and foremost for those who were wronged. For instance, it was Quinn's dogged determination that led to the city's libraries being open on Sundays.

Dey's plan had been nearly flawless. Even if Livingstone and Quinn had got the Canadian Hockey Association up and running, Dey would have ended up with control of a team. Because of Gorman's influence over the Ottawa media, Dey would have had to include him in any plans as well, or risk having his every move exposed in the *Citizen*. And Dey and Gorman wound up with the greater prize: the Ottawa Senators, a team on the verge of becoming the NHL's first dynasty. And with the playing pact signed in November 1918, they had managed to tie the other National Hockey League teams to them for an extended period. In so doing, Gorman and Dey ushered in an era of stability and expansion for the NHL — at the expense of Martin Rosenthal, Percy Quinn and Eddie Livingstone.

Chapter 16

The Short, Chaotic Life of the Toronto Arenas

*Livingstone has made us a real league. We were more or less
disjointed but now we are solid. We owe Eddie Livingstone a
vote of thanks for what he has done for us.*

— George Kennedy, 1918

*T*he NHL governors may have owed Eddie Livingstone a debt of
gratitude, as George Kennedy put it — no doubt with tongue
planted firmly in cheek — but Livvy was interested solely in the tangible assets the fledgling league owed him. And it would be up to the
courts to help him collect.

The man to whom Livingstone had entrusted his players, Charles
Huston, departed for a job in Ottawa in February 1918, leaving
Charlie Querrie as the interim manager of the Toronto hockey club.
The Arena had assumed responsibility for an NHL franchise for the
1917–18 season only, and was under orders to solve the Toronto
situation in that time or else return the franchise to the league.
A monkey wrench was thrown into the works when the Toronto
club won the 1918 Stanley Cup championship. Querrie had tasted
success — after failing in his previous attempts, most notably with
the Tecumsehs — and wanted more. To achieve that end, Eddie
Livingstone would have to be squeezed out once and for all.
Unfortunately, Livingstone was not willing to sell his NHA franchise
or its players.

The NHL was in a bind. The league had only been intended as a
means of buying time until the owners could get Livingstone safely
out of the way; once that was done, the NHA was to be resurrected

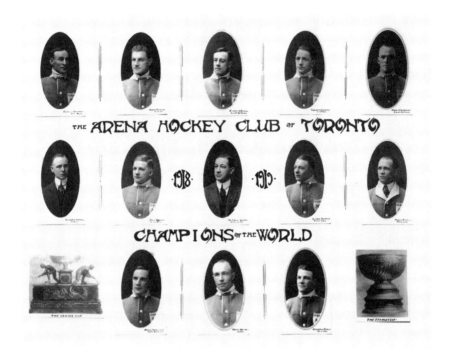

The 1918–19 Toronto Arenas
Top (l to r): Russell Crawford, Harry Meeking, Kenneth Randall,
Corbett Dennenny, Harry Cameron.
Middle: Richard Carroll (coach), Jack Adams, Charlie Querrie,
Alfred Skinner, Frank Carroll (trainer).
Bottom: Harry Mummery, Harry Holmes, Reginald Noble.
The composite features the team's two championship trophies:
O'Brien Trophy (lower left), and an early Stanley Cup, with the original rings.

for the 1918–19 schedule. The Torontos' success meant the cost of getting rid of Livingstone had gone up.

Way up.

The management of the Arena Gardens was already on the hook to hand over 60 percent of the club's profits. On March 7, Tommy Gorman estimated the total cost of renting Livingstone's team at about $9,000. It would have taken even more to buy Livingstone's team outright. And then there was the question of the Stanley Cup box office receipts, which amounted to more than $20,000. Yet, when it came time to cut a cheque, the Arena offered the princely sum of $5,958.54, along with a memorandum under which Livingstone would agree to relinquish any further claim on profits. Livingstone did not accept that deal, but kept on negotiating, through the spring and into the summer, to improve the amount offered and to extricate himself from the clutches of the NHA/NHL mess.

The Arena did make a $7,000 offer for the franchise and players, but this was well below the figure the Livingstone was expecting, and so on June 20, 1918, he sued the Arena Gardens for $20,400.50.[336] Livingstone had been preparing for an impasse with the Arena officials. By early July he was approaching Percy Thompson about operating his NHA team in Hamilton. The manager of the Hamilton rink was receptive to the idea of professional hockey being played at his facility.

As the summer of 1918 dragged on, so did Livingstone's lawsuit. He and his lawyer, John Boland, journeyed to Montreal in September to deal directly with the Arena Gardens ownership. Livingstone hoped that by going over Querrie's head a compromise could be reached, but he found the Montreal board was even more firmly set against him than the Toronto manager. In the end, Arena executive A. B. Claxton was served with a summons.

Querrie met with Claxton the next day for a briefing. The Arena was prepared to operate with Percy Quinn's transferred Quebec franchise as its tenant, but the two men soon found out that, because of the CHA connection, the Shamrocks solution would only serve to let Livingstone back into professional hockey. The only way of avoiding the man Gorman called hockey's "stormy petrel" was to return to the clutches of Calder and his cronies.

Livingstone, meanwhile, redoubled his efforts towards getting his team back into a restored NHA. With that in mind, he announced that he would be attending the September 28 gathering of the old Association — his first since February 1917. As noted in Chapter 15, Livingstone's first action at that gathering was to nominate Harvey Pulford to take Frank Calder's place as president. The ploy caught Tommy Gorman off guard and he actually seconded the motion. When his error was pointed out, Gorman withdrew his support, claiming that he thought the NHA post was vacant and that Pulford, an Ottawa man, would have represented the Senators' interests. Rebuffed, Livingstone withdrew his motion.

This led to a fierce exchange between Sam Lichtenhein and George Kennedy on one side and Livingstone on the other. The two Montreal magnates stated flatly that they would not play in any league with the man from Toronto. Then Kennedy softened his stance a bit, saying that he might reconsider if Livingstone dropped his court actions. Considering the way the meeting was going, there was little chance of this happening.

It is odd that Sam Lichtenhein was permitted to vote at the meeting, since he had all but abandoned his fellow owners after the Montreal Arena fire of January 1918, and had made no moves to show he planned to ice a team in the coming season. But Calder needed Lichtenhein's vote, and Sam was only too willing to help his fellow Montrealer freeze Livingstone out. As added insurance, Tom Wall's ballot was voided. The rationale was that Wall should only be an observer because he had not operated his old Tecumseh franchise for several seasons. The Montreal masters conveniently ignored that Livingstone kept the team active through 1915, and that the NHA had approved the use of the franchise by the 228th Battalion in 1916–17.[337]

The fireworks continued into the evening as various factions met independently until midnight.

The net result of the meeting was that the NHA again suspended operations for the 1918–19 season.

A hint of what the future might hold came on September 30 when Kennedy talked to the press. His comments would be the basis upon which the Arena Gardens built its defence against Livingstone. "This talk about Livingstone owning the Toronto players and Quinn owning the Quebec players is all rot," Kennedy said. "Livingstone owns no players at all, only fifty shares in the National Hockey Association. Quinn only owns such players as belonged to Quebec last season, and had not been bought by other clubs. The Toronto players belong as a body to the National Hockey League, for they were only loaned to the Toronto Arena Company, though Livingstone tried to make the Arena Company believe that he controlled those players."[338]

The Canadiens' owner did not elaborate as to the grounds on which the Toronto players belonged to the NHL.

Afterwards, the Toronto Arena Company recalled Charlie Querrie to Montreal to give him his instructions. The management was fearful that if Livingstone won a lawsuit, the company would not only lose the hockey team but the rink as well. Therefore it was spinning off the hockey club and putting Querrie in charge, giving him a free hand to act on the Arena's behalf against Livingstone. His first move was to declare that the Arena would book no professional hockey games that did not involve NHL teams.

This severing of ties between building and team signalled the birth of a new Toronto franchise, and provides further evidence that the Arena never had any intention of paying Livingstone. And even if Livvy won his case, the Arena reasoned, its liability would be limited to the 1917–18 season — the hockey team, now a separate corporate entity, would be hit with any damages assessed after that time.

Hubert Vearncombe, the Arena Company's treasurer, tendered the Toronto Arena Hockey Club's request for a franchise, written on Windsor Hotel stationery, when the NHL met on October 19, 1918.

> Dear Sir:
>
> We hereby make application for franchise rights to become a member and partner of the National Hockey League on terms to be mutually agreed upon.
>
> Yours Truly,
>
> Toronto Arena Hockey Club
>
> H. Vearncombe
> CEO, Treasurer[339]

Calder's acceptance of the agreement proves that the Arenas were born after October 19, 1918. What makes this particularly interesting is that all the record books, and indeed the Stanley Cup itself, show the Arenas as the 1918 Cup champions — but that series was played the previous March, *seven months earlier.* The engraving of champions' names into the coveted silver bowl wasn't a priority in those hectic, contentious days. The league finally corrected its oversight in 1947, when it added the names of all the teams that had originally been left off the trophy. Apparently, the history of the Toronto franchise had been forgotten, because the engraver dutifully etched the words "Toronto Arenas" — and not "Blueshirts" or even "Toronto HC" — in the space reserved for the 1918 champs.

An advertisement in the Toronto Daily News promoting the 1918 Stanley Cup championship series.

Querrie accompanied Vearncombe to the NHL's October meeting. On paper, the two men were to be the owners of the Toronto Arena Hockey Club, while the Toronto Arena Company would make its money by leasing the ice to the team. To perpetuate the charade, the temporary franchise held by the Arena Gardens Hockey Club, whose name first appeared in the minutes of the NHL meeting of February 1918, was returned to the league. The approval of a permanent franchise by George Kennedy and Frank Calder — the latter acting on behalf of the absent Martin Rosenthal — was a foregone conclusion. For no money down and the promise to split profits with the league until $5,000 was paid, the Toronto Arenas were formally born.[340]

There is no definitive record as to whether the league got that money or Calder pocketed it, but bankruptcy ledgers show there were cheques made payable to "Frank Calder, *NHA* President" (emphasis ours). Neither the NHL's books nor Calder's financial records were ever subjected to independent audits, so this is a mystery that will probably never be solved.

Upon returning to Toronto, Querrie set to work preparing the Arena Gardens for the new hockey season. Harry Holmes, the goaltender for the 1918 championship team, dropped by the rink for a visit; ominously, the former Seattle Metropolitan let it be known that he would return to the western league if the Patricks called. His loyalty to the Patrick brothers was greater than the draw of helping defend Toronto's Stanley Cup championship.

Querrie got more bad news when Mr. Justice Haughton Lennox ruled that Livingstone's suit against the Arena Gardens would go to trial. Lennox denied a request by the Toronto Hockey Club to have the $5,958.54 cheque from the Arena declared a "payment on account," so Livingstone did not cash the cheque.[341]

For a brief time it appeared as if the Arena Company might negotiate a settlement with Livingstone. Even Frank Calder was quietly optimistic when talking to reporters. Given that Livingstone was not making any headway in his appeal against the old NHA and its clubs, Eustache Bird, the Arena's managing director, figured he held the upper hand. Livingstone's appeal of his case against the NHA and its clubs went before the Supreme Court of Ontario on October 28, 1918, and after hearing arguments for one day the justices seemed to be showing little sympathy towards Livingstone's position. Bird used this as an excuse to kill the settlement talks and renew the rink's ban on Livingstone.

When Tommy Gorman visited Toronto a few days later, he found that even his legendary powers of persuasion could not reopen talks between the two sides. He returned to Ottawa.

The NHL meeting of November 9, 1918, would see one Livingstone innovation survive, at least temporarily: the split season was approved for another year. Later in the proceedings, Frank Calder was rewarded for his leadership as the board elected him to a five-year term as president. Perhaps emboldened by the long-term guarantee of a job, Calder waded into the war between the Toronto Arena Company and Eddie Livingstone, warning players not to sign with either the Toronto Hockey Club or Percy Quinn's team.

Livingstone continued to maintain that the former NHA players, as a body, all became free agents when the Association suspended. George Kennedy, never one to keep his opinions to himself, disagreed vehemently: "[Livingstone and Quinn] haven't a leg to stand on. The players they claim are free agents are no such thing. Let them rave. It doesn't worry any of the people associated with me in the National Hockey League."[342]

In typical stubborn fashion, Livingstone responded by sending contracts for the 1918–19 season to his Toronto Hockey Club players. The players, for their part, sat back and waited to see who would come out on top.

The eastern owners had reason to cheer on November 20. After several days of deliberation, Sir William Meredith, the Chief Justice of the Supreme Court of Ontario, dismissed Livingstone's appeal. The case against the old NHA and its member clubs seemed dead, and it also appeared unlikely that any similar action would have much chance of success. Livingstone had stated that he intended to appeal all the way to the Supreme Court of Canada, but he now retreated from that position. The Arena Gardens board was overjoyed with Livingstone's legal defeat and passed a resolution "that the Arena Gardens of Toronto, Ltd., has decided not to consider leasing of the ice during the coming season to any professional hockey teams other than those of the N.H.L."[343] With this statement, the board made a formal policy of the position Charlie Querrie had been espousing for weeks.

Undeterred, Livingstone stepped up his efforts to sign his players to CHA contracts. By now he was promising to pay them a salary even if the upstart league did not operate. Querrie took the news in stride. "So the C.H.A. is going to hire and pay players, whether they play or not. That's nice — for the players. No wonder they won't sign up to now. Still, we will open up practices at the Arena December 10 and I shouldn't wonder if we had a team."[344]

Early December found Livingstone conferring in Ottawa with Tommy Gorman and Ted Dey, the Senators owners, hoping they might influence Calder to convince the Arena Company to settle the Toronto situation. "Have talked with Calder re: your suggestions," they informed him. "He is willing to help straighten things out, but declines to move until you make out proposition in writing, on receipt of which he will call us to Montreal to try and carry out your plans. Believe this would be most satisfactory plan."[345]

There was just one hitch in the Ottawa mediation. Gorman and Calder twisted the situation to make it appear as if Livingstone was desperate to get out of the hockey business.

Livingstone replied to Gorman: "In view of Dey's and your voluntary statement, which resulted from Calder's urgent request for me to communicate with you two when in Ottawa, that the Ottawa club were anxious to do anything on earth to bring the Arena Company to its senses, I am at a loss to understand what you refer to by my proposition. I believe you also wired me that I was at full liberty to publish your letters. Many thanks for this privilege, which I shall avail myself of shortly no doubt."[346]

Within days, Frank Calder would use his deciding ballot at the NHA meeting to scuttle any hope Livingstone might have had of resurrecting the old league.

On the west coast, a new storm was brewing for Frank Calder.

The Patrick brothers were not impressed with the NHL's 1918–19 schedule, which called for the regular season to end on March 13, to be followed by a league playoff series. The problem was that the Pacific Coast Hockey Association's schedule had been drawn up and forwarded to the eastern owners with word that the NHL champions would be expected on the west coast to begin the Stanley Cup finals on the *fourteenth*. The NHL had completely disregarded the Patricks' request. For the time being, Calder refused to revise his league's schedule. The only alterations he made were to schedule an exhibition game to test some new rules and to repeal the split-season format that Livingstone had introduced. The Patricks were displeased, but they elected to let the issue drift to the background while they prepared for the new season.

Meanwhile, Eddie Livingstone could only watch as his players defected to the Arena club. One by one they appeared on the Arena Gardens ice, trusting the people who had paid them the year before. Livingstone again threatened injunctions against the NHL, this time to bar his players from taking the ice in any league game. "Any negotiations we will have with the N.H.L. will be in the nature of an ultimatum," he warned. "We have them where we want them, and we are going ahead with our injunctions and other legal proceedings."[347]

With opening night fast approaching, Charlie Querrie responded quickly. Said the Arenas manager: "The hockey public can take it from me that there will be no interference by E. J. Livingstone, or those who are associated with him, in Monday night's opening professional game between the Toronto team and the Canadiens of Montreal. A lot of people have the idea that Mr. Livingstone is going to tie the Arena up Monday night with an injunction. Eminent legal authorities have assured me that he cannot do that. He may annoy us, but he cannot stop us from playing, and there will surely be a game here on Monday night."[348]

Livingstone issued a statement contradicting Querrie's assertions, and threatened to file an injunction to prevent the Arenas' home opener from being played. Livvy's ally, Percy Quinn, even tried to fine the Canadiens' Joe Hall, who had been Quebec property, for playing in the game. But Hall didn't take the punishment seriously, and the game went off without incident. On December 23, 1918, the Toronto players took the ice in new uniforms — which borrowed from the colour scheme of a local amateur team, the Ashalantas — signifying the change in ownership and the severing of their ties to the Blueshirts legacy.[349] Harry Mummery, who was hospitalized with influenza, was the only player who would miss the game.

The match itself was an indifferent affair, with only goaltenders Harry Holmes and George Vezina appearing to be interested in the proceedings. Livingstone's threats of legal action — and the game's proximity to the Christmas holiday — scared away all but 2,500 fans, who witnessed the Canadiens beat Toronto, 4–3.

The defending Stanley Cup champions were dealt another blow on Christmas Eve, when Ken Randall was arrested and charged with receiving stolen goods, namely a scarf and a pair of neckties from the Robert Simpson Company's department store on Yonge Street. Randall compounded the situation by jumping bail to play in Ottawa on Boxing Day when he should have been at his court hearing. A warrant for Randall's arrest was issued, while Querrie, who had put up the bail money, was out of pocket to the tune of several hundred dollars.[350]

The game in Ottawa, a 5–2 Arenas loss, was Harry Holmes's last in a Toronto uniform. The goaltender, on loan from the Seattle Metropolitans, was recalled by his PCHA club after the man who had taken his place in the Seattle net, Hec Fowler, signed up for military service. Despite losing his first two games of 1918–19, Holmes's 4.50 goals-against average was actually better than the 4.73 mark he had posted the year before, when he led Toronto to a Stanley Cup title over his old team. The transaction left Querrie scrambling for a netminder. He found a willing substitute in Bert Lindsay, the former PCHA All-Star and Renfrew Millionaire who had first come to prominence in 1908 as one of the ringers recruited for Edmonton's Stanley Cup challenge. Unfortunately for both Lindsay and Querrie, the 37-year-old netminder was rusty — he hadn't played since the previous January, when the Wanderers withdrew from the NHL — and he would prove to be well past his prime.

On the last day of 1918 the Arenas finally won a game, pulling off a 4–2 victory over Ottawa and ending their three-game losing skid. It didn't stop the gossip from flying. On January 3, Charlie Good of the *Daily News* quoted manager Dick Carroll as saying that none of his players was under contract. Carroll claimed that they were waiting to see how the conflict between Livingstone and the Arena played out before making any commitments.[351] Then came word that Ken Randall, who still faced a charge of receiving stolen goods, was on the trading block. Randall seemed reconciled to the idea, and even said he looked forward to playing with a contender, but the spirited defenceman turned out for practice on January 6 after being assured he would play for the Arenas the next evening. He would continue to press management to trade or release him throughout the rest of the season.[352]

On January 8, Randall was remanded on $200 bail and ordered to appear in court five days later. The charges were eventually dropped when it could not be proved that Randall knew the items, which he had received from a Simpsons employee, were stolen.

By January 13, the Arenas were mired in last place with a 1–6 record, their latest indignity being a 13–3 pasting in Montreal at the hands of the Canadiens. Elmer Ferguson couldn't help but notice, and as a culprit he nominated the Quebec government's refusal to date to declare Prohibition.

> Either the players are not trying to win or they are in no condition to play, possibly a combination of both. One player of the club, an athlete noted for his conscientious efforts and who invariably gives his best, is quoted as having said that three members of the team have forgotten all thought of training rules and routine the instant they left Toronto, and on striking a "wet" territory had promptly made a gallant effort to drown out the memories of a long drought in Dryville.

However true this may be, Toronto certainly looked anything but a champion hockey team Saturday night. They played like a collection of Class XX amateurs. They were out-footed in a pitiable manner by the shifty Canadiens, and early in the game gave up any effort at checking back.[353]

Two of the revellers, Harry Cameron and Reg Noble, were suspended indefinitely for breaking training. Noble would return to the lineup a week later, while Cameron, the last of the original Blueshirts, was sent to Ottawa. He had been deemed expendable after Querrie signed up Dave Ritchie, the former Quebec defenceman who had split the 1917–18 season between the Wanderers and Senators. It was hoped that Ritchie and the recovering Harry Mummery would shore up the defence corps that had been less than spectacular with Randall, Cameron and Noble.

The shake-up worked as the Arenas took Ottawa in their next game, 5–2, despite Randall being ejected from the game by referee Steve Vair.

In Montreal, President Calder found himself under increased pressure from Stanley Cup trustee William Foran to reorganize the NHL schedule to suit that of the PCHA.

While others had been making plans to ring in the new year of 1919, Frank Patrick was campaigning to get the Stanley Cup scheduling conflict settled. Said the coast league president, "Unless the National Hockey Association rearranges its schedule to permit the winning team [to be] on the coast in time to meet the Pacific Coast Hockey Association champions in the world's series, in the first game around March 17, an appeal will be taken to the Stanley Cup trustee, William Foran, and the Easterners asked to comply with the conditions governing cup series set forth in the agreement drafted and signed by the rival leagues three years ago."[354]

Calder's response had been to send a letter to the NHL owners seeking a discussion on the topic at their January 5, 1919, meeting.[355] A proposal to drop the last three games of the schedule and the playoffs was considered, but still nothing concrete was approved.

On January 23, Calder finally buckled under the pressure and released a new timetable. The revised race for the championship would feature a playoff series, yet still allow the winner time to travel west for the Stanley Cup series. Aware of the flagging fan interest in Toronto,

Calder opted to revive that Livingstone innovation, the split season, and immediately declared the first-place Montreal Canadiens, with a 7–3 record, the winners of the first half.

The first half ended, despite home-ice victories of 5–2 against Ottawa and 11–3 against Montreal, with the Toronto Arenas in the cellar. The loss of goalie Hap Holmes, who was on his way to an outstanding season in Seattle, was proving to be the most significant setback for the defending Cup champions. Despite all of Querrie's wheeling and dealing of defencemen and forwards, he simply could not overcome the void left by Holmes. Things were no better in the second half, when Harry Cameron came back to haunt his old team by scoring the game-winning goal for Ottawa after 16 minutes of overtime. Flying through the Toronto lines, Cameron fired a bullet into the top corner to seal a 2–1 win for the Senators. The defenceman had played the full 76 minutes en route to exacting a measure of revenge against his old team.

At the same time, the Montreal *Star* reported that the Toronto Arena Company had offered Livingstone $12,000 to drop his suit.[356] The Arena balked when Livingstone requested that the offer be put in writing. Within days, Hubert Vearncombe and Charlie Querrie were testifying in court about their business activities and those of their employer, the Arena Gardens of Canada, Ltd. It was the third time that Vearncombe had been called as a witness in a Livingstone lawsuit.

On the same day that the two Toronto magnates were testifying, January 30, the principal game officials for matches played in Toronto, Lou Marsh and Steve Vair, tendered their resignations to Frank Calder,[357] citing their disgust with the state of professional hockey and the ongoing abuse they faced from fans and players at the Arena Gardens. Calder managed to persuade the two officials to return to duty and, in a face-saving statement to the press, managed to insinuate that Livingstone was behind their decision. He suggested that a series of anonymous letters, written on King Edward Hotel stationery, had influenced Marsh and Vair.[358] It was common knowledge in hockey circles, and widely reported through the media, that Livingstone often frequented the King Edward.

On February 3, the Arena filed its statement of defence against Livingstone, while the team's players followed suit a day later. On the eighth, Livingstone submitted his response. The stage was set for the courtroom showdown.

The Arenas' on-ice situation didn't improve any with the February 1 game in Montreal. The Canadiens smothered the Toronto team 10–0, making them look like a bunch of schoolboys. Querrie, who had received Livingstone's statement of claim, was in a surly mood when the team gathered the following Monday in Toronto for practice. One by one he called the players on their performance in Montreal and drew special attention to those who had again broken the training rules. At the end of the session, six players were fined for their indiscretions.

If the players had any doubts on where they stood with management, Querrie was quick to reassure them. "If the players cannot live up to the training rules, then we do not want them on the club. I have fined several of them for what they have done and have told them plump and plain that unless they show something tonight against the Canadiens here that they will not play for us any more this season. The public won't stand for this kind of stuff and neither will we. It makes it hard for us and gives pro hockey a bad name, something that should be prevented, especially in this city where the amateurs have such a stronghold. With a fine tacked on and a warning issued at the same time, the local players can probably be depended upon to stick to their knitting for the balance of the season. They are paid for their hockey services and should give value for their salaries. If they do not, then there should be other players who can take their place."[359]

When the Canadiens came to town on February 4, the attendance numbered in the hundreds. One of the few in the stands was Frank Calder, who had made the trip to observe first-hand the situation in Toronto. The Arenas responded with their best performance of the year, a 6–3 victory that was notable for its chippiness: Newsy Lalonde speared Toronto's Reg Noble, while Russell Crawford did the same to Montreal's Jack McDonald.

The pitiful "crowds" at the Arenas' games were becoming a source of no small concern to the players, most of whom demanded copies of their contracts to determine whether there might be any way out. When the requested paperwork was not forthcoming, doubt began to set in as to whether the team would complete the season. There was also a groundswell of frustration with Querrie's managerial style, which relied largely on fines and intimidation. The first player to be shown the door was Harry Meeking, followed quickly by the newcomer Dave Ritchie. Meeking's suspension came as a surprise to him, as the only apparent transgression he had committed was to ask for a copy of his contract — a request that had been denied. After his dismissal, Meeking said, "How they can do it and get away with it, I don't know. It's a funny league."[360]

Coach Dick Carroll was surprised to hear that Meeking was gone. In his estimation there were far worse performers on the team than Meeking. The Toronto *Telegram* caught up to the Arenas boss later the same day.

"Why was Meeking suspended?" was asked of Manager Querrie.

"For a very grave offence," was the answer given.

"Will you tell us what the offence was?"

"You can get that information from Meeking, but if he does not wish to tell and the public desires to know, I am quite ready to say what it was."

"Why do you not want to say now?"

"Because I am not desirous of doing any harm to the player, who has always played fair with us up until this infringement."

"What about the other players being sore?"

"I have just had a talk to them that if anyone does not like the way things are being run, they can quit whenever they want."

The first player to take Querrie up on that offer was Ken Randall, who had received a tempting offer of $700 to finish out the season with a team in the Nova Scotia coal-mining town of Glace Bay. The sturdy defenceman had played on Cape Breton Island earlier in his career and enjoyed his time there. Querrie was given a chance to match the offer, and when he couldn't do so, he gave the player permission to head east. In return, Randall agreed to play in the Arenas' home game on February 18. Meeking, who was also unable to get any satisfaction from Querrie, accepted a similar offer from Glace Bay.[361]

On February 20, the Arenas' season came to an abrupt end. Querrie informed Frank Calder that his team would drop out of the NHL race, and Calder agreed on the condition that Toronto play that night's game in Ottawa, as it would give each team a total of eight matches in the second half. Calder then directed the Ottawa and Montreal owners to schedule a playoff series, to begin in Montreal on the twenty-second. The NHL was down to two teams — and both made the playoffs!

The news lifted Livingstone's spirits. "It was tipped off to me some time ago that something like this would happen," he told the *Daily News*. "I knew the players were dissatisfied, also that the club was losing money, hand over fist. It's a fine black-eye for pro hockey."[362]

Querrie left the remaining players twisting in the wind. Reg Noble tried to hook up with the Canadiens, while several others approached the Senators for work, but Calder — using the excuse that only players already on team rosters could take part in playoffs — derailed this plan. Of all the Arenas, only Randall and Meeking emerged with jobs for the balance of the 1918–19 season,[363] although Bert Lindsay did appear in an exhibition game played in memory of Hamby Shore, the Ottawa defenceman who died of influenza on October 14, 1918.

The Senators and Canadiens certainly didn't suffer from the loss of the Arenas. Both rinks were packed for the first best-of-seven playoff series in NHL history. The Canadiens, winners of the first half, took the series in five games. As the series ended, plans were underway for both clubs to travel west. The Senators would play exhibition games in Victoria and Vancouver, while the Canadiens would have a rematch of their 1917 series with Seattle.

The Stanley Cup series got off to a magnificent start, as the Metropolitans won the first and third games, while the Canadiens took the second and fifth. As a further testament to how evenly matched the two teams were, game four was tied 0–0 after two overtime periods, before bad ice conditions forced the game to be called.

The series would go unresolved, however. During the fall of 1918, as World War I hostilities were winding down, a flu epidemic of unprecedented proportions was just hitting its stride. The influenza had been at its deadliest in October, but it was still claiming victims across the continent — and around the world — in March 1919, when the Canadiens arrived in the Pacific Northwest. Several players on both sides had come down with the illness, although the Canadiens were harder hit: after game five, Louis Berlinquette, Billy Couture, "Bad Joe" Hall, Jack McDonald, Newsy Lalonde — Montreal's top scorer in the Cup series — and manager George Kennedy were too weak to continue. Canadiens owner George Kennedy suggested that the series be finished using players from Victoria's roster in place of the fallen Canadiens, but Frank Patrick turned down the suggestion. The series was abandoned, with a tragic footnote: on April 5, 1919, Joe Hall died of pneumonia, which was related to his bout of influenza. The veteran defenceman was thirty-six years old.

Despite the lack of NHL playoff hockey, Toronto's Arena Gardens was a hive of hockey activity in March 1919. Given its status as a hotbed of the amateur game, it was only fitting that the city hosted the Allan Cup series — the national senior hockey championship — and the first edition of the Memorial Cup finals for the junior championship of Canada. Both competitions filled the rink far in excess of what the Arenas had been drawing. (The Memorial Cup series would have been especially crowd-pleasing, as the team from University of Toronto Schools handily defeated the Regina Patricias, 29–8, in a two-game, total-goals series.)

Needless to say, the financial fate of the Arenas hockey team was not as bright. As Livingstone's case against the Arena Gardens came to trial, Vearncombe made sure to let the press know that the club had lost $2,200 on the season.[364] The Toronto *Daily Star* had already cracked wise on the subject shortly after the Arenas withdrew from NHL competition:

> One safe Wager — Eddie Livingstone will not be worried about the split of the profits of the local pro hockey club this season. Charlie Querrie and Hubert Vearncombe carried their share home tucked in alongside of their car tickets.[365]

The first witness to be called on March 24, 1919, was Livingstone's lawyer, John Boland. Under the questioning of his fellow counsel, W. R. Smythe, Boland testified that A. B. Claxton of the Arena Gardens had informed him of the NHL's formation on November 26, 1917. He also recalled that Claxton met with Livingstone and him on December 5, 1917, to sign the lease they had agreed to the month before. "The meeting was very friendly," he said.[366]

Claxton was not in a friendly mood when it was his turn to take the stand.

> Smythe: How much of the thirty per cent received for the first three Stanley Cup games would you be willing to pay?
> Claxton: Just the amount you are entitled to, and that is nothing. By the regulations thirty per cent goes to the rink for rental.[367]

The trial continued the next day, with the players' testimony being entered into the record. On March 20, Boland had examined the Toronto player Alfred Skinner.

> Boland: Mr. Skinner, you signed a contract under date of 19th day of December, 1917, with the Toronto Hockey Club Limited?

Skinner:Who had the team that year?

Boland:Well, that was the year the Arena ran the team.

Skinner:They took it from Livingstone. Yes, [I did sign,] but I wouldn't swear by the date.

Boland:That is the date. You signed a contract bearing the same date, December 19th, 1917, with the Arena Gardens of Toronto Limited?

Skinner:Well, yes.

Boland:That is, in that year you signed two contracts?

Skinner:I signed about five that year.

Boland:Anyway, you signed two. If you signed five, you signed two?

Skinner:Yes. They had a new one for every day of the week.

Boland:Now, both of those contracts contained an option for your services for the past season [1918–19]?

Skinner:They did, but I don't think they are worth anything.

Boland:You don't think they are worth anything?

Skinner:No. Querrie said they ain't.

Boland:When did Mr. Querrie tell you that?

Skinner:Oh, in the spring.

And more:

Boland:Between December 10th and the date of this contract, January 6th, 1919, was there any other contract signed by you?

Skinner:No.

Boland:Then under what arrangement were you playing between December 9th, 1918, and January 6th, 1919?

Skinner:We were under a verbal agreement.

Boland:With whom did you have your
    verbal agreement?

Skinner:Querrie.

Boland:Now, what assurance did Mr. Querrie
    give you that you would be paid?

Skinner:He gave us his word.

Boland:Nothing but his word?

Skinner:No, we took his word.

Boland:That you would be paid.

Skinner:Yes.

Boland:And were you paid?

Skinner:Well, I was paid all within $116.

Boland:Were you paid between December
    9th, 1918, and January 6th, 1919?

Skinner:Yes.

Boland:How were you paid, weekly or
    monthly?

Skinner:No, they drew $50 one day and
    maybe $100 the next day. It just
    depended. I couldn't state offhand.

Boland:You don't know how you were paid?

Skinner:One day I drew a $50 cheque and
    two days after I went back and got $50
    more, and maybe a week after that they
    gave me $100 more.

Boland:Were those in cash or cheque?

Skinner:The first two were in cheques and
    the other was in cash.

Boland:Now, whose cheques were given
    you for the first two payments?

Skinner:That I couldn't state.

Boland:You don't know?

Skinner:No. I think it was this fellow,
    though.

Boland:Whose?

Skinner:Vearncombe's.

Boland:You think it was Vearncombe's per-
    sonal cheque?

Skinner:I wouldn't like to state it because it
    is a little too far back. We didn't both-
    er with that.... We thought there was

something fishy, and to make it look strong they handed us a cheque.

Boland:Now, when did you get your first $50 cheque? Would it be after the first game or before?

Skinner:Oh no, before.

Boland:Are you sure it was a cheque of Mr. H. Vearncombe?

Skinner: I wouldn't swear it was Vearncombe's.

Boland:Would it be a cheque of the Arena Gardens of Toronto?

Skinner:We signed those blanks, Arena Gardens Limited, after we received the money.

Boland:When did you sign for Arena Gardens of Toronto Limited?

Skinner:After we received the $50 first.

Boland:How many vouchers did you sign for Arena Gardens?

Skinner:I think I signed three or four. They might have switched them back again. I don't know, but I signed three or four. In fact, all of them signed them. Every one of the players there signed them, eight or nine.[368]

Reg Noble testified that he had last signed a contract around January 15, 1918, with the Toronto Arena Hockey Club. Calder would testify that only this contract was valid, since it was authorized by him as NHL president.

In his summation, A. C. McMaster, the Arena Gardens' attorney, took pains to point out that the Arenas hockey team was a separate entity from the rink, and that "the only interest Arena Gardens had in the club was to see that they got the rent for the rink."[369] He also said, "The Arena Club has not made money."

Both points may have been true for the 1918–19 season, but clearly did not apply to 1917–18, when the Stanley Cup–winning Toronto Hockey Club, which was operated by Arena Gardens, took in receipts of $53,000. The Arena couldn't help but be interested in more than the rental fee for its rink.[370]

Or, as W. R. Smythe put it in his summation of Livingstone's case, "The club which has the players, and not the club which has the ice, has the upper hand."[371] And the Arena had taken Livingstone's players.

And what of the players/defendants?

Alf Skinner dealt to the PCHA on November 24, 1919.[372]

Jack Adams as sold to Vancouver on December 7, 1919.

Harry Meeking was sold to Victoria on the same day.

Harry Cameron was traded to Montreal on January 14, 1920.

Reg Noble was offered to Montreal on December 12, 1919, for George McNamara, but the Canadiens refused the trade. In 1924, he was sold to the Montreal Maroons.

Ken Randall and Corbett Denneny said nothing that would further indict Querrie, and so both men remained in Toronto, although they would both be traded to Hamilton in 1923.[373]

Less than a week after he disposed of the infidel defendants, Querrie recruited some new investors and applied to transfer the Toronto Arenas to the new ownership group. As of December 13, 1919, the owners of the team were Querrie, Paul Ciceri, J. P. Bickell and N. L. Nathanson.[374] Calder and the National Hockey League charged the new owners $5,000 for Livingstone's franchise, of which Querrie chipped in $1,200, while Ciceri and Fred and Percy Hambly put up the balance.[375] Where that money went is anybody's guess, but Livingstone didn't receive it. As Calder was the NHL's only employee, he had control of the league chequebook as well as its presidency — a suspicious combination at best, and one that would not pass the outside auditors' internal control test at any North American company.

For their $5,000, the four partners purchased the club's name, sweaters, sticks and rink privileges. Querrie dubbed his team the Toronto Tecumsehs, the original name of the Ontarios franchise that Livingstone bought when he first got into the NHA in 1914 — and the name under which Querrie had managed the team back in 1911. Calder cau-

Charlie Querrie

tioned Querrie about the name change, so Livingstone's former friend tried again, calling his team the St. Patricks. The club's articles of incorporation were filed in Ontario on December 22, 1919, just days before the 1919–20 season began. Listed as stockholders were Fred Hambly, Percy Hambly, Ciceri and Querrie, with 99 shares each, and Richard Greer, who held four shares.

Popular legend has it that Querrie chose the name because he was trying to change the team's fortunes — as if one Stanley Cup title in the past two years could be considered bad luck! — and that he could think of no better way to appeal to the significant Irish population in Toronto than by naming the team after that country's patron saint. In fact, the name was carried over from the St. Patricks senior amateur team which the Hamblys and Ciceri had operated for the previous couple of years.

Querrie embarked on the task of building the new team by re-signing those Arenas players who were still in town. By this time would they have no formal contractual obligations to Livingstone. Even by Livingstone's admission, his assets — the player's contracts and their option years — had been converted into personal property by Querrie.

Meanwhile, Calder stood by and watched.

And approved.

And cashed the cheques.

Chapter 17

The Battle for Hamilton

Then Eddie went into the courts, but got nowhere.
— Elmer Ferguson, 1965

On January 7, 1920, Mr. Justice Sir Glenholme Falconbridge rendered his decision in *Toronto HC v. Arena Gardens*.

He ruled that Livingstone's club was entitled to be paid $20,093.54, plus interest dating from April 1, 1918, plus legal costs. The Arena was also mandated to return all player contracts, or else pay damages. Furthermore, Falconbridge found that the Arena had entered a questionable agreement with Hubert Vearncombe — who had been promoted in May 1918 from accountant to auditor and controller of the Arena — to take over the Arenas hockey club, giving the rink's management an excuse not to fulfill its obligations to Livingstone.

The Arena appealed, but the petition was dismissed on October 20, 1920. The case was referred to the master-in-ordinary, who in those days was responsible under Canadian law for assessing damages.

Throughout the various lawsuits, Frank Calder had apparently been advising Toronto manager Charlie Querrie, a fact of which Livingstone seems to have been unaware — or, if he knew about it, felt that to pursue a case against Calder and the NHL would forever doom his hockey aspirations. Livingstone might have had a slander case against both Calder and the Montreal *Herald*, Elmer Ferguson's paper, although a Ferguson column from October 1918, which may be the most astute and poignant piece he ever wrote, would have made it difficult to prove:

Eddie Livingstone may be all the unprintable things that the professional hockey magnates say he is, writes E.W. Ferguson in the Montreal *Herald*. But our experience is that a knock from most professional hockey promoters is in reality a boost, for the average promoter has come to be so careless with the truth that his vocal stuff must be interpreted with a strong sprinkling of reverse English.

What Livvy is or isn't in the eyes of his one-time brothers-in-kale is neither here nor there. The one thing certain is this, that at the present time Livvy is proving a lively and exceedingly painful thorn in the flesh of the other hockey owners. Like a game little tyke battling against a horde of grim-faced bulldogs, he's scrapping and snapping, and if he isn't doing any great harm he's keeping the opposition casting anxious glances at the newspaper head-lines to see what this surprising young man will do next.

Our strong personal conviction is that the best thing for the other owners can do, for their own peace of mind, is to take Livvy back into the fold of organized hockey once more. This, of course, is assuming that Livvy wishes to return to the fold, which is by no means certain. The well-advertised "stormy petrel," without turning over a hand, was strong and astute enough to sit back last winter and allow the league from which he had been carefully excluded to earn some $6,000 or $7,000 for him. The other magnates deny that he was entitled to this, which is, of course, the bunk. No individual or collective promoters are going to hand over $6,000 or $7,000 to anyone who isn't entitled to it. If he can make that much money sitting out, why should he return?

Not only did Livingstone thus prove just as shrewd a financier as the other dollar-seekers in the game, but he was a far better judge of raw hockey material than any one of the others, if results count for anything. In his brief and meteoric stay in the select circles, Eddie Livingstone uncovered and developed more high-class material than all of the others put together. While the other clubs were content to slip along in the worn grooves with the time-scarred veterans, Livingstone was continually on the hunt, and that he plucked few lemons is attested by the fact that he unearthed the Meeking boys, Noble, Skinner, Brown, the Dennenays, and Keats — the latter would have been a second Nighbor had he not responded to the call of the bigger game.

A great baseball player once said: "If I owned a baseball club, I would hire a $5,000 manager and a $15,000 scout."

He meant that finding championship baseball talent was far more important than directing it after it had been discovered — and the same thing goes for hockey. Livingstone has proven his value in judging players. Nearly all of the really good young stars of the last two seasons were dug up by Livvy — men worth thousands of dollars to the N.H.L. clubs.

Meanwhile, refusing to profit by the sorry example of professional baseball, the magnates continue to do their dirty linen washing in public. Expulsions, suits over cash alleged to be due, suits for libel, for conspiracy, and what-not, furnish a sinister comparison to the circumstances under which professional baseball began to wane in popular esteem.

The public doesn't want, and won't stand for it.

What the game sadly needs are owners of the Patrick type, who keep the sporting spirit rather than the ledger to the fore, and who show some other capability than getting the money without giving anything in return.

The worm will turn presently, and the box office will be as empty as the threats of a new league.[376]

Ferguson must have forgotten he even wrote this piece when he penned the 1965 article on the NHL's origins.

In the wake of Falconbridge's decision, Livingstone's ally Percy Quinn took over the job of managing the Arena Gardens from Charlie Querrie. With a friend in control of the Arena, Livingstone tried once again to launch the Canadian Hockey Association.

On August 26, 1920, the Hamilton *Herald* trumpeted the imminent arrival of major-league hockey in Steeltown:

Hamilton will be represented in the newly organized professional hockey league. The directors of the Abso-Pure Ice Co., after wrestling with the professional problem for some time, last night decided to operate.

Toronto, with two clubs, Hamilton and one American city, probably Cleveland, are already assured, and the chances are that Ottawa will also be included. Next year it is planned to have four American clubs represented — Boston, Pittsburgh, Cleveland and New York. The artificial ice plant in New York is to be erected in connection with the new baseball grounds being built by the New York American league club.

The new league is a certainty. Those connected with the Toronto clubs have control of the Toronto arena, and they say that the National Hockey association, which has operated for many years, cannot place another team in the Queen City. The officials feel that the N.H.L. is none too popular and that a general house-cleaning is in order.[377]

The battle for Hamilton, and its shiny new ice arena, was underway. Percy Thompson, manager of the rink, would also run the proposed team. He liked what Livingstone's league had to offer, particularly the proximity to rivals in Cleveland and Toronto. "If Hamilton had entered the N.H.L. and been forced to make the long jumps to Montreal and Quebec," the *Herald* said, "the gate receipts here would have to be mighty big to meet the travelling expenses."[378]

If the gate receipts were indeed to be "mighty big," the *Herald* offered a prescription that is as common today as in 1920:

What is required now is a team that will be made up with the leaders throughout the season battling for the championship. That's all that is needed to make Hamilton's first year as a professional centre a successful one. The management of the local club are very reticent in the matter, but they can be relied upon to get the best available. They are already working on several stars.[379]

Three weeks later, Livvy and Quinn felt emboldened enough to predict the NHL's demise. According to the *Herald*, they believed the established league "will make one kick and then keel over and play dead. They assert that the old league has gone its limit, that it will never again be able to operate a club in the Queen City, and that Ottawa, Montreal and Quebec will have to struggle among themselves or throw up the sponge." The *Herald's* reporter wasn't so sure. "There's no doubt that the pair have the upper hand in that they have Toronto in their mitts, but we have a suspicion that the old league will put up a fair fight before going under."[380]

Hamilton's new indoor arena had some interesting amenities, according to the Hamilton *Spectator*:

> The new structure has a seating capacity of 4,500 and standing room for 3,000 more. On the north side of the structure will be a rest room for the ladies as well as a check room. On the south side those gentlemen who are addicted to the soothing weed will find a place to enjoy their favourite brand during the intermission between periods. On this side will be located five dressing-rooms which all contain shower baths for the players, a convenience that was sadly lacking in the past. There will be six entrances all told. Three will be on Barton street, and the other three on Bristol street. The ice surface will be lighted by twenty-eight 500 candle-power lights. The building will be steam heated. The press box will be on the south side.
>
> In former seasons the local team was handicapped owing to the size of the rink, and every time they went to Toronto the question was asked, "How will they size up on the larger ice surface?" There will be no need to ask that question this year, for the ice surface is even larger than that in the Toronto arena. In fact, it is one of the largest sheets in Canada.[381]

It is only natural that such a state-of-the-art facility would also have been attractive to Frank Calder's NHL. And by late September, Percy Thompson, a neophyte when it came to managing a hockey team, had seemingly reconsidered his earlier enthusiasm about Livingstone's CHA. "The professional hockey outlook in Hamilton has taken on quite a change since the situation was reviewed in the *Herald* as of last Friday," the *Herald* reported.

> The C.H.A., which looked so strong then, doesn't appear to be quite the same league now, and all because the N.H.L. officials have been busy to stall off the

Livingstone-Quinn moves. Representatives of the N.H.L. were in Hamilton on Saturday afternoon, talking over the matter with the directors of the Hamilton arena, and, while nothing definite has been decided on, it looks very much as if Hamilton will be found in the N.H.L., with the C.H.A. a dead issue.

Manager Percy Thompson, of the local arena, will not be quoted in the matter. He says something definite will be announced before the end of the week, but further than that he will not talk. However, it is learned that Hamilton has been offered the Quebec franchise in the N.H.L., and that St. Patricks of Toronto are negotiating for the use of the Hamilton arena in case Livingstone and Quinn refuse to allow them to play on the Toronto arena ice.

The N.H.L., as the *Herald* predicted, refuses to die without a fight. And, as a matter of fact, the Ottawa and Montreal clubs have moved so quickly to stave off defeat that they stand a mighty fine chance of winning out and putting the Livingstone league out for the full count. The Hamilton arena authorities look with favour on the N.H.L. because it is a league that has been a success, while the C.H.A. will be more of an experiment than anything else. It will suit the local men if the N.H.L. wins out.

Hamilton is sure to have professional hockey, regardless of what league it is in, but the situation has taken such a turn that it is almost a certainty now that the N.H.L. will be plenty good enough for Thompson et al.

The N.H.L. has promised Hamilton everything within reason if Percy Thompson will agree to including this city in the old league, thus frustrating the plans of Livingstone and Quinn.[382]

Not to be outdone, Livingstone showed Hamilton he meant business, dangling $1,500 contracts in front of three of Hamilton's top players: Carson Cooper, Leo Reise and Herbie Reaume. The *Herald* quoted Reaume as saying he was not interested in "affiliating with such a league [as the CHA] until he is sure that it will materialize," but that Reise and Cooper were keeping their options open.[383]

Meanwhile, just up the road to the north, the battle for Toronto raged on. Lou Marsh, the sports editor of the *Star*, was being courted by Livingstone to manage one of the Toronto CHA teams. Livvy also signed Cully Wilson, who was under contract to the St. Pats, a bold stroke that prompted Charlie Querrie to fight back.

> Yesterday, the contracts of the St. Patrick players were taken to a lawyer for an opinion as to legality. They were pronounced as ironclad. Last season, the St. Patrick players were given $100 each in advance of this year's salary, which adds to the strength of the St. Patricks' claim. The St. Patricks' solicitor also stated that because E. J. Livingstone had not offered Reg. Noble and Corbett Dennenay contracts for the last two years it might interfere with his hold on them.[384]

On October 21, D. R. Scanlan of St. Paul, Minnesota, met with Livingstone and Quinn to check on the progress of the new league and investigate the possibility that it might expand southward. The Canadian pair did have its eye on such American sites as New York, Philadelphia, Boston, Cleveland and Pittsburgh for expansion when conditions were right, and Scanlan wanted St. Paul included on that list.[385]

On November 1, an article appeared in the Hamilton *Herald* that suggested Scanlan would be waiting some time for conditions to be right. The headline read "Hamilton has secured Quebec's N.H.L. franchise."

> Percy Thompson has the credentials safely tucked away in the Arena safe, after several months of dickering.
> This morning he made the announcement that clears up the air and gives Hamiltonians a chance to consider themselves residents of a really live hockey town.
> The N.H.L. will be composed of Hamilton, Toronto, Ottawa and Montreal, the same four cities that are represented in the Big Four Rugby union. Hamilton gets the Quebec franchise, players, and everything else that goes with it.[386]

In his later years, Thompson recalled, "We got the franchise and players of the Quebec club for $5,000, lock, stock and barrel."[387] But exactly who sold the team to Thompson is unknown; in fact, over the course of the next three weeks the newspapers printed story after story claiming that the deal had not gone through. An article moved over the Associated Press wire on November 3, quoting an unnamed Quebec official as saying "the announcement was a little premature, as the local club had not held a meeting and had taken no steps in the matter."[388]

Even as late as November 24, the Canadian Press reported, "A movement is on horn to interest a number of business men in the Quebec Hockey Club and retain the franchise in the N.H.L. Meetings were held yesterday and there will be further conference today. Should the negotiations come to a head, the Quebec club will most likely be represented at the annual meeting of the N.H.L. in Toronto."[389]

Even so, the Bulldogs' move to Hamilton was looking more and more like a done deal. For instance, according to the Toronto *Daily Star*, "It was reported that 'Goldie' Prodgers and 'Joe' Matte, last year with St. Patricks but who belonged to the Canadiens, have been traded to Hamilton for Jack McDonald and 'Joe' Malone of Quebec. Harry Cameron, who finished last season with the Canadiens, will return [to Toronto] as part of the trade for Prodgers and Matte. It is said that Prodgers will manage the Hamilton team."[390]

Meanwhile, Eddie Livingstone admitted to the *Star* that the question of which league survived depended upon who ended up in control of the Mutual Street Arena. "Getting ice in Toronto, or not getting it, means the death of the one league or the other," he said. "This has been admitted by both, and is beyond controversy. That we have right on our side is incontrovertible in the light of the sweeping judgment of Chief Justice Falconbridge as confirmed by the Court of Appeal."[391]

Being right in the eyes of the courts was one thing. To actually collect the judgment to which he was entitled would be quite another matter. Predictably, the Arena tried another gambit to avoid paying Livingstone. The owners of the Arena Gardens filed bankruptcy, claiming the company could not meet its financial obligations.

That drove Livingstone back into court, trying to wrest control of the Arena away from the Montrealers, thereby guaranteeing him a place for his team to play, even if he had no league. The Toronto *Daily Star* tried its best to explain the whole messy situation.

> If any layman, except E. J. Livingstone, can make head or tail of the legal tangle in which the Arena Gardens, the National Hockey League, the Canadian Hockey Association, the Arena bond holders, the Toronto General Trust Co., and the receiver in charge of the Arena, are con-

cerned, he is a wonder. The case came up before Justice
Latchford at Osgoode Hall to-day, and after everything was
all through and the platoon of legal luminaries concerned
in the case had filed out, Paul Ciceri of the St. Patricks
Hockey Club, which is trying to pry its way into the
Arena, summed it all up when he said, "It's as clear as
mud." Anyway, everybody had something to say about
everything from hockey as a brutal game to receivership
bonds and then toddled on their way when Justice
Latchford remarked:"I will give the matter early consideration, and deliver judgment as soon as possible. I understand the necessity for expedition in the case."

It was Justice Latchford who handed hockey a rude
jolt and called it a brutal game. Justice Latchford has not
been to a hockey game for more than eleven years, and
he considers the sport worse than the revels of the
Roman amphitheatre.

His Lordship this morning heard the hockey case on
the motion made by the Toronto General Trust Co. to set
aside the receivership of the Arena Gardens, Limited, the
move by which the St. Pats club and the N.H.L. expects
to get ice at the Arena and oust the C.H.A. forces.

"I saw a hockey slaughter at Ottawa once, and such
brutal conduct was tolerated by the crowd that I haven't
been near a game since," remarked His Lordship.

"Something like the old Roman amphitheatre," said
W. R. Smythe, representing the Toronto Hockey Club.

"Worse," replied His Lordship. "I remember now I
saw a game in Toronto eleven or twelve years ago, and
my impression was confirmed."

"I think the evidence before Your Lordship shows
the whole affair is collusive, not in good faith, and to
hinder the Toronto Hockey Club in the realization of its
judgment," said Mr. Smythe in presenting his clients'
end of the issue.

"I can see that it will hinder in the realization of the
judgment, but that is not all your client wants. What he
wants is the exclusive right to run this rink this winter
for professional hockey."

"That is something that is far from my mind," said
Mr. Smythe.

"I can see through a millstone as far as the next person," came from the bench.

The argument was lively from both sides, and the crux of the affair seemed to be as to whether the legal moves of the Toronto Hockey Club were bona fide efforts to satisfy the definite judgment for $24,000 obtained by the club against the Arena for using his players in the N.H.L. after his club was frozen out, and for an indefinite judgment for damages variously estimated from $100,000 to $300,000.

The [Arena] argued that the Toronto Hockey Club did not want payment so much as they wanted control of the pro hockey privileges at the Arena, and even the Arena itself. On the other side, the Toronto Hockey Club counsel argued that certain moves made by the bondholders were for the purpose of euchring the Toronto Hockey Club out of the settlement.

When it comes down to a showdown, all the sporting public wants to know is: "Does the St. Patricks Hockey Club get the ice for N.H.L. games, or will the C.H.A. have full control and the proposed three-team league here, or two teams here and one in Hamilton, provide the pro hockey for Toronto fans this winter."

On the judgment of Justice Latchford this depends. If it goes one way the C.H.A.'s contract for exclusive pro. hockey privileges holds good and the N.H.L. crowd is out in the cold. If it goes the other way, both N.H.L. and C.H.A. clubs will get ice and Toronto is likely to be the scene of a pro. hockey war.[392]

Livingstone and Calder waited anxiously for Mr. Justice Latchford's decision. Either way, as inconceivable as it might seem, a Canadian judge who knew little about hockey, and didn't like what little of the sport he had seen, was in a position to alter forever the course of hockey history.

The combatants did not have to wait long — one day, to be exact.

"Assuming that the applicant [Livvy's Toronto Hockey Club] is a party affected by this order, a point upon which I express no definite opinion, the application must, in my opinion, fail," Latchford said.

It is obvious, however, from the evidence before me that the motion is made, not in the Toronto Hockey

Club's interest as a judgment creditor, but in the interest as a lessee of the Arena during the hockey season of
1920–21, under an agreement alleged to have been
made with the managing director of the Arena.

From the financial statement in evidence it is plain
that the Arena is not in a position to pay its debts in full,
though it can probably arrange to pay the hockey club the
amounts due under the judgment so far as ascertained.

If the Hockey Club holds a valid contract for the
use of the Arena during the approaching season it will
no doubt subsist as against the receiver, just as it would
if a receiver had not been appointed. As a creditor, the
Hockey Club is in no way prejudiced.

The motion is dismissed with costs."[393]

Even before the decision was handed down, Calder had been
manoeuvring, working in conjunction with the Arena's receiver, Charles
Robin, and William Hewitt's Ontario Hockey Association to lock up all
the available ice time at the Arena. "The St. Patricks have their contract
for ice signed, sealed and delivered, and have called for a practice for
Monday morning," said Hewitt's newspaper, the *Daily News*, on
December 10. "They will play their first N.H.L. championship match
Christmas night at the Arena.

"The Ontario Hockey Association will have four nights and four
afternoons a week for games in addition to practice hours for the teams.

"The Bank League will have one night a week for hockey games.

"This takes up all the ice accommodations at the Arena this winter."[394]

Apparently, Quinn and Livingstone had never put their agreement
to lease the Arena ice into writing, and Justice Latchford's decision had
left Livvy out in the cold. A week later, Hamilton was brought into the
NHL, and Livingstone's league was unceremoniously extinguished.

Chapter 18

Livvy Wins, but the NHL
Gains Some Relief

As the boys declared, it was all quite legal. They didn't throw
Eddie out. They just resigned, left him a one-team league of his
own, complete with franchise. All very legal. Pretty shrewd, too.
— Elmer Ferguson, 1965

O n **October 8, 1923, the** master-in-ordinary of the Supreme Court of
Ontario, Mr. Justice George Alcorn, fixed damages at $100,000 to
compensate Livingstone for the money he could have expected to earn had
he been allowed to operate his club for the five seasons that had passed.

Amongst Alcorn's remarks was a stinging condemnation of
the defendants:

> The damages the plaintiff has sustained by reason of the
> non-delivery of contracts in the pleadings mentioned,
> and by reason of the plaintiff company being deprived
> of the services of the defendants Corbett Dennenay, E.
> Reginald Noble, Harry Cameron, Harry Meeking,
> Kenneth Randall, Alfred Skinner and Jack Adams, as
> hockey players, in breach of the contract between the
> plaintiffs and the defendant the Arena Gardens of
> Toronto Limited in the pleadings mentioned, in the
> sum of $100,000.
>
> [Querrie and Vearncombe] have left nothing
> undone that could be done to the injury of the plain-
> tiffs, by long, drawn-out, cold-blooded conspiracy, to
> ruin the plaintiffs. They should, therefore, pay exempla-

ry and punitive damages.... In fixing the sum, I am awarding damages with due regard to the punitive character they should bear under special circumstances of the case as detailed in the evidence, and to the defendant's position as trustee....[395]

On the evidence I find that the Arena Gardens of Toronto Limited and Vearncombe and Querrie, using and working through the National Hockey Association and National Hockey League, were also one and the same interest and brought the tort by conspiracy to its final culmination in depriving the plaintiff of its team and players.[396]

In other words, Alcorn believed that Vearncombe and Querrie were taking their orders from Calder, but that they were still the ones responsible for committing a tort against Livingstone. This point will become significant in a moment.

The ruling was appealed to the Supreme Court of Ontario, where Mr. Justice Orde reported that he could think of no precedent to justify the granting of punitive damages — it had never been done before. Furthermore, he could see no grounds for such a large award. It was his opinion that, given the recent history of Canadian hockey leagues, there was no guarantee the NHL would exist from one year to the next. Between 1904 and 1923, when Orde made his ruling, elite hockey had been dominated by no fewer than seven leagues: the Canadian Amateur Hockey League, the Federal Amateur Hockey League, the Eastern Canada Amateur Hockey Association, the Eastern Canada Hockey Association, the Ontario Professional Hockey League, the National Hockey Association, and finally the National Hockey League. Stability was the exception rather than the rule. Therefore, the defendants had made some money by operating a hockey team in the intervening years, but there was absolutely no guarantee Livingstone would have been able to do so.

Next, Orde made note of a letter that Livingstone had written to A. B. Claxton of the Arena Company on December 12, 1917, in which he offered to sell the franchise, its players and other rights for $15,000. According to the letter, the offer was good until April 15, 1918. In Orde's mind it did "provide a test of [the team's] capital value at the commencement of the season of 1917–18"; however, because the offer was not accepted, it could not be considered as representing the true value of the franchise. He therefore reduced the award to $10,000.[397]

Orde let Vearncombe and Querrie off the hook, ruling that the damages should be paid by the Arena Gardens Hockey Club — which, of course, was out of business by this time. In doing so, he seemingly ignored Alcorn's opinion that Vearncombe and Querrie *were* the hockey club, and that Querrie, after winding down the Arenas, had resurfaced as a partner in the Toronto St. Patrick's Hockey Club Ltd.

Livingstone appealed Orde's ruling, only to have Mr. Justice Masten agree with Orde about the amount of damages, but not the reasoning he had used to set them:

> The judgment below is founded largely on an offer made by plaintiffs in December 1917 to sell for $15,000, but in addition there is, if I understand the evidence right, a sale by Vearncombe to the St. Patrick Club made in 1919 for $7,000. This was a year after the breach of contract, and Livingstone's offer was a year before the breach of contract. It is plain, therefore, that in 1917 the undertaking was not worth in cash more than the $15,000 for which Livingstone offered to sell it; that offer was not accepted, presumably because the buyer thought it was too high; and on the other hand, the undertaking was worth in 1919 not less than $7,000 because it was sold for that sum in that year. It should be remembered that in 1918 the team reached its highest point of value, having won the championship in the 1917–18 series of games.[398]

In a nutshell, Masten was saying that the team couldn't possibly be worth as much as Livingstone wanted for it, but a Stanley Cup champion *must* be more valuable than a team that couldn't even complete the schedule. Using deductive skills worthy of Sherlock Holmes, he observed that $10,000 was firmly between the two extremes. Judgment rendered.

Masten did provide Livingstone with a moral victory when he fired this zinger at Frank Calder and the NHL:

> While I look on the conduct of the defendants as utterly dishonest and despicable, and would be glad to find a legitimate basis on which to increase the findings of $10,000 damages made by the Court below, yet I find myself unable to discern any warrantable basis in law on which to base such an increase.[399]

Despite those powerful words from a judge on the bench of the province's highest court, Calder's reputation never suffered. With journalists such as Elmer Ferguson, Mike Rodden, Tommy Gorman and Charlie Querrie — all of whom were on the league's payroll in one form or another — to defend his image, the president of the NHL could rest assured that few if any members of the public would consider him dishonest or despicable.

Public opinion of the president may have changed drastically had it been widely known that President Calder was receiving payment from the Toronto Arena Company — to the tune of $15,000. The information came to light, at least amongst officers of the court, when that enterprise filed for bankruptcy and its books were examined. Livingstone's lawyers were apparently unaware of these transfers, because they never brought them to the Ontario Supreme Court's attention. It stands to reason that, had Justice Orde been aware of this bit of financial chicanery, he would have taken with a grain of salt the Arena's protests that it had been losing money for many years. He might even have hesitated to reduce the Alcorn award to Livingstone by 90 percent.

The creation of the St. Patricks franchise wasn't the only bit of subterfuge that Querrie employed — with Calder's active involvement — to avoid paying the Livingstone judgment. Under Justice Falconbridge's decision back on January 7, 1920, Livvy was entitled either to 100 shares of Arenas stock, or the proceeds from the sale of those shares, as partial payment. It occurred to Querrie that, if the shares no longer belonged to him, the courts couldn't make him surrender them to Livingstone. So, on October 8, 1923, he transferred his 99 shares of Toronto St. Patricks stock to his wife Ida, thereby making her the first female owner in hockey history, and only the second in all of sports.[400]

Even though Livingstone wasn't being paid, Querrie's lawyers were. On June 30, 1922, the master-in-ordinary, George Alcorn, increased the damages to $23,404.33, prompting Querrie's representatives to appeal. On September 17, the Court of Appeals reduced the award to $13,271.52.

A couple of months later, on November 7, Alcorn wrote a memo that read, in part, "Subsequent acts of defendants or those representing them show only that the breach was persistent and do not constitute fresh cause or causes of action. There was one breach of contract, one breach of trust and such amounted to a conversion of plaintiff's property right in the services of the players."

By January 14, 1924, Livingstone still had not been paid. On that date, Mr. Justice Kelly restrained the Querries from "selling, hypothecating, mortgaging or otherwise transferring the 99 shares of stock."[401] With that decision, Livingstone filed yet another suit, this one naming Charles and Ida Querrie and the St. Patrick's Professional Hockey Club Ltd., as defendants.

While that action was ongoing, Justices Orde and Masten reduced Alcorn's award of punitive damages from $100,000. Livingstone was, understandably, less than thrilled with this outcome, and so he took the case before the highest court in the British Empire: the Judicial Committee of the Privy Council in London, England. Before this body, Livingstone's lawyers asked that Alcorn's rationale be respected — that damages be assessed as though Livvy had maintained control of the players and hockey club. The panel — Viscount Hardane, Lord Atkinson, Lord Darling, L. J. Warrington, and the chief justice of the Supreme Court of Canada, Francis Anglin — issued their decision on July 27, 1926, and they sided with Orde. The crux of their decision was that:

> It would have been impossible to make a satisfactory estimate of the amount of such profits. Moreover, they had no "Franchise" for those seasons and no ice unless they could obtain it from the Arena. They might, of course, have succeeded in getting over these difficulties, but the position was much too uncertain and speculative to form a basis of assessment.[402]

In essence, the court had given Calder carte blanche to command the NHL by fiat, because he could lift franchises at will. We might consider it theft of private property, but as far as Calder and the Privy Council were considered, it was all perfectly legal. An ironic footnote: less than two months after this decision was brought down, Charlie Querrie and his partners put the Toronto St. Patricks up for sale.

Elmer Ferguson's tale of the NHL's origins stops at this point, but the league's very survival depended on Calder's actions during the NHL's formative years. Calder would not rest until his dream of hockey's manifest destiny was fully realized: when the National Hockey League had permanent possession of the Stanley Cup.

Chapter 19

Hamilton is Hoodwinked

"Hamilton has to have a strong team, and it's up to the N.H.L. to see that we get one."
— Percy Thompson, 1920

By the fall of 1920, National Hockey League president Frank Calder had tired of dealing with Mike Quinn and his on-again, off-again Quebec Bulldogs. So, he stripped Quinn of his franchise and sold it to the Abso-Pure Ice Company of Hamilton, Ontario. Abso-Pure enticed Percy Thompson to manage the club, renamed the Tigers — a nickname it shared with the city's football and senior hockey teams. There is no evidence that the dapper and classy Quinn, one of the founding fathers of organized hockey in Quebec, with interests in the sport that dated back to the 1890s, received a cent out of the transfer. Abso-Pure made its cheque payable to Francis Calder, *not* Quinn and not even the NHL. By now Calder found it easy to use the threat of expulsion and loss of one's franchise to keep the once-fractious owners in line. Led by Calder's Montreal crony, the Canadiens' George Kennedy, the owners quickly got on the same page as Calder.[403]

On the ice, the Tigers were anything but fierce. And this posed a problem, because Hamilton was used to a winner after its senior Tigers brought home the Allan Cup in 1919. Thompson tried to sell several members of the Sudbury Wolves on the merits of moving south, but Red Green and his mates were not biting. They were perfectly happy playing senior hockey — the money was all right, and perhaps most importantly, they were being treated honestly and fairly. The Sudbury players had been reading about what was going on in Ottawa and Toronto and wanted no part of the NHL. Thompson was left with no choice but to make do with a lineup stocked largely with the same old retreads that had gone 4–20 in Quebec the year before.

As part of the bargain that brought the NHL to Hamilton, the other NHL teams agreed to help Thompson ice a competitive team. The goal was not necessarily to develop a Tiger powerhouse, but to prevent Thompson from having second thoughts about his decision to freeze Eddie Livingstone and Percy Quinn out of the new barn on Barton Street.

Thompson fully intended to make sure the NHL lived up to its word. The first test came when all-star forward Joe Malone declined to leave Quebec City for Hamilton. Reported the Hamilton *Spectator*:

> Percy Thompson is suffering from a severe headache today.
>
> The early morning mail is responsible.
>
> The first letter he picked up today was dated "Quebec."
>
> "Ah, good news!" he mumbled, as he hurriedly opened the envelope.
>
> But the epistle carried news that was exactly opposite to what was expected.
>
> It was a letter from Joe Malone notifying him that he would not be here this season to play for Hamilton's N.H.L. club. The only thing that prevented H. P. from cussing was the fact he doesn't cuss.
>
> "I am in the skate-making business game down here and will not play hockey this year," said Malone's letter.
>
> It proved a great shock to Thompson. He had been counting heavily on Joe. As a matter of fact, he wanted him as player-manager of the club. Malone is a handy player and a fine shot.
>
> But, while the shock almost bowled Thompson over, it did not dull his senses. He very quickly made up his mind on what plan of action to pursue, with the result that he immediately wired George Kennedy of Canadiens, asking him to send him a centre man, and to take Malone if he can induce him to play for the Frenchmen. Malone may consent to play for the Montrealers, rather than come all the way to Hamilton. Thompson followed up his request with similar wires to St. Pats and Ottawa, and topped it off with a request to

President Calder of the N.H.L. notifying him of his predicament. He expects to be aided.

"Hamilton has to have a strong team, and it's up to the N.H.L. to see that we get one," he said.[404]

Not surprisingly, the other owners did not respond.

The Hamilton *Herald*'s P. J. Jones — who, along with the *Spectator*'s W. C. McMullen, was named an official scorer at Tigers home games — wrote on the eve of the new season that Thompson was fit to be tied over the lack of support from his new colleagues.

> Percy Thompson, business-manager of the Hamilton N.H.L. club, realizes that the local team isn't strong enough to make a successful fight for the championship. He declared today that he wants a half dozen more players lined up so that the present crew will have to work for their places. The failure of Joe Malone to come here leaves a big hole. It takes Prodgers out of his position on the defence. What the Hams need is a goalkeeper and several forwards. The defence will just about do. Lockhart, the present goalie, may not be here long. He is helping the club out until some person else can be secured. Thompson was in Toronto yesterday in his effort to strengthen up for tonight's opener. The result of his visit was the decision of the St. Pats to loan "Babe" Dye for tonight. President Calder and the other league officials will also hear from Thompson. He intends to read the riot act. He was promised a strong team and he says he is going to get it if at all possible.[405]

Hamilton also missed an important opportunity to aid its own cause. It is an old hockey truism that winning teams are built from the net out. In this regard, the Hamilton owners were having as much luck as their Quebec predecessors. In 1909, the Bulldogs played an exhibition game against the senior team in Chicoutimi, Quebec, defeating a skinny little goaltender named Georges Vezina. The Bulldogs passed on the opportunity to sign him, and Vezina became a member of the Montreal Canadiens, for whom he would play the next fifteen years without missing a single game (although he did spend a few minutes in the penalty box).

The Hamilton Tigers also looked a goaltending gift horse in the mouth when they visited nearby Kitchener to play the senior Greenshirts in an exhibition game. Defending the home team's net was a 25-year-old George Hainsworth. The *Spectator* noticed what Tigers management apparently overlooked.

> Goldie Prodgers will be in charge of the team and he is going to attempt to change the style of play of some of the players. He realizes that the Bengals must be taught to bore in closer to the nets when shooting, as their longs on Saturday proved easy for Hainsworth.[406]

Instead of signing Hainsworth, the "Hams" stuck with Howard Lockhart, who was also 25, but whose nickname, "Holes," reflected his career goals-against average of 5.05 (or, if his season with the 228th Battalion of the NHA is counted, 5.17). Hainsworth played in Hamilton's backyard for a couple of more years before heading off to Saskatoon to play for the Crescents and Sheiks. In 1926, at the age of 31, Hainsworth made his NHL debut, starring with the Montreal Canadiens. In 1928–29, he posted 22 shutouts in a 44-game season — a league record that still stands. Although Terry Sawchuk eclipsed his NHL total of 94 career shutouts, Hainsworth's 10 whitewashes in the Western Canada Hockey League mean that he continues to hold the all-time major-league record with 104 — one more than Sawchuk.

On the subject of shutouts, in its five-year NHL existence, the Hamilton Tigers blanked the opposition a total of eight times.

The first was in the team's very first game. Lockhart, a native of North Bay, Ontario, recorded his only NHL shutout much to the surprise and delight of the Hamilton locals.

> There were numerous disappointed folks at Percy Thompson's Arena last night — disappointed because they went to see a slaughter and didn't see anything of the kind.
>
> So much had been heard locally of the slicing of the paid performers that a lot of the gang were on to see a few samples. Tigers and Canadiens, however, played the winter pastime as it should be played, and fooled the gore-seekers.
>
> And Hamilton won.

What better debut could Hamilton make in the N.H.L.?

They gave Newsy Lalonde and his fellow Frenchmen an old-fashioned coat of kalsomine that carried a decisive sting with it. While the Canadiens were straining their creaky, weary limbs in a vain effort to notch a sole counter, Tigers smashed in, given two in the first period, a like number in the second and one for good measure in the final dash, thereby proving that their first victory was well-earned and decisive.

For the Canadiens it must be said they stepped on to the ice for the first time this season. It took them ten minutes to get their legs moving properly, and by the time they had satisfied themselves that they were skating well enough, their wind gave out. When that is taken into consideration they did mighty well. At times they showed flashes of their old form, but they lacked the punch they will show before the N.H.L. season is far advanced.

The struggle attracted a very fair-sized crowd. And every moment of the affair was interesting, even if both teams slowed down to a walk at times. The fans were in a good mood and lenient. They fully realised that neither team could be expected to show mid-season form in the opener and they refrained from chiding those who faltered most. As a matter of fact, the majority left the Arena firmly convinced that professional hockey is going to make a hit in Hamilton and that is isn't such a bad old game to witness.

"They beat us fair enough tonight, but wait," said Eddie "Newsy" Lalonde, the Canadien captain after the scramble was over.

Lalonde told the truth. There wasn't a bit of doubt about the clear-cut win. Whether or not Canadiens will turn the tables later remains to be seen. For the present, suffice to say that they had no right to win the first game — and didn't.

Tigers — every team that sports Hamilton colours gets that moniker — were best from goal out. Georges Vezina, credited with being the best goaler in the game, was good in spots, but off in others. Some easy shots beat him. Lockhart, in the Hamilton nets, was a treat — a veritable stone wall. When the Canadiens worked their way to on top of him, which was seldom, they couldn't fool him, when they shot from well-out they met the same barrier; and when they tried to sneak 'em by the defence and follow the disc in, "Locky" was there to meet them and beat them to the rubber. He put up one of the greatest exhibitions of net-guarding ever seen in Hamilton.[407]

According to the *Spectator*, Quebec City apparently didn't miss the Bulldogs, and in fact wished them well: "The Hamilton team received a message from the mayor and city council of the city of Quebec, extending New Year's greetings."[408]

One Tiger whose stay in Steeltown would be brief was Babe Dye, who was on loan from Toronto. After he scored two goals and an assist in that opening game Charlie Querrie's eyes must certainly have been popping out. Dye had been deemed expendable because Corb Denneny was holding down the St. Pats' left wing spot. He starred in Toronto's 6–3 opening-night loss to Ottawa, but suffered a fractured hand when Senators captain Eddie Gerard — while trying to check Denneny — accidentally struck him heavily with his stick and broke one of the bones. He would not be able to play again for two weeks. As a result, Querrie was quick to recall Dye from Hamilton.

Even after Frank Calder applied some pressure to the reticent owners (and the Canadiens loaned Billy Coutu to the Tigers), Tommy Gorman's Senators refused to help. It's not that the Senators were unable to comply: the team was carrying five substitutes, an embarrassment of riches.[409] Finally, after Christmas, the Senators agreed to supply the Tigers with one of their spares. The Tigers had been interested in 24-year-old defenceman George Boucher, but the Senators would not release him. Instead, they offered right winger Punch Broadbent.[410] On December 30, the NHL assigned Broadbent's rights to Hamilton.

But Calder's generosity didn't stop there. Charlie Querrie had mentioned he could use some help on the St. Pats blueline, so Calder plucked Sprague Cleghorn off the Senators roster and reassigned his rights to Toronto. Perhaps he was trying to punish Ottawa for its reluctance to answer the original call to help Hamilton; perhaps he felt the Senators were too strong for their, or the league's, own good. In any event, Calder had gone from effectively stealing franchises — and awarding them to those with cheques made payable to Francis Calder — to moving players around the league as casually as if he were managing a rotisserie league or a hockey card collection. According to the Hamilton *Herald*, the league meant business: "… if [Broadbent] doesn't report immediately he will be placed on the suspended lists. Likewise, Sprague Cleghorn will have to go to the Toronto St. Pats or suffer the same treatment."[411]

Despite the threat, the two men refused to report to their new teams, creating a major obstacle to Calder's "equalization" plan. The hand of Ottawa manager Tommy Gorman can be detected here: the situation was partially reminiscent of 1916, when Gorman stole Cy Denneny from Eddie Livingstone's Blueshirts, then griped relentlessly in his Ottawa *Citizen* sports section that Denneny could not afford to go to Toronto to play. Four years later, Broadbent was quoted as giving the same excuse — the Hamilton *Herald* reported that Punch had "a lucrative position in Ottawa that he doesn't care to give up, and says he doesn't care what action is taken against him."[412]

Having won their first four games of the season, the Ottawa Senators naturally had no interest in having their team split up. Reported the Ottawa *Journal*:

> Week-end developments stated that Cleghorn was still obdurate regarding his stand not to report to St. Pats. He received no less than four telegrams ordering him to report, but ignored them all. Sprague is going to stand firm, he says. Broadbent will not report to Hamilton under any consideration. The players are still considerably peeved over the stand taken by the league in grabbing one of their star players.
>
> They point out, not without reason, that the demand for Boucher is an unreasonable one. They commended the fight put up by the Ottawas to retain the brunette star, and while admitting that it might have been impossible to retain Cleghorn, unanimously back him in his stand against going to Toronto. Ottawa is in a peculiar position so far as the league is concerned. It is practically a home brew outfit, and unlike Canadiens, St. Pats or Hamilton, have not been recruited from all over, but represent the steady development of players and fulfillment of an idea.
>
> "They couldn't beat us on the ice, so they tried some committee room strong arm work, but that won't beat us, either," stated one of the players. It was hinted

that the players would go on strike and refuse to play, but obviously the better way is to go through and show the "other fellows" that they are going to win.[413]

On January 4, the Tigers gave up on Punch Broadbent, trading him to Montreal for cash. Broadbent never joined the Canadiens. His suspension was lifted on February 21, 1921, and he rejoined Ottawa, scoring four goals in nine games.

If Hamiltonians were disappointed that Broadbent would not be suiting up for the Tigers, they would quickly rejoice at the impending arrival of a legitimate NHL superstar. "Joe Malone is in town," the *Herald* proclaimed on January 5. "And there's joy in the camp of the Hamilton 'pros.'"

> In less than an hour after his arrival at the Arena this morning, Malone was out on the ice with the rest of the squad, working as if he had been training for a month or more. His presence seemed to lend added life to the lads and the result was a rousing gallop.
>
> The coming of Joe Malone to Hamilton means that "Punch" Broadbent, of Ottawa, reverts to the Canadiens. He is now the property of George Kennedy, and pudgy George will have to do the worrying as to whether or not he can get him to report to duty.[414]

Any fears that, in the absence of Cleghorn and Broadbent, the Senators players might go on strike proved to be unfounded. Indeed, the Senators marched into Hamilton and walloped the Tigers, 5–1, before a crowd of 5,500, the largest to witness a hockey game in the Steel City to that date. Newcomer Malone tallied the lone Tigers goal. Commented one fan, "The N.H.L. can take away one or two more from [the Senators] and they'll still give the others cards and spades."[415]

Frank Calder was in no mood to say anything complimentary about the Senators. He was incensed at Gorman, who had helped him ascend to the presidency just a few years earlier, over the Sprague Cleghorn affair. Calder hastily called for a meeting between himself, Tommy Gorman and George Kennedy at Montreal's Windsor Hotel. The Hamilton *Herald* reported:

> The Ottawa secretary informed the president of Cleghorn's refusal to go to Toronto and asked that the defence man be allowed to return to his club. George

Kennedy, who was present, would not hear of it and threatened to take his team out of the league. He further added that the owners of both the Hamilton and Toronto clubs would back him to the limit and stated that, unless the Ottawas would drop the case altogether, they will find themselves out of the league.[416]

When it came to this meeting, Gorman resorted to one of his old tricks. Instead of reporting on the actual events of the meeting in the *Citizen*, Gorman bubbled over with praise for Kennedy's Canadiens, who handed the Senators their first loss of the season on January 8. The win was the Canadiens' first of the season, and evidence indicates the Senators may have intentionally lost. Wrote Gorman:

> Canadiens performed Saturday night like a new team. [Georges] Vezina gave a hair-raising exhibition in the nets and [Bert] Corbeau showed the finest hockey he has put up this winter. [Harry] Mummery blocked cleverly and was useful on the offensive, while "Newsy" Lalonde showed a complete comeback. His rushes were always thrilling. [Amos] Arbour and [Didier] Pitre were good on the wings and Odie Cleghorn proved one of George Kennedy's most valuable men. It was "do or die" with Canadiens, and they gave no quarter.[417]

Towards the end of January, Cleghorn finally reported to the St. Pats. He was a rock-solid addition to the Toronto blueline who added three goals in thirteen games to lead the St. Pats to the second-half title. Toronto would face Ottawa, the winners of the first half and the defending Stanley Cup champions, in the NHL playoffs.

The Senators won the first game of the home-and-home, total-goals series, 5–0. Cleghorn's replacement, George Boucher, notched a hat trick. Charlie Querrie had his doubts about Cleghorn's play, and benched him for game two. On March 14, the Senators defeated Toronto, 2–0, to claim the NHL title. The very next day, Gorman advanced Cleghorn enough money to buy his release. If that weren't enough, Cleghorn, now a free agent, signed with the Senators and travelled west to Vancouver to face the Millionaires in the Stanley Cup series.

Gorman argued that, because Cleghorn had been with the Senators before Calder stripped him away and assigned his rights to Hamilton, he should be considered eligible to play for the Cup. PCHA president Frank

Patrick agreed, and Cleghorn starred in a tightly contested series that went the full complement of five games, with each match decided by a single goal. Before the fifth game, more than 2,000 fans were turned away from the gates of Vancouver's 11,000-seat arena. That night was also remarkable because of a brief appearance in a Millionaires jersey by Cyclone Taylor, who was playing against the team with whom he first achieved fame.

The Senators' victory celebration was short-lived. Two days after the Cup series ended, Calder again stripped Cleghorn from the Ottawa roster, stating that his buyout from Toronto had been handled improperly. On April 6, 1921, Calder claimed that, because Cleghorn had been on the Montreal Wanderers roster when that franchise folded, he was the property of the NHL! Desperate to make good on his pledge to help Hamilton build a competitive squad, Calder this time awarded Cleghorn to the Tigers.

Tragedy struck the NHL, and robbed Frank Calder of his staunchest ally, before the start of the 1921–22 season. George Kennedy had never fully recovered from the bout of influenza he contracted in the spring of 1919, and on October 19, 1921, the pudgy owner of the Montreal Canadiens died. Three weeks later, Kennedy's widow sold the team to a Quebecois trio for $11,000. The syndicate consisted of Joseph Cattarinich (the Habs' original goaltender and the man credited with discovering Georges Vezina), Leo Dandurand and Louis Letourneau.

This was not the highest bid for the team: Thomas J. Duggan of the Mount Royal Arena had previously offered the Kendall estate roughly $20,000. It was only when Duggan sent his agent to finalize the deal with Nap Dorval, who was acting on the estate's behalf, that he learned the team would not be his. It was not clear why, unless there was extreme pressure to keep the team in French-Canadian hands, Dorval would turn down an offer that would have added nearly $9,000 to the Kendall estate. Duggan, however, was given a consolation prize: the right to sell two NHL franchises, which were ultimately placed in Boston and New York.

Less than four years after Frank Calder took over the National Hockey Association and reorganized it as the National Hockey League, only one original ownership group remained: the Ottawa Senators' Tommy Gorman and E. P. Dey.

Soon after acquiring his rights, Percy Thompson found out that Sprague Cleghorn was even more adamantly opposed to a move to Hamilton than he had been about Toronto. The Tigers business manager ultimately gave in and asked Cleghorn just where, other than Ottawa, he might like to play. When Sprague expressed a wish to be reunited with his brother Odie, Thompson struck a deal with the new owners of the Montreal Canadiens, acquiring Harry Mummery and Amos Arbour in return.

The new players were not much help much as the Tigers finished in the cellar for the second year in a row — the third, counting Quebec's dismal performance in 1919–20. By this time, Thompson had learned he would have to help himself if the Tigers' fortunes were to be improved upon.

Chapter 20

The Steeltown Strike

Sportsmanship is demanded of hockey team owners as well as hockey team players, and there is no more reason for expecting a hockey team player to play for his employers for nothing than there is reason for expecting a professional actor to work for his employers for nothing.

— Philip Ross, 1925

Percy Thompson's efforts to rebuild the Hamilton Tigers would take several seasons to bear fruit. The 1922–23 and '23–24 seasons both ended with the Tigers holding down their customary spot in last place. But there were important signs that improvement was imminent. In the autumn of 1923, Thompson finally succeeded in signing the Green brothers, Red and Wilf (also known as Shorty), whom he had coveted since the club's first season. It cost Thompson $12,000 to lure the two brothers south, at a time when NHL stars were earning $1,500 per year. By now, the stakes had got so high that Tommy Gorman, lacking the funds to compete, was forced to sell his interest in the Ottawa Senators.

A year later, Alex McKinnon and Charlie Langlois also moved from Sudbury to Hamilton, and there was a new coach in place. After watching Art Ross and Percy LeSueur have no more luck than he himself had enjoyed, Thompson called upon Jimmy Gardner. It was perhaps Thompson's most astute hockey move: Gardner had an illustrious track record that dated back to the turn of the century. As a player, he twice won the Stanley Cup with the Montreal Amateur Athletic Association, and was a champion on two more occasions with the Montreal Wanderers. In 1905 he was an all-star with Calumet, the champions of the International Hockey League, and when the Patricks formed the Pacific Coast Hockey Association they tapped him to coach the New Westminster Royals. He guided that squad to a first-place finish, then did the same with the Montreal Canadiens in 1913–14.

The year 1924 saw many changes take place throughout the hockey world. The National Hockey League expanded from four teams to six, with the addition of the Montreal Maroons (an English-Canadian team to rival the Canadiens) and the Boston Bruins, the circuit's first U.S. venture. In the west, there was consolidation. The Seattle Metropolitans folded, leaving the Patricks' Pacific Coast Hockey Association with only two teams, the Vancouver Maroons and Victoria Cougars. Those clubs joined the Western Canada Hockey League, which already had teams in Calgary, Regina, Saskatoon and Edmonton. (The two western leagues had been playing an interlocking schedule for the past two seasons.) The NHL, meanwhile, extended its regular season from 24 to 30 games, and revamped its playoff format. The second- and third-place finishers were slated to battle each other in a semifinal series, with the winner advancing to play the first-place team for the NHL championship. The winner of this series would play the WCHL champions for the Stanley Cup.

The 1924–25 edition of the Hamilton Tigers stormed out of the gate, winning their first four games, and losing only once in their first ten. In mid-February they sat comfortably atop the NHL standings. By this time, rumours were circulating that George "Tex" Rickard, the legendary New York–based boxing promoter who had been granted an NHL expansion franchise, was interested in buying the Hamilton team. Rickard had made and lost a fortune during the Klondike gold rush, learning how to operate a gambling hall and stage boxing promotions. After a short period in San Francisco, the former Texas Ranger moved to Nevada, where he became a fight promoter.

An even more fanciful piece of gossip out of Buffalo had Tommy Gorman planning to jump to a new hockey league based in the United States and organized by Eddie Livingstone. The Hamilton *Spectator* was skeptical.

> The story sent from Buffalo was probably founded on the same crop of dreams which had Rickard buying the Hamilton franchise and players for $110,000, if they won the Stanley Cup. Tex has never communicated with the Hamilton club on the matter, and would get

little satisfaction if he did, for the franchise is not for sale at any price, and as for the players — well, they're good enough for Mister Thompson.[418]

With two games left to play in the regular season, Hamilton led the second-place Toronto St. Patricks by only three points, meaning that it was still possible for Toronto to steal first place from the Tigers. On March 7, in their final home game of the regular season, the Tigers lost 2–0 to the lowly Boston Bruins. However, the St. Pats were also blanked, 3–0, by the Ottawa Senators, giving Hamilton the regular-season crown and a bye into the NHL finals. Although they won their final four games, the Senators failed to overtake the Canadiens, who secured the other available playoff berth by finishing third.

On March 11, the Canadiens took the first game of their two-game, total-goals series against the St. Pats, 3–2. When Calder tried to dictate that Montreal's home dates in the NHL playoffs should be played at the brand new Forum rather than the Canadiens' home rink, the Mount Royal Arena, Leo Dandurand warned him not to interfere. "If Canadiens get into the league elimination," the Montreal *Gazette* reported, "the Canadien Club will decide where it is going to play its home game or games, and does not need the league to run its purely club affairs.

"[Dandurand] further added that the club was out to retain the Stanley Cup, and that every energy would be directed in that direction, and if it were deemed wise to play their home game at their regular home ice at the Mount Royal Arena, the team would play there. He made it clear, however, that no decision as to rink arrangements has been made, and left the impression that the question of transferring any possible home play-off games from the Mount Royal Arena to the larger Forum would be given careful consideration, as the management wanted to look after as many spectators as possible who might wish to see the contests, but stressed the point that home games were home games, indicating the Canadiens' chance of success would be better in their own rink, and that winning the cup again was the object which the club had in mind."

Calder backed down.

The next day's Toronto *Mail and Empire* also carried a report that should have raised some eyebrows about the way the Tigers were conducting *their* business. A Hamilton lawyer and Tigers season ticket subscriber by the name of C. W. G. Gibson filed suit against Percy Thompson, Andrew Ross, William Yates and R. B. Harris, who operated under the name Hamilton Professional Hockey Club. Gibson sought damages of $120 for "breach of contract and wrongful conversion of goods" after the club confiscated his season tickets and refused to grant him admission to the March 7 game.

> The case will be heard on April 8 in Division Court. Mr. Gibson held two season books, each providing for the purchase of two tickets and the option of getting two more for every game. Last Saturday night Mr. Gibson used the two book tickets and it is alleged the ticket seller insisted he purchase two additional tickets, which he refused to do. The ticket seller then held the book, it is alleged. The question of whether or not the club could force book-holders to buy extra tickets will be one of the points which the judge will have to decide.[419]

Meanwhile, the players were getting restless.

> Hamilton players informed Percy Thompson, head of the Tiger club, that unless each player on the team got $200 for his services for the play-off finals of the N.H.L., they would refuse to play. As the playoffs are conducted under the direction of the N.H.L., Percy Thompson immediately informed President Frank Calder, of the league, regarding the players' demands. The league head had given the Hamilton players until 11 o'clock [on March 13] to decide to play under the old arrangements. He left for Toronto last night and will meet a delegation of the Hamilton players there this morning. If the Tiger players are not prepared to go on under the old arrangements, President Calder has given them to understand the league will not countenance what he terms a "holdup," and that rather than give in to the players, the team will be suspended from the play-off and the Ottawa team will be sent in to replace them in the finals against either Canadiens or St. Patricks. In the meantime, also, President Calder has informed the Ottawa management of their possible inclusion in the series and the team has resumed practices in case they are called upon to take Hamilton's place.
> Tigers claim that their contract for the season expired with the playing of the last scheduled game, and that they are entitled to extra money for the playoff. As the receipts

for the game are divided between the six clubs, the local owners feel that it would be working a hardship on them and that they would not profit as much as the club which did not figure in the finals.[420]

The players received telegrams from Calder threatening suspension and the holding up of back pay, after which the players met once more and decided to stick with their decision. Captain Shorty Green broke the news to Thompson.[421]

Green — whom Doc Stewart, the Boston Bruins' dentist-turned-goaltender, called "the trickiest and fastest-thinking forward" he ever encountered[422] — pointed out the facts from the players' point of view, based on the two-year contracts he and his brother Red had signed. "We signed to play 24 games. This year the N.H.L. schedule calls for 30 games. We have played them without receiving one cent more money. We reported for practice two weeks earlier than our contracts called for and had to pay our own expenses right up to the time that the league season got under way. We feel that we are not asking for anything that doesn't belong to us. The management now requests us to stay here an extra week and take part in two games for the benefit of the league. We would have to pay our own expenses during that time, too. We regret very much that the management wasn't big enough to come to us and admit the money was due us. They said when the show-down came they intended to 'fix us up.'"[423]

Thompson refuted Green's charges, noting that, with the exception of the Green brothers, the players had signed new contracts prior to the start of the season, and were therefore aware that the season would be thirty games long. He was silent about whether he renegotiated with the Greens.

Following his standard operating procedure, Calder criticized the players, stating that their contracts obligated them to perform between December 1 and March 31, regardless of the number of games in the regular season. The argument blithely ignored Green's assertion that the 1924–25 regular season opened on November 29, and that training camps opened a couple of weeks before that.

Calder told the Hamilton players they would be fined or suspended if they did not play the winner of the Toronto-Montreal series. The players countered that they would rather quit or be suspended than be taken advantage of. Calder expressed his fear that to capitulate, or even compromise, would jeopardize the owners' "large capital investment in rinks and arenas," and he maintained that "this capital must be protected."[424]

According to the Hamilton *Herald*, Tigers manager Percy Thompson tried to plead poverty.

The Hamilton club officials say that they cannot afford to pay the players anything for their participation in the series. If each player were to receive $200 it would mean an outlay of $2,000, and Mr. Thompson declares that not more than that amount would be realized on the games. The money of the games between the Canadiens and St. Pats, also the winner of that series [against] Hamilton, was to have been pooled and divided equally among the six clubs in the league. Because of that, Thompson says, Hamilton could not afford to pay the players.[425]

He also protested that his hands had been tied by Calder. "I've nothing to say except to express the greatest regret that such situation should have arisen. The next move will be made by President Calder," the Tigers manager said.[426]

The Ottawa *Journal*, normally a pro-ownership paper given that its publisher, Phil Ross, doubled as a Stanley Cup trustee, started the media avalanche against Calder.

Had [the Tigers players] waited till the day of the first game and then "struck," fandom would have justly condemned them. They apparently waited for a move from Thompson, and at first none came. Thompson admitted their demand somewhat by agreeing to give half of the amount. This solidified the players' position. Thompson's position is now untenable, because if he does not come through, the Hamilton public will be aroused, and if Ottawas go into a play-off, the future of the National League might be imperiled. It is a situation fraught with danger, and the easiest way out seems to be the best. Mr. Thompson will be well advised to take the elastic off his bank roll and "pay." Next year is another year and he can protect himself [then]. In the meantime, the National League moguls had better get together and devise some scheme by which the "financial" side of these manoeuvres will not be made so painfully apparent in the future.[427]

Meanwhile, Shorty Green tried to explain the players' rationale for the strike.

Professional hockey is a money-making affair. The promoters are in the game for what they can make out of
it and the players wouldn't be in the game if they did-
n't look at matters in the same light. If we weren't producing the kind of hockey to draw the crowds we
wouldn't be paid accordingly. Why, then, should we be
asked to play two games merely for the sake of sweet-
ening the league's finances?…

[W]e have given the club fair warning. We might
have waited until the night of our first game with the St.
Pats or Canadiens and then made known our demands.
That wouldn't have been fair to the public, and that's
something we took into consideration. Unfortunately, a
lot of happenings in the camps of the professional teams
never got out to the public. We are often called upon to
take abuses that are hard to stand, but we say nothing. The
management seems to think that we have to take those
abuses as well as play the game. We think we have taken
a proper stand and we think that the local management
acted unwisely in calling in the league president to
threaten us. Mr. Thompson said he would suspend us,
hold back our salaries and probably sue us for damages.
We refuse to be intimidated.[428]

"The Hamilton players can suit themselves what they do," Calder
retorted. "If they don't care to play against either St. Pats or Canadiens, they
don't have to. We will easily overcome the trouble."[429] Calder told the *Herald*
that it was the league's intention to allow the fourth-place Senators to play
the St. Pats–Canadiens winner if Hamilton was not going to compete.

Calder added: "I hear, however, that the Hamilton players have been
talking to St. Pats' players, pointing out that they would be foolish to
stand for Ottawa getting a chance, particularly when they finished fourth
and should not be granted a bye. If St. Pats kick over the traces I will send
the Canadiens west to represent the N.H.L. in the Stanley Cup series.
However, I do not look for trouble from the St. Pats."[430]

In this last statement, the league president was indulging in some
"table talk," sending a friendly warning through the press to the St. Pats
co-owner and manager Charlie Querrie that the Livingstone lawsuits
were not yet completely settled.

Calder's playoff plan didn't sit well with either of the two semifinalists.
"President Calder's original idea of allowing the Ottawa team to meet

tonight's winners was objected to strongly by Managing Director Leo Dandurand of Canadiens and all the officers of the St. Pats' club," the Ottawa *Citizen* reported. "In fact, the players on each of these two teams positively refused to meet the Ottawas, claiming that it was absolutely unfair to allow a team which finished fourth in the standings at the end of the N.H.L. schedule to have a bye, such as proposed, or even be allowed to enter the playoffs."[431]

On March 13, Shorty Green, the players' spokesman, travelled to Toronto to meet with Calder, who was in town for the second game of the NHL semifinal. He found that the league president's position was as steadfast as the players'.

The next day's editions of the Hamilton *Herald* suggested that Calder did not speak on behalf of *all* the owners: "One of the club owners hinted that the club had practically decided to give in to the players and it was announced that a meeting of owners and players would be held last night to clarify the air. The meeting wasn't held for two reasons. The players were in Toronto watching the St. Pats–Canadiens game and the other club owners wouldn't listen to the suggestion that they pay the $2,000 necessary to ensure the players' participation in the final series."[432]

Both sides were cutting off their noses to spite their faces. To satisfy the Hamilton players, the six league owners would have had to shell out less than $350 apiece — money they would have easily recouped by having the league finals proceed. Nor was there any truth to the Tigers' protests that they couldn't afford to meet the players' demands. The Tigers and the Hamilton arena were owned by the same company. Therefore, when the rink withheld its share of the gate receipts for the games played in Hamilton during the NHL final series — to cover "incidental expenses" — it would effectively be robbing Peter to pay Paul. Meanwhile, the team stood to receive one-sixth of the profits from the St. Pats–Canadiens semifinal, in addition to a similar share for the finals. On the other hand, the Hamilton players were holding out for $200 each, when, thanks to a generous gate-splitting arrangement, they stood to earn four times that amount if the Tigers advanced to the Stanley Cup series.[433]

Both sides tried to make their case in the pages of the Hamilton papers. The *Spectator* had the players' view:

> The players feel that as it was their efforts that put the club
> in a position to benefit greatly from a financial standpoint,
> not from the N.H.L. final play-off series alone, but from
> their share of the Stanley cup series gates, they should not

be overlooked in making this possible. Their stand is that they put in two weeks of training previous to the opening of the season and two weeks between the finish of the regular schedule, practically a month that they are compelled to play gratis, so they contend. This is strictly a matter between players and club. They do not feel they are holing the club up, rather that they are asking justice, and the amount requested, $200 to each man, is merely to cover their activities extending over the period not provided for, as they believe.[434]

The *Herald* quoted Percy Thompson, who seemed confident that the owners would not be blamed for the dispute:

Each and every contract signed by the National Hockey League players calls for a season ending "on or about March 31." This in itself is sufficient to prove that we were not asking the players to do something that their contract didn't call for. If any of the clubs taking part in the championship series are entitled to extra pay, why didn't St. Pats and Canadiens ask for it? In my opinion, they had no just right to additional salary.[435]

P. J. Jones of the *Herald* pointed out a flaw in Thompson's reasoning: "If the N.H.L. officials claim that their contracts call for the players to play hockey until 'on or about March 31,' why are the players paid extra for participation in the Stanley Cup series that is usually completed before March 31?"[436]

And a small wire service story picked up by the *Herald* might have answered Thompson's questions about the Toronto and Montreal players:

Montreal fans on the whole seem to support the Hamilton players in their demands in view of the recent facts made public as to the contracts signed by the Tiger players. From statements made from St. Patrick and Canadien camps, the players of the two semi-finalist teams have been taken care of financially as far as the extra games are concerned, and it is thought among fans here that the Tigers should be treated on a par with their rivals in the post-scheduled series.[437]

After all, you don't have to ask for something you've already been given.

Prior to the second game of the semifinal series, it was the St. Patricks' turn to grumble about Frank Calder's plan to have the series winner play Ottawa. Reported the Montreal *Gazette*:

> If St. Patricks win from Canadiens tonight in the National Hockey League play-off by more than one goal and take the round from the Montrealers, they will not play Ottawa as stated by President Calder, should the Hamilton team be thrown out because of a demand for a bonus. The St. Patricks management are determined on this point. And so are the players. Just what stand the Canadiens will take is not known, for the Montrealers are now on the train bound for Toronto. But it seems likely that Leo Dandurand and his players will likely adopt the same attitude as St. Patricks should they eliminate the Irish tonight.
>
> Why should Ottawa, the fourth place team in the standing, be now injected into the play-offs to replace Hamilton, and not only get a chance for the championship, which they do not deserve, but have the bye in the semi-finals, and come in fresh to the final after St. Patricks or Canadiens have engaged in two hard contests? It is not fair on the face of it. St. Patricks' claim is that if Hamilton is thrown out, Ottawa should not replace them, but the winners of the St. Patricks–Canadiens semi-finals should be declared champions and go west after the Stanley Cup.
>
> The St. Patricks players are not raising any fuss about a bonus for the play-offs and are satisfied to take their chance on winning the honours and then sharing in the Stanley Cup playoff receipts.[438]

Even the wife of Canada's governor general had taken an interest in the affairs of Canada's game. In March 1925, Lady Evelyn Byng had written a letter to Calder:

> Feeling a great desire to help your effort to "clean hockey" and eliminate the needless rough play that at present is a threat of the game, and also to leave a tangible record of the enjoyment I personally have had from the game

during our sojourn in Canada, I am writing to ask if you will let me offer a challenge cup for the man on any team in the league, who, while being thoroughly effective, is also a thoroughly clean player.

I am convinced that the public desires good sport, not the injuring of players, and if by donating this challenge cup I can in any way help towards this end it will give me a great deal of pleasure.[439]

The president of the NHL would likely have accepted Lady Byng's offer in any event, but the controversy surrounding the Hamilton strike made it impossible to refuse any opportunity to improve the league's image. Thus was born the National Hockey League's second award for individual effort (the first was the Hart Trophy, awarded to the league's most valuable player). In short order, Calder announced that the first Lady Byng Trophy was to be awarded to Ottawa's Frank Nighbor — who, coincidentally, was also the first winner of the Hart in 1924. Lady Byng personally presented the award to Nighbor before a postseason exhibition game between the Ottawa Senators and a team called the "Combines," which was made up of such former Senators such as goalie Clint Benedict, now with the Montreal Maroons, right wing Punch Broadbent, and the four Boucher brothers.

As it had been in the past with those who crossed him, such as Eddie Livingstone, Calder's response to the Hamilton situation was vindictive. On March 16, the *Mail and Empire* reported that he had suspended the Hamilton players and fined each of them $200. Three days earlier, the Canadiens had defeated the St. Pats, 2–0, to give them a victory in the semifinal series by an aggregate score of 5–2. Calder therefore awarded the NHL championship to Montreal.[440]

Lifetime suspensions were Calder's favourite way of dealing with players who were out of line, although these bans were usually meaningless. Invariably, the players would beg Calder for forgiveness, and he would quietly concur, as if he were doing them a favour out of the goodness of his heart. Those who chose not to grovel had few options, other than senior hockey or the Western Canada Hockey League. The latter was better suited to younger, single men without families that would have to be uprooted. And when the Seattle Metropolitans folded in 1924, it signalled the beginning of the end for major league hockey in the west.

Phil Ross's Ottawa *Journal* kept up its barrage against Calder, the Hamilton owners, and the playoff system itself.

[T]he arrangement whereby a team which completes the season's playing schedule at the head of the race is compelled to play off with the winner of a playoff between the second and third place teams is wrong because it is not a genuine test of the league championship.

The winner of two games, or the team which scores the most goals in two games, is proclaimed champion over the team which has won the majority of and scored the most goals in thirty games. The thing is simply absurd.

One dislikes questioning motives, but it does seem as if this strange rule was fathered solely by one thing, a desire on the part of the owners, or some of them, to draw down extra gates — totalling thousands of dollars — to be distributed among six club ownerships. Under this arrangement every club benefits after the expenses incidental to the games have been taken out.

There is another thing. The Hamilton club owners closed the season with an excellent financial balance. They are reputed to have had a net profit of $25,000. If that be so, or even partially so, why should these owners ask the Hamilton players, who have fulfilled their contract when they concluded the league schedule of games, to play two extra games and risk their hard-earned honours to chance, to provide two extra gates to their prosperous owners? Surely, at the very least, they were entitled to some small share in the gates?

It may well be held, of course, that there is something in hockey besides money, and that the Hamilton players might well have gone into a playoff just for the sake of the game. But the answer is that sportsmanship is demanded of hockey team owners as well as hockey team players, and there is no more reason for expecting a hockey team player to play for his employers for nothing than there is reason for expecting a professional actor to work for his employers for nothing.

It would have been better, more satisfactory, if the Hamilton team had been bigger than their owners and played off with the Canadiens. But the greater blame, we think, attaches to the men who made such an absurd play-off rule; and for the sake of hockey and its future success, they will be wise if they eliminate it next year.

The whole episode is regrettable — bad for professional hockey. President Calder may proclaim Canadiens champions of the league, but that doesn't make them champions. All it does is to create bad feelings, to leave a bad taste in the public's mouth, and to do injury to hockey.[441]

A couple of days later, *Journal* columnist Philip McCann called for Calder's head:

It's certain that there must be a house-cleaning, with the work beginning at the top. President Frank Calder is a fine fellow personally, but he has shown weakness upon several occasions during the past two or three seasons. It has been said in his behalf that it is the constitution of the National Hockey League that has hampered him. If this is a fact then there should be a general shake-up. President Calder's appointment of referees has been open to criticism, and his failure to curb the three or four "bad men" in the league has been quite noticeable. However, this is now a matter of history. The hold-out of the Hamilton players will doubtless be responsible for a searchlight being thrown on the entire workings of the National Hockey League which must result in vast improvement or utter ruin. Two years ago this writer said that the game was bigger than the men in control of it, and since then the game has grown, and the men in control have shown little, if any, improvement.[442]

In the face of this backlash against him, Calder tried to exercise some damage control by explaining his position.

"Because of the many conflicting reports and statements being circulated in connection with the recent impasse between the Hamilton Hockey Club and its players, the following authentic facts may be of interest to the hockey fans," said Calder.

In the first place it is not — and never was — a question of bonuses to the Hamilton players. It was — and still is — a question of contracts. Each of the players of the Hamilton club is bound under a contract to play hockey for the Hamilton Club for a certain period, expiring on or about March 30 next....

The ring-leaders of the Hamilton "strikers" have chosen to disregard this clause of their contract and to contend that the play-off series, of which they were all advised and knew about when they signed their contracts, was an additional task imposed upon them — which is not a fact.

The whole incident, then, resolves itself into a question whether the clubs and the league shall insist that players fulfill their contracts or whether the clubs and league shall permit the players to interpret their contracts in their own way and to suit the whims and fancies of those who imagine that they have grievances.

The clubs, whether they lose money or not, are bound to fulfill their part of the contract by paying the players the sums contracted for. Should the club meet financial difficulties of a nature which makes it impossible for them to meet their obligations to the players, then those obligations are met by the league.

The "strike" might have presumably have been ended by the yielding of the Hamilton Club to the demands of the players. To have acceded to the players' demands, however, would have established a precedent which would have been seized on in years to come. The majority of the club members of the National Hockey League are directly interested in large capital tied up in hockey rinks and arenas — investments which must be protected.

The Hamilton players, whatever the future may have for them, cannot claim that they were unjustly or unfairly treated in this incident. The greatest patience was exercised with them in an effort to persuade them of the error of their ways and some of them have admitted individually that they had done wrong. Because of an ill-advised compact, entered into with the ring-leaders, however, they chose to remain out rather than fulfill their contracts....

In the face of the persistent refusal of the Hamilton players to carry out their contracts, the only alternative was to declare them to have defaulted in their series with the Canadiens and to declare the latter club champions

of the league for the season 1924–25, an inglorious ending to an otherwise brilliant season for which the directors of the Hamilton Club are in no way to be blamed.[443]

Nowhere in that statement is any apology made to the supporters of
the Hamilton Tigers, who were now being deprived of a chance to see
their team compete for the Stanley Cup. Instead, Calder focused on his
league's losses. "I would like to point out that the league will lose close
to $8,000 from Hamilton's action," he said. "This money would have
been taken in at the two games between Canadiens and Hamilton. By
the payment of $2,000 to Hamilton, the amount asked by the players, we
could have carried on the series and taken in that $8,000. It can thus be
seen that we are paying dearly from a money end for our action, but we
are willing to take it to make an example of the Hamilton players and a
warning for all future time."[444]

No discussion of Hamilton's 1924–25 season would be complete without noting that it has been reported for decades that the Tigers strike was
the NHL's first labour dispute. Those reports are inaccurate; the dubious
honour actually belongs to the Toronto St. Pats, in 1921. As related by
Philip McCann of the Ottawa *Citizen*:

> It was only four years ago that a similar strike, or hold-
> up, occurred, but that one was timed effectively by mem-
> bers of the St. Pats team, who waited until they were
> about to go on the ice for their first play-off game before
> making their demands, and, with the Arena filled with
> cash customers, management of the club found them-
> selves with the pistol to their head and had to pay the
> players. In the present case, the plans of the Hamilton
> players are said to have been the same but a leak some-
> where brought the case to a head sooner than the players
> intended, which is responsible for them all now being on
> the suspended list.[445]

While the Canadiens travelled west to play for the Stanley Cup — a series
the Victoria Cougars won, in what would prove to be the western league's
last hurrah in the postseason — Calder and the NHL were confronted with

the return of an old nemesis. Eddie Livingstone was once again announcing plans to launch a rival league, the International Hockey League, with teams slated for Montreal, Toronto, New York, Boston, Springfield (Massachusetts), Pittsburgh, Cleveland and Philadelphia. Roy Schooley, the mayor of Pittsburgh and a former hockey magnate and referee dating back to the days of the Western Pennsylvania Hockey League in 1901, would own his city's franchise. Livingstone and Percy Quinn signed a contract with the City of Toronto to add ice to the Coliseum on the Canadian National Exhibition grounds.[446]

Just as Livingstone was making waves, Shorty Green of the Hamilton Tigers raised a ruckus of his own with a damning statement published in the Hamilton *Herald*.

> Be it known to the public of Hamilton that we, the playing members of the Hamilton professional hockey club, regret the fact that they who so earnestly and whole-heartedly supported us throughout the regular season must be denied a chance to see their team in the finals. We have enjoyed being here with you and, to a man, would rather play to a Hamilton audience than any other on the circuit. Knowing the players intimately, as I do, I feel this that this year the enthusiasm and support of the Hamilton public has brought forth a concerted and great effort from each and every man to give of his best, and I might add that this support was sadly lacking from the executive end of our club. Personally, I know of certain occasions when the help of this executive along certain lines could have made our climb to the top rung of the championship an easier matter and, forthwith, are a few facts to substantiate the above statement:
>
> Upon our second visit to Ottawa, which resulted in a 2–0 victory for the Ottawa club, I had occasion to question hockey rulings and decisions made by Referee Dr. O'Leary, and the fans here will remember that, at this particular time, there was a split between the owners of the Capital team and general conditions there were not very favourable. This was probably the reason for the following letter, which was never before made public:

Dear Percy,

No doubt you would like a victory for your club, but don't be disappointed if you lose. You will never know the extent of the favour you are doing your old side-kick, T. P. Gorman. Your coming up has cheered me a lot. I also want to thank Mr. Ross and the rest of your confreres.

T. P. Gorman

Mr. Thompson, the local manager, told me it was useless to question decisions made by Dr. O'Leary and showed me the above letter, which had been delivered to him by T. P. Gorman's son while the game was in progress.

I could quote many other instances with which I am personally acquainted, which did not appear to me to be in the best interests of the players, but we have been given this space to express our feelings towards the sport-loving public of Hamilton and there is just one thing we wish to say. We would be more than pleased to represent Hamilton again in the N.H.L. for the benefit of the fans who have so generously patronized our games, but this is final: We do not ever intend to ever play again for the present management.

In conclusion, we desire to thank the sporting public of Hamilton and trust that the unbiased fans can see our side of the argument.[447]

Green later added that the players would only play again if they were sold en masse to a club they were willing to go to. He also said that Mickey Roach and Jess Spring, married men who held summer jobs in Hamilton, could withdraw from the players' pact if they chose to.

"We realize that married men have more responsibility than we single fellows and can't do quite the same thing in a crisis of this kind. For that reason we told Mickey and Jess that anything they might do next year would not cause any ill-feeling. If they see fit to sign with Hamilton again, they will not be doing anything against our wishes. Billy Burch, Red and myself, however, are determined not to play here again unless there is a change in ownership."[448]

Thompson, in trying to pave the way for a compromise, violated Calder's order and summoned the Tigers to the Barton Street Arena. "We decided to clean the situation up and try to forget the sorry mess," he told the *Herald*. "It's something we are all eager to bury."[449]

On May 1, the Abso-Pure Ice Company agreed to erect a new hockey arena, one that would seat 8,000, on the site of the Barton Street Arena. "The directors will erect the most up-to-date building of its kind in Canada," the *Herald* crowed. "All the latest improvements as installed in Montreal, Ottawa, Boston and other big centres will be included in the local plans, as well as a few wrinkles that should make the Arena a credit to the city."[450]

That arena was never built, and Hamilton would never again host an NHL team after the 1924–25 season. And we would argue that the city Calder abandoned has never forgotten the slight. Despite its location near such fertile hockey territory as Toronto, Detroit and Buffalo, the city has never welcomed professional hockey. (See Appendix B for Hamilton's pro hockey history after the strike of 1925.) Since the completion of the 18,000-seat Copps Coliseum in 1985, Hamiltonians have turned out in droves for such international events as the Canada Cup and the World Junior Championships, but otherwise the city has had a checkered history. Minor pro teams such as the Canucks and Bulldogs and major junior teams such as the Dukes and Steelhawks have come and gone without leaving any impression.

The Tigers' walkout was the last catastrophe that would strike the NHL for quite some time. By cancelling the finals and, ultimately, cutting Hamilton out of the league, Calder sent a clear message to anyone thinking about crossing him: they would risk losing their career or their franchise. The president's scare tactics ensured that the owners and players would be careful to toe the line for years to come.

Chapter 21

Stop Spreading the News

But thousands of spectators pay good money every winter to cheer on the champions (sometimes to jeer at the other side) in what they believe to be genuine contests between Ottawa and "Boston" or some other club which carries on the business of hockey. They must naturally feel disturbed when the captain of the Hamilton team ... gives the public a little peep behind the scenes.
— Ottawa *Citizen*, March 18, 1925

*S*horty Green's accusations that a game between Ottawa and Hamilton had been rigged did not sit well with Frank Ahearn, the new owner of the Senators. Ahearn had bought out his partner, Tommy Gorman, who also left his job with the *Citizen* to go to New York and help Tex Rickard operate the new Madison Square Garden, which was rapidly taking shape at the corner of Eighth Avenue and 49th Street.

Gorman's departure from the *Citizen* brought with it a change in editorial policy toward the hockey team. No longer would the newspaper be the Senators' unofficial house organ, as evidenced by this editorial, which appeared on March 18, 1925:

**New York Americans owner
Tex Rickard donned goalie gear for this
promotional photograph.**

After all, the commercial hockey clubs represent only a small number of the hockey players in Canada. The roots of the great winter game are really in the thousands of school rinks, and the outdoor rinks that are cleared by small boys in every town and village wherever skating is possible.

But thousands of spectators pay good money every winter to cheer on the champions (sometimes to jeer at the other side) in what they believe to be genuine contests between Ottawa and "Boston," or some other club which carries on the business of hockey. They must naturally feel disturbed when the captain of the Hamilton team, speaking on behalf of the players who won the championship this year, gives the public a little peep behind the scenes.

Commercial hockey is described as something like vaudeville. The players put on shows at the different arenas, much as acrobats do at the variety halls, to earn an honest livelihood. Sometimes they doubt, according to the Hamilton captain's statement, whether they have the full support of the management in that honest endeavour. He cites as an instance one visit to Ottawa this season, when the Ottawa club needed a victory. He added:

"I could quote many other instances with which I am personally acquainted, which do not appear to me to be in the best interests of the players…"

Perhaps they might as well be left unsaid. Even the youngsters are remarking that it is the western league's turn to have the Cup this year, at any rate. Ottawa, Toronto, Canadiens and Hamilton have all had turns as National Hockey League champions. But the managers of Hockey Clubs, Limited, would be well advised to put on the soft pedal when they set out to disparage players who have earned fat dividends for them through the season.[151]

Frank Calder shared Ahearn's irritation over Green's comments and the *Citizen* piece. Back in the early days of the National Hockey League, such allegations probably wouldn't have seen the light of day, let alone carried the potential to damage the league's image. But the American media could not be counted on to play ball the way Elmer Ferguson's Montreal *Herald* or Gorman's *Citizen* had done. And now that the NHL had established an American outpost in Boston and was hopeful of making a foray into New York, a higher degree of professionalism around league affairs — or at least the appearance of same — would be needed. So it was that, with Calder's blessing and attendance, the Ottawa Senators sued the Ottawa *Citizen* for libel, seeking damages of $45,000. Ahearn believed Quebec's laws to be stricter than Ontario's, so he filed the suit in Hull, just across the Ottawa River from the nation's capital.[452]

The case did call into question the *Citizen's* integrity, but not for the reason Ahearn might have intended. Ahearn testified that the team paid the *Citizen* $1,000 for the season — for advertising *and* for the write-ups of the hockey matches. A copy of the contract was produced as evidence.[453] Also introduced was a letter from Ahearn to F. W. Crabbe, the *Citizen's* former advertising manager, in which the Senators owner expressed the opinion that $1,000 is "a lot of money for news the public demands."[454]

Crabbe's reply was also read into the record: "In any event, the $1,000 which you pay does not nearly cover what it would cost if we charged our regular advertising rate of 25 cents a line."[455]

The newspaper's attorney, Harold Fisher, questioned Ahearn about his expectations. Fisher asked, "You also wanted some advance stuff, which is advertising under another name?"

"I call it news," Ahearn replied, "not advertising."

"Do you know that the advance stuff is called 'bally-hoo'?"

"Yes. I expected to get as much bally-hoo, for example, as the Royal Humane Society."[456]

Judge Rose agreed that the *Citizen* had libelled the Senators, and awarded the team $100 — or one-tenth of the amount the paper had received from the hockey team for "advertising." Curiously, the newspaper's publishers, Wilson Southam and H. S. Southam — who just happened to be Ahearn's brother-in-law — congratulated Ahearn on his victory.[457]

As far as the National Hockey League was concerned, Tex Rickard's interest in joining was a major coup. The former Texas Ranger seemed gifted with the Midas touch as a boxing promoter. His first brush with that sport came in 1898, when he arranged a bout involving Joe Boyle, the man who went on to lead the Dawson City challenge for the Stanley Cup. He later moved to Reno, Nevada, where he organized a 1910 match between Jim Jeffries and Jack Johnson, then travelled through Central and South America before settling in New York. In 1916, he staged a contest between Jess Willard and Frank Moran at the old Madison Square Garden. The gate receipts — $150,000 — set a record for an indoor fight.

After orchestrating the 1919 fight in Toledo, Ohio, in which Jack Dempsey gained the heavyweight crown, Rickard's next project was the famed bout between Dempsey and Georges Carpentier in Jersey City, New Jersey. A crowd of 90,000 paid a total of $1,600,000 for the privilege of watching the contest, which was staged in an immense wooden stadium constructed especially for the occasion.

The only problem for the NHL was that Rickard was less than enthusiastic about hockey. Even if he did want the sport to be played in his new arena, it was less than certain he would choose Calder's league — he was also being wooed by Eddie Livingstone.

Not even the success of the NHL's first U.S.–based franchise, the Boston Bruins, could fully convince Rickard.

Tom Duggan, acting as the league's agent, had found a willing convert in the Boston grocery store magnate Charles Weston Adams. Adams left the management of his club to Art Ross, who had been fired as coach of the Hamilton Tigers in 1924. All he asked was that the team's colours match the brown and gold of his grocery stores. He even delegated the naming of the team — the Bruins were the first NHL club to be nicknamed by their fans.

In New York, Tommy Gorman kept up the pressure on his new boss, who, after some additional urging on the part of his close friend John Hammond, agreed to give hockey a chance. On April 17, 1925, the NHL granted a conditional franchise, to be called the New York Americans. Three months later, Gorman was introduced as the first manager of both

Opening night for the expansion New York Americans, and the first hockey game ever played at the original Madison Square Garden.

Madison Square Garden and the New York Americans.[458] Perhaps still uncertain about the sport's prospects, Rickard flipped the franchise to Bill Dwyer, who, in those days of Prohibition, was serving time for bootlegging whiskey.

Working with Frank Calder, Gorman opened negotiations with Percy Thompson to purchase the playing rights of the striking members of the Hamilton Tigers. On September 15, Gorman abruptly broke off these talks. Duggan, who by now was now also part of Rickard's management team, told the New York *Times* that two of the players, Mickey Roach and Billy Burch, could not be obtained as the former had retired and the latter was under contract to coach a team in Pittsburgh.[459] Percy Thompson contended that the deal had failed because Gorman and Duggan did not have any cash — they wanted to pay on terms. As far as he was concerned, everything was off.[460]

Gorman's next gambit was to approach the cash-strapped Edmonton Eskimos of the Western league, from whom he purchased Joe Simpson, Crutchy Morrison and Roy Rickey for $10,000.[461] The Eskimos owner, Ken McKenzie, offered to sell Gorman the remaining players, including future Hall of Famers Duke Keats, Eddie Shore and George Hainsworth, for $45,000. Gorman and Duggan made a counter-offer of $25,000, which was rejected.[462]

Four members of the Edmonton Eskimos. Left to right: Eddie Shore,
Art Gagne, Barney Stanley, Gordon Keats.

Meanwhile, they put a little pressure on Calder by hinting that they just might join up with Eddie Livingstone's proposed International Hockey League.

"According to the N.H.L. constitution," said Duggan, "a club that defaults on a game loses its franchise. At the last meeting of the league, when Art Ross of Boston moved that the [Hamilton] franchise be taken up by the league, we fought against it, and the motion was shelved, but at the September 26 meeting we will vote with Ross, and we have six clubs in the league to line up with us. If the league officials cannot see it our way, then we will pull out and start a new league. It may be the birth of the International League."[463]

Gorman and Duggan also returned to Hamilton in mid September in hopes of convincing Percy Thompson that Frank Calder was not about to lift the strikers' suspensions. Thompson tried to raise the ante, by saying he had another buyer willing to pay $85,000 for his players, but Gorman and Duggan called Thompson's bluff.[464] A few days later, Gorman made a trip to Toronto, where he and Thompson closed the deal. At the first NHL meeting to be held on American soil — in New York on September 26 — Dwyer ended up paying $75,000. Thompson and his partners received $18,000 cash, with the balance to be paid off over six months.[465]

With the favourable outcome of the Senators' libel case against the Ottawa *Citizen*, Calder felt sufficiently empowered to suggest to the newly acquired Americans that they fall into line or find another line of work. Shorty Green, who presented the note that showed Hamilton's game against Gorman's Senators had been rigged, would now have to play for Gorman in New York City — unless he wanted to return to the Sudbury Wolves.

Prior to the 1925–26 season, Calder required each of the suspended ex-Tigers to petition him in writing — along with explanations and apologies for their strike action — if they wished to be reinstated. The president was miffed by the tone of the responses he received. He told Gorman that "most of these young players want to give me an argument."

Still, he could afford to wait for their *mea culpas*. And after five weeks and dozens of letters, Calder was finally satisfied with the sincerity of the apologies and promises of good behaviour he received. The Tigers-turned-Americans were allowed to return to active NHL duty — but only after Calder ordered Gorman to ensure that the players paid their $200 fines from the year before. And, as insurance against any relapses of rebellion, Gorman was to hold back $300 in salary as a bond of dutiful conduct. The players would only get this money at season's end if they played in every game as required.[466]

Not that the players would miss the $500; they would make far more as members of the New York Americans than they could have dreamed possible. Billy Burch, who had just won the Hart Trophy with Hamilton, was considered a particularly valuable property because he had been born in Yonkers, just north of New York City. He signed a three-year contract worth $25,000.[467]

Oddly enough, as late as September 27, 1925, Percy Thompson's Hamilton franchise was still a member of the National Hockey League; in fact, a schedule that included the Tigers was drawn up.[468] But by November, they were playing in the minor Canadian-American Hockey League. Hamilton had officially lost its major-league team.

Chapter 22

The Original Ten

"He had a sense of duty and loyalty that you would find only too seldom in people. He was straight forward, and he had a code of ethics that would benefit us all to follow."
— Lester Patrick on Frank Calder, 1943[469]

By 1925, it could be argued that Frank Calder was at the peak of his powers as president of the National Hockey League. (His detractors may argue that he was also at his most meddlesome; he had by this point stripped four owners — Eddie Livingstone, Mike Quinn, Percy Quinn and Percy Thompson — of their franchises, levelled lifetime bans against an entire team's roster, then reinstated those same Hamilton players when their contracts were sold to New York interests.) And, as if to prove that he was not chastened by the controversy over the extended schedule of 1924–25, he announced that NHL clubs would play 36 games in 1925–26 — six more than the year before, and twelve more than two seasons ago.

On the positive side of the ledger, he had overseen the creation of a pair of successful new teams in Montreal and Boston, while additional expansion teams were soon to emerge from the pipeline.

The expansion of 1924 marked the return of James Strachan to the hockey world. His new Montreal club, which would play its home games in the brand new Forum at the corner of Atwater and Ste-Catherine in Westmount, was designed to appeal to the city's English-speaking community and therefore create a rivalry with the Canadiens along cultural lines. As the man who had once owned — and named — the defunct Montreal Wanderers, Strachan hoped to revive the nickname for his new team. His negotiations with Sam Lichtenhein and Dickie Boon (ownership of the trademark was uncertain) were unproductive, however, and the team went nameless for most of its first season. Eventually, sportswriters picked up on the Montreal Hockey Club's deep red sweater emblazoned with a giant capital M, and took to calling them the Maroons, a name that stuck.

The club would never be confused with their francophone counterparts, who were known simply as Canadiens in those days. In their maiden season, the new team stayed around the middle of the six-team NHL, and in the playoff hunt, until the midway point of the schedule.

Boston had long been recognized as a hotbed of the amateur game, and pro teams from Canada had journeyed there to play exhibition games as early as 1910. It had first been discussed as an expansion site back in 1911, when Eddie McCafferty's Toronto Hockey Club offered to move there for one season because of delays in the construction of Toronto's Arena Gardens. The offer was turned down because the other National Hockey Association owners did not want to incur the travel costs. Instead, the Toronto club made its debut in 1912. Three years later, Livingstone threatened to move his Toronto Shamrocks to Massachusetts amidst a dispute with the management of Arena Gardens.

The NHL began the 1925–26 season without the Hamilton Tigers, but with two new teams in New York and Pittsburgh. The latter city had pioneered the concept of professional hockey with the Western Pennsylvania Hockey League during the first decade of the century. And more recently, the Pittsburgh Yellow Jackets were the amateur champions of the United States for the 1924–25 season. Perhaps more importantly, by putting a club in western Pennsylvania, the NHL was preventing Roy Schooley from claiming the territory for Eddie Livingstone's rival league.

Pittsburgh's roster was intact when it joined the NHL, although there would be one significant change: the NHL version would be known as the Pirates, a nickname that was as synonymous with Pittsburgh as its steel mills. It already belonged to the major-league baseball team that Honus Wagner had led to prominence, and in 1933 the National Football League team that came to be known the Steelers began life under the Pirates moniker. Some of the eastern papers continued to refer to the hockey team as the Yellow Jackets, but it was officially the Pirates.

Odie Cleghorn, formerly of the Montreal Canadiens, joined the team as a player and coach, replacing Dick Carroll — Livingstone's friend who coached Toronto to their 1918 Cup win — in the latter capacity. Cleghorn was an innovator, reintroducing a technique he had first seen practised by Jack Marshall of the Toronto Tecumsehs back in 1913: changing players on the fly. Cleghorn rotated his players every couple of minutes, ensuring that the skaters on the ice would always have fresh legs. While it was unusual enough to make heavy use of a second platoon, it was even more radical not to wait until the whistle blew to make substitutions. Under Cleghorn's tutelage, the Pirates made the playoffs twice in their first three seasons.

In New York, the Americans were an off-Broadway hit, which prompted Tex Rickard to take a second look at the sport and decide that he wanted a team of his own. (Despite contemporary newspaper accounts to the contrary, Rickard did not own the Americans — it was the bootlegger Bill Dwyer who paid the bills, including rent to the Madison Square Garden Corporation.) Rickard understood the advantages that a team the Garden owned outright would enjoy. There were also parties in the midwestern cities of Detroit, Chicago and Cleveland who were interested in buying into the NHL, but further expansion would have to wait until next year.

While the NHL boomed, the outlook was not as bright in western Canada. After the 1924–25 season — in which the Victoria Cougars won the Stanley Cup — the Regina Capitals moved to Portland, prompting the Western Canada Hockey League to drop "Canada" from its name. The Saskatoon Crescents — having made a deal with James Strachan to offer their players to the Montreal Maroons if the team could not continue — were so desperate at the box office that they changed their name to "Sheiks," hoping to cash in on the hairstyle of the same name that Rudolph Valentino had popularized in his movies.

When Frank Calder granted three additional franchises to begin play in 1926, it marked the end of the Western Hockey League. The Patrick brothers knew what Calder knew: that the injection of new money from owners in Chicago, New York and Detroit meant the NHL could easily trump any offer the western clubs could make to a talented young amateur. And if the world's best hockey players all elected to remain east of the Mississippi, the NHL would be guaranteed a monopoly over both the Stanley Cup and major professional hockey.

The WHL's demise did not spell financial ruin for the Patricks. Over fifteen years, the teams of the west had evolved from raiding eastern rosters to developing their own stars, including: George Hainsworth and Eddie Shore in Edmonton; the Cook brothers, Bill and Bun, in Saskatoon; and Herb Gardiner and Harry Oliver in Calgary. These players and many others were proven, valuable talents whose services would be in great demand back east. Sensing as much, Frank Patrick sold the entire roster of the Victoria Cougars, winners of the Stanley Cup in 1925, for $100,000 to Charles Hughes, who proceeded to name his new NHL franchise the Detroit Cougars. He also dealt the contracts of all of the Portland Rosebuds to Major Frederic McLaughlin, who owned the new NHL franchise in Chicago, for the same amount. The balance of the WHL's players were auctioned off individually, netting a further $160,000. The proceeds, $360,000 in all, were divided among the six members of the Western league.

Frank Patrick reserved the best of the litter for his old Montreal friend Art Ross, who was now managing Boston. At a postseason exhibition game against Lester's Cougars, Frank had given Ross a complete scouting report on his league's players. On the basis of that report, Ross acquired Shore and Oliver, who would provide the foundation for a powerful Boston team that won the Cup in 1929 and 1939. Ross repaid Frank Patrick by hiring him as coach of the Bruins in 1934.

There was only one problem with the WHL fire sale: the Patricks were selling the rights to players they didn't exactly own. Unlike the NHL's moguls, the brothers had never adopted the reserve clause, which bound a player to his team through a one-year option that could be renewed indefinitely at a team's discretion. That meant that the WHL players were, effectively, free agents after their 1925–26 contracts expired. Frank Calder didn't find this out until it was too late to do anything about it.

The passing of the Hamilton Tigers and the WHL from the scene meant that Canada had lost seven major professional hockey teams in only two years (Appendix C offers a summary of the carnage). It would be forty-four years before it got one back (see Appendix D).

The country lost something even more valuable, however.

Ever since the Dawson City challenge of 1905 captured the fancy of the Canadian public, civic dreams, pride and hope hinged on the belief that any Canadian community — from Halifax, Nova Scotia, on through Kenora, Ontario, all the way to Victoria, British Columbia — could form a team and mount a challenge for the Stanley Cup. This would not be true now that the West was closed up.

Chapter 23

Livvy's Comeback

"We are not worried. These leagues come and go, coming in the spring and going in the fall."
— Frank Calder, 1925[470]

By *1925, the five-year*-old United States Amateur Hockey Association — of which Roy Schooley's Pittsburgh Yellow Jackets were two-time defending champions — was on the verge of collapse. At a May 15 meeting in Winnipeg, the Canadian Amateur Hockey Association formally broke off relations with its American counterpart and voted to tighten residence rules governing its players. The effect of the move was to prevent players from crossing the border. The decision forced the USAHA to consider reorganizing itself as a full-blown professional league.

At the same time, Eddie Livingstone was still trying to get a pro league to rival the National Hockey League off the ground. With an eye on that goal, Livvy met with Schooley — and with Newsy Lalonde, the former Montreal Canadiens star who was now manager of the Saskatoon Crescents of the Western Canada Hockey League. On April 9, the Toronto *Mail and Empire* quoted Canadiens co-owner Leo Dandurand as confirming that Lalonde had held discussions with Livingstone: "Newsy is known to have conferred with Livingstone when the latter was here, and made no secret about it. He also did missionary work on behalf of Livingstone on behalf of the proposed new circuit with Montreal parties."[471]

"We are not worried," Frank Calder replied. "These leagues come and go, coming in the spring and going in the fall. The new league cannot get into Montreal. They may get into Toronto and Ottawa, and perhaps Pittsburgh and Cleveland, but where will they get players?

"I would not be surprised if Roy Schooley of Pittsburgh was the moving spirit behind Livingstone. Schooley has already applied for a League franchise, but wants it for nothing, and this may be part of his propaganda. The amateur league in the United States, a farce as regards amateurism, is breaking up, and some of the cities on the amateur circuit no doubt will wish to get into out-and-out, honest professionalism."[472]

The NHL's behaviour during this period — ordering players to play additional games without additional pay, arranging for a referee to rig a game in favour of the home team — suggests that Calder wouldn't recognize "honest professionalism" if it hit him with an open-ice hip check.

For a moment, it appeared that he was right about one thing, however: Eddie Livingstone and Percy Quinn's efforts did fail once again. Demoralized, Quinn bowed out of hockey altogether and got into local politics, where he dedicated the rest of his life to making Toronto a better place to live. Livingstone left town.

The move caught Frank Calder by surprise. When Charles Hughes set up shop in Detroit with the transplanted Victoria Cougars, Calder asked J. L. Woods, one of Hughes' partners, if Livingstone was connected with the arena's architect.

He was assured that he wasn't.

Livingstone may not have been able to get a league off the ground, but Schooley announced that a professional hockey league would rise from the ashes of the USAHA: the American Hockey Association. "It is understood that St. Paul, Duluth, Eveleth and Cleveland will be given berths in the new league," the Hamilton *Spectator* reported. "These teams, together with a Pittsburgh team, will make up the western group. There will be an eastern group made up of Boston, New York, Philadelphia, Pittsburgh and probably some Canadian towns."[473]

When Schooley sold his Yellow Jackets to Henry Townsend, the owner of Duquesne Gardens, and the attorney James F. Callahan, and the pair entered the team into the NHL as the Pittsburgh Pirates, the remaining USAHA teams in communities such as Minneapolis, Cleveland and St. Louis were left scrambling. The teams proposed for the east did not play, while the midwestern teams reorganized as the Central Hockey Association.

Meanwhile, in Winnipeg and Sault Ste. Marie, Ontario — cities that were closer to the American Midwest than to most Canadian centres — there was dissatisfaction with the CAHA's split with the USAHA.

After one season, the Central Hockey Association changed its name to the American Hockey Association. The CHA team in Eveleth sold eight players to the Minneapolis Millers, who also lured the ageless Ernie "Moose" Johnson from the west. Meanwhile, the Winnipeg Maroons, headed by W. J. Holmes, turned pro and joined the AHA, as did the Soo Greyhounds, who announced plans to relocate to Detroit.

As rumours of the AHA's emergence circulated, Livingstone wrote Calder denying any connection with either Frank Patrick or the proposed league. Livingstone had already told this to Calder in person, but was careful to confirm the conversation with a telegram.[474]

Still, Livingstone's fingerprints were all over the AHA. For instance, his former right-hand man, Dick Carroll, was the head coach in Duluth. Carroll had been coach of Schooley's Pittsburgh Yellow Jackets, but did not accompany his players into the NHL. And the owner of the Detroit (née Sault Ste. Marie) Greyhounds was none other than the former Toronto Shamrocks defenceman George McNamara.

And perhaps most importantly, nearly ten years after he had been frozen out of the National Hockey League, Eddie Livingstone was back in hockey as the owner of the Chicago Cardinals. The AHA was up and running, Livvy had his team, and a solid six-team league seemed well positioned to compete head-to-head with the National Hockey League in two of its three newest markets: Detroit and Chicago.

In the autumn of 1926, Frank Calder met with the heads of the four leading amateur leagues, convincing them to assume minor pro status. In return, he promised them the right to challenge for the Stanley Cup, provided they sign an agreement that would name him commissioner of hockey, a role similar to that held by baseball's Judge Kenesaw Mountain Landis. The aim of the move was twofold: to undercut the powers and responsibilities of the Stanley Cup trustees, and, because he never intended to uphold his end of the bargain, to ensure that the winner of the NHL playoffs would automatically be crowned Stanley Cup champions.

The *Mail and Empire* covered the meeting, held at Toronto's King Edward Hotel.

> The special committee appointed to take up the matter of affiliation of the minor leagues presented a report, which was adopted, and as a result the Central Hockey Association, the Canadian Professional League, the Prairie League and the Canadian-American [league] are now

affiliated with the N.H.L. There will be no draft clause in operation this season, but it will come into action next year. At present, and for this season, the only way an N.H.L. club can secure a player from the minor league club will be by purchase.

President Calder is the commissioner of hockey, and will be the final judge of all disputes among the minor leagues and clubs.[475]

This announcement would have come as news to Stanley Cup trustee Billy Foran, who had held the role of commissioner for the previous ten years. Nor did Calder apparently bother to tell Foran, because six weeks later he was still claiming the title he thought was his. "The only differences between Judge Landis and myself," Foran told the *Sault Star*, "is that he gets a salary of $50,000 per year while I work without emolument. I expect to have more disputes to settle now with all these American teams in. There [are] bound to be fights over players, but I will continue to act without fear or favour."[476]

Chapter 24

The Real Curse of Muldoon

No hockey player, no man in fact, ever had a better friend than Pete Muldoon.

— Hall of Famer Jack Walker[477]

One of the most enduring pieces of hockey folklore, cooked up by the *Globe and Mail* sports columnist Jim Coleman, has to do with the fallout from the Chicago Blackhawks' inaugural season of 1926–27. Over the years the story of the "Curse of the Muldoon" has woven itself into the fabric of hockey history, and has become as important a part of Chicago mythology as Al Capone, deep-dish pizza, great steak houses and crooked politicians.

That the tale is a complete fabrication seems not to matter to many, who write it off as harmless fun. But the unfortunate truth is that the story of the curse is the only reason Pete Muldoon is remembered by modern-day fans, if he is remembered at all. As such, a good hockey man is deprived of his proper place in the sport's history.

As is often the case, the truth about what happened in Chicago during its first season of professional hockey is more interesting than Coleman's fiction.

In May 1926, Major Frederic McLaughlin, an associate of Tex Rickard's — the two men had teamed up to promote boxing cards in Chicago and throughout the midwest — was granted the NHL franchise for the Second City. The former military man and polo player, who served as secretary-treasurer of the highly successful coffee company his father had founded, reached back into his past to name his team. During the First World War, he commanded a battalion that was part of the 86th Division, also known as the Blackhawk Division.[478]

The design of the Blackhawks' black-and-white-striped uniforms was also an in-house affair; they were created by the Major's wife, Irene Castle, who had achieved worldwide fame as a ballroom dancer during the ragtime age. The sweaters featured a round emblem, with the now-familiar Indian head encircled by the words "BLACKHAWKS" and "CHICAGO." The two halves of the nickname didn't quite meet at the top of the circle, which made it appear as if the name was composed of two words. When eastern sportswriters saw this, they assumed that "Black Hawks" was the correct spelling, an error that wasn't officially corrected until 1986, even though the team's charter read "Blackhawk Hockey Club" and the Chicago papers had been correctly using the one-word style all along.

As noted in Chapter 22, McLaughlin stocked his team by purchasing the playing rights of the Portland Rosebuds of Frank Patrick's Western Hockey League. Coach Pete Muldoon, who had been connected with the Patricks since the PCHA's first season in 1911, was part of the package.

Pete Muldoon demonstrates his skill on stilt skates —
a novelty that never quite caught on.

Seattle Post-Intelligencer Collection, Museum of History and Industry

Nobody in Portland bothered to tell the Rosebuds' fans that one of the only two WHL teams to show a profit in 1925–26 was picking up stakes and heading back east along the Oregon Trail.

Even after news of the WHL's demise was made public, Portlanders thought they would still have a team. It fell to Pete Muldoon to pay a visit to his good friend, the *Oregonian* sports columnist L. H. Gregory, to set the record straight.

Muldoon told Gregory that he had received an offer from Chicago that was too good to pass up, and that he planned to take eight of the ten Rosebuds players with him to the Windy City, leaving only Ken Doraty and Joe McCormick behind. Muldoon added that his Chicago team would be bolstered by eight other WHL players.

"There was no hope that we could maintain our major hockey ranking in competition with the big population centers and bigger salaries the National league could pay," Muldoon said.

> We did make an effort to save the league. Frank Patrick went to San Francisco and interested $400,000 backing for a club there. But to make hockey a success in San Francisco, it was essential that Oakland also have a team, and there he was unable to put it over.
>
> Had San Francisco and Oakland entered, Wee Coyle and interests affiliated with him in Seattle would have built the ground floor of their projected rink in Seattle, put circus seats around it and enclosed it in a big circus tent to enable them to get by for next year, completing the building later. Then Vancouver, Victoria, Seattle, Portland, San Francisco and Oakland would have made a strong league. But without Oakland such a league was foredoomed to failure."

Muldoon denied emphatically that Frank Patrick had sold out western pro hockey.

> Nobody was betrayed. The plain facts of it are that it was a case of sell and get our price or be raided, get nothing and be forced into bankruptcy.
>
> Had we not sold our players, it was a practical certainty that new interests coming into hockey in the east, in the great scramble for players, would have got our men one way or another — they'd have gone outlaw

and then taken them from us had we held out. This was plain from the start.

We were in no position to start a war, much less to finance one. Only two clubs in the Western Hockey League, Vancouver and Portland, made any money last season. The Canadian prairie cities were hit by warm weather at the wrong time, which ruined their season and reduced their intake. They simply could not have gone another year.[479]

The interests Muldoon was talking about were the American Hockey Association, which included Eddie Livingstone, the man whose Toronto Blueshirts had been heavily raided by Frank Patrick in 1915. The Rosebuds had already been raided by St. Paul of the AHA who signed McCormick.[480] Doraty was signed by Minneapolis, but he later found his way to the Blackhawks.

Livingstone's Chicago Cardinals opened their 1926 training camp at the Mutual Street Arena, and the Toronto *Telegram* couldn't help but notice that Gordie Brydson, Ted Graham and Marvin "Cyclone" Wentworth were being auditioned. Two of the three — Graham and Wentworth — had been playing senior hockey in London and Windsor, respectively. Brydson, a former junior player with the Toronto Canoe Club, was slated to play in Stratford. All three Ontario cities were members of the new Canadian Professional Hockey League, one of the leagues Calder had co-opted. "The relationship between the N.H.L. and the minor leagues, which latter includes the American [Association], is likely to develop not a little business for High Commissioner W. Foran of Ottawa," the *Telegram* observed. "The difficulty is arising from drafting from the amateurs."[481]

London and Windsor both felt entitled to retain the rights to their players, even though neither had ever been paid to play, nor had they signed professional contracts. At the same time, the Montreal Canadiens set their sights set on Leo Lafrance, who had played with Duluth of the old USAHA, and Ottawa had signed Milt Halliday, on whom the Stratford Nationals held a claim. According to Roy Brothers, the Stratford manager, both Halliday and Brydson rightfully belonged to his club.[482]

The *Sault Daily Star* picked up an article from the Chicago *Herald-Examiner* that outlined why Graham was choosing to play for the Cardinals. Having graduated from London's University of Western Ontario and then spent a season as a lumberjack, he was going to study law at Northwestern University in Chicago. The situation was somewhat reminiscent of the fiasco that ensued in 1910, when the Ottawa Senators loaned Gord Roberts to the Montreal Wanderers so that he could study medicine at McGill University, and then tried to use him as leverage to pry Cyclone Taylor away from the Wanderers.[483]

Frank Calder was placed in a precarious position. As president of the NHL, he had to defend the actions of the Canadiens and Senators, whether they were right or wrong. But as commissioner of pro hockey, he was equally responsible for protecting the best interests of the newly minted minor pro clubs in Stratford, Windsor and London.

Major Frederic McLaughlin's knowledge of hockey could have filled an espresso cup. Lacking the slightest idea of where or how to begin building a team, he bought the Portland Rosebuds, a rather ordinary team that finished fourth in the six-team WHL in 1925–26. He augmented the lineup by purchasing Babe Dye, sight unseen, after Tex Rickard recommended the former Toronto scoring star. Fortunately for the Major, Dye would lead Chicago scorers with 25 goals.

The National Hockey League welcomed McLaughlin's money, but not his input; he was routinely excluded from important NHL meetings. His naïveté was on display when he entered into an agreement with Eddie Livingstone to share the ice at the Chicago Coliseum. He wouldn't have known Livingstone from Howie Morenz or Cyclone Taylor, and so he couldn't have known he was co-operating with Frank Calder's number one enemy.

Concerned that he might incur Calder's wrath, Livvy kept a low profile as he got his Chicago Cardinals underway. The only preseason coverage was a brief item in the October 29 editions of the Chicago *Tribune*.

> The Chicago Cardinals entry in the American Hockey Association will play twenty-two games on the Coliseum rink this winter, it was announced yesterday by E. J. Livingstone, president of the Chicago team, on his return yesterday from St. Paul, where the league meeting was held. The season will open on November 21, and close March 27.
>
> Charles R. Hall, president of the Coliseum commission, also attended the meeting and assisted in the schedule making in order to avoid clashes of dates between the Cardinals and the Blackhawks hockey

team of the National league, which will also use the Coliseum rink.

Detroit will open the local season with the Cards, games being scheduled on November 21 and 23. Each team of the league will play [in Chicago] in a series of two games while a similar arrangement has been worked out for the 22 games the Cards have scheduled for the road.

The Cardinals' squad of fifteen players will take the ice at Toronto on November 17 for its first workout. President Livingstone and H. J. Caldwell are arranging three exhibition games for their team to be played prior to the league opening.[484]

The coach McLaughlin inherited, Pete Muldoon, was a seasoned — and well-travelled — hockey man, who was born in 1881 in St. Marys, Ontario, a small town between Stratford and London. Had Jim Coleman been so inclined to research his "Curse of the Muldoon" story, he might have uncovered this December 1926 story in the London *Free Press*:

Chicago is just getting acquainted with Pete Muldoon, manager of the Blackhawks hockey team, but it seems a large portion of the rest of the world has known him well for many years. Pete is a young-looking man, tall and slender, with all the appearances of an athlete, and one feels rather surprised when he begins telling about things he did in athletics almost 20 years ago.

For instance, in 1907, Pete was living in San Francisco and entered the amateur boxing tournament which was put on by the old San Francisco Athletic Club. Pete was just above the middleweight limit, so he competed in the light heavyweight class, and after knocking out one opponent after another cold, he found he had won the championship of the Pacific coast in that class and was presented with a fine-looking watch as a trophy.

Pete was proud of his prize and took it to a place to have it engraved with his name, the names of the men he beat to win it and the year of the event. It cost Pete about $4 for the engraving. Then he met a jeweller friend and proudly showed him the trophy. "What is it worth?" asked Pete after the jeweller had given the prize a close inspection.

"Do you really want me to tell you?" said his friend.

"Sure," said Pete.

"Well, I can buy them at wholesale for $3.75," was the answer, and then Pete turned pro.

Pete played hockey 22 years ago at Regina, and he played in the Ontario Hockey Association as an amateur before that. Since 1911 he has devoted most of his time to hockey. It was that year he won the championship on the coast with his [New] Westminster club.

In 1914, he managed the Portland club and the next year went to Seattle. In the season of 1916–17, he won the world's championship with his Seattle hockey team, beating the Montreal Canadiens in the final play-off. He won again in 1919 and was to have played the Montreal club once more, but players on each team came down with the flu and the series had to be called off. Again in the season of 1920–21 his Seattle team won in the West and played the Ottawa team for the world's championship, this time being beaten in three out of five games.

Last year he went back to Portland to manage the team there, and then the Portland club was purchased outright along with him and transferred to Chicago....

In summer, Pete passes the time as he pleases, and it pleases him most to go to the race tracks and watch the horses run, especially if he has a small wager.[485]

Does this sound like a man who would place a curse? One suspects that if Muldoon were truly upset with McLaughlin, he would have knocked the boss on his keester!

In November, the Blackhawks faced off against some of the AHA teams. On November 8, they travelled to Minneapolis, where the Millers took a 5–0 lead into the third period before Chicago came back to earn a 5–5 tie. That performance was followed with a loss against Winnipeg and a 3–2 come-from-behind victory over Duluth.

An article by the *Tribune*'s main hockey reporter, Frank Schreiber, discussed the return of hockey to Chicago after a long absence.

After a lapse of nearly ten years, ice hockey will make its reappearance as a major sport in Chicago Wednesday night at the Coliseum when the Chicago Blackhawks of the rebuilt National Professional Hockey League meet the St. Patricks sextet of Toronto in the opening game of the regular league season.

Except for a few scattered amateur teams of more or less ability, hockey has been a dead sport in Chicago for the last ten or twelve years. The last real attempt to rally the sport was in 1917, when the Great Lakes Naval Training station mustered a squad and played a few games at the Broadway arena, now the Broadway armory.

The re-establishment of the hockey sport comes with the installation of an ice plant and rink floor in the Coliseum.

The rink in the Coliseum was built by a syndicate of Chicago men, headed by Frederic McLaughlin and John J. Mitchell. This syndicate also purchased a franchise in the National Hockey League and the entire player squad of the Portland Rosebuds of the old Western Canadian league.

The opening game between the St. Pats and the Blackhawks is being played for the benefit of the Chicago Junior league. The advance sale of tickets forecasts a heavy turnout of society for the initial contest.

After the Coliseum rink had become a reality, a second hockey club invaded the city. The Chicago Cardinals, owned by two veteran Canadian hockey men, will play in the American Hockey association circuit, an organization built from the old Central Hockey League. The American association teams are Chicago, Detroit, Minneapolis, St. Paul, Duluth and Winnipeg.

E. J. Livingstone and H. J. Caldwell, both from Toronto, are the Cardinal owners and managers.[486]

A couple of interesting points become apparent to those willing to read between the lines. First of all, the *Tribune* was careful to give the Blackhawks and Cardinals equal time, as if Schreiber might be uncertain as to the delineation between major- and minor-league status. One also gets a sense as to why McLaughlin was willing to rent the Coliseum to Livingstone's team: simple economics. Having paid to install ice in the old barn on South Wabash Street, and purchased what was the NHL's remotest franchise, McLaughlin hoped to recoup his investments in part by landing a second hockey tenant for his building. Little did he know the can of worms he was opening.

On November 17, 1926, the Blackhawks played their first game at the Coliseum, a 4–1 victory over the Toronto St. Pats. According to the *Tribune's* Schreiber:

> The sport was accorded a great reception. More than 7,000 pushed their way into the new building, and there were cheers from the time the game started until the final whistle.
>
> The play of the rival goalkeepers, Lehman for Chicago and Roach for Toronto, furnished the biggest thrill of the evening. Time after time these heavily padded warriors of the ice beat off attacks of their enemy forwards, and many times they seized the puck in midair with their hands or batted it back into center ice with their broad bladed sticks. When the battle was over Lehman and Roach were equal in stops, each having staved off scoring attempts on their respective goals 36 times.
>
> Both teams fought hard, but neither displayed more than an average attack or defense. As it was the first contest of the season, many substitutions were made, as the men are not in their best condition. The softening of the ice in the second period made skating harder than in the first and third sessions, when the ice making plant was going at top speed.[487]

Coincidentally, a photograph printed next to this story showed Tom Hammond kicking a field goal in a 1903 football game between the universities of Minnesota and Michigan. Hammond's brother, John, was president of the New York Rangers. The *Tribune* did not remark on the connection. The next day, the *Trib's* sports editor was enthused by the Hawks' debut, even if he admitted to not understanding the sport.

> Professional hockey, as exhibited by its cleverest exponents at the Coliseum Wednesday night, lived up to its advance notices in speed, skill and excitement. There was a capacity house, with a generous proportion of

fashionables because the Junior league received the profits and helped dispose of many tickets. We dare say that every one present felt the evening was well spent.

That was the first night. Now the question is how soon those first nighters will be impelled to go again. There are many hockey enthusiasts in Chicago who have known the game in other cities. But there must be new followers developed to support a schedule of twenty-two home games in the National league and twenty-two home games in the American league. In our opinion, it will require time to put the sport on a solid, self-supporting basis.

There were lightning speed and marvelous skating skill. There was almost unbelievable dexterity in manipulating the puck. There were thrilling stops by heavily armored goalkeepers. There was body contact, with resultant spills. All those features appeal. Our only unfavorable reaction was that hockey lacks variety in play despite constantly changing possession of the puck. After one period you feel the next two will be about the same thing. Perhaps that is because we do not understand all of its niceties and strategy.

Enthusiasts say the game grows on you. We can see how that is probable, as you become a team partisan with a liking for one or two individual players. At any rate, we advise every sport-loving Chicagoan to see at least one of these league contests.[488]

Despite the praise, only 4,000 turned out to see the Blackhawks beat the Boston Bruins, 5–1, in their second home game. The Bruins goal was Eddie Shore's first in the NHL.

Boston's lone goal came off Shore's stick with only one minute and a half left to play in the final period, when he emerged from a six-man scrimmage in front of the Chicago goal and hooked the puck into the net.

One bit of battling not on the original program took place after the match, when Shore of Boston rushed over and struck Gordon Fraser, Chicago defense player, on the chest. Referee Ritchie and the rest of the players separated the men before damage was done.[489]

To prepare Chicagoans for the debut of his Chicago Cardinals, Eddie Livingstone took out small ads in the newspapers that read "HOCKEY" in large, capital letters, followed by, "The World's Fastest Game by Two of the Country's Fastest Teams." The Cards were to open their season against the Detroit Greyhounds, owned by the former Toronto Blueshirt George McNamara. McNamara had retired to his hometown, Sault Ste. Marie, Ontario, where he led the Soo Greyhounds to the Allan Cup championship in 1924. McNamara took many of his players with him when the Greyhounds joined the AHA.

Unfortunately for McNamara, his charges were no match for the Cardinals, who played the game wearing maroon sweaters with "Chicago Americans" embroidered on them. The Greyhounds managed just eight shots on net the entire game, as the Cards won their inaugural, 3–0, before a crowd of 3,000.

The Chicago *Herald-Examiner* came away with a favourable opinion of the AHA brand of hockey, as this piece reprinted in the *Sault Daily Star* attests:

> Chicago is going to like its Cardinals hockey team. It has entertainment, speed, but more important than anything else, it has youth — the recklessness of youth.
>
> A combination of these three sets gave the Red Shirts a 3 to 0 triumph over the Detroit Greyhounds in the opening game of the American Professional League at the Coliseum last night.
>
> Only about 3,000 spectators witnessed the match, but they went away singing the praises of this up and going sextet.
>
> The Cardinals do not effect team play that the Black Hawks do, perhaps, but what they lacked in this department of play was more than made up for in sheer speed and daring.
>
> A fair sample of just how much speed the Cardinals generated during the evening is evidenced in the fact that Flat Walsh, the enemy goal tender, made a total of sixty-three stops during the sixty minutes of play. Bud Fisher, the Card goalie, only had to halt enemy goal tries eight times during the combat.[490]

As was the case for the Blackhawks, the Cardinals played their second game before a smaller crowd. Barely 2,000 showed up to see the

Cardinals beat Detroit 3–1, with Gord Brydson scoring all the Chicago goals. Still, by mid-December the London *Free Press* was reporting that

> Eddie Livingstone's Central League pro team is out-drawing the Black Hawks. The reason is said that the Livingstone crowd, while perhaps not as finished performers as the Black Hawk boys, display more "pep" and the Chicago fans, who don't know the first thing about hockey, take to that brand better than the real clever stuff.[491]

Faced with the embarrassing prospect of having one of his expansion teams fail, Frank Calder decided to get involved. As "commissioner of hockey," Calder took a two-pronged approach, ruling on the one hand that Livingstone had no right to sign Teddy Graham, while at the same time convincing the London Panthers to sell Graham's rights to the Blackhawks for $1,000. The same process was repeated with Windsor, this time for Cy Wentworth, who was also on the Cards roster.[492] Goldie Prodgers, the London coach, claimed no knowledge of the deal, but the *Border Cities Star* set the value of the entire transaction at $3,250, and said that the Panthers would get the rest if McLaughlin was successful in signing Graham to an NHL contract.[493]

On December 15, the *Tribune* noted that Calder had struck back against Livingstone.

> Opening guns of a hockey war, with the Chicago Blackhawks of the National Professional Hockey league and the Chicago Cardinals of the American Hockey association as the chief combatants, were fired yesterday.
>
> The conflict, which is the first to be experienced in Chicago hockey and which brings to a head six weeks of unsettled conditions in local circles, broke out when Maj. Frederic McLaughlin of the Blackhawks announced a communication from Frank Calder of Montreal, president of the National league. Calder's statement follows:
>
> 1. That Edward Livingstone, president of the Chicago Cardinals, had started a suit against several members and clubs of the National Hockey league, charging conspiracy.

2. That the working agreement held between the National Hockey league and the Central Hockey association, now known as the American Hockey association, had been declared void by Mr. Calder.
3. That all clubs in the American Hockey association are now considered as outlaws by the National league.
4. That the Chicago Cardinals had illegally signed players Marvin Wentworth and Teddy Graham and had not paid for their releases and would therefore be obliged to give up these two men.[494]

McLaughlin also alleged that Calder, as head of what he characterized as "the only major hockey organization in the world," had not authorized the Central Hockey Association to change its name to the AHA.

In the *Tribune* article, Livingstone countered McLaughlin's claim. He said that, at a September 25 meeting of the pro leagues in Montreal, the NHL had entered into an agreement that recognized the AHA as a major league and put it on an equal footing with the NHL. He also reported that Calder and Alvin Warren, president of the AHA, had drawn up plans for the two leagues to compete for the Stanley Cup and appointed the Cup trustee William Foran to head an arbitration board that would rule on disputes between the two leagues.

Livvy also denied that he had filed any suit against the NHL, and that the case McLaughlin referred to must have been one of the old ones involving his Toronto Blueshirts. He was, at this time, still busy trying to collect the money the courts had awarded him in previous lawsuits. Finally, he insisted that Graham and Wentworth were the Cardinals' property, having "signed legal contracts, both having been clear of any obligation to either the Windsor or London teams."[495]

In the same story, Teddy Graham took issue with Calder's ruling. "Graham last night declared that he never had a contract with the London team and that London had no call on his services. Both London and Windsor were amateur teams, Graham said."[496]

Calder arranged a meeting in Chicago with Alvin Warren. If he was expecting to flush Livingstone out, he was disappointed. Instead, he ended up in a bigger war than he imagined.

"Chicago has a clear title to these players," Warren said, "and our association will back the Cardinals in their stand."

Calder protested that Graham and Wentworth had both received cash advances from London and Windsor during the months of May and June, a fact that would, according to organized hockey rules, bind the men to these clubs. Yet Calder hadn't followed any such protocol when he stripped Livingstone's Blueshirts of its players, who were under contract, in 1917. Livvy's entire roster was stolen from again him in 1918, after the Blueshirts were leased to Charlie Querrie and Toronto captured the Stanley Cup. Calder was also overlooking the Canadiens' signing of Lafrance and Ottawa's signing of Halliday.

The lack of ice in Detroit, which was a temporary inconvenience for the NHL's Cougars, proved fatal for the AHA's Greyhounds. Delays in the construction of Olympia Stadium had forced Charles Hughes and his Cougars to take up temporary residence across the border in Windsor, Ontario, while the AHA responded by drawing up a schedule that would keep George McNamara's team on the road until February. The team would therefore represent Detroit in name only.

By mid-December, when the opening of the rink was pushed back until the autumn of 1927, McNamara decided it would be prudent to pack up his team, which had lost all six of its league games, and — according to the Toronto *Mail and Empire* — wait until next year.

> Although the Detroit Greyhounds have been withdrawn from the American Professional Hockey League, and the team broken up for the season, the possibility that the team will reorganize next year is hinted in a statement made by George McNamara, part owner of the club. McNamara stated that the club would still hold its franchise in the league as the Detroit entry.
>
> The withdrawal of the Detroit team was caused by the failure of the Olympia Club of Detroit, owners of the Detroit Cougars in the National Hockey League, to have their rink completed in time for any home games there this year, McNamara stated. An arrangement had been made with the Olympia Club for the use of the Arena for home games with the understanding that the club would have the rink completed by February 1. The schedule was drawn up accordingly with the Greyhounds on the road until the rink was completed.[497]

The sudden withdrawal meant that a number of games would have to be defaulted, which is why the Greyhounds appear in the 1926–27 standings with a record of 0–10–0.

For the most part, the members of the Detroit Greyhounds caught on with other teams in the AHA or the other minor leagues. What stands out, however, is the fact that three players from this winless minor-league club — Flat Walsh, Babe Donnelly and John Woodruff — were signed by the Montreal Maroons, the defending Stanley Cup champions.[498] This move did not go unnoticed: the *Border Cities Star* announced that the three had been drafted by other AHA teams, with Walsh and Donnelly set to go to Chicago and Woodruff to St. Paul.[499]

In another time and league, Livingstone would have reacted to the doublecross by quickly filing a lawsuit. But now that his fellow owners were becoming aware of his past, Livingstone let the matter pass. He had other, more pressing problems — the Cardinals' cash flow, for one. Despite the club's initial on-ice success, and the relatively low salaries he was paying compared to his NHL counterparts, Livvy was finding it a challenge to keep the turnstiles spinning. One strategy he employed was to cut ticket prices in midseason. Under the new plan, all balcony seats would be sold at $1, tax included, down from $1.75 and $1.10. Seats on the lower level that had been priced at $1.75 and $2.75 were reduced to $1.50 and $2.50. Box seats remained at $3.30. The new prices took effect for the two-game series against Minneapolis, played on December 31 and January 2.[500]

McLaughlin responded by doing some price cutting himself, lowering the cost of balcony seats for Blackhawks games to $1, effective with the December 29 match against the Montreal Maroons. Although the move could have been misinterpreted as an admission that the NHL product was no better than the AHA's, the gambit did work to McLaughlin's favour. More than 6,000 fans jammed the Coliseum to see Mickey MacKay score thirteen minutes and thirty seconds into overtime, completing a Chicago comeback in one of the most incredible games ever played in the Windy City.

It had taken the Maroons little more than two minutes to jump ahead, 2–0. The Chicago *Tribune* reported that "Montreal's maroon-clad puck chasers had all the better of the battling in the first period because Billy Phillips, a small but stocky fellow who played out of his regular position at wing to fill the place of Nels Stewart, drove home two fast goals."[501] In fact, Phillips scored off the opening faceoff, just five seconds into the game. It was an NHL record for the fastest goal from the start of a game, a mark that stood for many years.

The Maroons went up 4–0 before the Hawks woke up. Babe Dye scored twice in the second period to cut the Maroons lead to 4–2. With 1:15 left in the third period, Dick Irvin scored to make it 4–3, and Rabbit McVeigh tied the game with five seconds on the clock. The overtime rule in 1927 was that a full ten-minute period was played, after which, if the score was still tied, the teams would switch ends and play a sudden-death period of ten minutes. Neither team scored in the first overtime period, but in the second, Mickey McKay took a pass from Babe Dye and beat Clint Benedict to end the game. Both goalies made 49 saves.

The game did much to make the Blackhawks the toast of Chicago. More than 6,000 were on hand to see the Hawks' next effort. "The crowd was so great that even the old circus band stand, perched high against the north wall of the old building, was crowded with folks who viewed the struggle."[502] The New York Rangers also took a 4–0 lead, but there was no comeback this time. So desperate was Pete Muldoon to generate some scoring that he resorted to a strategy first conceived by Livingstone by putting a platoon of five forwards on the ice. If the loss cooled the fans' enthusiasm for the Blackhawks, Livvy's Cardinals would be unable to capitalize — they were scheduled to spend the next three weeks on the road.

Livingstone had concluded that his financial difficulties were insurmountable. His Cardinals were locked into a five-year lease at the Coliseum, were battling the Blackhawks for a limited number of Chicago hockey fans, and were looking at a seven-week stretch during which the Cardinals were on the road for all but two games. In March 1927, Livingstone decided to sell the team to the former secretary of the Chicago Cubs, thus leaving the club in local hands.

> Harry Herendeen, president of the Herendeen Milling company, and known for his interests in golf clubs in the Chicago district, is president of the new organization. Harold Wallace is the vice president, Rube Cook treasurer, and Ritchie W. Scott, secretary. Cook was ticket manager of the Cardinals under Livingstone and Scott was business manager.
>
> No announcement was made as to the cash given Livingstone for his holdings, but Mr. Cook said President Herendeen probably would make known the sum on his return to Chicago Saturday. The new president is now en route from Europe. The board of directors also will be announced by President Herendeen on his return. It is understood, however, that the directorate

will contain the names of several wealthy and socially prominent men of the city.

The new company has already taken control of the club and temporary quarters have been established in the Morrison hotel. All of the players of the squad will be retained and Coach Nip Dwan remains in charge of the players.

A charter and incorporation papers have been granted to the Chicago Americans Hockey Club, Inc. Livingstone has completely withdrawn from the local hockey field, along with his secretary, Harry Caldwell. Both will return to Toronto, where Livingstone was one of the pioneers of the hockey sport.

Included with the purchase of the Cardinal club was a five year lease on the Coliseum rink and this is to be retained by the new owners.

Mr. Cook is in active charge of the club until the return of President Herendeen. Cook for several years was secretary of the old Cubs' baseball team under Charles Webb Murphy and later was in charge of ticket sales for the Chicago National League club.[503]

Although the new owners called their corporation the Chicago Americans Hockey Club, the reporters did not stop calling the team the Cardinals, nor were the club's ruby-red sweaters — which were already embroidered with the words "Chicago Americans" — abandoned.

On March 16, President Herendeen's last-place club welcomed him home with a 1–1 overtime tie against the Duluth Hornets. One player missing from the Cardinals lineup was Ted Graham. Now that Livingstone was out of the way, it seems that the London Panthers management "found" a contract it could not locate during the previous five months. When it was presented with this document, the AHA suspended Graham. According to the *Tribune*, he was also fined $1,850, "the difference between the money end of the London and Chicago contracts."[504]

After selling the Cardinals, Livingstone intended to race back to Toronto to take care of some old business with Charlie Querrie, who had just sold the St. Pats. Before he could do so, his business in Chicago hit a snag.

On March 20, Livvy was called upon to attend a meeting of the AHA directors at Chicago's Morrison Hotel. The others in attendance included AHA president Alvin Warren, Paul Loudon of the Minneapolis Millers, and

William F. Grant of Duluth, as well as members of the syndicate that agreed to buy the Cardinals. James Gemmel of Detroit and W. S. Holmes of Winnipeg were absent. According to the *Tribune*, after "an all-day session, the directors refused to approve of the proposed transfer of the franchise.

> … It was said last night that consent to the purchase of the franchise by the Cook syndicate required a unanimous vote of all directors and that, two directors being absent, this was impossible. Another meeting of the directors will be held in St. Paul today or tomorrow.[505]

Livingstone responded by cancelling that night's game between the Cardinals and St. Paul.

> Although the officials of the Chicago Cardinals last night asserted that the game had "just been postponed" and that the remainder of the schedule would be played, wiseacres of the local hockey situation were of the opinion that the developments at the league meeting were such that the American association was through with hockey in Chicago this year.[506]

There was more to this story than meets the eye. Livvy cancelled the game because the opponent was St. Paul, whose owner, A. H. Warren, ran the American association. And the league was seeking to prevent Livingstone from selling his club, more than a full week after the deal had been consummated. Livvy anticipated that, by cancelling the game, thus depriving Warren of the visitors' share of the gate receipts, the approval process might be speeded up.

The man in charge of the Coliseum, Charles R. Hall, provided a different perspective on the cancellation of the game. He told the Chicago *Tribune* that, in his opinion, the Cardinals were behind on the rent. "When Mr. Livingstone and members of the new syndicate refused to guarantee the expenses of the game with St. Paul, I could not permit the use of our ice rink," he said.[507]

Despite the Herendeen group's insistence that the team would finish the season, the players, who had not been paid for the past two weeks — Livingstone felt the new owners would be covering the payroll, so he had stopped doing so — were not so sure. Still, the *Tribune* said, "The contracts of the players, however, are ironclad, and regardless of the franchise tangle, their salaries are guaranteed by the league."[508]

Left with no choice, and unable to battle two leagues in the courts simultaneously, Livingstone folded the Cardinals, much to the delight of Blackhawks owner Frederic McLaughlin.

Whether the Teddy Graham incident or Eddie Livingstone's circumstances were part of the problem, Pete Muldoon never said. On March 17, 1927, the Blackhawks coach had had enough of the man he referred to as "Solomon's Successor"[509] and gave his two-weeks notice to McLaughlin. Although he quit on St. Patrick's Day, there is no evidence to support Jim Coleman's claim that he was in "a black Irish snit."

In fact, if anyone could be accused of being given to fits of temper, it is McLaughlin, as an incident that took place during his 1923 honeymoon with Irene Castle illustrates:

> Maj. Frederic McLaughlin of Chicago soundly thrashed a traveling salesman on board the steamship *President Taft* because of the comments the latter made regarding his bride, Irene Castle, according to passengers on board the liner, which reached Japan yesterday.[510]

Muldoon finished the season, guiding the Blackhawks to a record of 19–22–3 — good enough for third place in the NHL's five-team American Division, as well as a playoff berth. The Hawks took part in a two-game, total-goals playoff series with the Boston Bruins, who eliminated them by a combined score of 10–5. In the regular season, Chicago's offence, spearheaded by Dick Irvin and Babe Dye, led the NHL in goal scoring. Unfortunately, the club also led in goals against.

Coleman's tall tale depicted a wild-eyed Muldoon cursing McLaughlin out. "Fire me, Major," he is supposed to have said, "and you'll never finish first! I'll put a curse on this team that will hoodoo it till the end of time." The hoax gained more and more currency the longer the Hawks failed to top the standings — although they won the Stanley Cup three times in the intervening half-century, Chicago did not finish in first place until 1966–67.

But just a week after the playoff series against Boston, Muldoon gave an interview to the Seattle *Post-Intelligencer* in which he displayed none of the animosity of which Coleman would accuse him years later.

"Our worthy president wanted to run the club, the players, the referees, etc. He learned the game very quickly. In fact, after seeing his first game, he wrote me a letter telling me what the players should do and should not do," he said. "The country is too large and life is too short to battle all the time in unpleasant conditions. If my team would have been in the basement, it would have been different."[511]

In other words, McLaughlin was a control freak, and Muldoon could think of better ways to make a living than to humour his boss. Hardly the stuff that "hoodoos" are made of.

McLaughlin accepted Muldoon's resignation and wasted no time in replacing him. A few days after the Hawks' season ended, he raided the AHA yet again and signed the Winnipeg Maroons' player-manager, Barney Stanley.[512]

If anyone was the victim of a curse after Pete Muldoon left Chicago, it was the ex-coach himself. He returned to the Pacific Northwest with his wife and young sons, Dick and Lynn. He acquired the right to operate the concessions at the Portland Arena and a couple of racetracks, and in 1928 he helped Frank Patrick relaunch the Pacific Coast Hockey League. Muldoon, along with former Seattle mayor Hugh Caldwell and boxing promoter Nate Druxman, owned the Seattle Eskimos and built a new ice arena, located at the corner of Fourth Avenue North and Mercer Street, just north of where the Space Needle is currently located. (The arena was still standing in 2002, when it was serving as the temporary home of the Seattle Opera and the Pacific Northwest Ballet.)

The middle of March was a busy — and stressful — time for the popular Muldoon. On March 11, he helped Frank Patrick negotiate a deal with the Montreal Canadiens and New York Rangers that would bring the two teams to Seattle for a postseason series of exhibition games. On the same day came word that Patrick, the man who *was* hockey on the west coast, was considering an offer to go to Chicago and manage a transplanted Ottawa Senators club (see Chapter 26).[513]

A day later, Muldoon made a move to further the development of hockey in the Pacific Northwest by guaranteeing ice time at the Arena to four fraternities at the University of Washington so that they could form a hockey league.[514] That evening, the Portland Buckaroos leapfrogged past the Seattle Eskimos to claim the last available berth in the PCHL playoffs.

On March 13, Muldoon and his business partners drove to nearby Tacoma to inspect a vacant strip of land where they planned to build an arena to host a PCHL expansion team. The men were driving up Puyallup Avenue when their attention was caught by another vacant plot near 24th Street and Pacific Avenue.

"This," exclaimed Muldoon, "looks like a good site. Let's look it over."

He was sitting in the front seat with Druxman, who was at the wheel.

"Take down the real estate agent's name and address," suggested Druxman, pointing to a sign on the property.

"I haven't any paper," said Muldoon.

"Here's some," said Druxman, producing a piece from his pocket.

Druxman later said that he heard Muldoon breathe oddly and then saw his head fall forward, his chin resting upon his chest. "I thought he was jesting at first, then I saw his face become discolored," he told the Tacoma *Spokesman-Review.* "I knew something was wrong, thinking perhaps that Muldoon had suffered from an epileptic attack."[515]

His companions lifted him from the car and attempted to revive him on the grass, but in vain. An ambulance rushed Muldoon to Pierce County Hospital, where he was pronounced dead due to an acute dilation of the heart.[516]

Frank Patrick was crushed.

"Nothing has ever affected me like this," he said. "Pete was like a brother to me." His voice broke as he paid his late associate a final compliment: "In eighteen years of association with Pete, I have never had one cross word with him. Not one. He was always smiling and happy and well liked by everyone. He had not an enemy."[517]

Only on his death was it revealed that Pete Muldoon was not the man's real name. Linton Muldoon Tracy was forty-seven years old at the time of his death.[518]

Leo Lassen, the sports editor of the Seattle *Times*, was covering baseball spring training in San Clemente, California, when he heard the news, and he took time out to commemorate Muldoon in print. "Hockey has lost a great organizer and a great manager. But, more important, athletics in Seattle has lost a man who put loyalty to his associates far above whatever financial gain he might have ahead. In the very prime of his life he sacrificed it to the game he loved."[519]

The Canadiens did not play their series in Seattle. Instead, they ended up in Vancouver, playing Frank Patrick's Lions for what was billed as the "Championship of Canada." Vancouver won the set, two games to one.

Lester Patrick's Rangers did not make the trip west at all — they backed out, their place taken by Tommy Gorman's Americans. The Americans beat the Portland Buckaroos, shortly after which Gorman bolted for Mexico.

Chapter 25

Leafs of a Different Colour

A change of the name, but not the letter, is a change for the worse and not the better.

— C.C. Milne, 1926[520]

Eddie Livingstone wasn't the only hockey owner with financial problems in the early months of 1927. The National Hockey League's greatest source of concern came from Livvy's old stomping grounds in Toronto, where Charlie Querrie's court-ordered obligations to Livingstone had made it impossible for him to continue operating the St. Pats.

By February, Querrie had located a willing buyer for the team in the recently deposed manager of the New York Rangers, Conn Smythe. Smythe had already developed a reputation around Toronto as a hockey man. After graduating from high school in 1912, he attended the University of Toronto, where he lined up at centre for the Varsity Blues junior hockey team. In 1915, the Blues won the provincial junior hockey title. That year, he joined the army. During World War I he served as a lieutenant, was taken prisoner and was decorated with the Military Cross. After the war he returned to his studies, earning a degree in engineering from U of T in 1920, and then entered the sand and gravel business.

In his 1974 book *The Fastest Sport*, Gerald Eskenazi recounts the next part of the Smythe story.

> It began for Smythe in 1926. He was 31 years old and already a veteran executive of amateur hockey. The New York Rangers were to enter the league that winter and the Rangers' president, Colonel John S. Hammond, on

the recommendation of Charles Adams, the Boston Bruins' president, elected Smythe to bring hockey players to New York....

The kind of team Smythe selected was made up of men much like himself. "I wanted guys who loved to play the game, to whom money was secondary," he explained. Seeking "sportsmen," he convinced many amateurs to turn pro. But his stubbornness toward this ideal proved his undoing before the Rangers ever played a league game.

Colonel Hammond wanted Babe Dye for his new club. Smythe objected. "Dye was more like a union man than a sportsman," Smythe insisted. "He wanted to organize the players." They continued to argue about Dye. Smythe got as far as the Rangers' training camp in Ontario (training camp was a Smythe conception). A few days later he met the colonel at the local train station. Accompanying Hammond was Dye — and Lester Patrick. It was the first Smythe had heard that Patrick had been appointed the Rangers' coach and general manager, that Dye was staying — and that Smythe was not.

In later years, Smythe said that the Chicago Black Hawks' coach, Pete Muldoon, had whispered bad things about Smythe, that Muldoon convinced Hammond that the Rangers needed a man with a professional background, and one with a name to lure fans if they were to succeed in New York. Smythe, bitter over the setback, nevertheless accepted the Rangers' invitation to attend their opening game in Madison Square Garden. It was there that his fortunes changed.

At the game he ran across Tex Rickard, renowned boxing impresario and builder of Madison Square Garden. Rickard could hardly help noticing that Smythe was miffed. When asked why, Smythe told Rickard that his Rangers contract had called for $10,000 but that he had received only $7,500. Although Smythe hadn't actually fulfilled his contract, Rickard immediately gave him a check for $2,500.[521]

There can be no question that part of this story was concocted. For one thing, if Smythe had any aversion to professional players, he sure concealed it on October 18, 1926, when the National Hockey League's board of governors met at the King Edward Hotel in Toronto to divvy up the unclaimed players from the Western Hockey League. On the same day, the Toronto St. Pats sold Dye to Chicago for "a good price,"[522] making it impossible for him to have surprised Smythe by showing up for training camp in the company of Hammond and Lester Patrick. It is also anyone's guess as to why Muldoon would have been talking to anyone from the Rangers about personnel decisions.

Other versions of the story have Blackhawks owner Frederic McLaughlin bragging to Hammond about his acquisition of Babe Dye, prompting the Colonel to ask Smythe about it. Smythe insisted that Dye was past his prime, but Hammond did not appreciate being shown up by McLaughlin, so he fired Smythe.

In any event, the one point we cannot contest is that Smythe attended the Rangers' first game as a guest of the club, and that Rickard had Hammond write Smythe a cheque for $2,500 after the Rangers beat the Maroons 2–0 in their opener. Eskenazi says that, one week later, Smythe attended a football game between U of T and McGill University, and that he bet the whole $2,500 on the Varsity Blues. He won the bet. Another week later, the Rangers came to Toronto to play the St. Pats. Smythe got odds of 3-to-1 on his former team and won. Eskenazi writes, "By then he had to admit, 'I was feeling pretty good toward the Rangers.'"[523]

Smythe, who was coaching the Varsity senior hockey team in 1926–27, decided to use his $15,000 stake to get back into the pro hockey business. He raised a further $145,000 from thirteen partners to purchase the last-place St. Pats from Querrie and his three associates. To ensure an orderly transition, J. P. Bickell held onto his shares in the hockey club. Bickell had bought into the St. Pats in 1924, along with N. L. Nathanson, by snapping up the shares of Fred and Percy Hambly. According to the Toronto *Mail and Empire*, rumours indicated that Smythe's other partners were all Varsity alumni.[524]

According to the official version of events, the first thing Smythe did upon taking over the team was rip the St. Pats crest off the club's green and white sweater and replace it with a maple leaf. Smythe named the team after the World War I fighting unit, the Maple Leaf Regiment, of which Smythe was a member.[525] Although Smythe did not become involved in the operation of the club until the following season — when his obligations to the U of T hockey team were fulfilled — this was one change he made immediately.

That's the official version, anyway.

In fact, as early as December 1926, Smythe's predecessor Charlie Querrie was considering changing the team's nickname to Maple Leafs, to match that of the local minor-league baseball team. C. C. Milne of the *Sault Daily Star* had the story.

> *A Change of the Name, but not the letter,*
> *Is a change for the worse and not the better.*

So says the old adage, but the Toronto St. Pats are said to be changing both in an effort to bring the club some of the breaks of the game. The St. Pats are holding down the tail end of the National Hockey League procession, with but five points in eight games played, and are out to find the meaning of it. Charlie Querrie, manager of the club, did his best when he dyed the old red blankets of the club a vivid green and gave the club a 5–2 win over Chicago on Thursday night last, and now he proposes to change the name to "Maple Leafs." While the name has become famous by reason of its baseball association, there is no reason why it should not be taken over by the Toronto Club and brought to the fore in the hockey world.

The name St. Patricks, unlike the Canadiens, signifies nothing. Canadians have made their name famous by the use of only players of French Canadien extraction on their lineup, but the St. Pats is merely a name for a hockey club. Maple Leafs, with a symbolic emblem on the sweater, would convey more to the uninitiated hockey fans of the American cities.[526]

Querrie never did change the name, however. Instead, he sold the franchise to the Varsity group on February 14, 1927. The Valentine's Day transaction marked the beginning of an enduring love affair with the city of Toronto. As the Toronto *Daily Star* saw it:

The name St.Patricks will be used for the last time at Detroit to-night.

The team will be known henceforth as the Maple Leafs of Toronto.

New uniforms of white will be used, with a green maple leaf on the breast and the word Toronto underneath, something like the Canadian Olympic sweaters at Chamonix in 1924.

The club changed hands late yesterday afternoon after a day of negotiations being swung by E. W. Bickle and Co. and Campbell, Stratton and Co. Of the former owners of the club, only J. P. Bickell and N. L. Nathanson will retain an interest, and it will be small compared to what they previously held.

The sum paid for the franchise, players and assets of the St. Patrick's Hockey Club was $160,000.

Charlie Querrie, who has been in charge of St. Patrick's for the last couple of seasons, took the team to Detroit this morning for to-night's game with the Cougars and was accompanied by Alex Romeril, who has been appointed manager of the new club and who will be in charge for the first home game on Thursday night against the New York Americans.

It was officially stated that the St. Patrick's club could have sold their holdings for as much as $40,000 more than the $160,000 they received had they chosen to dispose of them to Montreal or Philadelphia interests, but both the old and the new owners were loath to see the franchise and players leave Toronto.[527]

The Philadelphia bid may have seemed greater, but not when one takes into account that Smythe and company were acquiring only 75 percent of the team. That would put the total value of the franchise at a little over $213,000. Bickell and Nathanson's stake alone would have been worth more than $50,000 — a healthy gain over the $30,000 they had paid less than three years before.[528]

The *Star's* Lou Marsh, who was also an NHL referee and a Livingstone ally, was underwhelmed by the midseason name change: "You can't make an onion into a rose by calling it an American Beauty or a Crimson Rambler." He also railed against the blue laws governing Ontario. "They play pro hockey in New York Sunday night. BUT IT IS AGAINST THE LAW TO BROADCAST IT [in Toronto]!"[529]

On February 16, the St. Pats were in Windsor for what was to have been their farewell game before becoming the Maple Leafs. According to the *Telegram*, it was one of the worst attended games in the sport's history.

The Toronto St. Patrick's celebrated the change of ownership of their club by losing out here last night.

About 200 fans saw Detroit win 5–1 from the Toronto aggregation.

The contest was to have been the last under the name "St. Pats," but the new owners learned from the N.H.L. meeting in Toronto Tuesday afternoon that a change in name now would make all the present members of the team free agents, as they all had signed St. Patrick contracts last November.

So we will have the St. Patricks with us for the remaining games of this season.[530]

By the next day, the *Telegram* had corrected its attendance figure and come up with a hypothesis as to why fans of the fledgling Detroit Cougars fans were staying away:

Only about 150 people turned out for the contest, showing that you can't fool the people all the time. Detroit are weak and are not trying to strengthen. They see disaster written for this season and are content to take it.

Next season they will be in their own rink in Detroit. Work did start on it early this winter, but was suspended when it was found that if even if rushed it would not be ready until the last of the season. It was figured wise to lay off and complete the work in the better weather.

And not only have Detroit a poor team, but they have strong opposition from the Windsor pros., who pack them in every time they play. Another thing, Detroit charge prohibitive prices for admission. For example, the bleacher or rush seats are one dollar. These are the same as in Toronto for fifty cents.

And the top price is $3.75 for the best. There is no doubt the prices are high and the Detroit owners know it. But they are afraid to reduce them because if they do and then want next season to boost them up again when they move to Detroit, the public will squawk. So, as said before, Detroit are content to go along and lose their shirt this winter, hoping for better things next winter.

Tomorrow the green-and-white St. Patrick uniforms will be left in the lockers by one Thomas Daly. And out the local boys will trot with brand new "jumpers" bearing the Maple Leaf. It is hoped the new uniforms will bring luck, for the Leafs will find strong opposition from these New York Americans.[531]

The newly named Leafs would wear those new sweaters until the end of the season. They began the 1927–28 schedule in the now-familiar blue and white.

Having paid the last $10,000 instalment against the damages Eddie Livingstone had been awarded, and then sold the Toronto St. Pats, Charlie Querrie was now free of the hockey business.

Almost.

Less than six weeks after the sale, Livingstone was back in front of a judge in Toronto, suing Querrie for interest on the debt that had just been retired. Livvy's lawyer, William B. McHenry of MacDonell & Boland, summarized his client's problems with Querrie, to whom the legendary Montreal *Herald* columnist Elmer Ferguson referred as a "respected sportsman":

> On January 7, 1920, Livingstone was awarded $21,871.64, and directed to the Master in Ordinary for damages.
>
> 1. On June 30, 1922, Assistant Master George Alcorn amended the award to $23,404.33.
> 2. On September 17, 1922, the Appeals Court reduced the award to $13,271.52.
> 3. The Arena Gardens of Toronto then paid $15,861.87, including interest and proceedings costs.
> 4. On October 8, 1923, Alcorn awarded Livingstone $100,000 in damages, which was reduced to $10,000 by Justice Orde on April 26, 1924.
> 5. The Arena Gardens made a payment of $10,000 plus interest from May 14, 1924, but refused to pay interest prior to that date.[532]

Despite being called "dishonest" and accused of having exhibited "despicable behaviour" by the Ontario Appellate Court, Querrie emerged from the case with his reputation intact.

Chapter 26

Conspiracy, Chicago Style

In your wildest flight of imagination would you have believed such things possible today in sport or business?
— Eddie Livingstone, 1919[533]

In the summer of 1927, Alvin Warren, the president of the American Hockey Association, met in Chicago with Frank Calder, his National Hockey League counterpart, for a game of golf and to discuss the terms under which the NHL would continue to recognize the AHA. Warren submitted a draft agreement that was similar to the ones the other minor leagues had signed. Calder subsequently wrote a memo to Frederic McLaughlin of the Chicago Blackhawks advising that the NHL should not sign this document until the AHA "have shown us that they have officially severed connections with this lunatic [Livingstone]."[534]

We can only wonder at the words Calder might have used to describe Livvy that he didn't care to commit to paper!

On August 24, the AHA passed a resolution terminating Livingstone's membership in the league. Warren sent a copy of the resolution to Calder, with a cover letter that read: "I hope that matters are now adjusted to your satisfaction, and that the agreement may be renewed along the lines we discussed in Chicago, and which I believe are covered to your satisfaction in the agreement submitted."[535] The AHA ousted Livingstone on the grounds that he failed to abide by the contract made between his franchise and the league. Two specific charges were the non-payment of a $750 franchise fee before the January 1, 1927, deadline, and the failure to book the Coliseum for the requisite number of dates.[536] Obviously, since Livingstone had folded the club when Warren refused to allow its sale, these were moot points.

On December 23, the New York *Times* observed that Livingstone was fighting back yet again.

> Charging that his Chicago hockey league franchise and star players were taken from him, Edward J. Livingstone of Ontario, Canada, filed suit today in Federal Court for $700,000 damages against Major Frederic McLaughlin, owner of the Chicago Black Hawks and husband of Irene Castle, the dancer.
>
> Two associates of Major McLaughlin in the promotion of hockey here, William J. Foster and John S. Keough, were named defendants with him.
>
> Livingstone charged that two years ago he organized the Chicago Cardinals franchise and made a contract for a Chicago franchise in the American Hockey Association. He said he also made arrangements to lease the Coliseum for games. A year ago, he asserts, the three defendants went to Canada, where the Cardinals were playing, and induced four of his star players, Edward Graham, Marvin Wentworth, Robert Burns and Ralph Taylor, to break their Cardinal contracts and sign with a Chicago team that was to be in the National Hockey League.
>
> Because of that, he alleges, he lost the local franchise in addition to his players. He asks $500,000 in actual damages and $200,000 for malicious practices.
>
> In September, 1927, at a meeting of the National Hockey League in Chicago, Frank Calder, President, and Alvin H. Warren, Jr., President of the Hockey Association, with the approval of both organizations, ratified an agreement that eliminated him from organized playing, Livingstone contends.[537]

The evidence presented in *Livingstone v. McLaughlin* centred around Wentworth, whom Livingstone had nicknamed Cy (as in Cyclone) in an effort add some sizzle to his Chicago Cardinals. One exhibit was a notarized statement Wentworth signed in Toronto on November 12, 1926.

> I, Marvin P. M. Wentworth, of the Town of Grimsby in the County of Lincoln, Hockey-Player, do solemnly declare that

1. I played hockey for the Windsor Amateur Hockey Club for the season 1925–26.
2. I made no contract or agreement to play hockey for the Windsor Professional Hockey Club and I received no money on account of my hockey services for the Season 1926–1927 from the Windsor Amateur Hockey Club or the Windsor Professional Hockey Club, except as explained hereinafter.
3. I did take a position in Windsor in May 1925 (about a year and a half ago), which was obtained for me by the Windsor Amateur Hockey Club, with the Canadian Salt Company, the Windsor Amateur Hockey Club having assured me a position at $50.00 per week. They secured the position for me, but the salary was not what was assured to me and the difference was made up to me, I believe, by the Border Cities Arena Company. I merely continued in this position till on or about the 1st of July, 1926, when I gave up my poisition in consequence of the disbanding of the Windsor Amateur Hockey Club and the formation of the Windsor Professional Hockey Club, which latter club wanted me to play professional hockey for it during the season 1926–1927, which I declined to do.
4. Later and before the 25th of September, 1926, I signed a bona fide contract to play for the Chicago Americans Hockey Club.[538]

After the Chicago Americans disbanded, the Blackhawks signed Wentworth, paying him a $500 bonus on March 22, 1927. Wentworth, who believed he was suspended from organized hockey, was left no choice but to sign the following document in front of Cook County Notary Public M. C. Travers on March 21, 1927:

I, Marvin Wentworth, being duly sworn, do hereby testify that during the months of April, May and June, 1926, I accepted from the Border Cities Arena Co., Ltd., of Windsor, Ontario, sums of money aggregating approximately Two Hundred and Fifty ($250.00) Dollars as advance part payment for my professional

Hockey services with the Windsor Hockey Team for the season of 1926–1927.[539]

Wentworth's most damning statement against McLaughlin and Calder came in his own handwriting, followed by his signature: "The above is an accurate copy of a falsely drawn affidavit typed from copy written by Frederick McLaughlin himself and who knew the real facts but influenced me to sign this."[540]

McLaughlin, meanwhile, was beginning to enjoy his new hobby. Calder and his cronies had initially shunned the coffee baron as a know-nothing, but his work in ridding Chicago of Eddie Livingstone provided him an entrée into hockey's powerful inner circle. Things hit a snag however, during the 1928–29 season, when McLaughlin, expecting Chicago Stadium to be completed, allowed his lease on the Coliseum to lapse and had to scramble for a place to play. On January 21, 1929, the Chicago Blackhawks embarked on an extended road trip, one which would last eleven months. The night before, fans had flocked to the Coliseum to bid their team farewell. "More than 7,000 fans, who occupied every seat, stood up on against the walls and even sat on the steel beams far up near the ceiling, watched the Hawks lose their final game in Chicago this season," the Tribune reported, adding that "some 3,000 other folks didn't because the Coliseum lacks rubber walls. There wasn't anything approaching a riot, but all the coppers in the immediate neighborhood got together to keep in check the ticketless 3,000 surging at the doors."[541]

The Blackhawks' first stop was Detroit. The *Border Cities Star*, based across the river in Windsor, Ontario, told the story:

> Chicago Black Hawks, the "little Orphan Annie" of the National Hockey League and basement holders in the American division at the moment, have transferred six of their remaining home games to Olympia, according to an announcement made by Charles A. Hughes, president of the Detroit Hockey Club.
>
> The Black Hawks have been chased out of the Chicago Coliseum to make room for the extensive boxing program planned this winter. This action leaves the N.H.L. aggregation without a "home" until the new arena is completed in Chicago next fall.

> Only recently the Chicago moguls approached
> Olympia with a proposition to play the remaining Black
> Hawks home games in the Detroit ice palace.[542]

The Hawks also played some "home" games in Fort Erie, Ontario, before the season was done.

On January 13, the *Tribune* reported that Paddy Harmon, owner and builder of the Chicago Stadium, might present the Second City its second NHL team — one with a distinguished pedigree that included several Stanley Cup championships.

> Frank Ahearn, president of the Ottawa Senators Hockey
> club, said tonight he was awaiting the arrival of Chicago
> representatives regarding the possible sale of his team.
> He announced that he had received three offers to sell
> or transfer the team to the United States.
>
> Ahearn also stated that he had received flattering
> offers for the services of King Clancy, Hec Kilrea and
> Frankie Finnigan, but that he was not considering them.
> Ahearn, it is believed, feels he can sustain heavy losses
> here when American cities, especially Chicago, are
> offering excellent prospects.
>
> Though Paddy Harmon admitted last night he
> was one of the bidders for the Ottawa Senators, he
> declined to say how much he was offering for the
> Canadian club. Even should his bid be acceptable to
> the Ottawa owners, there is considerable doubt as to
> whether the club could be brought into Chicago.
> Under the rules of the National Hockey League,
> establishing a club in a new city requires a unianimous
> vote of the other franchise holders and it is practical-
> ly certain that the Hawks would not permit another
> club to come into the city.[543]

Harmon, who couldn't stand Major McLaughlin and who had missed out on the chance to land the Blackhawks franchise, must have been serious, as he recruited Frank Patrick to manage the team once it moved.

As it turned out, the Blackhawks and Senators both stayed put. Despite mounting financial losses, Ahearn kept his club in Ottawa. When the team finally did move, in 1934, it was to St. Louis, not

Chicago. McLaughlin's club, meanwhile, survived its lengthy absence and moved into the Chicago Stadium in December 1929. Chicagoans welcomed the Blackhawks back with open arms and hearts. They would be rewarded with back-to-back winning seasons, and a trip to the Stanley Cup finals in 1931.

Courtesy of the Hockey Hall of Fame

Frederic McLaughlin

Just before that 1930–31 season got underway, Livingstone's four-year-old lawsuit against McLaughlin came to trial. One of the issues of the case was the fact that McLaughlin signed four former Cardinals — including Teddy Graham and Cy Wentworth — prior to the 1927–28 season. Livingstone claimed that the players' professional rights were still his because of the option year on their contracts — a practice with which the "commissioner of hockey," Frank Calder, should have been familiar, since the National Hockey Association first instituted it in 1911. It was also the very tool the teams in Windsor and London had used, under Calder's supervision, against Livingstone in the original flap over the rights to Graham and Wentworth.

McLaughlin's lawyer, Fred Burnham, opened by informing the jury that Livingstone had been ejected from the Coliseum for failure to pay back rent and that his players were owed several months' worth of back salary when they signed with McLaughlin.[544] On this basis, it was argued that Livingstone had no rights to the services of the four players.

The truth of the matter was that Livingstone did not guarantee the rental of the Coliseum for the Cardinals' game against St. Paul, so Charles Hall, the president of the Coliseum, had refused to allow the game to go on. And the players were owed two weeks' salary, not months' worth: the only paycheque they had missed was the last one of the 1926–27 season. If they were not paid for "several months," it was only because players didn't receive paycheques during the off-season, regardless of what team they played for. That last payday had been missed because the new owners of the Cards agreed to assume responsibility for the payroll, but when the AHA vetoed the sale, and subsequently kicked Livingstone out of the league, there was no one to pay the players.

The trial was supposed to last for two days, but evidence was heard for five. Then came a strange twist in the case, as reported by the Chicago *Tribune*:

> Federal Judge Carpenter yesterday declared a mistrial in the suit for $700,000 brought by Edward J. Livingstone, Canadian hockey promoter, against Maj. Frederic McLaughlin, owner of the Chicago Blackhawks, and two of his employees. The court declared that one of the jurors, "either through ignorance or inadvertance," approached McLaughlin and talked with him.
>
> John Hodge, an insurance agent [from] Mundelein, [Illinois,] the juror involved, was questioned, but not detained, although the United States attorney's office was directed to investigate the case. It was stated that McLaughlin himself had reported the juror's remarks to Judge Carpenter. A new trial of the case will begin Monday.
>
> Livingstone had been on the witness stand for two days and had not been cross-examined.[545]

These were the days when Al Capone still ruled Chicago. The mayor of Chicago, the governor of Illinois, even federal judges, were on Capone's payroll. Capone's influence was such that anyone not party to the gangster could consider himself an enemy. Livingstone could not be sure where McLaughlin stood, so even the hint of jury tampering was enough for him to express his concern through his lawyer.

On the day after the mistrial was declared, the American Hockey Association announced that the St. Paul team would relocate to Buffalo, the dormant Detroit franchise would relocate to the Bronx and be known as the New York Stars, and that Tom Shaughnessy, the former Blackhawks coach who had purchased the Minneapolis Millers, would be granted an expansion franchise in Chicago.

On October 8, the trial began anew. After the testimony given by two of Livingstone's ex-players, McLaughlin might have been better off tampering with the jury again!

> Ralph Taylor and Robert Burns, former hockey players with the Chicago Cardinals, testified in Federal Judge

Carpenter's court yesterday that Maj. Frederic
McLaughlin, owner of the Chicago Blackhawks, offered
them bonuses and higher salaries to break their contracts
with Edward J. Livingstone, who owned the Cardinals.[546]

After giving this evidence, neither Taylor nor Burns would ever play
in the National Hockey League again. In fact, neither would play in a
pro league other than the AHA: both men were blacklisted from the
"organized hockey" leagues under Calder's control. Even when World
War II triggered a glaring shortage of talent in all of hockey's leagues,
neither player was called upon.

Two days later, Livingstone dropped another bombshell.

For the second time in as many weeks, the $700,000
damage suit of Edward J. Livingstone, of Toronto, Canada,
against Maj. Frederic McLaughlin, owner of the Chicago
Blackhawks hockey team, was declared a mistrial.

Attorney Cecil C. Erickson, counsel for the plaintiff,
made the motion for a non-suit because of the "frag-
mentary manner in which the evidence was allowed to
go in." After the motion was granted, he said he would
refile the suit.[547]

The lawsuit was never refiled. Without giving any reason,
Livingstone left for Toronto. As we have seen, it was certainly unchar-
acteristic of Livingstone to give up so quietly. There is no record that the
case was settled, so one can only speculate on what happened. Was Livvy
paid off by Tom Shaughnessy, owner of the AHA's new Chicago
Shamrocks franchise, or even by William Grant, the new president of the
AHA? Instead of cash, could he have been on the receiving end of
threats from Chicagoland gangsters?

After the Livingstone suit was dismissed, Shaughnessy, who was having
trouble selling his Minneapolis team, was faced with the additional challenge of organizing his Chicago club. He signed the former Cardinals
Ralph Taylor and Bobby Burns, as well as a couple of other players who
had worked for Livingstone: Gord Brydson and Corb Denneny.
Shaughnessy also took a page out of Livingstone's book by recruiting
American college stars — young, swift-skating, hard-working, and inex-
pensive talent — to fill out the ranks. These included the centre Don

McFadyen and right winger Clarence "Pudge" MacKenzie, both of whom had played for Marquette University in Milwaukee. Their coach, John Farquhar, would join them in the same role as well.

The reaction from NHL headquarters to the presence of the Shamrocks in Chicago was not surprising. Calder ruled that, by placing a team in Chicago, where there was already an NHL club, and in Buffalo, where there was an NHL-affiliated International Hockey League franchise, without his consent, the AHA had earned outlaw status. "Such action was a direct challenge to organized hockey," Calder said. "From the date of its outlaw action the American association automatically has cut off itself and its members from any player deals or other transactions with clubs in the National, Canadian-American, International, Pacific Coast and California Hockey leagues."[548] The NHL's board of governors also ruled that those who played in the AHA were automatically barred from joining an "organized" hockey team.

Calder also raised the spectre of the unpaid Chicago Cardinals players to threaten anyone thinking of breaking ranks. "Outlaw players cannot expect organized hockey to help them collect their salaries, and that help is one of the special benefits enjoyed by players under National league control."[549]

Chapter 27

Calder Steals the Cup

*Many deals of importance were closed on Calder's word alone.
Once his word was given, it was as good as any bond in the
country. You do not always find that, in business or in sport,
but on Calder's word, you could place absolute reliance.*

— Frank Patrick, 1943[550]

*A*fter growing rapidly in the
mid 1920s, the early thirties
were rocky years for Calder and
the National Hockey League.
The Pittsburgh Pirates' early
success soon fizzled, and in 1928
the team was sold to the New
York Americans' owner, "Big
Bill" Dwyer. Dwyer paid cash
and did not publicize his ownership of the club, using the former lightweight boxing champion Benny Leonard as a front
man. Although the National
Hockey Association had objected to Eddie Livingstone's ownership of the two Toronto teams

**The Stanley Cup in the late 1920s.
The trophy was the subject of battles on and off the ice.**

in 1915, Calder was either unaware of the Dwyer transaction or, given that Tex Rickard supported the bootlegger, afraid to cross him.

By 1930, financial conditions were such that the Pirates were no longer sustainable in Pittsburgh, and they were moved to Philadelphia. The city that had raised the world's first artificial ice rink, given hockey its first permanent foothold in the U.S., attended at the birth of professional hockey, and — thanks to coach Odie Cleghorn's line changes — revolutionized the sport for all time, would be absent from the world's top hockey league until 1967, when it gained the expansion Penguins. (In the interim, Pittsburgh would become one of the strongest markets in the minor leagues.)

Despite the cross-state move, the franchise fared no better in Philly. Playing under the Quakers nickname and coached by Cooper Smeaton, the Hall of Fame referee and future Stanley Cup trustee, its 4–36–4 record in 1930–31 was one of the worst ever in hockey.

During the off-season, the Great Depression began to erode Calder's big league. The Philadelphia Quakers and Ottawa Senators both asked for — and were granted — one-year leaves of absence. Both teams' players were loaned out via a dispersal draft, with the draft fees going to the two clubs. Ottawa returned to active play in 1931–32, but the Pennsylvania franchise did not.

Meanwhile, after Calder declared his organization an "outlaw league," AHA president William F. Grant fired back. Grant, a friend of Livingstone's who had owned the Duluth Hornets before heading south to start up the Kansas City Pla-Mors, fired back. He replied that the AHA's establishment of the Chicago Shamrocks did not violate any territorial agreement with the NHL. He asserted that it was the AHA's refusal to renew a three-year agreement with the NHL that had brought about the outlaw charges.

> The American league had a three year agreement with the National which expired on Sept. 24, and directors of the American league decided that if a new agreement were entered into certain objectionable features of the old agreement must be obviated.
>
> Our league felt that the draft was unjust and also that it was unwise to have the president of the National league acting as "commissioner of hockey," to whom all disputes, whether involving National league clubs or not, were referred.

> Our club owners are responsible business and
> professional men. We intend to operate independent-
> ly and will respect the rights of other leagues as
> regards legal contracts.[551]

On that last point, Grant was foolish for not seeking the input of
Eddie Livingstone, who had taken the high road with Calder for fifteen
years and lost.

He might also have asked Percy Thompson, the Hamilton Tigers
owner who lost his NHL franchise when his players went on strike and
he followed Calder's advice. Thompson's Tigers set up shop in the minor
leagues, but by 1930 Hamiltonians were staying away in droves. The team
announced on October 21 that it was moving to Syracuse, New York.

Having gone head to head with the NHL in Chicago and Detroit,
the AHA announced its intention to invade the New York Rangers territory. And another former Livingstone employee, George McNamara,
was the one about to make inroads.

> At a special meeting of the American Hockey League at
> the Morrison hotel yesterday, New York became a
> member of the circuit and the Minneapolis franchise
> was sold to Minneapolis interests.
>
> The New York franchise was granted to the New
> York American Hockey Club, Inc., of which George
> McNamara, of Toronto, Ont., is president and F. Harland
> Rohm, former *Tribune* sports writer, secretary.
>
> The Minneapolis franchise was purchased by R. V.
> Huth, secretary of the Minneapolis American association
> baseball club, and associates, from Thomas J. Shaughnessy,
> president of the Shamrocks.
>
> President McNamara of the New York club
> announced the purchase of Minneapolis players for a
> reported $55,000. Home games will be played in the
> new New York Coliseum in the Bronx. The contract
> already has been let for the ice plant and the rink will
> be open by Dec. 15. The seating capacity of the New
> York rink is 12,000.[552]

The New York team never competed in the AHA.

One player who would be at the centre of the AHA–NHL cold war
was Gord Brydson, who at the age of twenty-three was involved in his

second inter-league controversy. In 1926 he had left Stratford to play for Eddie Livingstone's Chicago Cardinals. After the collapse of the Cards, Brydson returned to Ontario, playing for the Hamilton Tigers and Buffalo Bisons of the Canadian Professional Hockey League. After a cup of coffee with the Toronto Maple Leafs, Brydson was back in the Can-Pro league — which had renamed itself the International league — with the London Panthers. In November 1930 he signed with the Chicago Shamrocks. It was the second time Brydson would be scooped off the roster of a team managed by Roy Brothers.

> The hockey war between organized and so-called outlaw leagues has been declared. Manager Roy Brothers of the London club of the International Professional Hockey league announced today that he will seek injunctions in Illinois and New York state courts restraining Gordon Brydson, former London right winger, from playing with the Chicago Shamrocks of the American Hockey league, regarded by the National Hockey and affiliated leagues as an outlaw organization.
>
> The London team purchased Brydson from the Toronto Maple Leafs for the sum of $3,500 last year. This year he was tendered a contract but refused to sign and yesterday the announcement was made that he had signed with the Chicago Shamrocks.
>
> Brothers has already held a conference with Frank Calder, president of the National Hockey League, about Brydson's case. The London manager announced a few days ago that Brydson could purchase his outright release if he desired, but the release was not purchased and he made the jump without first being declared a free agent.[553]

Shaughnessy resorted to the same defence McLaughlin had used in *Livingstone v. McLaughlin et al.*, at the same time throwing Frank Calder's words back in his face. "We signed Gordon Brydson as a free agent," he told the *Tribune*. "At our last meeting with President Calder of the National Hockey League it was agreed that we would respect existing contracts. At the same time, Mr. Calder himself stated plainly that he would consider all players who had back salary coming as not under contract, as being free agents. In this case we merely acted in accordance with Mr. Calder's own rule.

"Brydson represented to us that the London club had broken his contract by failing to pay his salary in full. We investigated fully. As evidence of his contention there is in our possession a check for $800, the amount due the player, made out to Brydson by the London club and returned several times marked 'not sufficient funds.' This player's claim is further supported by correspondence, which Brydson carried on all summer in an effort to collect his salary."[554]

William Foran, who was still one of the Stanley Cup's two trustees, was in attendance at the 1930 meeting where the AHA was branded an outlaw league. He was there in his capacity as the Ottawa Senators' representative on the NHL board of governors.

Soon enough, he would make a decision that would see him kicked out of the NHL.

Prior to the 1930–31 season, the AHA claimed major-league status under a new name, the American Hockey League.[555] Players would now have an alternative to the NHL, although Calder threatened any player who jumped with lifetime expulsion. The circuit also announced its intention to challenge the NHL's playoff champion for the Stanley Cup.

Grant filed a challenge on behalf of the 1931 champions, the Tulsa Oilers, but did so too late for Stanley Cup trustees Phil Ross and William Foran to demand a series. The next season, Grant was prompt, issuing the league's challenge in December 1931. He announced that the American league was willing to meet the NHL champion "any place and at any time" after the end of the regular season.[556]

One of the movers and shakers behind this challenge series was James Norris, a former hockey player for the storied Montreal Amateur Athletic Association who, like Tex Rickard, had become a prominent figure in the boxing world. Norris, now based in Chicago, was one of Shaughnessy's partners in the AHL Shamrocks.

In the AHL, the trustees saw a going concern, with attendance figures rivalling the NHL's. (The Chicago Shamrocks made their debut at Chicago Stadium before a crowd of 7,500.) Ross and Foran were also aware of the immense national interest in the World Series, and saw the potential to create an equally successful series for hockey. In the early weeks of 1932, Foran wrote Grant advising him of the trustees' decision to accept the AHL challenge.

> This is to advise you that the challenge of the American League (of Professional Hockey Clubs) for a series of

games with the championship club of the National
Hockey League at the close of the present season, for the
Stanley cup, has been accepted by the trustees. A letter
conveying this decision by the trustees was dispatched
today to the president of the National Hockey League,
and I shall be glad to communicate with you again when
I have received a reply from Mr. Frank Calder.[557]

Calder refused to acknowledge the trustees' decision and refused to
play a series. Ross responded by threatening Calder.

"The next move is up to the National League president, and unless
the challenge is accepted, the Montreal Canadiens — winners of the
National League race last year — must forfeit the Stanley cup which
they hold as present hockey champions of the world."[558] The trustees also
threatened legal and criminal action if the series was not played.

Calder, who was more accustomed to issuing threats than receiving
them, plotted his revenge. First, Frank Ahearn fired Foran as the Ottawa
Senators' rep on the board of governors. Next, the NHL declared war
against the American Hockey League. Frederic McLaughlin told the
Chicago press that the AHL was on the verge of collapse.

Grant was in Chicago, and when he learned of the Major's comments he called reporters in the other AHL cities to exercise damage
control. "The American Hockey League will positively finish its schedule. The situation at St. Louis was never brighter. Kansas City is ahead in
its attendance over last season, while the Shamrocks in Chicago have
been going strong," he told the St. Louis *Post-Dispatch*. "Buffalo is our
only weak point, and it may be necessary to drop that city from the
league, but if we do, the other five clubs will play each other oftener to
make up the forty-eight games which each team is to play."[559]

The St. Louis Flyers, coached by Eddie Livingstone's former right-
hand man Dick Carroll, had become something of a success story after
a slow start. The team went on a seven-game winning streak, and crowds
of up to 12,000 had started turning out at the St. Louis Arena. An
extremely popular promotion was Ladies' Night, when all women were
admitted free. On each of the three occasions the Flyers ran this promotion, it put 2,000 additional spectators in the stands. The team's success
prompted Flyers president Harry Taber to offer Carroll a new two-year
contract just before the team's January 26 game against the Buffalo
Majors. It was the last game the Majors played.

The Flyers went on to lose back-to-back games in Tulsa, where Carroll
had coached the three previous seasons, winning two championships. But

W. J. McGoegan of the *Post-Dispatch* seemed more concerned about the Flyers' loss of star defenceman Burr Williams than the two games.

> Williams, according to reports with Tulsa, has agreed to play with the Chicago Blackhawks of the National League, along with Bob Trapp, veteran defense man of the Tulsa team. The two were said to have made the agreement after last night's game in Tulsa, with Frank Naylor, scout for Col. [sic] Frederick McLaughlin, owner of the Blackhawks, who was sent to Tulsa to fire the first gun in what apparently is the opening of war between the National and American leagues.[560]

Grant did his best to give the impression that it was business as usual in the struggling AHL, while painting the NHL as the aggressors. He told the Kansas City *Star* that Naylor had also been seen at Pla-Mors games. "The same fellow saw our last game in Kansas City, I believe. He talked with our players in the dressing room between periods. Told me he was a goalie from Toronto."[561]

McGoegan suggested revenge was the motive:

> It was said the rubber band was off the Colonel's bankroll and while figures were unobtainable, it was learned that Williams and Trapp had declared their salaries were to be doubled. Also, Blackhawk officials from Chicago stated the players were not "jumping," but that their clubs had failed to pay the players their salaries, thereby making their contracts null and void.
>
> The action of the National League appears to be a follow-up of the Stanley Cup trustees' action Wednesday in accepting the American League's challenge for the trophy, emblematic of world hockey supremacy, for the National League declared that in view of the situation existing they wished to strengthen their teams for the Stanley Cup competition and were going to negotiate with any players in the American League with whom they had a right to deal.
>
> William F. Grant of Kansas City, president of the American League, declared the charge that the players had not been paid was untrue, asserting that there was nothing in the contracts specifying any particular

dates of payment and that the clubs were paying their men regularly.

"We are fully protected by law," Grant told the *Post-Dispatch* over the telephone, "and if the players attempt to go through with the jump we will apply for an injunction to prevent them from playing for Chicago and sue the Blackhawk management for damages."[562]

The AHL president had taken legal action against the NHL before. When he owned the Duluth Hornets, the Detroit Cougars went after one of his players, Herbie Lewis. Grant obtained an injunction against the NHL, then filed a lawsuit, alleging conspiracy, against the league and the Detroit owner Charles Hughes. The court sided with Grant, who later sold Lewis to the Cougars.

"We can do the same thing over again if they want it," Grant said, "but I don't think that will be necessary."[563]

To replace Williams, Harry Taber signed Eddie Bouchard — who had seen NHL action with Pittsburgh — and Billy DePaul, both of whom had last played for the extinct Buffalo Majors. Then, as suddenly as McLaughlin had gone after Williams, he broke off negotiations abruptly. It would seem that the Blackhawks weren't interested in Williams at all, but only wanted to force the Flyers to spend money on players they wouldn't have needed had the Blackhawks not tampered with Williams. The *Post-Dispatch* noted, however, that McLaughlin did sign Bob Trapp.

> The Chicago Blackhawks, which were dickering for Williams' services, dropped their negotiations today when they learned that the player signed a new contract with the St. Louis club.
>
> It appeared this afternoon that the "raid" of the Chicago Blackhawks and other National League clubs on American League teams is off. Bob Trapp of the Tulsa club, who was named with Williams as the two players sought by the Blackhawks, was in Chicago today, but officials of the Blackhawks had taken no action in his case. The Blackhawk office announced they were not figuring on using Trapp, but plan to use him in a trade.[564]

The Blackhawks sent Trapp to Providence of the Canadian-American Hockey League. And on February 5, they explained their change of heart in the Williams case:

It was represented to us that, inasmuch as Burr Williams had not been paid his salary, that his contract with the St. Louis club was void. It now appears that, although his salary had not been paid, that he was induced by the St. Louis club to sign a new contract on Jan. 27. This contract, of course, has not had enough time to be broken, and we therefore regard Williams as morally and legally bound to the St. Louis Club.

Under no circumstances can we have business dealings with him. Our position remains exactly the same as outlined yesterday. Any player of sufficient ability, who either has no contract or whose contract has not been lived up to, will be welcome to our club if we can use him. But we will not engage or aid any player to break a bona fide contract with anyone.[565]

Five weeks after Foran and Ross approved the Stanley Cup challenge series, the matter came to a head. Foran was irritated by Calder's latest attempt to bully him, and he threw a couple of punches back. The National Hockey League came very close to losing the Cup.

"We have accepted the challenge of the American League," he told the New York *Times*. "I am going to Montreal to meet Frank Calder and learn what is his attitude."[566]

Calder hinted that Foran's trip would be a waste of time. He had made up his mind that the NHL would rather forfeit the trophy than take part in a series with an "outlaw" league.

"I have nothing more to say. I have expressed my opinions before."[567]

On the eve of the AHL championship series between Chicago and the Duluth Hornets, the *Tribune* reported that the Shamrocks considered themselves the logical challengers for the Stanley Cup, and that they were not averse to using the Cup challenge to force a showdown between Calder and the Stanley Cup trustees.[568]

Five thousand fans came to Chicago Stadium to see the Shamrocks slip past the Duluth Hornets 2–1 in the series opener. A crowd of the same size returned a couple of days later to see the Shamrocks take a 2–0 series lead with a 4–2 victory. The action shifted to Duluth, where the Hornets won 4–2, delaying Chicago's Stanley Cup hopes. After that game, Chicago coach Babe Dye gave his star right winger, Gordie Brydson, the day off. Brydson hopped a train to Toronto, where he was to be married the following day. When Brydson and his fiancée set the date, they hadn't apparently accounted for the possibility of his being involved in the playoffs. Still, he would not make his bride wait.

When Shaughnessy, the club president, learned of Brydson's furlough, he fined the player $1,000 and fired Dye. That night, as the Shamrocks played for the AHL championship, Tom Shaughnessy was behind the bench. After taking a 3–0 lead midway into the third period, Chicago almost choked, allowing Duluth to tie the score and force overtime. A rookie forward by the name of Tony Prelesnik scored a minute and forty-one seconds into extra time, giving the Shamrocks the title.[569]

What went on behind closed doors was not reported, but the Chicago Shamrocks never got to play for the Stanley Cup.

In May 1932, Shamrocks owner James Norris applied for an NHL expansion franchise in St. Louis, but his bid was rejected. It was explained that such an addition would render the other team's travel costs excessive.[570] As the Depression deepened, the NHL and AHL were both plagued by financial problems. The American league had lost its Buffalo franchise, while the NHL's Detroit Falcons (formerly the Cougars) had filed for bankruptcy. At the same meeting at which the league rejected Norris's expansion bid, Detroit owner Charles Hughes resigned from the NHL board of governors, turning the team over to Arthur Pfleiderer, a young banker whom the bankruptcy court had appointed as receiver. He was also a friend of Jim Norris's.

Pfleiderer admittedly knew nothing about hockey, but he did understand finance. So he contacted Norris, and the two developed a plan that Pfleiderer presented at a special meeting of the board of governors in Toronto in August. The feud he triggered almost led to the creation of yet another rival league.

Leo Macdonnell of the Detroit *Times* covered the meeting.

> When Arthur B. Pfleiderer, representing the Detroit Hockey Club, emerged from a nine-hour verbal battle with other governors of the National Hockey League here last night, he said to Jack Adams, manager of the Detroit Falcons:
> "Jack, I don't know whether you have a job or not with Detroit."

Fatigued and plainly disappointed with the outcome of negotiations by which the Detroit banker hoped to effect a deal which would bring the Chicago Shamrock team players to the Motor City, Pfleiderer said he was "not sure what Detroit would do in hockey."[571]

The trouble started when Pfleiderer proposed that Detroit — which had drafted Art Gagne, Hec Kilrea, Danny Cox and the Hall of Fame goaltender Alex Connell in the Ottawa dispersal draft, and stood to lose them when the Senators returned to the NHL for the 1932–33 season — be allowed to replenish its ranks with members of the Chicago Shamrocks. To do so, the National Hockey League moguls would have to reinstate the players.

Frederic McLaughlin of the Blackhawks led the charge against the idea, claiming that two of the Shamrocks players in question, "Pudge" MacKenzie and Don McFadyen, were *his* property, due, in Macdonell's words, "to some sort of agreement made with the players several years ago." The players didn't sign with McLaughlin because the Shamrocks made better offers, so "McLaughlin wrote the players 'to go back to school and forget about hockey.'"

> "Now two years later McLaughlin lays claim in the players," Shaughnessy said. "After this being dismissed by the owner of the Hawks, the boys applied to the Shamrocks and were signed for a salary of $4,000 a year each with a $4,000 bonus each, costing the American League club $12,000 all told. Naturally, Mr. Norris was not desirous of relinquishing rights to players developed and owned by his club. At least without recompense."

The other players the Detroit Falcons hoped to acquire were Walter Buswell, Paul Armand, Burr Williams and Gordie Brydson. The Montreal Canadiens claimed rights to Buswell and Armand, but were ready to negotiate with Pfleiderer, "and there was no disposition to quarrel over Brydson, supposedly London property, and Williams."[572]

> As a reaction to the action of the governors of the National Hockey League it was said here that a new "outlaw league" may be organized.
>
> A. B. Pfleiderer said he had heard the rumour, but was not identified with it.

Tom Shaughnessy, associate of James F. Norris, in control of the Chicago Shamrocks, denied he was sponsorer of the proposed league, but said, "it was very feasible."

The Chicago men pointed out that hockey interests outside the ranks of the National League loop controlled the Chicago Stadium, that it might be possible to interest those who rule the Detroit Olympia and that the old Toronto Maple Leaf Gardens [i.e., the Mutual Street Arena] could probably be secured. St. Louis, too, could be counted on to join a new circuit and Kansas City, if asked, Shaughnessy said.[573]

His plan rejected, Pfleiderer placed the responsibility for the fate of the Detroit franchise at the feet of Calder and the NHL governors. Macdonell wrote:

It was when your correspondent asked the Detroit man if he planned to close the Olympia that he said he was "not sure what Detroit would do."

"Of course, the bondholders of Olympia will be protected," he added.

While Pfleiderer said he had hopes that there would be a renewal of negotiations, President Calder declared that as far as he knew, all negotiations were off for an agreement with the Chicago "outlaws."

"National League and territorial rights must be protected," Calder said.

After the meeting it was the consensus of newspapermen, including the Toronto writers, that the governors had acted unwisely, or at least hastily, in turning down an opportunity to bring new blood and money into this league and help Detroit ...

To such argument Calder announced that it was "nobody else's business" what those clubs wanted to do — "territorial rights must be protected."[574]

The Detroit media had Calder and the NHL for dinner. Although it was late August, Tigers baseball and University of Michigan football were knocked off the sports pages by news of the Falcons' perilous situation.

On August 24, Bud Shaver wrote a particularly scathing column in the Detroit *Times*. The subheading read, in part, "Still Plucking Hen that Lays the Golden Eggs."

> The National Hockey League's callous indifference to the problems of the Detroit Hockey Club, one of its franchise holders, is but another example of the small-mindedness of the men who run our professional sports.
>
> Detroit paid $50,000 for a franchise in the National Hockey League. It discharged all its obligations to the league, mustered the best team its resources would admit, suffered arrogant and incompetent referees, endured unfair schedules, and what does it get for its $50,000?
>
> It gets practically kicked out of the league, all because of a petty feud in which Detroit is no party at all.
>
> The National Hockey League is so infested with dogs in the manger that no sensible argument can be heard above the uproar of their yappings.
>
> Ottawa closed up shop last season because the hockey fans in that city would not patronize in sufficient numbers to make the enterprise profitable. Four Ottawa players were loaned to Detroit. Without at least two of them Detroit would have been hopelessly outclassed.
>
> As it was, the Detroit Hockey Club could not escape a receivership. That was not because hockey was unprofitable in Olympia. It was profitable, but it could not carry the entire load of the enormous cost of maintaining an enterprise that was capitalized for close to two million and a quarter dollars.
>
> The Detroit Hockey Club tried to rent Ottawa players for this season. The price demanded for a year's rental would have been a fair price to have bought them outright. The Detroit club could not operate at a profit and pay that much rental for four players.
>
> In short, Ottawa's rental terms would be called, even in polite business circles, a "holdup."[575]

Shaver called Pfleiderer's proposition to use Norris's players "an intelligent move, the kind that intelligent businessmen make every day." In his assessment, the NHL had turned down a chance to transform Norris from a costly competitor into a well-heeled ally. He also suggested that an end to the AHA–NHA war could have provided Ottawa and Pittsburgh with the players they needed to reverse their fortunes at the box office. Pfleiderer's diplomacy failed, Shaver said, "not because his case lacked merit, but because members of the board were not large-minded enough to forget personal enmities." As for Calder's assertion that the NHL's territorial rights must be respected, Shaver wrote, "That is sheer poppycock."[576]

Has a league president or commissioner ever been criticized more strongly in the press? But there was more. Branding Calder an out-an-out liar, Shaver went on to explain:

> No one's territorial rights would be invaded. Norris did not propose to operate in Chicago in competition to Maj. Frederic A. McLaughlin's Blackhawks. He proposed to cease operating the Shamrocks in opposition to the Chicago club of the National League. Norris would have transferred his hockey interest to Detroit, had he been permitted to enlist in the National League.
>
> The deal was not turned down to "protect territorial rights." It was turned down because Norris and McLaughlin were involved in a minor dispute over the property rights to two players. The money represented by those two players is negligible along side of the vast investments which will suffer because of the league's action.
>
> Because of it, Detroit is left helpless with a $50,000 franchise, a beautiful arena and not enough players of caliber to make a decent showing in the league. Ottawa and Pittsburgh probably will operate at a loss. All this because of mulishness.
>
> During all of the debate, the most important party of all was not even mentioned. That is our old familiar, and somewhat seedy, friend, John Q. Public. While the National Hockey League was sounding off sonorous phrases about "territorial rights," they might have paused to consider the rights of our little friend. He is the lad who built those stadiums. He pays the salaries of every man in hockey. He gets trampled between periods, gets the wrong seats and occasionally gets hit by a stray egg aimed at a truculent referee. And suffers it all uncomplainingly as long as he can see a decent hockey

game for a fair price, or even for an unfair one. What about his "territorial rights," Mr. Calder?

Organized baseball had to learn the lesson that hockey is ignoring now. It cost the ball-yard moguls millions before they declared a truce in their silly quarrels. After that they bent a more attentive ear to the modest wants of the patrons and less to their own gas pains. As a result they have benefited greatly.[577]

Given Calder's commitment to "territorial rights," his next move is interesting: he reinstated three members of the AHL's Tulsa Oilers, Paddy Byrne, Emil Hanson and Syl Acaster. Hanson had just been signed by the Shamrocks, who had an interest in the other two players as well.[578]

Then, as the summer neared its end, President Grant of the AHL signed an agreement with Calder to retract his league's claims of major league status and the right to challenge for the Stanley Cup. On August 31, Grant and Calder met with Pfleiderer, Norris and Shaughnessy.[579] The New York *Times* told the world what had transpired behind closed doors:

> The long-standing hockey feud between the National and American leagues came to an end tonight with the American league resuming its minor league status and becoming subject once more to the N.H.L.'s player draft.
>
> Announcement of an agreement whereby the American league returns to the "organized" hockey fold as an affiliate of the National league was made tonight by Frank Calder, president of the N.H.L.
>
> The effects of the agreement, in general, were twofold:
>
> First — the American league, a so-called "outlaw" organization for several years, again recognizes the right of the National league to draft American league players.
>
> Second — the American league agrees to abandon operations in any city where the game has been established by clubs which are members of the National, Canadian-American, or International leagues.
>
> As a result of the agreement, the American league will abandon its operations in Chicago, where the Black Hawks represent the National League, and in Buffalo where the Bisons are members of the International league.

Until its revolt of a few years ago, the American league was, like the International and Canadian-American, a minor league outfit subject to draft by the N.H.L. After it broke away and sought to gain equal standing with the National as a major circuit, the leagues in "organized" hockey declared it an "outlaw" outfit and placed all its players on the ineligible list.[580]

While this may sound as if the agreement would force the American league to make some fundamental changes, it did not. The AHL's "hands-off" policy towards Buffalo was more a formality than anything else, as the last-place Buffalo Majors had folded on January 31, 1932. The city was also too far from its league rivals, which were scattered about the Midwest, for the circuit to resurrect a team there. The AHL's withdrawal from Chicago would also be relatively painless: in exchange for disbanding his Shamrocks, owner Jim Norris had been given the right to purchase the NHL's Detroit Falcons at a bargain price. The team would remain in the Norris family for more than fifty years. (Norris would later own portions of the New York Rangers and Chicago Blackhawks as well.) The only other significant item was that the league agreed to revert to its old name, the American Hockey Association, under which it operated until 1942, when the shortage of players created by World War II forced the league to fold.

It had taken a bit longer than expected, but Pfleiderer and Norris had secured the future of hockey in Detroit, the city that today bills itself as Hockeytown. Few, if any of the fans who watched the Red Wings win their tenth Stanley Cup championship in 2002 would be aware of how close Detroit came to following Hamilton into hockey obscurity. Or that the man they should thank for their team's survival in 1932 was none other than Conn Smythe, managing partner of the Toronto Maple Leafs. Smythe, who viewed Detroit as a natural rival for his team, pressured Frank Calder and Frederic McLaughlin to put their egos aside and avoid making what would have been a monumental mistake.

When Norris joined the NHL fraternity, he brought sixteen of his Shamrocks players with him. They were: goaltender Mike Karakas; defencemen Walter "Buster" Buswell, Fern "Curley" Headley, Ralph "Bouncer" Taylor and Emil Hanson; centres Robert Clayton and Jack Riley; right wingers Paul "Babe" Armand, Gordie Brydson, Charles "Tip" O'Neill, Eddie Wiseman and Gus Marker; and left wingers Robert Burns, Tony Prelesnik, Ronn Moffatt and Otto Hanson (Emil's brother).

Three of the Shamrocks — Clarence "Pudge" MacKenzie, Donald McFadyen and Burr Williams — were assigned to the Chicago Blackhawks.[581]

Williams was drafted from St. Louis by the Blackhawks, then sold a few weeks later to St. Louis's AHA rival in Duluth, a team that was upset about the Flyers' signing of Eddie Bouchard, an eight-year NHL veteran, despite Duluth's having come to a verbal agreement with him.

On October 6, 1932, Louis Giffels, the manager of the Olympia, announced a trade. Goalie John Ross Roach had been acquired from the New York Rangers for cash, and would replace Alex Connell, whom the Ottawa Senators had recalled from their loan. The Detroit *Times* article contained this passage, which seemed to be included as a complete afterthought:

> The Falcons will be garbed in new livery and will not
> be the Falcons. They will wear all-red uniforms and will
> be called Red Wings.[582]

That was all.

No explanation. No press conference to unveil the new sweater and logo. No mascot. Indeed, when the former Shamrocks reported at the Olympia a few weeks later, they were all still clad in old Falcons sweaters.

With few exceptions, the ex-Shamrocks who became Detroit Red Wings were the only AHL players to make it to the National Hockey League. Mike Karakas, sent to the St. Louis Flyers, who were weak in goal — another move to appease manager Harry Taber — made his NHL debut in 1935 with the Chicago Blackhawks. Burr Williams, who had been claimed by the Toronto Maple Leafs in the 1930 Inter-League Draft — a draft the AHA did not recognize in those days — had an NHL career that lasted only 19 games, played between 1933 and 1937. Don McFadyen played four years with the Blackhawks, helping them win their first Stanley Cup title in 1934. The blacklist on the remaining AHL players continued, even after the truce was called.

For instance, not one of the Kansas City Pla-Mors — whose owner William Grant was the AHL's president and one of the driving forces behind the Stanley Cup challenge that never came to be — ever returned to the NHL. Yet the club was a competitive one that had finished second to the Shamrocks in 1931–32. And the only members of the Tulsa Oilers who broke into the big league were players whom Norris had signed to Shamrocks contracts prior to joining the NHL.

The Stanley Cup had been conceived in 1893 as a challenge trophy for the amateur hockey championship of Canada. Over the intervening four decades it had come to symbolize a professional hockey championship, competed for by teams in Canada *and* the United States. And although no one had actually challenged the defending Cup champion since the mid teens, when the NHL and PCHA formalized a playoff arrangement between the champions of the two leagues, well, no one had ever said definitively that a team *couldn't* issue a Cup challenge.

Until 1932.

With this, Calder's last power play, the Stanley Cup was finally the exclusive preserve of the NHL, and the trustees appointed by Lord Stanley became nothing more than figureheads.

Chapter 28

Frank Calder Dies

Frank Calder died quietly, after being stricken with a heart attack. He was in his Montreal hospital bed, the League books spread around him one morning. He was ready to carry on the business of the league, when death tapped him on the shoulder.
— Elmer Ferguson, 1965

In the decade after the battle with the American Hockey League, Frank Calder, the grand manipulator of the scheme to rid hockey of Eddie Livingstone, would emerge as a strong leader and become recognized as the backbone of the National Hockey League.

He donated a trophy that bore his name, and awarded it to the best first-year player in the NHL. The first winner, in 1933, was Carl Voss, a centre for the Detroit Red Wings who, after his playing days were done, would become referee-in-chief of the NHL. Two years later, the prize was awarded to Chicago Blackhawks goalie Mike Karakas, a native of Aurora, Minnesota, who had played in the outlaw AHL.

Which highlights another interesting inconsistency in hockey history. In 1979, when the NHL took on four teams from the defunct World Hockey Association, one of the most talked-about stars in hockey history entered the league: Wayne Gretzky, an 18-year-old centre with the Edmonton Oilers. Gretzky's first NHL season was phenomenal, as he tied Marcel Dionne for the league scoring lead with 137 points. Yet, because of a new rule the NHL enacted prior to the season, Gretzky was ruled ineligible for the Calder Trophy because he had played in the WHA, an "outlaw" league much like the old AHL. Instead, Raymond Bourque of the Boston Bruins was named the rookie of the year.

The NHL was a much more harmonious operation after Livingstone and the AHL were finally vanquished. Which is not to say it was a more successful league. The Ottawa Senators, who had withdrawn from the league and then come back to life, finally played their last game in Ottawa in 1934. They were victims of the Great Depression. At the urging of Jim Norris, the club was placed in St. Louis and renamed the Eagles. After one dismal season, in which they competed head-to-head with the AHA's Flyers for the hearts of St. Louis hockey fans (so much for Calder's insistence that territorial rights be protected!), the franchise retired for good.

The harsh economic times also claimed the Montreal Maroons. In 1937, the team's owners, the Canadian Arena Company, asked Calder for permission to make a move of their own to St. Louis. Calder refused, and the Maroons sold most of their players to the Montreal Canadiens.

The New York Americans were also in trouble. In 1936, after the bootlegger "Big Bill" Dwyer suffered a financial reverse, the league was forced to take over the club. Thirty-eight-year-old Mervyn "Red" Dutton, a tough defenceman who had played fourteen years for the Calgary Tigers, Montreal Maroons and New York Americans, retired to assume the managerial reins. The team hit a high point in 1938, when it eliminated the New York Rangers in the first round of the Stanley Cup playoffs. In 1941, the Amerks' future looked just as bright. Hoping to intensify the rivalry with the Rangers, Dutton changed the team's name to the Brooklyn Americans, even though it would continue to play at Madison Square Garden.

By October 1942, however, the United States had entered World War II, and a youth movement on which Dutton had embarked was now a liability — only four of his players were exempt from serving in the military. Although the war had claimed players from every NHL team except the Canadiens, the last-place Americans were the least likely to survive. Dutton asked for, and was granted, a leave of absence for the team until the end of the war.

The NHL's general meeting of January 25, 1943, was supposed to have been a non-event. The only news story expected to arise out of the conference at Toronto's Royal York Hotel was that the Stanley Cup playoffs were scheduled to begin on March 20, and that, for the first time, all playoff series would be best-of-seven. The playoff arrangements were settled during the morning session of the all-day affair. Five minutes into the afternoon session, Calder had just finished explaining to Red Dutton the status of the reserve player list of the suspended Brooklyn Americans when Toronto Maple Leafs coach Hap Day noticed that Calder appeared to be in pain.

"I'm all right," Calder insisted when two governors moved towards him. Then his face contracted as though he was in pain. He rose to his feet, took a step or two, and exclaimed, "My God, there *is* something wrong."

Day and Detroit's Jack Adams helped Calder to his hotel room upstairs. He was examined by the Maple Leafs' team physician, a Dr. Galloway, who sent for a cardiac specialist, Dr. J. Hepburn. Despite his protestations, Calder was persuaded to go to St. Michael's Hospital, where he had suffered a second heart attack.[583]

In addition to his duties as league president, Calder also acted as the NHL's secretary and treasurer. For years, he was the league's sole employee. It was only after Tex Rickard pointed out a piece of business that was missing from the minutes of one meeting that Calder agreed to hire a stenographer to keep track of the proceedings. In time he hired a secretary for the league office in Montreal. So it is hardly surprising that the league had no vice president, or that Calder had never thought about grooming a successor. (Although he had taken a liking to a young lawyer by the name of Clarence Campbell, who had gone overseas to join the war effort.)[584] Dutton agreed to chair what remained of the meeting.

Dr. Hepburn, who confirmed Dr. Galloway's diagnosis, ordered Calder to rest for two or three months, but observed that Calder was not in any immediate danger. "If he follows that advice, there is reasonable assurance that all will be well," he said.[585]

On February 3, Calder felt well enough to travel, and was brought to Montreal's General Hospital so he could be closer to his family. Elmer Ferguson had visited with his old boss earlier that morning, and reported that Calder was feeling fine and was able to eat a small breakfast upon his arrival at the hospital.

According to Ferguson's newspaper, the Montreal *Herald*, "members of his family who were with him while he had breakfast had just left the hospital to have something to eat themselves when he sank back on the pillows and died."[586]

After his family left him, the 65-year-old Calder had apparently defied doctor's orders and begun looking over some papers outlining the military draft status of the NHL's players.

The first person to the room was Tommy Gorman, who was one of the catalysts in the NHL's founding and who was now serving as general manager of the Montreal Canadiens. Gorman reached Calder's bedside just a few minutes after the NHL president died.[587]

The testimonials poured in. The Montreal *Gazette* lauded the late NHL boss on its editorial page:

> If Canada has any one outstanding agency of Canadianization it is its universal national sport, hockey, where for once the many schisms which beset the nation vanish. It was typical, then, that the executive leader of this pre-eminently Canadian game, Frank Calder, was the English-born son of Scottish parents. Under him, hockey flourished as never before, and under him, too, it set standards of honour which served as a worthy ideal for the thousands of youngsters from coast to coast striving to do their best with blade and stick to reach that goal of goals, a call to the majors.
>
> Frank Calder's name never meant a great deal to the average hockey follower. He made no spectacular head-lines in the Landis fashion, and generally was outshone as a public figure by the directors of the clubs whose association he headed. But all the time he was quietly directing and advising, and in its 25 years of existence he steered the National Hockey League through many a difficult passage, and with never a "Black Sox" scandal.[588]

Dick Irvin, the Hall of Fame player and coach, said, "In his dealings with difficult and knotty problems which were legion, he never once rendered an unfair decision."[589] Irvin can be excused for not knowing about Calder's track record, since he was playing hockey in the west at the time the NHL was formed.

Acting president Red Dutton said, "I can truly state that during all my dealings with him I have never heard him say an ill word against anyone."[590] Dutton must never have mentioned the name of Eddie Livingstone to Calder.

Said Lester Patrick, "He had a sense of duty and loyalty that you find only too seldom in people. He was straight forward, and he had a code of ethics that would benefit us all to follow."[591]

We beg to disagree.

Calder single-handedly elected himself president of the NHL, and then engaged in power struggles to remove any and all obstacles in his way. He was the guiding force behind the theft of Eddie Livingstone's franchise, by guiding the Toronto Arena Company in its decisions. Thanks to his machinations, the Toronto Arena ended up in bankruptcy, largely because it refused to pay the court-ordered damages to Eddie Livingstone. A high court judge even described Calder's behaviour as "utterly dishonest and despicable."

Calder is credited as a builder of the sport. If one builds by tearing down, then Calder was a master builder. Within five years of the league's foundation, six of the seven men who owned stakes in NHL clubs had sold out or been forced out. He received kickbacks for the conversion of Eddie Livingstone's property. He should be held accountable for the loss of ten Canadian major league franchises — Quebec/Hamilton, Ottawa, Edmonton, Calgary, Vancouver, Victoria and Saskatoon, Toronto and two Montreal teams. Three U.S. teams also disbanded on his watch.

His quest for power led to aggressive expansion into the United States, with teams owned by deep-pocketed backers who had little knowledge of or respect for hockey. While the Tex Rickards and Frederic McLaughlins brought large bankrolls to the NHL, they also drove proud franchises such as the Ottawa Senators and the teams of the Western Hockey League, which could not afford to compete in the same financial arena, out of business. The closing of the WHL, in particular, helped stymie the development of the game in the west. Under Calder's leadership, major league hockey contracted from thirteen teams in 1926 to six at the time of his death.

Calder promised other leagues that they would be able to challenge for the Stanley Cup, but when they signed the minor league agreements, he appointed himself commissioner of all of pro hockey and reneged on the promise. Stanley Cup trustee Billy Foran gave Calder one last challenge and threatened to take the Stanley Cup away from the 1931 winners, the Montreal Canadiens. Calder showed little regard for the trophy and told Foran to go ahead. Then he worked a deal behind Foran's back to merge the Detroit Falcons with the Chicago Shamrocks, which would cripple whatever power the Cup trustees had left.

By 1948, original trustee Phil Ross was ninety-one years old, and after fifty-six years as a vigilant guardian of the trophy, he knew it was time to move on. Ross had long since retired as publisher of the Ottawa *Journal*, and over the years had become so highly regarded in the sports world that he was asked to serve as trustee of Canadian football's Grey Cup — a task he refused — and of lacrosse's Minto Cup, which he had accepted. He and fellow trustee Cooper Smeaton signed an agreement that allowed the NHL to take stewardship of the oldest trophy continuously competed for by professional athletes — for as long as the NHL remained the dominant hockey league in the world.

Even though the event took place more than five years after his death, Frank Calder's dream had now officially come true. The National Hockey League had complete control of the Stanley Cup.

Chapter 29

Livingstone at Peace

*Livingstone developed a championship club and probably had
more to do when all is said and done in making the sport what
it is hereabouts than any other individual.*

— Charlie Good, longtime
Toronto *Daily Star* columnist[592]

Throughout his career as a sportsman, Eddie Livingstone played,
coached, managed and operated his teams in the same manner:
with absolute fairness for all. In nearly twenty years as a manager, only
two of his players held out. Players may not always have agreed with
everything he did or said, but only one, Cy Denneny, ever admitted publicly — and even then under the influence of Tommy Gorman — to
have disliked playing for Livvy.

Like a working-class sportsman who crashed a society gathering,
Livingstone was unceremoniously ejected from the hockey business. After
returning to Toronto in the midst of the Great Depression, he moved into
an apartment at his sister's hotel and helped run the Toronto Victorias,
who played out of the Arena Gardens. The team was taken over by the
Toronto Lions Club, renamed the Young Lions, and moved to the brand
new Maple Leaf Gardens. Conn Smythe, who operated the arena, seemed
to be willing to overlook whatever beef the NHL and Calder had with
Livvy. Smythe, who would have been playing junior hockey for the Varsity
Blues when Livingstone got involved with the Toronto Ontarios, would
no doubt have been aware of his exploits and accomplishments.

With his return to the local amateur hockey scene, the bespectacled
coach began to attract some of the respect that had been denied him in

the pro ranks. In a 1929 article for the Toronto *Globe*, Mike Rodden (who is also an honoured member of the Hockey Hall of Fame as a referee), credited Livingstone with many innovations in the sport. His rotation of two forward lines in a 1916 game against Ottawa was declared "bush-league tactics" at the time, yet the technique would be commonplace years later. Rodden correctly recognized Livvy as the man who pioneered the concept of playoffs by introducing the split season.[593]

Charlie Good, who moved to the Toronto *Star* after the *Daily News* folded, continued to speak well of Livingstone. When the Mutual Street Arena (formerly the Arena Gardens) was sold for back taxes in 1936, Good reminded readers about the way Livingstone's teams had fired fan interest in the rink's early days. In fact, Good stated that Livingstone "probably had more to do, when all is said and done, in making the sport what it is hereabouts than any other individual."[594]

In the mid-thirties, Livingstone joined the Toronto office of the Ontario Hockey Association and helped keep junior hockey alive in the Queen City through the Great Depression. Whether because of a lack of funds, or burnout after some forty years' involvement in the game he loved, Livingstone finally stepped away from hockey at the end of the decade.

On September 11, 1945, at the age of sixty-one, Eddie Livingstone died in Toronto of arterial sclerosis, the same ailment that had taken his brother's life, and his father's.

There was no lengthy front-page story for Livingstone, as there had been when Calder died. His passing was marked in one of the four Toronto newspapers with a standard three-line notice on the obituary page. There was no outpouring of grief from Elmer Ferguson, or a week-long procession of tributes from hockey greats. His death was not even noted in the Montreal press.

He left no children — indeed, he had never married.

His estate consisted of $1,110 in stocks and a bank account with a balance of $32.49. In today's dollars, that would be about $12,000. Hardly a fortune.

His sister handled the funeral arrangements, and he was buried in Toronto's Mount Pleasant Cemetery, where he rests amongst the likes of former Prime Minister William Lyon Mackenzie King, Timothy Eaton of Canadian department store fame, and the legendary hockey broad-caster, Foster Hewitt. Despite such august company, the Livingstone family plot is rather humble.

The plot measures sixteen feet by twelve feet, and is the final resting place not only for Eddie, but for his parents, the Welsh-born David and American-born Rita, and his aunt, also an American émigré. Eddie's sister and her husband's cremains are also buried there.

There is a family stone with the Livingstone surname, as well as David and Rita's names engraved on it. Instead of being buried perpendicular to the stone, as is customary, Rita and David are buried parallel to it. Between Rita and the headstone lies Eddie. There is no individual marker for their son, who never married, although there are ground plates bearing initials for the patriarchs.

Puzzling how a man who had owned three professional hockey teams over the years wouldn't have a gravestone.

Next to Eddie, the guiding spirit of Toronto hockey in the 1910s, there could be seen, growing perpendicular to the stone, a five-year-old maple

The Livingstone family plot

tree. While this might be considered a random act of horticulture, we must point out that it was the only maple to be found within 60 metres in any direction. As well, the most recently departed of the Livingstone clan had been dead more than forty years. And neither Eddie nor his sister ever had children.

Could it have been placed there by a former player? That player would have to be no younger than seventy-five years old, and he would have had to carry the young tree about two kilometres into the cemetery without being noticed — the planting of trees by anyone other than cemetery personnel is forbidden. He would also have had to know exactly where Livingstone is buried, since his name does not appear on the grave site.

Seeds and trees get planted in many ways. Cemetery personnel stated emphatically that they had no record of planting this tree, and that they would never have done so in this particular spot, since the tree's roots would one day topple the headstone, damage for which the ceme-tery would be liable.

This humble maple tree, whose leaf is the symbol of Canada, is the prominent feature of the country's flag, and lends its name to Toronto's current NHL team, was the only marker for the final resting place of the man who built and nurtured professional hockey in the city, paving the way for English Canada's most storied franchise. In any sport.

Without Eddie Livingstone's involvement in the 1910s, professional hockey might have gone no further west than Ottawa and gone the way of pro lacrosse.

And yet, this man is not even afforded the dignity of having his name on a tombstone.

It is sad.

It is time for Elmer Ferguson's version of hockey history to be com-pletely recanted, and to let the record show clearly that Edward James Livingstone made professional hockey work in Toronto.

Humbly.

And without ever getting the credit he deserved.

We felt a sense of accomplishment at discovering his grave, but it was tempered by our disappointment at not seeing something more tangible to show that he ever existed.

And at the time of this writing, more than two years after work began on this book, and ten months after our initial visit to Mount Pleasant Cemetery, the tree is gone — removed by cemetery staff.

They didn't dig up all the roots, however, as there still remains a bunch of surviving maple shoots which strive to reach the light. Like the man they protect, these mysterious tree remnants are unwilling to give up.

Appendix A

What Happened to Them

Jack Adams became the legendary coach and general manager of the Detroit Red Wings, winning seven Stanley Cup championships after helping to rescue a franchise that was almost a victim of the Depression. He was fired unceremoniously in 1962 after a thirty-five-year run with the team, during which it was known as the Cougars, Falcons, and finally Red Wings, after which "Jolly Jack" became president of the Central Hockey League. He died while working at his desk on May 1, 1968. He was seventy-three.

Edwin Peter "Ted" Dey sold his interest in the Ottawa Senators to Franklin Ahearn in 1923. Born in Hull, Quebec, on April 21, 1864, Dey severed all ties with hockey after selling the team and the old arena on Laurier Avenue. Dey's greatest contribution, one which is still used today, is the way in which goals are officially confined. During World War I, Dey decided that there must be a better method than the time-honoured custom of a goal umpire signalling a score by raising his hand or a white handkerchief. Accordingly, he commissioned Stanley Lewis, who went on to become mayor of Ottawa, to outfit a pair of flashlights with red bulbs. These were the first goal lamps. Some time later Dey had electric wires strung along the top of the netting behind the goals and a switch installed to allow the umpire to turn on a red light whenever the puck entered the cage.

After leaving the hockey business, Dey lived in New York City until 1932, when he moved to New Westminster, British Columbia. He died there at the age of seventy-eight on April 15, 1943.[595]

William A. Foran, hockey executive and Stanley Cup trustee from 1908 until 1945, died in Ottawa on November 30, 1945. Frank Boucher was sent to his funeral to represent the National Hockey League. The rest of the mourners were civil servants and politicians who had known the former secretary of the Civil Service Commission.

Tom Gorman managed the New York Americans for four years before he left. He was also a successful horse racing promoter, and he moved to Tijuana, Mexico (less than ten miles south of San Diego), where he became assistant general manager of the Agua Caliente racetrack. (In Spanish, *agua caliente* means "hot water," reflecting its location near a hot spring.) The track was part of a hotel/casino/spa complex frequented by the Hollywood set looking for a temporary respite from Prohibition and a California ban on betting on horse races. In 1932, Gorman brought the legendary Austrailian race horse Phar Lap to Mexico, where he won the $100,000 Agua Caliente Handicap before dying under mysterious circumstances near San Francisco one month later.

In 1933, the president of Agua Caliente, Gorman's boss, survived a plane crash but was forced to sell the track to Hollywood interests. Two months later, Gorman was coaching the Chicago Blackhawks. The former sportswriter won the Stanley Cup in 1934, then left amidst the possibility that the franchise might be sold — and a rift that had developed between Gorman and a Chicago resident by the name of Al Capone. The franchise was never sold, but Jimmy Strachan, who had known Gorman since 1909, hired him to manage the Montreal Maroons. The Maroons won the Stanley Cup in 1935, making Gorman the first man to coach consecutive Stanley Cup winners with different teams. Gorman, who never actually learned to play hockey, managed the Montreal Canadiens in the early 1940s and saved them from going broke before settling back in his native Ottawa to manage senior hockey teams. Gorman died in Ottawa on May 15, 1961. He was seventy-four, and was survived by his wife Mary — the sister of Silver Seven star Harry "Rat" Westwick.

Wilfred "Shorty" Green, who led the Hamilton Tigers strike, suffered a career-ending injury when he broke his leg during the the 1928–29 season as a member of the New York Americans. He coached the Tulsa Oilers of the American Hockey League/American Hockey Association, and later served as the longtime trainer of the Boston Bruins. Green died in Sudbury, Ontario, on April 19, 1960.

Colonel John S. Hammond, friend and aide to "Tex" Rickard, was president of the Madison Square Garden Corporation from 1929 to 1932. He returned in that capacity from 1934 until September 1935, and sold his stock in the arena on March 4, 1936. Hammond, who was one of four athletic brothers, played football at the University of Chicago under the legendary coach Amos Alonzo Stagg and competed in the 100- and 200-yard dashes in the 1904 Olympics in St. Louis. He was also widely known as an artillery expert. Hammond wrote the *Gunner's Handbook of Field Artillery*, which sold more than 100,000 copies. He was the great-grandson of Charles F. Hammond, who chose the mounts for the Fifth New York Calvary in the Civil War, mined and forged the plates for the famed warship *Monitor* and later shipped the first cargo around Cape Horn. Hammond died on December 9, 1939, just days after his fifty-ninth birthday.[596]

Gordon "Duke" Keats was considered the finest stickhandler of his era. He was recruited from the northern mining country by Eddie Livingstone, played in the NHA, and served in World War I with the 228th Battalion. After meeting Deacon White in the army, Keats moved to Edmonton and was the first star of the Edmonton Eskimos, a team that would later feature Eddie Shore and George Hainsworth, amongst others. Sold by the Patricks to Boston, Keats played three seasons in the NHL before buying out his contract for $5,000 and trying for the Stanley Cup with the AHA's Tulsa Oilers. After breaking an ankle, Keats moved back to Edmonton and became the manager and owner of the North West Hockey League's edition of the Eskimos. When that league failed, Keats went to work for the Royal Canadian Navy in Victoria. An avid hockey fan from the day he was born to the day he died — he even travelled frequently to Oakland to watch California Seals games with his son, a season ticket holder — Keats was elected to the Hockey Hall of Fame in 1958. He died January 16, 1972, in Victoria, at the age of seventy-six.

George Kennedy contracted influenza during the 1919 Stanley Cup series in Montreal. He never fully recovered, and died at 7:30 in the morning on October 19, 1921. Three weeks later, his estate sold the franchise to Leo Dandurand, Leo Letourneau and Joseph Cattarinich.

Samuel Edward Lichtenhein had a history of businesses that went up in flames. Born in Chicago on October 24, 1870, his family moved to Montreal after his father's department store was ruined in the great Chicago Fire. Besides the Westmount Arena, where the fire started in a locker room, Lichtenhein's baseball stadium also went up in smoke twice, as did one of his private businesses. He took over his father's Montreal Cotton and Wool Waste Company, and remained there until his death. His only child, Philip, died in 1930. During the winter of 1936, Lichtenhein moved to Miami Beach after contracting pneumonia. On May 10, 1936, he returned to Montreal, where he died six weeks later on June 21.

Frank Patrick tried to resurrect his Pacific Coast league in a minor-league form, but was never able to replicate the success he had enjoyed with the original PCHA. He is acknowledged as the author of some of hockey's most enduring innovations. He also displayed a visionary side in 1930, when he predicted, "I see the time when each team will have two goalies dressed for each game." (The NHL adopted such a rule thirty-five years later.) In 1933–34, Patrick served as the NHL's managing director, after which he went to Boston to work for his old boyhood friend Art Ross as the coach and governor of the Boston Bruins. In the late 1940s, while working for the Bruins, Patrick suggested that players raise their stick after scoring a goal so that spectators would know immediately who scored. It is yet another hockey tradition that endures. Frank Patrick died June 29, 1960, in Vancouver, at the age of seventy-five.

Lester Patrick was the general manager of the New York Rangers until 1946, leading the team to Stanley Cup titles in 1928, 1933 and 1940. (They would not win again until 1994.) Patrick's two sons, Lynn and Murray (better known as "Muzz"), would both play for the Rangers under Lester's tutelage. Lynn's son Craig was the assistant coach of the 1980 U.S. Olympic hockey team that won the gold medal, and has been the general manager of the Rangers and the Pittsburgh Penguins. Muzz's son Dick is the president and a minority owner of the Washington Capitals. Lester died June 1, 1960, in Victoria, at the age of seventy-six.

Charlie Querrie left the hockey business to manage the Palace Theatre, located at Danforth and Pape avenues in Toronto. A newspaper ad from the era contains a photograph of Querrie underneath this statement: "Won Two World's Championships as Manager of Hockey Clubs. Now He Manages Danforth's House Of Hits."[597] After he sold the St. Patricks to Conn Smythe, the Markham, Ontario, native stayed connected with the team. He wrote a weekly article for the Maple Leafs game program, and kept a box seat next to the bench. He also became friends with Art Ross, who was one of Smythe's fiercest rivals. The *Globe and Mail* said:

> The pair used to battle from the time they saw each other, but since Querrie's retirement from active sport, he and Ross have been exceptionally close. It was a treat for habitués of the press room at the Gardens to hear the pair insult one another and then lapse into a discussion of the "good old days."[598]

Querrie lived within walking distance of his theatre until his death in Toronto on April 6, 1950. He was seventy-one. Charlie Querrie is buried on the opposite side of Mount Pleasant Road from Livingstone.

Percy Quinn left the hockey business altogether in the 1920s and resumed his career as a financial broker. The famous hockey referee, coach, manager and administrator later became a director of the Hudson Bay Insurance Company.

Except for a five-year absence, he served on the Toronto City Council from 1927 until a heart attack prompted him to retire in 1942. While his sportsmanship had built his reputation before he entered politics, after he achieved public office he established himself as a humanitarian. Quinn's work on behalf of inmates of the Don Jail earned him few votes but much praise. He also lobbied for the city's libraries to be open on Sundays. He was a social reformer under the guise of a successful businessman.

J.V. McAree of the *Globe and Mail* summed Quinn up in this way: "He had to work out his own life in his own way, and we think that at the end he could take more honest pride in it than many more celebrated men who lived amid more public acclaim but felt very small and lonely in their own hearts."[599] He died in Toronto on October 28, 1944.

Thomas Emmett Quinn died in Montreal on February 9, 1930. After leaving the presidency of the NHA, he was often spotted as a judge at Mount Royal racetrack. Quinn was also appointed to the Montreal Fire Commissioner's Court. He attended George Kennedy's funeral in 1921, but otherwise kept out of the limelight. Always known as Emmett, and never Mr. Quinn, his death at age sixty-two was largely overlooked in Montreal.

George L. "Tex" Rickard, died in Miami after an operation for gangrenous appendicitis on January 6, 1929. Dr. William Mayo of the Rochester, Minnesota–based Mayo Clinic was called in from Havana to attend to Rickard, but a delay in his departure prevented him from arriving in time. Rickard's obituary was carried in just about every major newspaper in North America, as well as in Paris, Mexico City, Havana and South America.

Will Rogers offered this comment: "The world is full of men who do big things, but when you meet 'em they are not outstanding personalities. Pretty near everybody is almost alike. Tex Rickard was one of the very few outstanding personalities of our time. It's a loss that we didn't have his autobiography written by himself. He was a character. I wouldn't a missed knowing him for anything."[600]

There was little mention made of his involvement in hockey, even in the New York papers. Rickard disliked the sport, having been quoted as saying it had little action. It is interesting to note that, on the day he died, the two New York teams he was responsible for bringing into the NHL were scheduled to face each other.

Prior to the match there was a moment of silence, followed by the playing of taps. Fittingly, the Americans and the Rangers played a 0–0 tie before 16,000 fans, most of them Ranger partisans. The two goalies combined to make 106 saves. The Rangers were coached by Lester Patrick, while Tommy Gorman stood behind the Amerks bench.

The 58-year-old left the majority of his fortune to his three-year-old daughter Maxine.

Martin Rosenthal continued to run the family jewellery store where the Stanley Cup used to be put on display during the Ottawa Silver Seven's glory years of the early 1900s. Rosenthal died in Ottawa on December 26, 1958, at the age of eighty-five.

Arthur Howie Ross is considered the father of pro hockey in Boston. After he was fired as coach of the Hamilton Tigers, Ross began an association with the Bruins that lasted until the late 1950s. A long-running feud between Ross and Toronto's Conn Smythe made for some of hockey's most colourful moments. Ross left his mark in three important and enduring ways. He redesigned the puck so that it had bevelled edges, making it less harmful to players who get in its way. He also designed a B-shaped goal net that trapped the puck, making it easier to recognize that a goal had been scored. His design was the basis for nets used until the mid 1980s. And finally, he lent his name to the NHL's "Leading Scorer Trophy." That was the original, if somewhat uninspired, name of the Art Ross Trophy before the longtime Bruins general manager donated an award in 1948. Ross died August 5, 1964, at the age of seventy-eight.

Philip D. Ross, the Stanley Cup trustee who played hockey with Lord Stanley's sons, signed over the rights and obligations of trusteeship to the NHL just months before his passing on July 5, 1949, at age ninety-one. Ross granted the NHL a lease on the Stanley Cup, instructing that the league accept outside challenges once it is no longer considered the top league. To this date, the NHL has not accepted a challenge. Frank Ahearn, who had been out of hockey ownership for more than a decade, represented the league at Ross's funeral.

Conn Smythe, controlling owner of the Maple Leaf Gardens and the Toronto Maple Leafs, would become one of the legendary builders of the NHL. During World War II, he commanded the 30th (Sportsmen's) Battery, and his feud with Art Ross ended after two of Ross's children served under him. Smythe retired from the Maple Leafs in 1961. He was also a successful owner of thoroughbreds, and Smythe horses won the Queen's Plate in 1958 and 1967. He died in Toronto on November 18, 1980, at the age of eighty-five.

Jimmy Strachan managed the Montreal Maroons until 1938, when he was forced to fold them. Strachan wanted to move the team to St. Louis, but the NHL board of governors, mindful of the St. Louis Eagles' failure in 1934, turned him down. He sold off most of his players to the Montreal Canadiens so that they would not be forced to relocate.

Appendix B

Hamilton-born Players in the NHL

The theft of the Hamilton Tigers' shot at the Stanley Cup would appear to have left a sour taste among Hamiltonians. Surprisingly few elite players have hailed from Canada's Steel City, when you stop to consider a number of factors: Hamilton's proximity to hockey-mad Toronto, its size (about 660,000, according to the 1996 Canadian census), the long-standing hockey rivalry between Toronto and Detroit, and the city's nearness to the birthplaces of many of the greatest players to ever slip on skates: Wayne Gretzky, from Brantford; Cyclone Taylor, from Listowel; Howie Morenz, from Mitchell, near Stratford; and the Boston Bruins' Kraut Line of Milt Schmidt, Woody Dumart and Bobby Bauer, from Kitchener. All these towns are within an hour's drive of Hamilton. Yet the Steel City itself has produced relatively few NHL players. Meanwhile, an entire wing of the Hockey Hall of Fame could be devoted to superstars from nearby Toronto.

Such latter-day players as Dave Andreychuk, Ken Dryden, Don Edwards, Murray Oliver and Pat Quinn were born in Hamilton (and all of them, coincidentally, have had some connection with the Maple Leafs). Hamiltonians who were playing pro hockey before the NHL Tigers came into being include Hall of Famers Babe Dye and Dick Irvin. But Hamilton's NHL contribution of players born between 1913 and 1935 is very small, with only one Hall of Famer, defenceman Harry Howell.

Name	Year Born	Years in NHL
Walt Atanas	1923	1944–45
Bob Barlow	1935	1969–71
Ian Cushenan	1933	1956–60, 1963–64
Herb Dickenson	1931	1951–53
John Holota	1921	1942–43, 45-46

Harry Howell	1932	1952–73, 73–76
		(WHA) - HHOF
Ron Howell	1935	1954–56
Stan Kemp	1924	1948–49
Doug McKay	1929	1950 Playoffs★
Ron Murphy	1933	1952–70

★McKay's name is engraved on the Stanley Cup, even though he played in only one game in his career. It just happened to be in the 1950 finals, as a member of the Cup-winning Detroit Red Wings.

Whether intentional or not, it is obvious that Frank Calder and the NHL permanently scarred a market by forcing the Tigers strike. The city has never shown long-term interest in minor professional hockey, as the market seems to have been (and still is) too large for the minors, but not quite big enough to sustain a major-league franchise.

Hamilton Team	Years	League
Tigers	1926–29	Canadian Professional
Tigers	1929–30	International-American
Canucks	1992–94	American
Bulldogs	1996–	American

Appendix C

The Closing of Canada

Between March 1925 and October 1926, Canada lost seven major-league hockey teams. Listed below are the teams, the leagues they played in, the year they left their Canadian city, and the name under which they operated after the move.

Team	League	Year	New Name	New League
Hamilton Tigers	NHL	1925	New York Americans	NHL
Regina Capitals	WCHL	1925	Portland Rosebuds*	WHL
Calgary Tigers	WHL	1926	Players acquired by NHL teams	
Edmonton Eskimos	WHL	1926	Players acquired by NHL teams	
Saskatoon Sheiks	WHL	1926	Players acquired by NHL teams	
Vancouver Maroons	WHL	1926	Players acquired by NHL teams	
Victoria Cougars	WHL	1926	Detroit Cougars	NHL

* The Portland Rosebuds played one season in Portland before the team's roster was bought intact by Major Frederic McLaughlin. The team played in 1926–27 as the Chicago Blackhawks.

The 1930s were not kind to Canadian NHL clubs, either.

NHL Team	Year	Problem
Ottawa Senators	1931	Requested and were granted a one-year leave of absence
Ottawa Senators	1934	Relocated to St. Louis and renamed the Eagles for one season before folding in 1935
Montreal Maroons	1938	Folded after request to move to St. Louis was rejected
Montreal Canadiens	1942	Financial troubles almost forced them to relocate to Cleveland.

Appendix D

Calder's Damage

Frank Calder's reign as president of the NHL was disastrous for those who owned franchises. By comparison, the National Hockey Association's line-up had been relatively stable during that league's seven-year run. Of the five teams that started the 1910–11 season, only Renfrew dropped out. That club was replaced by two Toronto teams. Besides the merger of the two Toronto clubs, the league's only other defection was the Toronto-based military team that represented the 228th Battalion.

Under Calder's stewardship, things were much more chaotic. Only one franchise that started play in the NHL in 1917 is still a member: the Montreal Canadiens. They survived the Depression only because of what was effectively a merger with the Maroons in 1938.

NHA Team	Year	Result
Cobalt Silver Kings	1910	Left NHA and returned to Temiskaming League, October 1910
Haileybury Hockey Club	1910	Left NHA and returned to Temiskaming League, October 1910
Montreal Canadiens	1910	Joined NHL
Montreal Shamrocks	1910	Returned to amateur status, April 1910
Montreal Wanderers	1910	Joined NHL
Ottawa Senators	1910	Joined NHL

Renfrew Creamery Kings	1910	Sold franchise to Toronto, November 1911. Toronto began play November 1912.
Toronto Tecumsehs	1912	Changed name to Ontarios, 1914
Toronto Ontarios	1914	Changed name to Shamrocks, 1914
Toronto Shamrocks	1914	Merged with Toronto Blueshirts, October 1915
Quebec Bulldogs	1910	Joined NHL
Toronto Blueshirts	1912	Franchise revoked by other NHA owners, February 1917. Secretly revived when the renamed NHL was formed and a franchise was granted to Toronto.
228th Battalion/ Northern Fusiliers	1916	Club withdrew, February 1917
Montreal Canadiens	1917	Still in NHL
Montreal Wanderers	1917	Folded, January 1918
Ottawa Senators	1917	Requested leave of absence, September 1930
Ottawa Senators	1931	Franchise relocated to St. Louis, October 1934
St. Louis Eagles	1934	Folded, April 1935
Toronto Blueshirts	1917	Franchise revoked, May 1918
Toronto Arenas	1918	Franchise folded, February 1919
Toronto St. Pats	1919	Franchise sold, February 14, 1927
Toronto Maple Leafs	1927	Still in NHL
Quebec Bulldogs	1919	Franchise revoked, December 1920
Hamilton Tigers	1920	Franchise revoked, September 1925
Montreal Maroons	1924	Players sold to Canadiens, April 1938
Boston Bruins	1924	Still in NHL

Pittsburgh Pirates	1925	Relocated to Philadelphia, April 1930
Philadelphia Quakers	1930	Requested leave of absence, September 1931. Never returned.
New York Americans	1925	Changed name to Brooklyn, April 1941
Brooklyn Americans	1941	Requested leave of absence due to World War II, April 1942. Franchise revoked, September 1943
Chicago Blackhawks	1926	Relocated to Windsor, Ontario, January 14, 1929
Blackhawks Hockey Club	1929	Relocated to Chicago, September 1929
Chicago Black Hawks	1929	Officially changed name to Blackhawks, 1986
Chicago Blackhawks	1986	Still in NHL
Detroit Cougars	1926	Changed name to Falcons, 1930
Detroit Falcons	1930	Franchise filed bankruptcy, May 1932. Merged with Chicago Shamrocks (AHA), September 2, 1932.
Detroit Red Wings	1932	Still in NHL

Notes

Introduction and Acknowledgements

1   Ferguson, Elmer. "Following in Hockey's Foot-Steps." Montreal *Herald and Daily Telegraph*. 16 Feb, 1943.

2   "Citizen Bulletins at Rockland." Ottawa *Citizen*. 7 Mar 1910.

3   "Ottawa Hockey Team Might Be Taken Out of 'Ted' Dey's Hands." Ottawa *Journal*. 24 Nov 1916.

4   "Quebec Must Improve Lights; Ottawas Fyle Another Kick." Ottawa *Citizen*. 15 Feb 1911.

5   "On The Side." Ottawa *Citizen*. 5 Mar 1904.

6   Coleman, Charles L. *Trail of the Stanley Cup.* Vol. 3. Sherbrooke, Que.: Progressive Publications, 1976. p. vii.

7   Milne, C. C. "General O'Pinion." *Sault Daily Star*. 16 Dec 1926.

8   "Ed. Livingstone Has Developed Many Players." Ottawa *Journal*. 3 Oct 1918.

Chapter 1: Birth of the Legend

9   Moss, Marv. "Sportswriter Elmer Ferguson Dead at 87." Montreal *Gazette*. 27 Apr 1972.

10   "Star Sportswriter Elmer Ferguson Is Dead at 87." Montreal *Star*. 27 Apr 1972.

11   Ferguson, Elmer. "The Only One Left of NHL Originals." Toronto Maple Leaf program. 10 Nov 1965.

12   "Ottawa Hockey Assn., Versus The Citizen, Before Judge Rose." Ottawa *Citizen*. 23 Nov 1925.

Chapter 2: Frank Calder's Beginnings

13   Cosentino, Frank. *The Renfrew Millionaires.* Burnstown, Ontario:

General Store Publishing House, 1990. p. 48–49.

14   "Nationals Will Not Take over Franchise Les Canadiens Club." Ottawa *Citizen*. 19 Jan 1910.

Chapter 3: The Trash King and the Yarn Spinner

15   "'Late' Tommy Gorman Led Three Cup Teams." *The Hockey News*. June 1961. p. 4.

16   Gorman, Tommy. "Renfrew Earns First Victory of Season, 10–4." Ottawa *Citizen*. Jan. 20, 1910. The headline gave the score as 10–4, although it was actually 9–4.

17   "Ottawa Overcomes Creamery Town in Brilliant Game." Ottawa *Citizen*. 14 Feb 1910.

18   "Ottawa Won 8 to 5, in Overtime Play." Montreal *Gazette*. 14 Feb 1910.

19   "Ottawa Won 8 to 5, in Overtime Play." Montreal *Gazette*. 14 Feb 1910.

20   Cosentino. *The Renfrew Millionaires*. p. 149.

21   Goyens, Chrys, and Frank Orr. *Blades on Ice: A Century of Professional Hockey*. Markham, Ont.: Team Power Enterprises, 2000.

22   "Hockey Impressario, Too." Montreal *Gazette*. 31 Dec 1910.

23   "Hockey Impressario, Too." Montreal *Gazette*. 31 Dec 1910.

Chapter 4: The Western Raiders and an Ottawa Power Play

24   "Taylor Won't Play At All." Ottawa *Citizen*, 3 Jan 1912.

25   "In an Interview Mr. Lichtenhein Says Much." Ottawa *Journal*. 8 Jan 1912.

26   "Side-Lights On Many Sports." Ottawa *Journal*. 9 Jan 1912.

27   "Side-Lights On Many Sports." Ottawa *Journal*. 9 Jan 1912.

28   "Taylor Didn't Play." Ottawa *Citizen*. 15 Jan 1912.

29   "A Raw Deal." Ottawa *Journal*. 16 Jan 1912.

30   "Sporting Comment." Ottawa *Journal*. 25 Jan 1912.

31   Whitehead, Eric. *The Patricks: Hockey's Royal Family*. Garden City, N.Y.: Doubleday, 1980). p. 12.

32   "Demoralized Wanderer Sextet Easy for Champion Ottawas." Ottawa *Citizen*. 25 Jan 1912.

33   "Ottawas Show Reversal of Form and Win 10–6." Ottawa *Journal*. 25 Jan 1912.

34   "Demoralized Wanderer Sextet Easy for Champion Ottawas." Ottawa *Citizen*. 25 Jan 1912.

35   "$300 Fine If They Refuse to Play." Montreal *Gazette*. 26 Jan 1912.

36   "Should Let a Sleeping Dog Lie." Montreal *Gazette*. 27 Jan 1912.

37   "No Games in States." Montreal *Gazette*. 6 Feb 1912.

38   "Nothing to Do with Stanley Cup." Montreal *Gazette*. 9 Feb 1912.

39   "Challenge from Coast." Montreal *Gazette*. 23 Feb 1912.

40   "Sporting Comment." Ottawa *Journal*. 5 Mar 1912.

41   "Wanderers Beat Ottawa at Montreal by Means of Two Stolen Goals." Ottawa *Citizen*. 6 Mar 1912.

42   "Fred. Taylor Has Retired." Ottawa *Journal*. 13 Mar 1912.

Chapter 5: Livingstone, We Presume

43   "Eddy Livingstone Issues a Statement." Toronto *Daily News*. 7 Jan 1919.

44   "Our Weekly Gallery." Toronto Daily News. 18 Dec 1915. p. 8.

45   "Our Weekly Gallery." Toronto Daily News. 18 Dec 1915. p. 8.

46   "Statement by the O.R.F.U. Secretary." Toronto *Daily Star*. 7 Dec 1912.

47   "Our Weekly Gallery." Toronto *Daily News*. 18 Dec 1915. p. 8.

48   "Local Pro Teams Lost Some Money." Toronto *Daily News*. 18 Mar 1913. p. 8.

49   "Denies Rumours." Ottawa *Journal*. 1 Dec 1914. p. 4.

50   "N.H.A. Magnates After Livingstone." Toronto *Mail and Empire*. 4 Dec 1914. p. 8.

51   The Denneny brothers' surname has frequently been given as Dennenay, and this spelling variation has appeared game programs from Calgary, Toronto and the Chicago Blackhawks. However, Corb's brother Cy expressed a definite preference for the Denneny spelling. As such, and for the sake of consistency, we have chosen Cy's preferred spelling, but have not altered the name where it appears in news reports of the day.

52   Good, Charlie. "Charlie Good Says." Toronto *Daily News*. 16 Dec 1914. p. 8.

53   "Tommy Smith Is Out With Ontario Team." Ottawa *Citizen*, 12 Dec 1914. p. 8.

54   Good, Charlie. "Charlie Good Says." Toronto *Daily News*, 18 Dec 1914. p. 8.

55   "Tommy Smith Has Been Ordered to Report Back Again to the Ontario Hockey Club." Ottawa *Journal*. 21 Dec 1914. p. 5.

56   "Snap Shots on Sport of Various Kinds." Toronto *Evening Telegram*. 18 Dec 1914. p. 18.

57   "Skene Ronan Awarded to Ottawa Club but May Be Traded to Ontarios." Ottawa *Citizen*. 24 Dec 1904. p. 8.

58   "Smith Subject to Draft; Ronan Stays with Ottawa." Vancouver *Sun*. 24 Dec 1914. p. 6.

59   "Snap Shots on Sport of Various Kinds." Toronto Evening Telegram. 29 Dec 1914. p. 14.

Chapter 6: Livingstone's Battles Begin

60   "Rush Orders Sent for Tommy Smith." Vancouver *Sun*, 31 Dec 1914, p. 6.

61   "Endorse Action of President Quinn." Montreal *Gazette*, 26 Jan 1915. p. 10.

62   "Endorse Action of President Quinn." Montreal *Gazette*, 26 Jan 1915. p. 10.

63   "Endorse Action of President Quinn." Montreal *Gazette*, 26 Jan 1915. p. 10.

64   "Commission May Be Broken over the Tommy Smith Case." Vancouver *Sun*. 5 Jan 1915. p. 6.

65   "Ottawa for Down Grade." Toronto Evening Telegram. 12 Jan 1915. p. 14.

66   Toronto Evening Telegram. 9 Dec 1914.

67   "Side-Lights on Many Sports." Ottawa *Journal*. 1 Feb 1912.

68   "Will it Come to This?" Ottawa *Journal*. 23 Jan 1912.

69   Querrie, Charlie. "Querrie's Hockey Gossip. " Toronto *Daily News*. 11 Jan 1915. p. 8.

70   Good, Charlie. "'Ontarios' Are Now the 'Shamrocks' and Will Be 'Wearin' of the Green'." Toronto *Daily News*. 18 Jan 1915. p. 1.

71   Good, Charlie. "'Ontarios' Are Now the 'Shamrocks' and Will Be 'Wearin' of the Green'." Toronto *Daily News*. 18 Jan 1915. p. 1.

72   "Eastern Hockey Magnates Hope to Patch Up Trouble." Vancouver *Sun*. 15 Jan 1915. p. 6.

73   "Coast Will Not Compromise." Toronto Evening Telegram. 18 Jan 1915. p. 12.

74   "Still at Loggerheads over Tommy Smith." Victoria *Colonist*. 27 Jan 1915. p. 9.

75   "Tommy Smith Returns to the Quebec Club." Vancouver *Sun*. 30 Jan 1915. p. 6.

76   Roche, Wilfrid, ed. *The Hockey Book*. Toronto: McClelland & Stewart, 1953.

77   "Shamrocks After New Players." Toronto *Mail and Empire*. 1 Feb 1915. p. 8.

78   "McNamara Brothers Called Home, and Manager Ed. Livingstone Insists on a Postponement." Ottawa *Journal*. 2 Feb 1915. p. 4.

79   Querrie, Charlie. "Querrie's Hockey Gossip. " Toronto *Daily News*. 3 Feb 1915. p. 8.

80   "Wanderers Awarded Game by Default." Toronto *Daily Star*. 3 Feb 1915. p. 11.

81   Good, Charlie. "Charlie Good Says." Toronto *Daily News.* 2 Feb 1915. p. 8.

82   "Shamrocks Threaten to Resign From N.H.A.." Ottawa *Citizen*, 4 Feb 1915. p. 9.

83   "The N.H.A. Race." Toronto *Daily Star*. 4 Feb 1915. p. 14.

84   "No Bearing on the Championship. " Montreal *Gazette. 2* Mar 1915. p. 12.

85   "Statement from Ed. Livingstone." Montreal *Gazette*, 3 Mar 1915. p. 12.

86   "Statement from Ed. Livingstone." Montreal *Gazette*, 3 Mar 1915. p. 12.

87   "Mar. 6 Is Date for Wanderer Play-off." Toronto *Mail and Empire*. 10 Feb 1915. p. 8.

88   "Lichtenhein States He Will Not Participate in Game Mar. 6." Ottawa *Journal*. 13 Feb 1915. p. 6.

89   Good, Charlie. "Charlie Good Says." Toronto *Daily News*. 1 Mar 1915. p. 8.

90   "Sammy Changes His Mind." Toronto *Daily Star*, 1 Mar 1915, p. 10

91   "Shamrocks Have Demanded Play Off." Montreal *Gazette*, 2 Mar 1915, p. 12

92   "Statement From Ed. Livingstone." Montreal *Gazette*, 3 Mar 1915, p. 12

93   "Statement From Ed. Livingstone." Montreal *Gazette*, 3 Mar 1915, p. 12

94   "S. E. Lichtenhein Makes His Reply." Montreal *Gazette*, 3 Mar 1915, p. 12

95   "Raw Deal For The Shamrocks." Toronto *Daily News*, 2 Mar 1915, p. 8

96   Edwards, Henry P. "Pro Players Put Up Scrappy Game For Local Fans." *Cleveland Plain Dealer.* 19 Mar 1915.

97   Edwards, Henry P. "Tables Turned Upon Shamrocks By Toronto Pros." *Cleveland Plain Dealer.* 20 Mar 1915.

98   "Torontos Defeat Shamrocks Again On Elysium Ice." *Cleveland Plain Dealer.* 21 Mar 1915.

99   "Lichtenhein Is Pulling For Peace In Hockey War." *Vancouver Sun*, 28 Oct 1915, p. 6

100   "Hockey Squabble Spreads, Eastern Clubs By The Ears." Toronto *Evening Telegram*, 29 Oct 1915, p. 16

101   "Expects Shamrocks To Sign Contracts." Toronto *Mail and Empire*." 27 Oct 1915, p. 8

102   "Queen City Athletes Accept Terms Offered By Patrick." *Vancouver Province*. 5 Nov 1915.

103   "Queen City Athletes Accept Terms Offered By Patrick." *Vancouver Province*. 5 Nov 1915.

104   "Frank Patrick Makes A Statement Giving His Side Of The Case." Toronto *Daily Star*, 5 Nov 1915, p. 15

105   "Livingstone Buys Toronto Franchise." Toronto *Mail and Empire*, 8 Nov 1915, p. 8

106   "Livingstone Buys Toronto Franchise." Toronto *Mail and Empire*, 8 Nov 1915, p. 8

107   "Ten Thousand Dollars Of Offers Made To-Day To Coast Hockey Stars." Montreal *Herald and Daily Telegraph*. 4 Nov 1915.

108   "How Eastern Clubs Are Stealing Mar." Ottawa *Citizen*, 27 Oct 1915, p. 8

109   "M'Namara Boys Buy the Shamrocks." Toronto *Daily Star*, 9 Nov 1915, p. 13

110   "NHA Moguls To Meet To-Night." Toronto *Daily News*, 9 Nov 1915, p. 8

111   "Hockey War News On Eastern Front." *Vancouver Sun*, 11 Nov 1915, p. 6

112   "Claims H. Cameron For Toronto Club." Toronto *Daily Star*, 10 Nov 1915, p. 14

113   "N.H.A. Will Again Have Six Clubs." Montreal *Gazette*, 15 Nov 1915, p. 15

114   "Coach Smith Starts Roundup Of Local Men For Ottawas; Indoor Work Begins Monday." Ottawa *Citizen*, 16 Nov 1915, p. 8

115   "Shamrock Hockey Franchise May Be Transferred Here." *Hamilton Spectator*, 17 Nov 1915, p. 18

116   "Famous Stanley Cup Will Not Be Recalled By Trustees; Mr. Foran Outlines Plans." Ottawa *Citizen*, 9 Dec 1915, p. 9

117   "Cameron Reports To The Torontos." Toronto *Mail and Empire*, 2 Dec 1915, p. 8

118   "Wanderers Beat Tail-end Torontos." Montreal *Gazette*, 20 Jan 1916, p. 12

119   "Limit In Hockey Protests." Toronto *Daily Star*, 21 Jan 1916, p. 18

120   "'Pro' Hockeyist Is Committed For Trial." Toronto *Daily Star*, 22 Jan 1916, p. 2

121   "Kennedy After Quinn." Toronto *Daily News*, 26 Jan 1916, p. 10

122   "Extreme Penalty For Rowdy Players." Toronto *Daily News*, 1 Feb 1916, p. 10

123   "Randall's Case Source Of Worry." Toronto *Mail and Empire*, 22 Feb 1916, p. 8

124   "Speedy Pro Teams Will Show Wares Tonight At Rink." *Cleveland Plain Dealer*, 21 Mar 1916, p. 11

125   Dan Diamond, ed. The Official National Hockey League Stanley Cup Centennial Book. Willowdale, Ontario: Firefly Books, 1992. p. 47

126   "National Hockey Association Decided To Split Schedule; Single Referee System Adopted." Ottawa *Citizen*, 13 Nov 1916, p. 8

Chapter 9: Eddie Livingstone Goes to War

127   "Sixty-Three Players For The 228th Battalion, Toronto *Globe*, 13 Dec 1916, p. 12

128   "Hockey Team In Khaki." Toronto *Daily News*, 2 Sept 1916, p. 15

129   Examination of Frank Calder, The National Hockey Association of Canada Limited v. the Ocean Accident & Guarantee Corporation Limited, Ontario Supreme Court, 23 Sept 1918, p. 5

130   Examination of Frank Calder, The National Hockey Association of Canada Limited v. the Ocean Accident & Guarantee Corporation Limited, Ontario Supreme Court, 23 Sept 1918, pp. 3–4

131   "Calder Likely N.H.A. President." Ottawa *Citizen*, 5 Oct 1916, p. 8

132   "Double Schedule For N.H.A.; Will Play In Two Series." Toronto *Daily News*, 13 Nov 1916, p. 10

133   "Puckerings." Toronto *Globe*, 28 Nov 1916, p. 9

134   "Robinson Awards Keats To Toronto." Toronto *Mail and Empire*, 15 Nov 1916, p. 8

135   "Soldiers Show True Spirit." Toronto *Daily News*, 16 Nov 1916, p. 10

136   Roche, Bill (editor). "The Hockey Book." McClelland & Steward. 1953. p. 60.

137   "Cy Denneny States Positively He Will Not Play For Toronto This Winter." Ottawa *Journal*, 24 Oct 1916, p. 4

138   "Denneny For The Ottawas." Ottawa *Journal*, 20 Oct 1916, p. 4

139   "Sport Comment." Ottawa *Citizen*, 25 Oct 1916, p. 9

140   "Will Not Part With Nighbor." Ottawa *Citizen*, 24 Oct 1916, p. 8

141   "Ottawa Hockey Club Is Now Angling For New Men Though Veterans Are Expected Back." Ottawa *Citizen*, 7 Nov 1916, p. 6

142   "T. & D. Troubles." Charlie Good, Toronto *Daily News*, 8 Nov 1916, p. 10

143   "Denneny's Case." Charlie Querrie, Toronto *Daily News*, 10 Nov 1916, p. 10

144   "Pro-Hockey's Greatest Comedian." Ottawa *Journal*, 9 Nov 1916, p. 4

145   "Pro-Hockey's Greatest Comedian." Ottawa *Journal*, 9 Nov 1916, p. 4

146   "Cyril Denneny Is Suspended." Toronto *Mail and Empire*, 16, Nov 1916, p. 8

147   "Cyril Denneny Is Suspended." Toronto *Mail and Empire*, 16, Nov 1916, p. 8

148   "Hockey Gossip. " Toronto *Mail and Empire*, 16 Nov 1916, p. 8

149   "Frank Nighbor Has Refused To Accept Terms Of Ottawa Club; Returns Contract Unsigned." Ottawa *Citizen*, 17 Nov 1916, p. 9

150   "Coach Smith May Be Found With One Of The Opposing Clubs In National Hockey Assn." Ottawa *Citizen*, 18 Nov 1916, p. 8

151   "Ross A Free Agent." Montreal *Gazette*. 20 Nov 1916.

152   "Led Two Leagues." Charlie Good, Toronto *Daily News*, 20 Nov 1916, p. 8

Chapter 10: Toronto: Shipped Out and Drummed Out

153   "Soldiers' Team May Withdraw From Professional Hockey." Toronto *Daily News*, 30 Nov 1916, p. 14

154   "N.H.A. May Withdraw From This Territory." Toronto *Globe*, 1 Dec 1916, p. 11

155   "Sammy Lichtenhein Refused Permission." Ottawa *Citizen*, 16 Dec 1916, p. 8

156   "Ottawa Hockey Club Again Places Hebert In Market. May Trade Him For Denenny." Ottawa *Citizen*, 6 Dec 1916, p. 8

157   "Hold-Outs Were On Hand For Ottawa's First Practice." Ottawa *Journal*, 13 Dec 1916, p. 4

158   "228th Winners Over The Torontos." Toronto *Mail and Empire*, 4 Jan 1917, p. 8

159   "Notes Of The Game." Toronto *Daily News*, 4 Jan 1917, p. 10

160   "Notes Of The Game." Toronto *Daily News*, 4 Jan 1917, p. 10

161   "Ottawa Club Takes Action In Behalf Of Idle Players; Quebec Will Back Them Up" Ottawa *Citizen*, 6 Jan 1917, p. 9

162   "Ottawa Club Failed To Break Deadlock Over 'Cy' Denenny."
        Ottawa *Citizen*, 8 Jan 1917, p. 8

163   "Ottawa Club Failed To Break Deadlock Over 'Cy' Denenny."
        Ottawa *Citizen*, 8 Jan 1917, p. 8

164   "Soldiers Return To Form And Battle Back Into Running."
        Toronto *Daily News*, 22 Jan 1917, p. 10

165   "Two Form Upsets." Charlie Good, Toronto *Daily News*, 22 Jan
        1917, p. 10

166   "228th Will Be Unable To Finish Schedule." Toronto *Mail and
        Empire*, 26 Jan 1917, p. 8

167   Calder testimony.

168   "New Goaler Wanted By Toronto Team." 29 Jan 1917, p. 10

169   "Cy Denenny Signs To Finish Season With Wanderers." 29 Jan
        1917, p. 8

170   "Livvy Breaks All Change of Wind Records." Ottawa *Journal*, 30
        Jan 1917, p. 8

171   "Ottawas defied An Order From League In Using Denenny."
        Ottawa *Citizen*, 1 Feb 1917, p. 8

172   Roche, Bill (editor). "The Hockey Book." 1953. Toronto:
        McClelland & Steward. p. 48.

173   "Northern fusiliers At Ottawa." Toronto *Globe*, 31 Jan 1917,
        p. 10

174   "Soldier Battalion Will Finish The Season." Toronto *Daily News*."
        2 Feb 1917, p. 10

175   "Battling Pros." Charlie Good, Toronto *Daily News*, 3 Feb 1917,
        p. 10

176   "Offered 'Livvy' $3,000 To Quit." Ottawa *Journal*, 6 Feb 1917, p. 10

177   "Played Last Game." Charlie H. Good, Toronto *Daily News*, 8
        Feb 1917, p. 10

178   "228th Seniors Drop Out." Toronto *Mail and Empire*, 7 Feb
        1917, p. 8

179   "Hockey Gossip. " Toronto *Mail and Empire*." 8 Feb 1917, p. 8

180   "Soldiers May Not Finish Season." Toronto *Daily News*, 8 Feb
        1917, p. 10

181   "Played Last Game." Charlie H. Good, Toronto *Daily News*, 8
        Feb 1917, p. 10

182   "How Ottawa Players Regard The Situation." Ottawa *Citizen*,
        10 Feb 1917, p. 9

183   "Pro. Situation Is Unsettled." Toronto *Daily News*, 9 Feb 1917,
        p. 10

184   Examination of Edward J. Livingstone, Toronto Hockey Club v.

Ottawa Hockey Association et al, Ontario Supreme Court, 20 Apr 1917, p. 5

185 "Toronto Dropped By N.H.A. Moguls." Toronto *Mail and Empire*, 12 Feb 1917, p. 8

186 "Livvy Wants To Know Who opened His Tely."Toronto *Mail and Empire*, 13 Feb 1917, p. 8

187 "Probable Resignation Of 228th And Move To Exclude Torontos causes Tense Situation In N.H.A." Ottawa *Citizen*, 10 Feb 1917, p. 8

188 Statement of Claim, Toronto Hockey Club v. Ottawa Hockey Association et al, Ontario Supreme Court, 23 Mar 1917, pp. 2–3

189 "Livingstone Retiring From Toronto Club." Toronto *Mail and Empire*, 15 Feb 1917, p. 8

190 "The Sporting Periscope." Ottawa *Citizen*, 13 Feb 1917, p. 8

191 "Dropping Of Torontos Was Seen In The Offing." Ottawa *Journal*, 12 Feb 1917, p. 10

192 "Should Be Cut." Charlie Querrie, Toronto *Daily News*, 15 Feb 1917, p. 10

193 "Our Opinion." Charlie Querrie, Toronto *Daily News*, 16 Feb 1917, p. 10

194 "Hockey Gossip. "Toronto *Mail and Empire*, 17 Feb 1917, p. 8

195 "Oatman Alleges He Was Badly Treated."Toronto *Daily News*, 21 Feb 1917, p. 10

196 "'Lieut. Meeking Is Also Unmasking Hockey Scandal." Ottawa *Citizen*, 20 Feb 1917, p. 6

197 "'Lieut. Meeking Is Also Unmasking Hockey Scandal." Ottawa *Citizen*, 20 Feb 1917, p. 6

198 "Oatman's revelation May Cause Another Upheaval In National Hockey Assn.." Ottawa *Citizen*, 20 Feb 1917, p. 6

199 "Livingstone's Statement." Toronto *Mail and Empire*, 22 Feb 1917, p. 8

200 "War Looms Again On Hockey Horizon; More Trouble For N.H.A. Moguls." *Vancouver Sun*, 20 Feb 1917, p. 6

201 "Concealing Facts Of 228th Trouble Not Good For The Game." Ottawa *Journal*, 21 Feb 1917, p. 10

202 "Concealing Facts Of 228th Trouble Not Good For The Game." Ottawa *Journal*, 21 Feb 1917, p. 10

203 "N.H.A. Prexey Pleads Not Guilty In Case." *Vancouver Sun*, 23 Feb 1917, p. 6

204 "Ottawa Hockey Club Decided To Finish Out N.H.A. Season." Ottawa *Citizen*, 14 Feb 1917, p. 8

205 Examination of Frank Calder. The National Hockey Association of Canada Limited v. Ocean Accident & Guarantee Corporation Limited. Ontario Supreme Court. 23 Sept 1918, p. 10

206 Examination of Frank Calder. The National Hockey Association of Canada Limited v. Ocean Accident & Guarantee Corporation Limited. Ontario Supreme Court. 23 Sept 1918, p. 10

207 Examination of Frank Calder. The National Hockey Association of Canada Limited v. Ocean Accident & Guarantee Corporation Limited. Ontario Supreme Court. 23 Sept 1918, pp. 13–14.

208 "Will Appeal $3,000 Bond Case At Once." Montreal *Star*, 10 Oct 1918, p. 6

209 "Eddy Livingstone Issues A Statement." Toronto *Daily News*. 7 Jan 1919.

210 "Livingstone Retiring From Toronto Club." Toronto *Mail and Empire*, 15 Feb 1917, p. 8

211 "Eddie Livingstone Charges Frameup By Three Clubs." Ottawa *Citizen*, 27 Feb 1917, p. 8

212 "Brings Charges Against Wanderers." Toronto *Mail and Empire*, 9 Mar 1917, p. 8

213 "Wanderer Magnate After Livingstone." Toronto *Daily News*, 10 Mar 1917, p. 10

214 Charlie Querrie, "Sports In General by Charlie Querrie." Toronto *Daily News*, 10 Mar 1917, p. 10

215 "Resorts To The Courts." Toronto *Evening Telegram*, 12 Mar 1917, p. 14

216 "N.H.A. Magnates Just One Big Happy Family." Ottawa *Journal*, 12 Mar 1917, p. 10

217 "Ottawa Owners May Launch Counter Suits Against Livvy; No Word Yet From The Coast." Ottawa *Citizen*, 15 Mar 1917, p. 8

218 "Eddy Livingstone Issues A Statement." Toronto *Daily News*. 7 Jan 1919.

219 "Livingstone Insists On Going To Trial." Ottawa *Citizen*, 28 Apr 1917, p. 8

220 San Francisco never joined the PCHA; in fact, no competitive hockey would be played in the City by the Bay until July 21, 1926.

221 "Canadians Win Hockey Match From Seattle." *San Francisco Chronicle*. 31 Mar 1917.

222 "Seattle Evens Up With Hockey Win Over Canadians." *San Francisco Chronicle*. 3 Apr 1916.

Chapter 12: The Penny Drops

223   "May Freeze Out Toronto Team." Toronto *Daily News*, 22 Oct 1917, p. 4

224   "Jimmie Murphy To Manage Torontos." Ottawa *Citizen*, 2 Oct 1917, p. 7

225   "Pro Hockey Pot Is On The Boil." Toronto *Daily News*, 2 Oct 1917, p. 4

226   "Four Strong Teams Likely To Play In N.H.A. Next Winter; Toronto Asked To Withdraw." Ottawa *Citizen*, 22 Oct 1917, p. 22

227   Charlie Querrie, "Sports In General By Charlie Querrie." Toronto *Daily News,* 24 Oct 1917, p. 4

228   "Cannot Afford To Drop Blue Shirts." Toronto *Daily News,* 26 Oct 1917, p. 4

229   "Sporting Gossip. "Toronto *Mail and Empire*, 24 Oct 1917, p. 8

230   "Don't Want Toronto In Hockey Circuit." Toronto *Daily News*, 27 Oct 1917, p. 4

231   Solman was one of the city's top impresarios, period. Besides his stake in the Arena Gardens, he owned the baseball Maple Leafs and their home stadium. The ballpark was located on Hanlan's Point at the western tip of Toronto Island; to get there, baseball fans had to pay to ride one of the ferries Solman owned and operated. For those with non-sporting tastes, his holdings included the amusement parks at Sunnyside and Hanlan's Point and the Royal Alexandra Theatre.

232   "Has No Objection To Dropping Club." *Vancouver Sun*, 2 Nov 1917, p. 8

233   Charlie Querrie, "Sports In General By Charlie Querrie." Toronto *Daily News,* 2 Nov 1917, p. 4

234   "Hockey Gossip Here And there." Toronto *Mail and Empire*, 2 Nov 1917, p. 8

235   "Four Eastern Clubs Will Sucede From The N.H.A. And Form New Hockey Circuit." Ottawa *Citizen*, 3 Nov 1917, p. 9

236 "   Guarantees Strong Team For Toronto." Ottawa *Citizen*, 6 Nov 1917, p. 9

Chapter 13: Quebec Bows Out

237   Ferguson, E. W. "New League Line-Up Is Not Yet Certain: Toronto May Be In." Montreal *Herald and Daily Telegraph*. 12 Nov 1917.

238   Ferguson, E. W. "An Ear To The Ground." Montreal *Herald and Daily Telegraph*. 13 Nov 1917.

239   "Mike Quinn Is Out Of Hockey." *Quebec Chronicle*, 5 Nov 1917, p. 6

240   "Quebec Asked For A Meeting." Montreal *Herald and Daily Telegraph*. 19 Nov 1917.

241   "Ottawa Hockey Club Now Has Complete Team In Readiness For Coming Of Cold Weather." Ottawa *Citizen*, 20 Nov 1917, p. 8

242   "Very Stormy Session Expected To-Night To Form New League." Montreal *Herald and Daily Telegraph*. 22 Nov 1917.

243   "To-Night Quebec Will Give Answer." Toronto *Mail and Empire*, 24 Nov 1917, p. 9

244   Ferguson, E. W. "An Ear To The Ground." Montreal *Herald and Daily Telegraph*. 24 Nov 1917.

245   "Toronto Now Given Place." Toronto *Globe*. 26 Nov 1917.

246   "Quebec Still Asking Price For Its Players." Montreal *Herald and Daily Telegraph*. 26 Nov 1917.

247   "New League is Forming Here Today." Montreal *Herald and Daily Telegraph*. 26 Nov 1917.

Chapter 14: Lichtenhein Loses the War

248   Pro. League To Operate." *The Globe*. 27 Nov 1918.

249   Pro. League To Operate." *The Globe*. 27 Nov 1918.

250   "Interest In Hockey Is Aroused By The Arrival Of Winter." *The Globe*. 27 Nov 1917.

251   Affidavit of Frank Calder. The National Hockey Association of Canada Limited v. Ocean Accident & Guarantee Corporation Limited. Ontario Supreme Court. 15 Mar 1918.

252   "S. Cleghorn's Career Finished." Toronto *Mail and Empire*, 27 Nov 1917, p. 8

253   "After Quebec Players." Montreal *Gazette*, 7 Dec 1917, p. 18

254   "Sammy Adds His Little Ultimatum." *Quebec Chronicle*, 15 Dec 1917, p. 30

255   "Wanderers May Quit." Montreal *Gazette*, 11 Dec 1917, p. 16

256   "Wanderers Will Quit Unless Other Clubs Give Them Players." Montreal *Herald and Daily Telegraph*. 10 Dec 1917.

257   "Wanderers Will Quit Unless Other Clubs Give Them Players." Montreal *Herald and Daily Telegraph*. 10 Dec 1917.

258   "Wanderers Will Quit Unless Other Clubs Give Them Players." Montreal *Herald and Daily Telegraph*. 10 Dec 1917.

259   "Will Wanderers Back Out Of It?." *Quebec Chronicle*, 11 Dec 1917, p. 6

260   "Wanderers Will Quit Unless Other Clubs Give Them Players."
       Montreal *Herald and Daily Telegraph*. 10 Dec 1917.

261   "Wanderers Must Decide Quickly." Montreal *Gazette*, 12 Dec
       1917, p. 18

262   "Will Be Satisfied With Two Players." Toronto *Mail and Empire*,
       14 Dec 1917, p. 8

263   "Invalided Soliers Invited To Opening." Montreal *Herald and
       Daily Telegraph*. 18 Dec 1917.

264   "Mummery Reports To Blue Shirts." Toronto *Mail and Empire*,
       28 Dec 1917, p. 8

265   "Arena Is Completely Destroyed To-Day By Fire And
       Explosion." Montreal *Herald and Daily Telegraph*. 2 Jan 1918.

266   "Arena Is Completely Destroyed To-Day By Fire And
       Explosion." Montreal *Herald and Daily Telegraph*. 2 Jan 1918.

267   "League Meets Today To Take Up Demands Of The Wanderers."
       Montreal *Herald and Daily Telegraph*. 3 Jan 1918.

268   "Next Arena Not Likely To Be Built Out In Westmount."
       Montreal *Herald and Daily Telegraph*. 3 Jan 1918.

269   "N.H.A. To Play In Jubilee Rink." Quebec *Chronicle,* 3 Jan 1918,
       p. 6

270   "League Meets Today To Take Up Demands Of The Wanderers."
       Montreal *Herald and Daily Telegraph*. 3 Jan 1918.

271   "Wanderers Disband, But League Will Go On With Three Teams
       Left." Montreal *Herald and Daily Telegraph*. 4 Jan 1918.

272 " Wanderers Disband, But League Will Go On With Three Teams
       Left." Montreal *Herald and Daily Telegraph*. 4 Jan 1918.

273   "Wanderers Disband, But League Will Go On With Three Teams
       Left." Montreal *Herald and Daily Telegraph*. 4 Jan 1918.

274   As a result of this decision, many sources state incorrectly to this
       day that the Wanderers withdrew from the league after playing
       six games. Even an official NHL publication such as *Hockey Hall
       of Fame: The Official Registry of the Game's Honour Roll* (Dan
       Diamond, ed., Toronto: Doubleday Canada, 1996), says that the
       Arena burned down "[s]ix games into the season." In fact, the
       Redbands followed up their opening-night victory over Toronto
       with embarrassing losses to the Canadiens (11–2) and Ottawa
       (6–3 and 9–2) before the fire.

275   "Side-Lights On Many Sports." Ottawa *Journal*. 10 Jan 1912.

Chapter 15: Dey's Deceptions

276 "Pro Hockey Operations Were Resumed Here Yesterday With Big

Offer For Local Control." Ottawa *Citizen*, 4 Oct 1918, p. 9

277   "Proposed Change In Hockey Rules." Halifax *Daily Echo,* 10 Mar 1911, p. 10

278   "Percy J. Quinn Ex-Alderman Noted Athlete." Toronto *Globe and Mail*. 30 Oct 1944.

279   "Side-Lights on Many Sports." Ottawa Journal. 29 Jan 1912.

280   Among the numerous differences between eastern and western hockey, the most obvious was the number of players: the PCHA clung to seven-man hockey. The coast league had made some important innovations, however — most significantly, PCHA rinks were divided into thirds by a pair of blue lines, and forward passing was allowed in the middle zone. And western goalies were allowed to drop to their knees or flop around to make a save, while their NHA counterparts were still required to stay on their feet.

281   Examination of Percy Quinn, Percy J. Quinn v. E. P. Dey, Supreme Court of Ontario, 14 Jan 1919, p. 12

282   "Sports In General." C . H. Good, Toronto *Daily News*, 19 Jun 1918, p. 9

283   "Inside Dope On Hockey Convention." Montreal *Star*, 30 Sept 1918, p. 6

284   "Inside Dope On Hockey Convention." Montreal *Star*, 30 Sept 1918, p. 6

285   "N.H.A. Was Again Suspended But Pro Hockey Situation Is Still Far From Being Settled." Ottawa *Citizen*, 30 Sept 1918, p. 6

286   "Quinn Says He Owns The Flying Men." Montreal *Star*, 2 Oct 1918, p. 6. Dey later claimed to be in town for a boat-builders' meeting ("Said the Old Wanderers May Go Back." Montreal *Star*, 11 Nov 1918, p. 6).

287   "Calder Welcomes Suit." Ottawa *Citizen*, 2 Oct 1918, p. 8

288   "N.H.A. Was Again Suspended But Pro Hockey Situation Is Still Far From Being Settled." Ottawa *Citizen*, 30 Sept 1918, p. 6

289   "Dissatisfied Toronto Men Move For New Hockey League And Invite Ottawa Into It." Ottawa *Citizen*, 1 Oct 1918, p. 8

290   "New Pro Hockey League May Come Into Existence." Toronto *Daily News*, 2 Oct 1918, p. 9

291   Statement of Claim, Percy J. Quinn v. E. P. Dey, Supreme Court of Ontario, 13 Dec 1918, p. 2

292   Examination of Percy Quinn, Percy J. Quinn v. E. P. Dey, Supreme Court of Ontario, 14 Jan 1919, pp. 3–4

293   "Pro Hockey Operations Were Resumed Here Yesterday With Big Offer For Local Control." Ottawa *Citizen*, 4 Oct 1918, p. 9

294 "Ottawa Hockey Club Talk Rink At Lansdowne Pk." Ottawa *Journal*, 5 Oct 1918, p. 22

295 "Ottawa Not Dependent On Mr. Dey." Montreal *Star*, 5 Oct 1918, p. 6

296 "Looking 'em Over." C. H. Good, Toronto *Daily News*, 5 Oct 1918, p. 9

297 "N.H.A. Magnates Show No Fear Of New League." Ottawa *Journal*, 8 Oct 1918, p. 12

298 "Lansdowne Park Arena May Turn Out A Reality." Ottawa *Journal*, 8 Oct 1918, p. 12

299 "Lalonde Admits Receiving Offer." Montreal *Gazette*, 8 Oct 1918, p. 12

300 "Kennedy And Calder Laugh At New League." Ottawa *Journal*, 10 Oct 1918, p. 12

301 "'Ted' Dey Still Trying To Buy Ottawa Ass'n Stock." Ottawa *Journal*, 11 Oct 1918, p. 14

302 "Ottawa Hockey Club Were Highest Bidders For Franchise." Ottawa *Journal*, 19 Oct 1918, p. 18

303 "Saturday's Meeting Of N.H.L. Failed To Settle Situation; Ottawa Now Doubtful Club." Ottawa *Citizen*, 21 Oct 1918, p. 6

304 "Toronto Arena Given Franchise." Montreal *Gazette*, 21 Oct 1918, p. 12

305 "Main Building Not Available As Rink." Ottawa *Citizen*, 23 Oct 1918, p. 6

306 "Ottawa Rink Is Safe For Senators." Toronto *World*, 26 Oct 1918, p. 8

307 C. H. Good, "Looking 'em Over." Toronto *Daily News*, 9 Nov 1918, p. 8

308 "Said The Old Wanderers May Go Back." Montreal *Star*, 11 Nov 1918, p. 6

309 "National League Makes Agreement." W. M. Gladish, Ottawa *Journal*, 11 Nov 1918,

310 "Quinn Gets Very Short Shrift Here." Montreal *Star*, 11 Nov 1918, p. 6

311 "Colossal Bluff Says C.H.A. Chief." Toronto *Daily News*, 11 Nov 1918, p. 9

312 "Colossal Bluff Says C.H.A. Chief." Toronto *Daily News*, 11 Nov 1918, p. 9

313 "'Very Interesting' Says Percy Quinn." Ottawa *Citizen*, 12 Nov 1918, p. 8

314 "Toronto Promoter Threatens Action Against Ottawa Arena As

Last Salvo Of Hockey War." Ottawa *Citizen*, 12 Nov 1918, p. 9

315 "Hockey Promoters Threaten To Take Dey To Courts." Toronto *Daily News*, 14 Nov 1918, p. 8

316 Writ of Summons, Percy J. Quinn v. E. P. Dey, Supreme Court of Ontario, 15 Nov 1918

317 "Calder Today Gives Quinn His Private Ultimatum." Montreal *Star*, 15 Nov 1918, p. 6

318 "Quinn Discloses Some Timely Facts." Toronto *Mail and Empire*. 18 Nov 1918, p. 8

319 "Ottawa Club Has Requested National Hockey League To Redistribute Quebec Stars." Ottawa *Citizen*, 19 Nov 1918, p. 6

320 "Osgoode Hall News." Toronto *World*, 21 Nov 1918, p. 5

321 "Quinn May Still Return To Grace." Toronto *Mail and Empire*, 21 Nov 1918, p. 8

322 "Nothing Definite Results From The Montreal Meeting." W. M. Gladish, Ottawa *Journal*, 13 Dec 1918, p. 18

323 "Local Ice Situation Much Mixed." Montreal *Star*, 23 Oct 1918, p. 6

324 "Riopel To Vacate The Jubilee Rink." Montreal *Gazette*, 11 Mar 1919,

325 "G. Kennedy Laughs At Ashes On Ice." Montreal *Star*, 3 Dec 1918, p. 6

326 "Wind-up Order For Association." Ottawa *Journal*, 18 Dec 1918, p. 16

327 "Livingstone Says Few Things Anent Hockey Situation." Toronto *Daily News*. 7 Jan 1919.

328 "Livingstone Says Few Things Anent Hockey Situation." Toronto *Daily News*. 7 Jan 1919.

329 Examination of Witnesses on Motion, Percy J. Quinn v. E. P. Dey, Supreme Court of Ontario, 23 Dec 1918, pp. 4–5

330 Examination of Witnesses on Motion, Percy J. Quinn v. E. P. Dey, Supreme Court of Ontario, 23 Dec 1918, pp. 10–11.

331 Order, Percy J. Quinn v. E. P. Dey, Supreme Court of Ontario, 26 Dec 1918, pp. 1–2

332 Offers Use Of Ottawa Ice Arena To Those Represented By Quinn." Ottawa *Journal*, 28 Dec 1918, p. 16

333 Examination of Percy J. Quinn, Percy J. Quinn v. E. P. Dey, Supreme Court of Ontario, 14 Jan 1919, p. 10

334 *Ibid,* pp. 8–9.

335 "Percy Quinn's Suit Against E. P. Dey Was Dismissed." Ottawa *Citizen*, 23 Jan 1919, p. 8

Chapter 16: The Short, Chaotic Life of the Toronto Arenas

336   "Livingstone Sues Toronto Arena." *Quebec Chronicle*, 23 Jul 1918, p. 5.

337   "Inside Dope On Hockey Convention." Montreal *Star*, 30 Sept 1918, p. 6.

338   "Trying Hard To Wreck Pro. Hockey." Montreal *Star*, 1 Oct 1918, p. 6.

339   Minute Book of National Hockey League : Nov 22nd, 1917 to Nov 7th, 1925, Hockey Hall of Fame Collection, Toronto, p. 14.

340   Minute Book of National Hockey League : Nov 22nd, 1917 to Nov 7th, 1925, Hockey Hall of Fame Collection, Toronto, p. 17.

341   "Magnates Still Claiming Players." Toronto *Mail and Empire*, 23 Oct 1918, p. 8.

342   "Livingstone And Kennedy In War Talk." Montreal *Star*, 19 Nov 1918, p. 6.

343   "Arena Flings Hat Into The Ring." Toronto *Mail and Empire*, 26 Nov 1918, p. 8.

344   "Outlaw Organization Shows Hand With Latest Move In Hockey War." Ottawa *Journal*, 29 Nov 1918,

345   "Will Force Meeting Of The N.H.L. Clubs." Toronto *Mail and Empire*, 6 Dec 1918, p. 8.

346   "Will Force Meeting Of The N.H.L. Clubs." Toronto *Mail and Empire*, 6 Dec 1918, p. 8.

347   "More Threats From Livingstone Crowd." Ottawa *Journal*, 20 Dec 1918, p. 22.

348   "'We Will Play Game' Says Charlie Querrie." Toronto *Mail and Empire*, 21 Dec 1918, p. 8.

349   "Canadiens Beat The Blue Shirts." Toronto *Mail and Empire*, 24 Dec 1918, p. 8.

350   "Scandal For Tor.–Arena's Hockey Men." Montreal *Star*, 27 Dec 1918, p. 6.

351   "Looking Them Over." C. H. Good, Toronto *Daily News*, 3 Jan 1919, p. 10.

352   "Cameron And Noble Are Banished For Season By Toronto Arenas." Ottawa *Journal*, 14 Jan 1919, p. 14.

353   "Something Is Very Wrong." Toronto *Evening Telegram*, 13 Jan 1919, p. 20.

354   "Must Rearrange The N.H.L. Schedule." Toronto *Mail and Empire*, 27 Dec 1918, p. 8.

355   "Looking Them Over." C. H. Good, Toronto *Daily News*, 2 Jan 1919, p. 10.

356   "Arena May Pay 'Livy' $12,000 Now." Montreal *Star*, 24 Jan 1919, p. 6.

357   "Toronto Referees Hand In Their Resignations." Montreal *Star*, 31 Jan 1919, p. 6.

358   "Steve Vair Will Act Again As Referee In Toronto Game." Montreal *Star*, 3 Feb 1919, p. 6.

359   "Random Notes On Current Sports." Toronto *Daily Star*, 4 Feb 1919, p. 22.

360   Good,Charlie. "Looking 'em Over With C. H. Good." Toronto *Daily News*, 13 Feb 1919, p. 10.

361   "Arena Players Accept Offers." Toronto *Globe*, Toronto, 18 Feb 1919, p. 13

362   "C. H. Good, "Looking 'em Over With C. H. Good." Toronto *Daily News*, 21 Feb 1919, p. 10.

363   "Ottawa Objects To Officials Chosen." Montreal *Gazette*, 22 Feb 1919, p. 20.

364   "Arena Club Lost $2,200 On Season", Toronto *Daily Star*, 25 March 1919, p. 24.

365   "Random Notes On Current Sports." Toronto *Daily Star*, 21 Feb 1919, p. 23.

366   "Who Owns Hockey Players." Toronto *Evening Telegram*, 24 Mar 1919, p. 19.

367   "Who Owns Hockey Players." Toronto *Evening Telegram*, 25 Mar 1919, p. 15.

368   Examination of Alfred Skinner. Toronto Hockey Club v. Arena Gardens of Toronto, Ltd. Supreme Court of Ontario (1918).

369   "Who Owns Hockey Players." Toronto *Evening Telegram*, 25 Mar 1919, p. 15.

370   "Big Hockey Suit May End Soon." Montreal *Star*, 25 Mar 1919, p. 6.

371   "Who Owns Hockey Players." Toronto *Evening Telegram*, 25 Mar 1919, p. 15.

372   "Shake-Up Is Coming In Local Pro. Outfit" Toronto *World*, 25 Nov. 1919, p. 8. This refutes contemporary sources that indicate the deal was made on Dec. 9, 1919. Toronto was to get Victoria's goaltender, Tommy Murray, in the exchange.

373   Toronto actually dealt Denneny *twice*. In December 1922, his PCHA rights were traded to Vancouver for Jack Adams. But the St. Pats had retained his NHL playing rights, and a year later he was included in the deal that also sent Randall to Hamilton.

374   Podnieks, Andrew. "The Blue And White Book 1997." p. 5. Don Mills, Ont.: ECW Press

375   "Noted Canadian Sportsman; Lacrosse Ace; Hockey Figure." Toronto *Globe and Mail*. 6 Apr 1950.

Chapter 17: The Battle for Hamilton

376   "Ed. Livingstone Has Developed Many New Players." Ottawa *Journal*. 3 Oct 1918.

377   "Hamilton Entered in New Professional Hockey League." *Hamilton Herald*. 26 Aug 1920.

378   "Hamilton Entered in New Professional Hockey League." *Hamilton Herald*. 26 Aug 1920.

379   "Hamilton Entered in New Professional Hockey League." *Hamilton Herald*. 26 Aug 1920.

380   "Greatest Hockey Scrap in Years Sure To Come With New 'Pro' League." *Hamilton Herald*. 17 Sept 1920.

381   "Hockeyist's Long Felt Want Filled When New Arena Was Constructed." *Hamilton Spectator*. 3 Nov 1920.

382   "Talking Things Over." *Hamilton Herald*. 21 Sept 1920.

383   "Three Hamilton Hockey Players Get Bug Offer To Play With 'Pros.'" *Hamilton Herald*. 4 Oct 1920.

384   "Lou Marsh May Manage One of Livvy's Clubs." *Hamilton Herald*. 23 Oct 1920.

385   "In City To Organize International League", Toronto *Daily Star*, 22 October 1920, p. 22.

386   "Hamilton Gets Quebec Club." *Hamilton Herald*. 1 Nov 1920.

387   Dunnell, Milt. "An Unprofitable Team But A Big Profit." Toronto *Daily Star*. 4 Apr 1950.

388   "Quebec Says Report of Transfer Is Premature." *Hamilton Herald*. 3 Nov 1920.

389   "Trying To Keep Franchise In Quebec." *Hamilton Herald*. 24 Nov 1920.

390   "N.H.L. Schedule To Be Arranged This Week." Toronto *Daily Star*. 29 Nov 1920.

391   "'Livvy' Claims Pro. Arena Privileges." Toronto *Daily Star*. 29 Nov 1920.

392   "Hockey Is Brutal, Says Latchford." Toronto *Daily Star*. 9 Dec 1920.

393   "Toronto Hockey Club Loses Application." Toronto *Daily Star*. 10 Dec 1920.

394   "St. Patrick's To Play At Arena This Winter." Toronto *Daily News*. 10 Dec 1920.

Chapter 18: *Livvy Wins, But the NHL Gains Some Relief*

395   24 Ontario Law Reports p. 514.

396   24 Ontario Law Reports p. 515.

397   24 Ontario Law Reports p. 525.

398   25 Ontario Law Reports. p. 618–9.

399   25 Ontario Law Reports. p. 618–9.

400   Livingstone's Statement of Claim. Toronto Hockey Club Limited v. Charles Laurens Querrie, Ida Lucy Querrie and the St. Patrick's Professional Hockey Club Limited.

401   Justice Kelly's Injunction. Jan 18, 1924. Toronto Hockey Club Limited v. Charles Laurens Querrie, Ida Lucy Querrie and the St. Patrick's Professional Hockey Club Limited.

402   26-4 Dominion Law Reports, p. 1–5.

Chapter 19: **Hamilton Is Hoodwinked**

403   "Hamilton Gets N.H.L. Franchise." *Hamilton Herald*. 29 Nov 1920.

404   "Joe Malone Notifies Hamilton Club That He Will Not Play Here." *Hamilton Herald*. 10 Dec 1920.

405   "Sporting Comment." *Hamilton Herald*. 22 Dec 1920.

406   "Canadiens and Hams Open Professional Season To-morrow." *Hamilton Spectator*. 21 Dec 1920.

407   "Carey and Matte Star of Opening "Pro" Game Won By Hamilton, 5–0." *Hamilton Herald*. 23 Dec 1920.

408   "Hamilton and Saints Meet Here To-night in Professional Battle." *Hamilton Spectator*. 3 Jan 1921.

409   ""Babe" Dye Has Been Recalled." *Hamilton Herald*. 24 Dec 1920.

410   ""Punch" Broadbent May Play For Tigers In Tonight's N.H.L. Game." *Hamilton Herald*. 29 Dec 1920.

411   "Ottawa Star Has Been Ordered to Join the Toronto Irishmen," Hamilton *Herald*, 31 December 1920, p. 16.

412   "St. Pats Here Tonight To Meet Hamilton "Pros" – Big Crowd Assured." *Hamilton Herald*. 3 Jan 1921

413   Ottawa *Journal*. 4 Jan 1921.

414   "Malone Arrived This Morning and Took Part In Two-Hour Workout." *Hamilton Herald*. 5 Jan 1921.

415   "How To Play Hockey Was Ottawa's Lesson To Local N.H.L. Club." *Hamilton Herald*. 7 Jan 1921.

416   "Calder, Gorman and Kennedy In Wordy War Over Sprague Cleghorn." *Hamilton Herald*. 10 Jan 1921.

417   Gorman, T. P. Ottawa *Citizen*. 10 Jan 1921.

Chapter 20: The Steeltown Strike

418   McMullen, W.C. "The Sports Trail." *Hamilton Spectator*. 17 Feb 1925.

419   "Hamilton Pro. Club Sued by Season Ticket-holder." Toronto *Mail and Empire*. 12 Mar 1925.

420   "Ottawa May Take Hamilton's Place in N.H.L. Finals." Montreal *Gazette*. 13 Mar 1925.

421   "Tiger Players to Stand by Demand." Montreal *Gazette*. 13 Mar 1925.

422   Jones, P. J. "P. J. Jones Says –." *Hamilton Herald*. 14 Mar 1925.

423   "No Change In Local 'Pro' Hockey Situation." *Hamilton Herald*. 13 Mar 1925.

424   Siemiatycki, Myer. "The Stanley Cup Strike of 1925." <http://www.nhl.com/hockeyu/history/anniversary/25strike. html>.

425   "No Change In Local 'Pro' Hockey Situation." *Hamilton Herald*. 13 Mar 1925.

426   "Local N.H.L. Players Standing Firm In Demand For Bonus." *Hamilton Spectator*. 13 Mar 1925.

427   "Grist From The Sport Mill." Ottawa *Journal*. 14 Mar 1925.

428   Jones, P. J. "P. J. Jones Says –." *Hamilton Herald*. 13 Mar 1925.

429   "No Change In Local 'Pro' Hockey Situation." *Hamilton Herald*. 13 Mar 1925.

430   "No Change In Local 'Pro' Hockey Situation." *Hamilton Herald*. 13 Mar 1925.

431   "N.H.L. Hockey Tangle Remains Unsolved." Ottawa *Citizen*. 14 Mar 1925.

432   "Canadiens Declared Champions – Will Go West." *Hamilton Herald*. 14 Mar 1925.

433   "Hamilton Players May Go On Strike." Toronto *Mail and Empire*. 13 Mar 1925.

434   "Local N.H.L. Players Standing Firm In Demand For Bonus." *Hamilton Spectator*. 13 Mar 1925.

435   "Canadiens Declared Champions – Will Go West." *Hamilton Herald*. 14 Mar 1925.

436   Jones, P. J. "P. J. Jones Says –." *Hamilton Herald*. 16 Mar 1925.

437   "Montreal Fans Are With Local Players." *Hamilton Herald*. 16 Mar 1925.

438   "Hamilton Wants Peace." Montreal *Gazette*. 14 Mar 1925.

439   "Lady Byng Gives Cup To Pro League." *Hamilton Herald*. 9 Mar 1925.

440   "Strikers Suspended By N.H.L President." Toronto *Mail and Empire*. 16 Mar 1925.

441   "A Blotch On Professional Hockey." Ottawa *Journal*. 16 Mar 1925.

442   McCann, Philip. "Sports Leads and Counters." Ottawa *Citizen*. 18 Mar 1925.

443   "President Calder Issues Statement." Toronto *Mail and Empire*. 17 Mar 1925.

444   "Canadiens Are Champions." Toronto *Evening Telegram*. 14 Mar 1925.

445   McCann, Philip. "Sports Leads and Counters." Ottawa *Citizen*. 16 Mar 1925.

446   "Notes." Toronto *Evening Telegram*. 17 Mar 1925. p. 26.

447   "Players' Statement." *Hamilton Herald*. 17 Mar 1925.

448   Jones, P. J. "P. J. Jones Says-." *Hamilton Herald*. 18 Mar 1925.

449   Jones, P. J. "Players Received Back Salary." *Hamilton Herald*. 17 Mar 1925.

450   "Hamilton's N.H.L. Club To Have New Home." *Hamilton Herald*. 1 May 1925.

Chapter 21: Stop Spreading the News

451   "Hockey Clubs Limited." Ottawa *Citizen*. 18 Mar 1925.

452   "Ottawa Hockey Assn. is Awarded Damages of $100." Ottawa *Citizen*. 24 Nov 1925.

453   "Ottawa Hockey Assn., Versus The Citizen, Before Judge Rose." Ottawa *Citizen*. 23 Nov 1925.

454   "Ottawa Hockey Assn., Versus The Citizen, Before Judge Rose." Ottawa *Citizen*. 23 Nov 1925.

455   "Ottawa Hockey Assn., Versus The Citizen, Before Judge Rose." Ottawa *Citizen*. 23 Nov 1925.

456   "Ottawa Hockey Assn. is Awarded Damages of $100." Ottawa *Citizen*. 24 Nov 1925.

457   "Ottawa Hockey Association Gets Verdict From Judge In Libel Action." Ottawa *Journal*. 24 Nov. 1925.

458   "New Hockey Rink Largest In World." New York *Times*. 26 Jul 1925.

459   "Deal For Hockey Team To Play Here Fails." New York *Times*. 16 Sept 1925.

460   "Sale of Hamilton Club Failed to Materialize." *Hamilton Herald*. 16 Sept 1925.

461   "Buys Three Hockey Stars." New York *Times*. 19 Sept 1925.

462   "Edmonton Team Not Sold to New York." Montreal *Gazette*. 22 Sept 1925.

463   "Lack of Security Scares Hamilton." Toronto *Globe*. 18 Sept 1925.

464   "Hamilton Franchise Has No Ties To It." *Hamilton Spectator*. 18 Sept 1925.

465   Dunnell, Milt. "Burch Pioneered for Playoff Lucre." Toronto *Daily Star*. 4 Dec 1950.

466   Siemiatycki, Myer. "Stanley Cup Strike of 1925: The Aftermath." <http://www.nhl.com/hockeyu/history/anniversary/25after-math.html>.

467   "New York Sextet Rounding To Form." New York *Times*. 19 Nov 1925.

468   "Pro Hocky Body Completes League." New York *Times*. 27 Sept 1925.

Chapter 22: The Original Ten

469   "Frank Calder – A Canadian", *Montreal Gazette,* 5 Feb 1943, p. 8.

Chapter 23: Livvy's Comeback

470   "Schooley Behind New Pro. League Thinks F. Calder." Toronto *Mail and Empire*. 9 Apr 1925.

471   "Schooley Behind New Pro. League Thinks F. Calder." Toronto *Mail and Empire*. 9 Apr 1925.

472   "Schooley Behind New Pro. League Thinks F. Calder." Toronto *Mail and Empire*. 9 Apr 1925.

473   "Pro League Will Supplant Amateur." *Hamilton Spectator*. 4 May 1925.

474   Livingstone to Calder, telegram. 7 Aug 1926, 1925–26 Miscellaneous Correspondence file, *NHL Archives.* Courtesy of John Wong.

475   "Rangers and Boston Are Awarded Players." Toronto *Mail and Empire*. 18 Oct 1926.

476   "Pro. Referee Says Old Time Players Better." Sault *Daily Star*. 27 Nov 1926.

Chapter 24: The Real Curse of Muldoon

477   Harrison, Cliff. "Honest Pete Muldoon Gone." *Seattle Star*. 14 Mar 1929.

478   Nearly all published sources assign McLaughlin's 333rd Machine Gun battalion to the 85th Division. However, this unit, which trained at Camp Custer in Battle Creek, Michigan, was named

the Custer Division. The 86th was the Blackhawk Division.

479   Gregory, L. H. "Baseball Interested in Hockey 'Play-off' Plan for Deciding Pennants." *The Oregonian*. 20 May 1926.

480   Gregory, L. H. "Cy Townsend To Get Chance At Chicago." *The Oregonian*. 24 Jul 1926.

481   "Chicago Hockey Out at Arena." Toronto *Evening Telegram*. 29 Oct 1926.

482   "2 Amateurs To Turn 'Pro' At Stratford." *Border Cities Star*. 25 Oct 1926.

483   "Chicago Sign Another Star." *Sault Daily Star*. 30 Oct 1926.

484   "Cardinal Hockey Team Opens Here Against Detroit." Chicago *Tribune*. 29 Oct 1926.

485   Crusinberry, James. "Muldoon, Coach of Chicago Pros, Is St. Marys Boy." *London Free Press*. 9 Dec 1926.

486   Schreiber, Frank. "Ice Hockey To Make Comeback Here Wednesday." Chicago *Tribune*. 14 Nov 1926.

487   Schreiber, Frank. "Blackhawks Win Hockey Opener, 4-1." Chicago *Tribune*. 18 Nov 1926.

488   "In The Wake of the News: Hockey's Inaugural." Chicago *Tribune*. 19 Nov 1926.

489   Schreiber, Frank. "Blackhawks Beat Boston, 5–1, and Take League Lead." Chicago *Tribune*. 21 Nov 1926.

490   "Walsh Stops 63 Shots In First of 'Hounds Pro Games." *Sault Daily Star*. 24 Nov 1926.

491   "Sport Comment." *London Free Press*. 13 Dec 1926.

492   "Sport Comment." *London Free Press*. 15 Dec 1926.

493   "Get Balance When Teddy Quits Cards." *Border Cities Star*. 20 Dec 1926.

494   Schreiber, Frank. "Hockey Loops War; Chicago Battle Ground." Chicago *Tribune*. 15 Dec 1926.

495   Schreiber, Frank. "Hockey Loops War; Chicago Battle Ground." Chicago *Tribune*. 15 Dec 1926.

496   Schreiber, Frank. "Hockey Loops War; Chicago Battle Ground." Chicago *Tribune*. 15 Dec 1926.

497   "McNamara to Reorganize Detroit Hounds Next Year." Toronto *Mail and Empire*. 14 Dec 1926.

498   "Sport Comment." *London Free Press*. 17 Dec 1926.

499   "Maroons Are to Get Three 'Soo' Players." *Border Cities Star*. 15 Dec 1926.

500   "Cards Reduce Price of Seats at Hockey Tilts." Chicago *Tribune*. 26 Dec 1926.

501   Schreiber, Frank. "Blackhawks Beat Maroons in Overtime Game." Chicago *Tribune*. 30 Dec 1926.

502   Schreiber, Frank. "New Yoprk Rangers Hand Blackhawks 4-0 Beating." Chicago *Tribune*. 2 Jan 1927.

503   Schreiber, Frank. "Ed Livingstone Sells Cardinal Hockey Club." Chicago *Tribune*. 9 Mar 1927.

504   Schreiber, Frank. "Duluth Knots Score Late In Final Session." Chicago *Tribune*. 17 Mar 1927.

505   "Hockey Bosses Refuse To O.K. Sale of Cards." Chicago *Tribune*. 21 Mar 1927.

506   "Hockey Bosses Refuse To O.K. Sale of Cards." Chicago *Tribune*. 21 Mar 1927.

507   "Hockey Bosses Refuse To O.K. Sale of Cards." Chicago *Tribune*. 21 Mar 1927.

508   "Hockey Bosses Refuse To O.K. Sale of Cards." Chicago *Tribune*. 21 Mar 1927.

509   Boreham, Bruce. "Sport Salad." *Winnipeg Tribune*. 1 Apr 1927.

510   "Maj. M'Laughlin Whips Insulter of His Bride." Chicago *Tribune*. 23 Dec 1923.

511   Steedman, William. "Muldoon May Be Seattle Boss." *Seattle Post-Intelligencer*. 6 Apr 1927.

512   "Black Hawks Get Stanley." New York *Times*. 5 Apr 1927.

513   Mesher, Mose. "Post Season Series With Big Leaguers Looms for Eskimos." *Seattle Times*. 11 Mar 1929.

514   "College Ice Loop Forms; Four Fraternities Sign." *Seattle Times*. 12 Mar 1929.

515   Metcalf, Elliott. "Between You and Me." *Tacoma Spokesman-Review*. 14 Mar 1929.

516   "Pete Muldoon Dies." *Seattle Times*. 14 Mar 1929.

517   "Smiling and Happy Pete Muldoon Had Not A Single Enemy." *Victoria Times*. 14 Mar 1929.

518   "Hockey Game Held Off Until Saturday." *Seattle Times*. 14 Mar 1929.

519   Lassen, Leo H. "Pete Muldoon." *Seattle Times*. 15 Mar 1929.

Chapter 25: Leafs of a Different Colour

520   Milne, C.C. "General O'Pinion." *Sault Daily Star*. 14 Dec 1926.

521   Eskenazi, Gerald. "The Fastest Sport." p. 68. Chicago: Follett. 1974.

522   "'Babe' Dye is Purchased from Irish by Chicago." Toronto *Mail and Empire*. 18 Oct 1926.

523   Eskenazi, Gerald. "The Fastest Sport." p. 68–70. Chicago: Follett. 1974.

524   "Sporting Gossip. "Toronto *Mail and Empire*. 27 Jan 1927.

525   Podnieks, Andrew. "The Blue And White Book 1997." p. 6. Don Mills, Ont.: ECW Press.

526   Milne, C.C. "General O'Pinion." *Sault Daily Star*. 14 Dec 1926.

527   "New Owners Take Over The St. Patricks Club." Toronto *Daily Star*. 15 Feb 1927.

528   "St. Patrick's Effect Startling Changes", *Toronto Globe*, 10 December 1924, p. 12.

529   Marsh, Lou E. "With Pick And Shovel." Toronto *Daily Star*. 15 Feb 1927.

530   "Toronto Defence Shaky In Detroit Cougar Game." Toronto *Evening Telegram*. 16 Feb 1927.

531   "Pro. and Amateur Hockey Chatter." Toronto *Evening Telegram*. 16 Feb 1927.

532   Affidavit of W. B. McHenry. Toronto Hockey Club Ltd. v. Arena Gardens of Toronto Ltd. et al. Ontario Supreme Court. Mar 25, 1927.

Chapter 26: Conspiracy, Chicago Style

533   "Livingstone Says Few Things About Hockey Situation." Toronto *Daily News*. 7 Jan 1919.

534   Calder to McLaughlin, 7 Jul 1927, 1926–27 Chicago National Hockey Team Inc. file, *NHL Archives*. Coutesy of John Wong.

535   Warren to Calder, 24 Aug 1927, 1926–27 American Hockey Association file, *NHL Archives*. Courtesy of John Wong.

536   Warren to Calder, 24 Aug 1927, 1926–27 American Hockey Association file, *NHL Archives*. Courtesy of John Wong.

537   "Suit For $700,000 Filed Against Owners of Black Hawks By Canadian Promoter." New York *Times*. 23 Dec 1927.

538   Exhibit A. Notarized Statement of Marvin Wentworth. Livingstone v. McLaughlin, Foster and Keough. U.S. District Court, Case 36839, 1927.

539   Exhibit B. Notarized Statement of Marvin Wentworth. Livingstone v. McLaughlin, Foster and Keough. U.S. District Court, Case 36839, 1927.

540   Exhibit B. Notarized Statement of Marvin Wentworth. Livingstone v. McLaughlin, Foster and Keough. U.S. District Court, Case 36839, 1927.

541   Rohm, Harland. "Boston's Body Checking Keeps Chicago At Bay." Chicago *Tribune*. 21 Jan 1929.

542   "Hawks Move To Detroit." *Border Cities Star*. 28 Dec 1928.

543   "Chicagoans May Acquire Hockey Team At Ottawa." Chicago *Tribune*. 13 Jan 1929.

544   "Canadian Sues For $700,000 In Hockey Case." Chicago *Tribune*. 30 Sept 1930.

545   "Halt $700,000 Hockey Trial As Juror Talks." Chicago *Tribune*. 3 Oct 1930.

546   "Former Hockey Players Testify In $700,000 Suit." Chicago *Tribune*. 9 Oct 1930.

547   "Judge Declares Second Mistrial In Hockey Suit." Chicago *Tribune*. 11 Oct 1930.

548   "Hockey Moguls Decide A. A. Is Outlaw League." Chicago *Tribune*. 19 Oct 1930.

549   "Hockey Moguls Decide A. A. Is Outlaw League." Chicago *Tribune*. 19 Oct 1930.

Chapter 27: Calder Steals the Cup

550   "Sports World Mourns Late Frank Calder." Montreal *Herald*. 5 Feb 1943.

551   "Answers Hockey Chiefs." Chicago *Tribune*. 21 Oct 1930.

552   "American Loop Gives New York New Hockey Club." Chicago *Tribune*. 26 Oct 1930.

553   "Seek Injunction To Put Brydson Off Shamrocks." Chicago *Tribune*. 6 Nov 1930.

554   "Shamrock Head Answers Threat To Bar Brydson." Chicago *Tribune*. 7 Nov 1930.

555   This version of the American Hockey League is not to be confused with the current minor league of the same name, which was founded in 1938 after a merger between the Canadian-American Hockey League and the International Hockey League.

556   "Accept Ice Defy." *Kansas City Star*. 3 Feb 1932.

557   "Accept Ice Defy." *Kansas City Star*. 3 Feb 1932.

558   "Accept Ice Defy." *Kansas City Star*. 3 Feb 1932.

559   "Grant Denies Rumours That Hockey League Is Near Breakup. " St. Louis *Post-Dispatch*. 30 Jan 1932.

560   "Burr Williams Jumps Flyers, Goes To Chicago Blackhawks." St. Louis *Post-Dispatch*. 4 Feb 1932.

561   "To Act In Ice War." *Kansas City Star*. 4 Feb 1932.

562   "Burr Williams Jumps Flyers, Goes To Chicago Blackhawks." St.

Louis *Post-Dispatch*. 4 Feb 1932.

563   "To Act In Ice War." *Kansas City Star*. 4 Feb 1931.

564   "Burr Williams, Flyers Defense Star, To Remain With Club." St. Louis *Post-Dispatch*. 5 Feb 1932.

565   "Burr Williams, Flyers Defense Star, To Remain With Club." St. Louis *Post-Dispatch*. 5 Feb 1932.

566   "Will Hold Conference." New York *Times*. 25 Mar 1932.

567   "Reiterates His Opinion." New York *Times*. 25 Mar 1932.

568   "Shamrocks End Drill For Title Playoff Sunday." Chicago *Tribune*. 1 Apr 1932.

569   "Defeat Duluth 4-3; Prelesnik's Shot Triumphs." Chicago *Tribune*. 8 Apr 1932.

570   "Hockey Teams Face Drastic Economies." New York *Times*. 11 May 1932.

571   Macdonell, Leo. "Falcons May Be Out Of National Loop." Detroit *Times*. 23 Aug 1932.

572   Macdonell, Leo. "Falcons May Be Out Of National Loop." Detroit *Times*. 23 Aug 1932.

573   Macdonell, Leo. "Falcons May Be Out Of National Loop." Detroit *Times*. 23 Aug 1932.

574   Macdonell, Leo. "Falcons May Be Out Of National Loop." Detroit *Times*. 23 Aug 1932.

575   Shaver, Bud. "Shavings." Detroit *Times*. 24 Aug 1932.

576   Shaver, Bud. "Shavings." Detroit *Times*. 24 Aug 1932.

577   Shaver, Bud. "Shavings." Detroit *Times*. 24 Aug 1932.

578   "Hockey Stars Reinstated." Detroit *Times*. 25 Aug 1932.

579   "Hockey Truce Is Being Submitted By Club Owners." St. Louis *Post-Dispatch*. 31 Aug 1932.

580   "Dispute Is Ended By Hockey Leagues." New York *Times*. 3 Sept 1932.

581   Macdonnell, Lee. "Detroit Gets Big Grist of Puck Stars." Detroit *Times*. 3 Sept 1932.

582   Macdonnell, Leo. "Detroit Buys Goalie Roach From N.Y." Detroit *Times*. 6 Oct 1932.

Chapter 28: Frank Calder Dies

583   Lytle, Andy. "Frank Calder Stricken; Red Dutton Carries On!" Toronto *Daily Star*. 26 Jan 1943.

584   Lytle, Andy. "Speaking On Sports." Toronto *Daily Star*. 27 Jan 1943.

585   "Complete Rest For Mr. Calder." Toronto *Daily Star*. 26 Jan 1943.

586 "Death Removes N.H.L. Prexy." Montreal *Herald and Evening Telegram*. 4 Feb 1943.

587 "Hockey Heads Mourn Loss." Montreal *Herald and Evening Telegram*. 4 Feb 1943.

588 "Frank Calder – A Canadian", *Montreal Gazette*, 5 February 1943, p. 8.

589 "Frank Calder – A Canadian", *Montreal Gazette*, 5 February 1943, p. 8.

590 "Frank Calder – A Canadian", *Montreal Gazette*, 5 February 1943, p. 8.

591 "Frank Calder – A Canadian", *Montreal Gazette*, 5 February 1943, p. 8.

Chapter 29: Livingstone at Peace

592 Good, Charlie. "Haze of Memories Clouds Old Arena." Toronto Daily Star. 16 Dec 1936.

593 Rodden, Michael J., "On The Highways Of Sport", *Toronto Globe*, 7 Nov 1929, p. 12.

594 Good, Charlie. "Haze Of Memories Clouds Old Arena", Toronto *Daily Star*, 16 Dec 1936, p. 10.

Appendix A: What Happened to Them

595 Koffman, Jack. "Along Sports Row." Ottawa *Citizen*. 16 Apr 1943.

596 "Col. J. S. Hammond, Promoter, 59, Dies." New York *Times*. 10 Dec 1939.

597 Podnieks, Andrew. "The Blue And White Book 1997." p. 19. Don Mills, Ont.: ECW Press.

598 "Noted Canadian Sportsman; Lacrosse Ace; Hockey Figure." Toronto *Globe* and Mail. 6 Apr 1950.

599 McAree, J.V. Toronto *Globe* and Mail. 31 Oct 1944.

600 "Will Rogers Pays a Tribute To Personality of Rickard." *New York Times.* 7 Jan 1929.

Index

Duncan, Art, 104
Dunderdale, Tommy, 51
Dutton, Mervyn "Red," 330, 332
Dwan, Nip, 290
Dwyer, Bill, 263, 264, 268, 311–12, 330
Dye, Babe, 232, 235, 278, 296–97, 319–20, 347

Earchman, Archie, 102, 104, 105, 116, 120
Eastern Canada Hockey Association (ECHA), 31–32
East Hamilton Athletic Association, 56
Edmonton Eskimos, 263, 341, 349
Edwards, Henry, 81–82
Eskenazi, Gerald, 295–97

Falconbridge, Sir Glenholme, 131, 133–34, 214, 228
Farquhar, John, 310
The Fastest Game (Eskenazi), 295–97
Ferguson, Elmer, 13, 16, 21, 152–54, 331
    account of NHL's beginnings, 21–25
    backs Livingstone, 214–16
    conflicts of interest, 14, 26, 125, 154
    hired by Calder, 28–29
    sides with Livingstone, 98–99
Fleming, R. J., 173, 177
Foran, William, 49, 94–95, 173, 203, 286, 333, 340
    accepts AHL Cup challenge, 315–16, 319
    role usurped by Calder, 213
Foyston, Frank, 86, 88, 98, 173–74

Gardner, Jimmy, 32, 42, 49, 241–42
Gerard, Eddie, 63, 188, 235
Gibson, C. W. G., 243–44
Good, Charlie, 78, 120, 182, 336
Gorman, Tommy, 13, 24, 25, 47, 93, *102*, 156, *171*, 174, 195, 198, 236–38, 242, 331, 340, 344
    accused of rigging game, 256–57
    attacks Livingstone in print, 109–10, 115, 123
    becomes part-owner of Senators, 171–72
    becomes Senators manager, 102
    conflicts of interest, 14–15, 107–8, 111, 118, 123
    friendship with Calder, 36
    journalistic style, 37–39
    manages Madison Square Garden, 259
    manages New York Americans, 262–64
    sells stake in Senators, 241
Graham, Ted, 277–78, 290, 303
    playing rights disputed, 285–87
Grant, William F., 291, 309, 312–13, 315–18, 325, 327–28
Green, Red, 230, 241, 245
Green, Wilfred "Shorty," 241, 245–48, 264, 340–41
    accuses Ottawa of fixing game, 256–57, 259
    explains basis for Hamilton strike, 246–47
Gregory, L. H., 276–77

Haileybury Hockey Club, 32, 351
Hainsworth, George, 233, 263, 268

Hall, Charles R., 278–79, 291, 307
Hall, Joe, 24, 50, 207
Halliday, Milt, 277, 287
Hambly, Fred, 212, 213, 297
Hambly, Percy, 212, 213, 297
Hamilton
    arena, 94
    considered as site for CHA, 216–19
    gets Quebec NHL franchise, 220–21
    NHL players from, 347–48
    resentment at loss of Tigers, 258
Hamilton Alerts, 55–56
Hamilton Tigers (football team), 55, 56
Hamilton Tigers (hockey team), 237, 239–40, 348, 349, 352
    become minor-league team, 265
    finish first in NHL, 243
    first game, 233–35
    move to Syracuse, 313
    players sold to New York, 263–64
    players' strike, 244–49, 251–57
    sued by subscriber, 243–44
Hammond, John, 262, 295–96, 297, 341
Harmon, Paddy, 306
Harris, R. B., 243–44
Hebert, Sammy, 59, 63, 114, 117
Herendeen, Harry, 289–90
Herman, Jack, 29
Hewitt, William, 13–14
hockey
    business aspect, 12–13
    comparison across eras, 9–12
    ethics of team owners, 12, 16, 110–11
    historical research, 15–16
    violence, 96–97
Hockey Hall of Fame, 21
Hodge, John, 308
Holmes, Harry "Hap," 16, 88, 98, 204
    returns to PCHA, 198, 201–2
Holmes, W. J., 272, 291
Howell, Harry, 347, 348
Hughes, Charles, 268, 271, 287, 305, 318, 320
Huston, Charles, 193
Hyland, Harry, 42, 51, 158

influenza epidemic, 24–25, 207
International Hockey League, 14
International Hockey League II, 256, 262, 264, 267, 270–71
Irvin, Dick, 332, 347

Jubilee rink, 25, 168, 184, 186, 187
Judicial Committee of the Privy Council, 229

Karakas, Mike, 327, 329
Keats, Gordon "Duke," 263, *263*, 341
    playing rights disputed, 105–6, 112, 116, 119–20
Kendall, George Washington. *See* Kennedy, George
Kennedy, George, 23, 29, *30*, 34–35, 58, 96–97,

rules on Duke Keats dispute, 105–6
sells Blueshirts to Livingstone, 89–90
Rodden, Mike, 14, 336
Ronan, Skene, 61–64, 66, 93, 95, 96, 97
Rosenthal, Martin, 119, 141, 150, 171–72, 176, 345
   resigns from Senators, 182
   seeks alternative to Dey's Arena, 178–80
   takes Denneny dispute to NHA, 114–15
   tries to trade for Cy Denneny, 113–14
Ross, Andrew, 243–44
Ross, Art, 32, 163–64, 166, 241, 262, 264, 269, 343, 345
Ross, Phil, 13, 44–45, 68, 74, 94–95, 170, 173, 246, 315, 316, 333, 345

St. Louis Eagles, 330, 350, 352
St. Louis Flyers, 316–17
St. Paul Saints, 277, 308
San Francisco (California), 142–43, 276, 364*n*
Saskatoon Sheiks, 268, 349
Sault Ste. Marie Greyhounds, 271–72
   move to Detroit, 284
Savage, Ed, 99, 104
Scanlan, D. R., 220
Schooley, Roy, 267, 270–71
Schreiber, Frank, 280–81
Seattle Eskimos, 293
Seattle Metropolitans, 142–43, 242
   "raid" of Blueshirts, 88–91, 98
Sedgewick, G. H., 131–33
Shaughnessy, Frank, 83, 84
Shaughnessy, Tom, 308, 309–10, 313, 314–15, 320, 321, 322, 325
Shaver, Bud, 323–25
Sheppard, E. D., 168
Shore, Eddie, 263, *263*, 268, 269, 281
Shore, Hamby, 46, 165, 207
Skinner, Alf, 59, 64, 96, 137, 208–11, 212
Smeaton, Cooper, 97, 312, 333
Smith, Donald, 42, 43
Smith, Tommy, 59, 88, 89, 115
   playing rights disputed, 61–63, 65–67, 71–72
Smythe, Conn, 14, 295–97, 297, 326, 335, 345
Smythe, W. R., 208, 212, 222
Solman, Lol, 79, 92, 94, 148, 365*n*
Sons of Ireland, 145, 154
Southam, H. S., 261
Southam, Wilson, 261
Sparks, N. C., 45
split season, 100, 199, 200, 203–4
Spokane Canaries, 102, 149
Stanley, Barney, *263*, 293
Stanley Cup, *311*
   AHA challenge, 315–16
   controlled by ECHA, 31
   last non-NHL champion, 255
   Portland's "phantom" title, 99–100
   1919 series abandoned, 207
   taken over by NHL, 328, 333–34

trustees allow challenges from American teams, 94–95
trustees object to American challenges, 49
Stewart, Doc, 245
Strachan, James, 266, 268, 340, 346
Stratford Nationals, 277
Sudbury Wolves, 230–31
Supreme Court of Ontario, 198, 199, 225–26

Taber, Harry, 316, 318, 327
Taylor, Fred "Cyclone," 84, 87, 170, 238–39
   jumps to PCHA, 51
   playing rights disputed, 46–48, 51
   refuses to play for Wanderers, 42–45
   scores "backwards" goal, 37–39
   signs with Renfrew, 32
Taylor, James A., 62, 63, 72, 89
Taylor, Ralph, 303, 308–9
Tecumseh Hockey Club. *See* Toronto Tecumsehs
Temiskaming League, 32, 351
Thompson, Percy, 195, 217, 241, 243–44, 257, 263–64
   appeals to NHL for players, 231–32
   becomes Hamilton manager, 220–21, 230
   response to players' strike, 245–46, 249
   second thoughts about CHA, 218–19
   trades Sprague Cleghorn, 239–40
Toronto
   attitude toward NHA sours, 139
   considered as NHL market, 153, 158
   as hotbed of amateur hockey, 93, 207–8
   is granted NHA franchise, 32, 52, 57
   is granted NHL franchise, 159
   police crackdown on hockey violence, 96–97
Toronto Amateur Athletic Club, 55
Toronto Arena Company. *See also* Arena Gardens
   spins off Blueshirts, 196
   tries to settle with Livingstone, 204
Toronto Arenas, 24, 193–212, *194*, 352
   creation of, 196–98
   discipline problems, 202–3, 205
   name on Stanley Cup, 197
   on-ice performance, 201–3, 204–5
   players signed to multiple contracts, 208–11
   withdraw from NHL, 206–7
Toronto Blueshirts, 79, *85*, 103, 352. *See also* Toronto Arenas
   exhibition games in Cleveland, 81–82, 98–99
   expelled from NHA, 121–24, 132
   first game *vs.* 228th, 114
   founded, 57–58
   lose players to 228th, 104–5
   play in NHL's first game, 165
   put up for sale, 85–86
   "raided" by PCHA, 88–91
   sold to Livingstone, 89–90
   win Stanley Cup, 173, 193
Toronto *Daily Star*, 221–23